BUILDING TRUST

To our wives,
Barbara and Carol,
for all their support

Building Trust

An Introduction to Peacekeeping and Arms Control

RALPH M. GOLDMAN
University of Washington
and
WILLARD M. HARDMAN
Catholic University of America

Ashgate

Aldershot • Brookfield USA • Singapore • Sydney

Published by
Ashgate Publishing Limited
Gower House
Croft Road
Aldershot
Hants GU11 3HR
England

Ashgate Publishing Company
Old Post Road
Brookfield
Vermont 05036
USA

British Library Cataloguing in Publication Data
Goldman, Ralph M. (Ralph Morris), 1920-
    Building trust : an introduction to peacekeeping and arms
    control
    1.Security, International 2.Arms control 3.Peace
    I.Title II.Hardman, Willard M.
    327.1'7

Library of Congress Cataloging-in-Publication Data
Goldman, Ralph Morris, 1920-
    Building trust : an introduction to peacekeeping and arms control
    / Ralph M. Goldman and Willard M. Hardman.
        p.   cm.
    Includes bibliographical references and index.
    ISBN 1-85521-987-5 (hc)
    1. Arms control. 2. Security, International. 3. United Nations-
    -Armed Forces. I. Hardman, Willard M. II. Title.
    KZ5625.G65   1997
    341.7'33–dc21   97-20767
                                                                         CIP

ISBN 1 85521 987 5

Printed in Great Britain by Galliard (Printers) Ltd, Great Yarmouth

Contents

List of Tables and Figures

List of Tables

List of Figures

Preface

The leaders of the defense establishment of the United States are increasingly confronted by the dilemmas of their mission requirements. Are they war-makers, trained to overwhelm or destroy any enemy of the nation? Or, are they peacekeepers, trained to use force sparingly, if at all, and to maintain the agreements reached by the parties to a conflict? Or, are they deliverers of humanitarian aid, trained to act as angels of mercy carrying food, clothing, and shelter to the innocent victims of war or other human catastrophes? Or, are they all three. The missions of the U.S. military have become confusing. War-making and peacekeeping are merging functions. This introductory textbook aims to provide the history and the context of these dilemmas. Our main concern is the role of trust in responding to them.

Although Chapter VII of the United Nations Charter places responsibility for international security, peacekeeping, and disarmament under the aegis of the United Nations Security Council, over the last four or five decades peacekeeping and arms control have become distinct fields of study and policy making. Each field has its own specialists and its own professional literature; each offers distinct policies and panaceas. This survey of collective security developments since World War II will trace the parallel evolution of events in these two specialized fields - arms control and peacekeeping - and to reestablish the connection between them.

In making this survey, we shall be concerned with the subjective and objective aspects of the circumstances of "security" as well as with the relationship between political distrust and arms races. This approach will carry us into consideration of the bases of security other than military strength, the *internation* sources of distrust, the *intranation* sources of distrust, and some of the techniques currently used for confidence building, including third-party involvement in conflict resolution, the development of political institutions, peacekeeping, and the pursuit of arms control and disarmament agreements.

The underlying assumptions of the authors are these: disagreement among human beings is inevitable. Political conflict is perpetual. However, war and other forms of military violence are primitive, inefficient, and inconclusive techniques of conflict resolution. Weapons and warfare are the symptoms, not the disease. The disease arises from insufficiencies in human relationships, notably distrust, and from inadequacies in the modes of organizing and institutionalizing those relationships of distrust for purposes of conflict management and resolution. Our further motivation for preparing this book has been the demise of the other superpower, the former Soviet Union, an event that has generated many new challenges, but also aggravated older challenges for policy makers.

Our use of data is illustrative or historical rather than definitive. They are used to reveal trends rather than keep abreast of the rapidly unfolding events in the field of global security. We hope the reader will give his or her attention to the generalizations derived from the data.

Ralph M. Goldman
Willard M. Hardman

January 1997

About the Authors

Ralph M. Goldman, Visiting Scholar, Department of Political Science, University of Washington; Professor Emeritus, San Francisco State University; President, Center for Party Development; former director, International Affairs Program at the Pentagon, The Catholic University of America. Publications (partial list): *From Warfare to Party Politics: The Critical Transition to Civilian Control* (Syracuse University Press, 1990); *The National Party Chairmen and Committees: Factionalism at the Top* (M.E. Sharpe, 1990); *How to Build and Maintain a Democratic Party System* (Center for Party Development, 1993); *Promoting Democracy: Opportunities and Issues*, with William A. Douglas (Praeger/Greenwood, 1988); *Transnational Parties: Organizing the World's Precincts* (University Press of America, 1983).

Willard M. Hardman, Adjunct Faculty, The Catholic University of America; retired U.S. Army officer who has held various command and staff positions, including service in international headquarters; author of several specialized technical and training publications in the fields of military history, intelligence, and security.

1 Political Distrust as Generator of Arms Races

The phenomena of trust and distrust are among the most frequently mentioned elements in the problem of security and arms control. Distrust clearly leads to worst-case analysis, military buildups, and acceleration of the arms race. We have a great deal of evidence about how this process works. We have much less evidence to support a prediction that international political trust would produce arms control, security, and peace. Or perhaps there is evidence, but for political and social reasons, it does not get the attention it deserves. Substantial study is given to the causes of the world's conflicts, but relatively little study to the reasons that the U.S. and Canada have maintained the longest undefended border in the world for over 150 years.

This chapter will describe some of the components of trust and distrust that are identified in behavioral theory. The decision making predicament of the policy maker responsible for security will be analyzed and illustrated by the case of the Prisoners' Dilemma. Some examples of security policies that generate distrust and others that promote trust and cooperation will be considered. The chapter will conclude with an argument favoring attention to the socio-psychological aspects of trust and distrust, particularly in connection with the arms race.

Both Hawks and Doves, as the two extremes in the arms control debate are known, have much to say about political distrust. Hawks will identify an "enemy", call attention to that enemy's "misconduct and treachery", and conclude that greater military strength is necessary because that enemy cannot be trusted. Hawks will tend to interpret the designated enemy's behavior as "proof" of untrustworthiness. Hawks believe that trust must be "earned", not given. Doves, on the other hand, will tend to emphasize good faith and trust, argue that the circle of fear must be broken by a reduction in military forces, even unilaterally, and conclude that trust must be "given", even at some risk, in order to assure an anxious or fearful enemy.

Although the Hawk versus Dove rhetoric has died down with the end of the Cold War, it continues to lurk just below the surface. This is evidenced by attempts in early 1995 to eliminate, or at least substantially reduce, the U.S. Arms Control and Disarmament Agency by incorporating it into the State Department. There is the perpetual debate over military aid to foreign governments. Although Americans have concerned themselves primarily with the Soviet-American confrontation of the Cold War for the last five decades, Hawks and Doves exist in other countries as well and engage in the identical rhetoric, modified somewhat for their particular domestic and cultural circumstances.

While they may have used different names at different times, the Hawk-Dove controversy is not new. There were the equivalent of Hawks and Doves in Athens during the Peloponnesian Wars, for example. The Egyptian Pharaoh Ramses II faced the same debate when he set out on his expansion of the Egyptian Empire. There were Hawks and Doves in the American Civil War in both the North and the South. Where the historical record provides us the opportunity, a comparison of the rhetoric shows that it is not all that different. The following pages therefore are couched in terms of the Cold War rhetoric as a matter of history and familiarity, but are applicable to almost any similar confrontation.

The ending of the Cold War and other international crises demonstrates that a balance between the two views is achievable. The Arab-Israeli peace process, after years of direct confrontation and refusal even to speak to each other, was initiated through an initial gesture of trust by Anwar Sadat of Egypt. However, this was only possible after he had demonstrated to his own Hawks his willingness to employ force by waging the 1973 Arab-Israeli War. Though often, and arguably, considered a military defeat, it was for Sadat and Egypt a political victory, both domestically and internationally.

Similarly, after almost 40 years of distrust between the U.S. and Mainland China, the Nixon administration opened the doors to communication through gestures of trust, albeit limited at first. This was initially accomplished by the sounds of a ping pong match rather than saber rattling. On the other hand, conducting a massive military build-up, accompanied by Hawkish rhetoric, the Reagan administration simultaneously worked in incremental steps to make gestures toward the U.S.S.R. that engendered trust. One of the key elements in the process was continual communication between the protagonists.

Prisoners' and Security Dilemmas

The Prisoners' Dilemma, which is a special case of the theory of games of strategy, is an excellent model for better understanding some of the difficulties associated with the question of security and safety in this world. In the usual formulation of the Prisoners' Dilemma, two prisoners have been caught and charged with a crime. Lacking evidence, the prosecuting attorney realizes that he has a weak case against the two, whereupon he has the prisoners placed in separate cells and prevented from communicating with each other.

He then offers each prisoner the following deal. "The evidence against you is not complete, so each of you has a choice of confessing or not confessing to the crime. If you both confess, your sentences will be five years each. If neither of you confesses, your sentences will be one year each. If one of you confesses, the one who confesses will get a light sentence of only half a year for helping us clear up this case, but the other will be dealt with harshly and receive a sentence of ten years." Because the prisoners are kept separated, each must make his own decision about confessing without information about what the other prisoner has decided.

The first number in each cell of Figure 1.1 represents the possible sentence for Prisoner 1. The second is the possible sentence for Prisoner 2. Obviously each prisoner's greatest preference is likely to be the half-year sentence, followed by the one-year sentence, and then the five-year sentence. The least desirable outcome for each prisoner would be a ten-year sentence.

Figure 1.1 Prisoners' Dilemma Payoff Matrix

		Prisoner 2	
		Confess	Not Confess
Prisoner 1	Confess	5,5	1/2, 10
	Not Confess	10,1/2	1,1

Rational behavior, by definition, requires that a person strive exclusively for his own first preference on a scale of preferences. In this case, a rational prisoner must strive exclusively for the payoff that maximizes his own self-interest, that is, the half-year sentence, without regard for the other party. However, neither prisoner can escape the hard fact that the outcome for himself is also contingent upon what his partner in crime decides. In other words, the dilemma each has is how to reconcile the two self-interested "rationalities".

Ordinarily, individuals in such a situation proceed to communicate with each other in order to arrive at some collective action. Such is the central role that communication plays in the achievement of cooperation in human affairs. In our hypothetical Prisoners' Dilemma, however, communication is not possible. Each must consider other factors in arriving at his own decision to confess or not confess.

Each prisoner must consider two antecedent questions. First, what will be the other prisoner's probable behavior? Second, will that probable behavior have positive or negative consequences for himself? These two questions are, in fact, the principal elements of trust. *Trust has been defined as consisting of two elements: (a) predictability of another's behavior and (b) the positive or negative consequences of that behavior for oneself.*[1]

To predict another's probable behavior requires observation of the past behavior of that individual. This is an *empirical* process. One must also make a judgment as to whether or not the predicted behavior will have positive consequences for oneself. This is a *normative* judgment. Taken together, the empirical and the normative conclusions will generate an attitude of trust or distrust toward the other person. Obviously the possibility of error in predicting how another will behave depends a great deal on how well one knows the other. This kind of empirical knowledge is rarely perfect or without risk. Further, the extent to which one wishes to risk trusting another may depend a great deal upon the weightiness of the positive or negative consequences for oneself that may ensue from a trusting attitude.

This is the case for the two prisoners. Much will depend on how long they have been partners in crime, how well they have "stuck together" under trying circumstances in the past, the extent to which they share common goals, and the degree to which they like each other. If they trust

---

1   Morton Deutsch, "Trust and Suspicion", *Journal of Conflict Resolution*, 2 (1958), 265-279. One of the most recent and comprehensive treatments of trust in its many manifestations is Roderick M. Kramer and Tom R. Tyler, *Trust in Organizations: Frontiers of Theory and Research* (Thousand Oaks, CA: Sage Publications, 1996). The essential components of the definition remain the same almost 40 years after originally proposed by Deutsch.

each other not to confess, each would give up his rational first preference (the half-year sentence) in favor of a second best, but collective, preference: the one-year sentence. However, if they distrust each other, each is likely to try to "get the jump" on the other by confessing, and both are likely thereby to get their third preference, the five-year sentence. If one is trusting of the other while the other is distrusting of him, the trusting (not confessing) prisoner will be exploited in that he will receive a ten-year sentence while his partner gets off with only half year.

Distrust continues to be a major hurdle to cooperation in international affairs. In fact, distrust is the compelling central feature of the arms race. Consider the following observations by former U.S. Secretary of Defense Harold Brown in his annual report to the Congress. It is illustrative of Cold War perceptions and statements.

> There remains the question of how large the collective deterrent should be. The answer to that question depends, in turn, on how we interpret the policies and assess the capabilities of the Soviet Union. . . . We face great uncertainty as to the intentions of [the Soviet] leadership. . . . After reviewing the growth in Soviet military forces since 1964, the Soviets may be less well-intentioned than we would wish them to be. Our planning must take that possibility into account. . . . Exactly what the Soviets are trying to accomplish with their large and growing capabilities is uncertain.[2]

The Secretary of Defense said that the Soviet Union was not to be trusted. Its future behavior cannot be reliably predicted on the basis of its past behavior, particularly in the light of its rapidly growing military forces. The consequences of Soviet behavior for the United States are likely to be negative, that is, reduced American security as well as reduced American influence in world affairs. Of course, Soviet leaders were expressing a similar analysis, with certain variations, arguing that they are surrounded by past and present enemies, namely, Germany and NATO on the west and China on the east, not to mention the other superpower in North America.

Thus, the parties to an arms race are in a predicament similar to that described in the Prisoners' Dilemma. Thinking strictly on a unilateral, self-interested, rational basis, the leader of a nation might say: "We have

---

2   Secretary of Defense, *Annual Report to the Congress: Fiscal Year 1979*, 33-34, 62.

two choices: to arm or to disarm. If the other nation disarms, we are better off by remaining armed. If the other nation arms, we are even more obviously better off remaining armed." Hence, in an environment of international distrust, the outcome is an arms race, even though both parties may prefer to use their respective resources for other than military purposes.

Robert Jervis has reformulated this security dilemma as described in Figure 1.2.[3] In Jervis' formulation, the numbers represent the ranked order of preferences of Nations A and B, respectively. Thinking strictly in terms of its own maximum self-interest, each nation most prefers, as represented by the numeral 1, to defect and thereby exploit the cooperative inclination of the other nation. At the other extreme, however, each nation would least like (numeral 4) to be exploited for being cooperative while the other nation defects.

Figure 1.2 Payoff Matrix in the Security Dilemma

		Nation B	
		Cooperate	Defect
Nation A	Cooperate	CC (2) (2)	CD (4) (1)
	Defect	DC (1) (4)	DD (3) (3)

Each nation's second preference would be to cooperate if, and only if, the other nation can be trusted to cooperate as well. However, under conditions of distrust, each nation is likely to defect and go its own way, resulting in the third preference in the defect-defect cell, that is, carry on a competitive arms race.

Jervis' excellent analysis of the security dilemma makes it clear that the essential task of Nations A and B is to do all that is necessary and possible to increase each other's incentive to cooperate. In recent years, the popular

---

3   Robert Jervis, "Cooperation Under the Security Dilemma", *World Politics* (January 1978), 167-214. For an evaluation of the debate about deterrence theory and mutual assured destruction (MAD), Donald M. Snow, "Current Nuclear Deterrence Thinking: An Overview and Review", *International Studies Quarterly*, 3 (September 1979) 23, 445-486.

term for this type of effort has been "confidence building". In other words, engage in those gestures and efforts that lead to greater trust between the two adversaries. Deterrence theory goes a step further, requiring Nations A and B to make evident the unacceptable costs that each nation risks by exploiting the other nation.

What happens to nations that allow themselves to be exploited, as indicated in the DC and CD cells in Figure 1.2? The most serious results are loss of territory or loss of sovereignty. A more subtle consequence is the loss of international prestige and influence that, in the volatile and fickle world of international politics, may also have serious consequences for the security and prosperity of the victim. It is the profound fear of such exploitation that drives nations to arm, join alliance systems, or seek protection from each other and from superpowers. Nations that cooperate successfully may be able to achieve safety and security at reduced cost, allocate resources to desirable nonmilitary purposes, and achieve all the benefits of nonviolent human community. Disputed territory, for example, is more likely to be shared by the cooperating nations in a civilized manner for the economic and cultural good of all.

The debate over the North American Free Trade Area (NAFTA) is instructive in this context, notwithstanding that it dealt with economics rather than arms. Trust is still a major component. The debate is instructive because of the pairings. The U.S. and Canada have, over the last 150 years or so, constructed perhaps the most trusting relationship that exists between any two nations. On the other hand, relations between Mexico and the U.S. have been filled with warfare, exploitation, and distrust. In the development of NAFTA, cooperation between Canada and the U.S. was a given, while a great deal of difficult and often rancorous debate, on both sides, surrounded the involvement with Mexico.

There are profound obstacles to trustworthiness and cooperation. Nationalism, for one, will not leave the stage quietly. Elements of distrust and nationalism are evident in the continuing difficulties of cooperation in the European Union over any number of issues. On the other hand, the contest for prestige and political influence can, among cooperating nations, proceed in arenas other than the battlefield, for example, in national political party systems. There is abundant evidence of the latter approach, although the media seldom publicize it. Whereas the failures in peacekeeping in Somalia and the former Yugoslavia receive a great deal of attention from the media, little attention is given the successful efforts in

Mozambique, for example, where a nasty civil war ended when there was agreement to hold free elections, with the losing party accepting the results.

Policies for Promoting Cooperation

What are some of the factors and policies that are likely to encourage nations to cooperate successfully, that is, pursue the payoffs of the CC matrix? One consideration relates to the central problem of the security dilemma identified by Jervis. The security dilemma arises because an increase in one nation's ostensive security decreases the security of others. That is to say, every time a nation adds to its military or other security-relevant capacity, joins an alliance, or aspires to territory that may improve its safety, such actions automatically decrease the security of others. In these circumstances, security is seen as a form of zero-sum game, that is, winner-take-all.

The problem is further compounded in that it is the perception that is acted upon, a perception that may or may not agree with the reality. National defense administrators, particularly in the intelligence services, are by their very nature notoriously secretive. Thus, decisions in this zero-sum game are often made based on half-truths and deceptions. Because every nation must do its utmost to maintain and improve its security, the dilemma is how to avoid an apparently inevitable arms race, yet prevent inadvertent war.

To encourage the cooperation needed to resolve such dilemmas, one recommended policy is for a nation to give up some of its ability to inflict damage on the other. In some respects this is what the United States did when it leveled off its rate of military spending relative to its gross national product following the end of the Vietnam War. A similar policy was the American freeze on the number of its strategic delivery systems following SALT I, thereby allowing the Soviet Union to catch up and, according to the Hawks, possibly surpass the American arsenal. Even during the height of the renewed competition between the U.S. and U.S.S.R. in the 1980s, a major part of the American administrations' efforts continued to be devoted to pursuing arms control, particularly in weapons of mass destruction.

A second policy designed to encourage nations to cooperate is to understate the gains one's own side could achieve from ever exploiting the other. In other words, the leaders of powerful nations ought not go around, as Khrushchev did, bragging that "we will bury you", referring to the day when, in his opinion, the Soviet Union would win its contest with the

United States. Even while this kind of rhetoric was issuing from both sides of the Iron Curtain, it was regularly and repeatedly also noted that neither side would really gain much should they engage in a war. Both had the ability to inflict such severe damage on the other that war would bring little, if any, benefit for the one initiating such an action. Indeed, this understanding is probably what allowed some of the saber rattling to take place. For example, when both superpowers rushed to support their respective clients during the 1973 Arab-Israeli War, great pains were taken to let each other know that there was little to be gained by a direct confrontation of the superpowers.

A third policy promotive of cooperation is also an argument for an open society. The general availability of information about a nation's military and other resources, that is, the elimination of secrecy about security resources, can be a major contributor to the reduction of national anxiety about the capacity and intentions of another nation. In many areas of human behavior, information tends to reduce anxiety. A similar tendency applies in the security field. If information is not openly available, nations expend great sums, as we shall see below, on verification systems, KGBs, and CIAs in order to obtain the required information. Nevertheless, much of this secretive information, when obtained, is faulty and may lead to misperceptions.

A fourth cooperation-producing policy would be to break up large issues and big transactions into smaller ones, thereby reducing the scale of possible losses for each party if exploited by the other. This is a familiar principle in the theory and practice of negotiation. The principle assumes that there is small likelihood that suspicious and hostile adversaries can ever reach Grand Settlements of all their outstanding controversies at one time. The greater probability is that small issues, if successfully resolved, will tend to build attitudes of trust that encourage the resolution of larger issues at a later time. Often the larger issues lose much of their saliency as the momentum of smaller resolutions goes forward.

Such is the argument for the Camp David agreements that led to the treaty between Egypt and Israel. These agreements left such large issues as the disposition of Jerusalem and other lands claimed by the Palestinians for later negotiation. Such also is the argument for the SALT I and SALT II agreements and their replacements in the 1980s, the START I and II agreements. Even negotiations over matters not directly affecting security have a confidence-building component. Thus. successful trade negotiations tend to engender a greater degree of trust, as do agreements, even if nominal, on social issues and the environment. Opponents of these agreements insisted that all outstanding issues with the former Soviet Union needed to be linked one with the other in order to get the Russians to concede on any of them. Proponents of the SALT agreements, however, considered such linkages to be insurmountable obstacles to making any progress toward halting the arms competition. The nonlinkage posture is presumably the one that is more likely to advance the cooperative relationships required in the CC cell of Figure 1.2.

A fifth policy recommendation offered by Jervis was that each nation's leaders study and comprehend the nature of the security dilemma itself. An understanding of the security dilemma is likely to lead to humility and caution about this extremely complex and dangerous problem. In a world that resounds with bravado propaganda and strutting statesmen, such humility and caution could themselves be great contributions to the sense of world security.

Policies to Discourage Exploitation

In an imperfect world in which human judgment is fallible, it is necessary to make explicit that exploitation of one nation by another, as in the DC and CD situations, will incur grave costs for the exploiter. What policies are likely to accomplish this? The issue is essentially one of reward-and-punishment conditioning. Just as the several policies suggested above would reward nations for cooperating with each other, the policies below are intended to deter or punish exploitation of one nation by another.

"Drawing-the-line" is one of several familiar policies for making clear to a potential attacker or predator the risks of exploitation. This is one of the principal functions of geography and territorial boundaries. The military force that crosses a boundary is usually *prima facie* an aggressor. A hostile boundary crossing legitimizes such countermoves as "hot pursuit" or a counter-invasion of the attacker's territory. Thus, when Idi Amin's troops crossed over from Uganda into Tanzanian territory, this act legitimized the Tanzanian counter-invasion that ultimately unseated Amin and gave the Ugandans a new regime. Similarly, the principle of hot pursuit in international law permits the victim to not only resist the attack, but also to pursue the invader into the latter's own territory without necessarily embarking upon a general counter-invasion. This was the principle behind the decisions made in the Gulf War of 1990-1991. Part of the U.S. rhetoric was to "draw a line in the sand" beyond which Iraq should not go and beyond which the United States would not go.

Drawing-the-line is one of the functions of demilitarized zones. These zones are usually a result of military engagements at the end of which the parties separate in such a way as to minimize the recurrence of further military incidents. Presumably, entering or tampering with the demilitarized zone by either side signals a warning to the potential victim and is likely to provoke countermeasures. Border incidents and breaches of demilitarized zones are familiar techniques by which potential exploiters test the resolve and military capacity of a prospective victim. Buffer states, buffer zones, and boundaries made up of mountains, rivers, and oceans are geographical conditions that make such probes difficult for potential aggressors to carry off. These conditions also give the prospective victim an opportunity to mobilize his defenses.

"Trip-wire" arrangements are another type of punitive warning system. This usually involves a relationship between a powerful and a weak ally. The powerful ally will agree to defend the weaker ally by placing a small contingent of its troops or a few military installations at exposed and vulnerable places within the territory of the weaker nation. The presence of American troops and military installations in Europe and South Korea, although hardly large enough to have a winning battle capability, serve as trip-wires for NATO and South Korea, respectively. As a consequence, any attack on NATO or South Korea automatically is an attack on the forces of the United States and serves as grounds for immediate American military action against the attacker.

A third type of potential disincentive is preemption, that is, the offensive that presumably makes the best defense. When one nation observes a neighbor going through all the motions of military preparation for an attack, the best defense may be to attack first. Such was the basis for Israel's preemptive attack against Egypt in the Seven Day War of 1967. With the help of Soviet military equipment, Egypt had reoccupied Sharm-el-Sheikh, closed the Gulf of Aqaba to Israeli shipping, requested the withdrawal of the United Nations Emergency Force that had been patrolling the Israeli-Egyptian border, declared a state of national emergency at home, and agreed to carry on common military operations with Jordan, Syria, and Iraq. As a consequence of these hostile preparations and perceived threats to its security, Israel launched a preemptive attack. Within the week, Israeli forces captured the Sinai, the West Bank, and the

Golan Heights, destroyed the Egyptian air force, and captured or destroyed most of the Soviet-supplied military equipment.

Preemption is, of course, a high-risk policy. It requires starting a war on the basis of inferences about the probable military behavior of a potential attacker. In the case of the Seven Day War, were all the Egyptian maneuvers merely for the purpose of threat and pressure, or were they actual preparations for a military attack? Rather than wait and consequently have to fight a war on its own tiny territory, Israel decided that an attack was imminent, struck first, and carried the war into the enemies' territories. The cost to the Egyptians and their allies was devastating. Indirectly, it was devastating to Israel as well. The end of this war marked the real beginning of the Palestinian terrorist attacks on Israel and its allies. Internationally, Israel lost a great deal of support, particularly in the so-called Third World.

A fourth type of punitive action is publicity. In this approach, a potential or actual attacker is exposed as such to the entire world. The assumption is that exposure will trigger negative world opinion and thereby embarrass or otherwise hurt the aggressor. In such instances, the "smoking gun" scenario is the most damaging. The aggressor is either caught red-handed in the midst of an act of aggression or, after the deed, found with a "smoking gun" in his hand, that is, with overwhelming evidence that he committed the evil deed. The latter was the approach the United States was able to use during the Cuban missile crisis. The Soviet ambassador to the United Nations categorically denied American charges that the Soviets were building intercontinental ballistic missile sites in Cuba. For a few days it was the word of the United States against that of the Soviet Union. Then Ambassador Adlai Stevenson dramatically presented U-2 reconnaissance photographs revealing the Soviet missile launcher emplacements. The exposure did much to undermine Soviet credibility and eventually led to their agreement to withdraw the missiles.

Yet another approach intended to warn or deter a potential aggressor is explicitly and publicly to express concern over the other's behavior. If we glance back at the definition of distrust, such expressions amount to stating the belief that the other's behavior is predictable and likely to have negative consequences for the party expressing concerns. In the former Soviet Union, these statements of concern usually took the form of speeches before the Supreme Soviet or propaganda pieces in official publications such as Pravda. In the United States, the usual occasions for such statements were Senate debates over presidential appointments to agencies such as the Arms Control and Disarmament Agency or the approval of arms control treaties.

Anticipating statements of senatorial concern about Soviet behavior, the principal arguments in support of the SALT II treaty were that (a) it did not assume that the Soviet Union could be trusted and (b) American intelligence could amply verify all aspects of the treaty. Significantly, on the eve of the Senate debate, Soviet leaders made several moves obviously intended to demonstrate their trustworthiness, including the release of a number of Soviet dissidents and the first voluntary announcement of the precise type and size of their nuclear arsenal (which previously was known only from United States intelligence reports). Publicity also was used to great effect, albeit in a somewhat different manner, by the United States and its allies to place pressure on the Soviet Union during the 1980s. The United States went out of its way to publicize human rights violations in the U.S.S.R. and even linked trade agreements to the release of dissidents like Anatoly Sharkansky and other Russian Jews.

Another manner in which to bring a potential adversary to heel is to engage in saber rattling and gunboat diplomacy. Massive troop build-ups and military maneuvers, such as Team Spirit by the United States and South Korea, demonstrate to a potential aggressor the willingness of Country B to respond to Country A's threats. The appearance off a nation's coast of an aircraft carrier battle group can be extremely intimidating. Open threats of resolve and retaliation fall into this category as well. All of these means have been used throughout history. They are referred to as a "show of force", but they essentially intend to intimidate the potential adversary and cause him to back down and desist.

Gaining currency in the world is the use of peacekeeping forces to separate two adversaries, with their acquiescence. Usually the peacekeepers are international forces under the control of the UN or a regional organization. By standing between two potential or warring adversaries, they may deter or end aggression. In some cases, such as Liberia, regional organizations have actually been employed to impose peace by force of arms. Such occasions have so far been the exception rather than the rule. Peacekeeping forces have had mixed results thus far. The intent, however, is to enforce a cooling off period that will allow confidence-building measures to take effect.

A final, and in some ways ultimate, warning to potential aggressors takes the form of the arms race itself. A nation's willingness to expend its precious and limited resources in order to invent and stockpile vast quantities of weapons is presumably the most fundamental kind of demonstration of national resolve and capacity to defend itself and its allies under any and all circumstances. In traditional arms races, this has meant maintaining clearly visible and measurable military equality with one or any combination of potential attackers.

The escalatory trap of this approach is that a nation's leaders may hypothesize any one of a number of potential combinations of enemies. This worst-case analysis spurs the drive not only to match the principal adversary, but also to surpass the adversary in order to match the combined strength of the hypothesized hostile coalition. It was a favorite theme of Soviet arms control negotiators, for example, that Russia has more enemies, i.e., the United States, Western Europe, China, and others, than the United States, and hence Russia must arm itself sufficiently to be able to repel an attack from all of them at once.

It was exactly this fear that the United States capitalized on during the qualitative arms race it conducted in the 1980s. At the same time that the U.S. spent large sums on advanced technology and armaments, it put pressure - publicly - on several of its allies, notably Western Europe, to increase their defense spending. U.S. forces that had been decreased in Korea under the Carter administration were re-equipped, as were the Republic of Korea armed forces. The alliance of India with the Soviet Union was in part generated by a fear of the alliance between Pakistan and China. Israel spent enormous amounts of both its own and American money to counter the alliances among certain Arab states and the U.S.S.R.

In such situations, the security dilemma prevails; that is, any increase in one state's security (through the invention and stockpiling of arms, for example) decreases the security of others. In response to such situations, the other state or states respond with their own arms buildup. The traditional assumption in making such a response is that overt preparation for a strong defense will make clear to potential aggressors the high price they would pay if they were to launch an attack.

However, as Jervis points out, in an age of nuclear weapons and deterrence theories, the distinctions between offensive and defensive weaponry has become entirely obsolete. In any nuclear exchange, no side can adequately defend itself. This is the strategic conclusion that emerged from the 1960s debate over antiballistic missile systems. Under such circumstances of defenselessness, the number of missiles and warheads that a nation has can only serve as an index of its military capacity and political resolve. Indeed, this is what lies behind the policy of mutually assured destruction (MAD).

In view of the fact that nuclear weapons have never been employed since the end of World War II, it is important to note that technological advances in conventional weapons have probably exceeded those of nuclear weapons. With the advent of dual-use technology and the development of "smart" bombs, laser guidance systems and target acquisition, advanced communications, and all the rest, the conventional battlefield has become awesome in its destructive speed and power. The peril of the modern battlefield was exemplified in the Gulf War by the number of battle casualties caused by friendly fire, let alone those inflicted on the enemy by the U.S. forces in particular.

What emerges from this analysis is the central importance of trust and the extreme difficulty in designing political conditions that promote trust, deter physical attack, and improve the security of all. This is particularly true given that the tools outlined in this and the previous section often appear to be contradictory, but may not actually be so. It only illustrates that this is a highly complex dilemma that defies simple, single solutions. The overriding dimension of cultural perception and misperception has yet to be addressed.

The Behavioral Study of Trust and Distrust

The terms "trust" and "distrust" are frequently found in analyses of security and arms control. Consider the following quotations in which the term "trust" is the central, yet most ambiguous, element.

Item: At the conclusion of the joint meeting of NATO foreign and defense ministers in Brussels on December 12, 1979, at which it was decided to deploy 108 Pershing II ballistic missiles and 464 groundlaunched cruise missiles in Europe, Secretary of State Cyrus Vance commented: "The two years of intensive consultations which led up to these decisions give evidence of the mutual trust that prevails in the alliance". Here was a case in which trust is identified as a major element in a complex system of military cooperation.

Item: In his syndicated column, Jack Anderson cited a top-secret document on "Understanding Soviet Strategic Policy", prepared by Central Intelligence Agency analyst Fritz Ermath, in which three distinct perspectives were found in the American intelligence community. One contended that the Soviet leaders sought clear superiority over the United

States within as short a span as a decade. A second believed the Soviet leaders expected no superiority, but were determined to resist being placed in an inferior position. A third part of the intelligence community thought the Soviets wished to hedge against uncertainty and maintain overall parity with the United States. Ermath observed:

> The subject of Soviet strategic policy and objectives is very elusive. Pertinent evidence is voluminous, but it almost never speaks for itself. Interpretation of the evidence always involves *our preconceptions* (emphasis added) about the Soviet Union as a nation, international politics, the meaning of military power, and the condition of our own country.

Mr. Ermath's testimony highlights one of the most difficult aspects of developing trust in the security milieu. Because most, if not all, nations are secretive about their defense posture, or at least about parts of it, actions must be based on intelligence estimates. Intelligence estimates rely on the ability of the analyst to manipulate and interpret ever-growing volumes of raw information, often contradictory. It is imperative that such analysis be completely objective. Two major and linked factors often impede this process. The first is the tendency of people to "mirror image", in other words, to project their own cultural values on the analysis, often subconsciously. This tendency is often combined, particularly in established bureaucracies, with efforts to please the boss. The more established the bureaucracy, the greater this tendency is.

Item: In his 1985 State of the Union Address, President Reagan made the following statement. He was referring to the world being under siege by the U.S.S.R. and its allies.

> We cannot play innocents abroad in a world that is not innocent. Nor can we be passive when freedom is under siege. Without resources, diplomacy cannot succeed. Our security assistance programs help friendly governments defend themselves, and give them confidence to work for peace. . . . [D]ollar for dollar security assistance contributes as much to global security as our own defense budget.

The prevailing assumption in international relations is that *no nation* can be fully trusted; hence, nations insist upon procedures for verification of compliance with arms control agreements, inspection of military facilities, and creation of international police forces or collective security systems designed to constrain or punish "lawbreaking" nations. This was exemplified by President Reagan during a summit with President Gorbachev of the U.S.S.R., when he highlighted the alleged Russian proverb of "trust, . . .but verify". In an evaluation of the provisions of the SALT II Treaty, Thomas W. Milburn and Kenneth H. Watman stated the issue succinctly: "The first and most self-evident principle for verification is that we do not trust the Soviets. Indeed, it is precisely because we do not trust them that verification, a substitute for trust, is incorporated in the agreement."

The START treaties established an elaborate mechanism of mutual on-the-ground inspections and verification. To enhance the element of trust, short notice inspections were also included. A primary purpose of the International Atomic Energy Agency is to monitor and inspect the use of nuclear power to ensure its use only for peaceful purposes. Its effectiveness is subject to debate because of the ability of nations to disguise their programs and restrict movements of the inspectors. On the other hand, Argentina and Brazil provide examples of how such a regimen can work, as well as examples of how to build mutual trust. Both had substantial nuclear weapons programs under way. One of the first actions of both governments when democracy was restored to them was to sign an agreement to discontinue their nuclear weapons programs and set up a system of mutual verification and inspection.

If inspection and verification are difficult under treaties pertaining to the narrow and limited field of nuclear weapons, they are infinitely more difficult when it comes to conventional and chemical weapons. The U.S. has difficulty keeping track of *domestic* small arms sales. Imagine what it would take to keep track of all the AK-47 assault rifles that have been manufactured and distributed overseas.

In over 60 countries of the world, people walk down the street with great trepidation. Their countries have been polluted with small devices that will blow off an arm or leg, if they do not kill the victim. Antipersonnel mines are small enough to fit in a pocket; how does one verify them?

Similarly, production facilities for chemical weapons are easily and effectively disguised as fertilizer factories and biological facilities or as veterinary schools or blood laboratories. Under UN sponsorship, a Chemical Warfare Ban Treaty was agreed to by some 130 nations in January 1993. The treaty totally bans chemical weapons and provides for a verification regimen that includes both scheduled and short-notice inspections of military and civilian facilities. It also provides for sanctions against those nations found in violation. However, as the infamous "milk factory" incident[4] substantiates, it does not take much to evade the proposed inspections in either the chemical or biological warfare realms.

One verification and inspection system has been successfully implemented and has provided the institutional basis for promoting trust. The Agency for the Control of Armaments (ACA) is a council that has operated under the Western European Union. The WEU, consisting of Belgium, France, Germany, Italy, Luxembourg, Italy, the Netherlands, Spain, and the United Kingdom, was established as a defense alliance in 1948. ACA was created in order to monitor WEU arms control agreements. The verification system worked so well that both NATO and the then-Warsaw Pact were increasingly able to trust West Germany's military policies and operations. West Germany agreed not to manufacture in its territory nuclear, chemical, biological, or certain other classes of weapons. Given Germany's militaristic past over the last century, ACA's success made it possible to admit the Federal Republic of Germany to its council in 1954. The experience demonstrates how institutional arrangements may create an environment of trust in world security affairs.[5]

Despite the obvious and profound significance of political trust in these situations, the systematic study of the behavioral attributes and dimensions of political trust was late in coming. Morton Deutsch's theoretical formulation regarding the trusting process was early, seminal, and parsimonious.[6] Basic was his socio-psychological approach, which identifies two essential aspects cited previously: (1) the predictability of another's behavior and (2) the positive or negative consequences of that other's behavior for oneself. As we have noted before, the first is an empirical assessment. The second is a normative and subjective judgment.

---

4   During the Gulf War, the United States bombed what appeared to be an Iraqi milk factory on the outskirts of Baghdad to the great consternation of the world press and Doves. While it did produce powdered milk in part of the plant, another section of the plant was engaged in chemical warfare research.

5   Thomas W. Milburn and Kenneth H. Watman, "SALT II: Verification", *Mershon Center Quarterly Report*, 4 (Summer 1979) 1. The description of the work of the Agency for the Control of Armaments is from Harold K. Jacobson, *Networks of Interdependence: International Organizations and the Global Political System* (New York: Knopf, 1979), 183-185.

6   Deutsch, op. cit., in 1958. Also, his *The Resolution of Conflict: Constructive and Destructive Processes* (New Haven: Yale University Press, 1973), ch. 7. Kramer and Tyler, *Trust in Organizations*, op. cit., 3-4.

Early research used the prisoners' dilemma in games to test Deutsch's theory.[7]

Bernard Barber surveyed the early literature where he found different meanings of trust.[8] He reviewed the theoretical arguments and empirical research. He then examined the functions of trust in different American institutional settings, such as the family, the body politic, the philanthropic foundations, the professions, and business. Drawing upon the experiments of Harold Garfinkel,[9] Barber took as one meaning of trust the individual's expectation of persistence and fulfillment in the natural and moral social order. He added two other expectations: those of the other individual with respect to the fulfillment of technical competence and, further, with respect to carrying out fiduciary obligations and responsibilities. (These meanings are more simply and directly stated in Deutsch's formulation.) When Barber explored the functions of trust in American society, particularly in the political institutions, he found pervasive distrust. In this, he shared the perspectives of Phillip Shaver, who found that unrealistic expectations of leaders have led to a "crisis of confidence" in our politics.[10]

In the behavioral literature dealing with international politics, attitudes of trust are related to perception (what we see) and cognitive structure (what we already know).[11] Relationships among attitudes of trust, perceptions, and cognitive structure are identified and tend to underscore the significance of subjectivity, particularly subjective probability, in judgments of trust and distrust.

---

7   Mainly reported in the *Journal of Conflict Resolution.*

8   Bernard Barber, *The Logic and Limits of Trust* (New Brunswick, NJ: Rutgers University Press, 1983).

9   Harold Garfinkel, "A Conception of, and Experiments with, 'Trust' as a Condition of Stable Concerted Actions", in O.J.Harvey, *Motivation and Social Interaction* (New York: Ronald Press, 1963), ch. 7.

10 Philip Shaver, "The Public Distrust", *Psychology Today* (October 1990). In the same issue, Julian B. Rotter reports that "high trusters are no less intelligent or more gullible than others. However, they are happier, more likable-and more trustworthy." "Trust and Gullibility", *Psychology Today* (October 1980).

11 See Robert Jervis, *Perception and Misperception in International Politics* (Princeton: Princeton University Press, 1976) and David Finley, Ole Holsti, and R. Fagan, eds., *Enemies in Politics* (Chicago: Rand McNally, 1967).

Another body of behavioral theory that is importantly related to the phenomenon of trust has been exchange, or transaction, theory. According to this theory, trust is a principal attitudinal outcome of a series of successful (read: profitable) transactions of behavioral "currencies" over time.[12] The relevance of this theory to the problem of arms control and collective security was subsequently established in research on trust.

The collection of research reports edited by Kramer and Tyler adds the most recent (1980s and early 1990s) findings regarding the definition and implications of the concept trust. In their own words,

> The importance of trust in social, economic, political, legal, and organizational relations has been increasingly recognized. Why is trust becoming more important? One perspective on the evolving social landscape . . . is linked to rational choice. Axelrod argues that cooperation is sustained by the "shadow of the future". It is the expectation of an ongoing relationship that sustains trust in the actions of others. This rational perspective recognizes that declining trust in the existence of long-term relationships increases transaction costs, because people must engage in self-protective actions and be "continually making provisions for the possibility of opportunistic behavior" by others. From a rational perspective, trust is a calculation of the likelihood of future cooperation. As trust declines, people are increasingly unwilling to take risks, demand greater protections against the possibility of betrayal, and increasingly insist on costly sanctioning mechanisms to defend their interests.[13]

Kramer and Tyler refer to the social institutions that sanction those who violate trust. These institutions can exercise both formal and informal control over the behavior of individuals, making untrustworthy behavior costly.

A discussion of trust and distrust in human affairs must also make reference, albeit a disturbing one, to the views of social Darwinists and sociobiologists, particularly with regard to the issue of deception. More

---

12 George Homans, *Social Behavior: Its Elementary Forms* (New York: Harcourt, Brace & World, 1961), Peter M. Blau, *The Dynamics of Bureaucracy* (Chicago: University of Chicago Press, 1955) and *Exchange and Power in Social Life* (New York: Wiley, 1964), and Ralph M. Goldman, "A Transactional Theory of Political Integration and Arms Control", *American Political Science Review*, 63 (September 1969) 2, 719-33.

13 Kramer and Tyler, op. cit.

precisely, sociobiological theories tend to be significant modifications of the Darwinian theory of natural selection. Sociobiologists evaluate apparently altruistic self-sacrificial acts by individual members of a species as acts intended to protect the survival chances of the species' gene pool, particularly from attacks by predators.

To illustrate, consider what is genetically involved in some acts of human altruism. A mother has, on the average, half her genes in common with her offspring and a quarter with her grandchildren. Siblings share half their genes, cousins one-eighth, and so on. An act of sacrifice by an individual member of the family increases the survival and reproductive prospects of related individuals carrying some of the same genes. If the cumulative increase in fitness of the survivors exceeds the loss of the altruistic individual organism, the species is the beneficiary.

In the case of organisms that are not related, one organism helps another in the expectation of receiving help in return, that is, on an assumption that the beneficiary of the original help may be trusted to reciprocate. Cheating - defined as a failure to reciprocate - happens often and is likely to be selected against, that is, cheating organisms will be less trusted and less helped in the future. Sociobiological theory thus replaces current notions of individual altruism with one that emphasizes the collective survival of the species.[14]

In the view of sociobiologists, confirmed, they claim, by the entire evolutionary process, deception about reality and exploitation of the trusting individuals have been widely prevalent throughout the animal kingdom and a key factor in the demise or survival of species. In a world rampant with betrayal, exploitation, and violence, the deceiver usually appears to have an impressive advantage and success rate, particularly in the short run. However, does the deceiver have the same advantage over the long run? Are not deception and exploitation the principal stimuli for propelling animals of all kinds into coalitions and cooperation designed for protection and survival? And is not trust an essential component of such cooperative systems, including those we call political communities? If the answers to these questions are affirmative, then beliefs about cooperation and trust, too, may claim to be confirmed by the entire evolutionary process since it

---

14   Richard Dawkins, *The Selfish One* (New York: Oxford University Press, 1976) and R. L. Trivers, "The Evolution of Reciprocal Altruism", *Quarterly Review of Biology*, 46 (1971) 1, 35-37.

preserves those species with the greatest skills in developing cooperative systems.

A major criticism of sociobiological theory is that for every species that survives by cooperation, one can point to one or more others that have survived without cooperation and trust. Lions are unique in the cat world, for example. They are the only species of the cat family that hunts and operates in a cooperative manner. All of the other species of cat, both large and small, are essentially solitary and "distrustful" even of their own species. Neither argument is completely valid - *except for humans.*

Humankind has two distinct differences from all other species in this regard. It has cognitive reasoning and language. The first allows for rational consideration of the advantages and disadvantages of a course of action. The second permits the communication of abstract ideas between the parties concerned. There are those who maintain that human history is a story of repeated conflict. However, human history also clearly and amply demonstrates a process of increasing cooperation and amalgamation. Family groups have evolved into clans, which in turn have associated with others to become tribes, and so forth, until reaching the point of nation-states. Humans are now moving into associations of regions and, prospectively, the entire world. While there has been great conflict throughout history, the overall trend has been toward greater and wider cooperation and unification.

One must conclude from this chapter's analysis that the Doves clearly have the harder row to hoe. In a world beset by long histories of distrust and enmity among peoples and nations and by the chauvinistic language of nationalism and patriotism, the Hawks can readily make a strong case for their suspicions and their policies. On the other hand, history has also provided evidence of increasing trust and cooperation as societies evolve. Part of the evolution has been military readiness, which increases in cost exponentially and must compete for limited resources. Consequently, the competition between guns and butter is never ending.

The Doves must face the equally countless theoretical and practical difficulties of trying to create unprecedented universal conditions that promote political trust among peoples and elites at the same time that they assure everyone's safety and security. As noted above, however, the Doves have with them historical precedent as mankind has continually evolved into ever larger polities, sometimes by force, but more often by cooperation. In short, it falls to the Doves to produce globally the same conditions that have made human order and self-governance possible in communities of smaller size - a large and frustrating undertaking at best. At the same time, and until such world order evolves, it remains the primary duty of a polity to protect its citizenry from predators and aggression. The degree of balance that must be maintained between the Hawk and Dove positions is the essence of the debate.

Part I

SOURCES OF DISTRUST

2 Warfare: A Permanent Human Institution?

Warfare is a highly complex form of international and national politics. Wars are not fought over a single issue, but rather find their roots in a diverse, and often contradictory, complex of reasons and rationalizations. Nor is combat a new phenomenon in the history of humankind. Archaeological evidence of warfare indicates that violence has been with us since at least the time of the Neanderthals. Is warfare therefore inevitable? Given the enormous power of mass destruction that technologically advanced nations, and some not so advanced, can unleash, can we rationally afford to accept the assumption that war is inevitable? Is, as Clausewitz states, and Sun Tzu implies, war "merely" an extension of politics? And can politics become nonviolent?

Just as war is not new, neither are efforts to control the tools of war. Arms races and arms control are two sides of the same coin - and the coin on which they, and indeed, war itself are based, is insecurity. Arms races occur as one nation, feeling insecure, devotes resources to advancing its military capability. Its neighbor responds in kind and the race is on. On the other hand, arms control is used to accomplish the same end - security. Simply stated, "if the other guy doesn't have a gun, then do I need one?" This question, of course, presents the age-old philosophical dichotomy of whether humankind is inherently pacifist and social or whether humankind is inherently violent and therefore must create institutions to control violence in order to preserve the species.

To understand the problems of war and national security, we need first to examine the principal human institution for war making; that is, the military organizations that have evolved and the weapons technologies that have so profoundly influenced the development of military organization and the conduct of warfare. Although the case will not be made here, it may well be that the technology of violence has promoted in human beings their unique opportunities and willingness to kill members of their own species. Of one thing we may be sure: weapons motivate distrust.

This chapter has a simple purpose, namely, to describe some of the major developments in the history of military organization, weapons

27

technology, and warfare, to identify some of the relationships among these three factors, and to appreciate the scope of the challenge that this evolution of military institutions and warfare now presents to the human talent for creating systems of self-governance and nonviolent conflict. This brief institutional history, by implication, states the problems as follows: How may humankind hasten the obsolescence of warfare as a technique of human conflict? How may governments assure that military organizations become agents of domestic political order, freedom, and justice, rather than agents of war? More immediately, how may the U.S. and other military organizations reconcile war-making with peacekeeping and humanitarian aid?

There are those who accept the inevitability of war. Consequently, they pursue policies that enlarge their military institutions and that ensnare them in costly and risky arms races. At the other extreme, there are those who reject the inevitability of war, deride their military protectors, and become ensnared in an unsafe theology of peace. The middle path among these opposites is difficult to find. The working solutions that would provide physical safety, nonviolent conflicts, and ordered self-governance have yet to be clearly recognized. We need to provide background against which we may better portray the reasons it is so difficult to feel safe in the world as it is today. The demise of the Soviet Union and the emergence of the "New World Order" compel us to take up this challenge in earnest.

At the present time, only the United States has the ability to project military power worldwide. However, can the United States, politically and economically, afford to assume the role of principal international arbiter of all conflicts? Who decides, and on what basis, whether or not the United States should intervene between adversaries? Is greater use of the United Nations the solution? Or should there be greater participation by regional alliances such as NATO, the European Union, the Organization for Security and Cooperation in Europe (OSCE), OAS, and others?

The New World Order is envisioned by various thinkers as evolving in one of three different ways. "Pragmatists" (represented by Morgenthau, Waltz, and Mearsheimer) expect a breakdown in the perceived international stability that characterized the bipolar world of the Cold War. They foresee competition among states, supported by the re-emergence of nationalism, resulting in substantial chaos in the international system.[1] Others, such as

---

1   For example, see Hans J. Morgenthau, *Politics Among Nations* (5th ed.; New York: Knopf, 1973); Kenneth Waltz, *Theory of International Politics* (New

Keohane, Jervis, and Hoffmann, are encouraged by the increasing unity of purpose displayed by such regional organizations as the European Union and ASEAN. Members of this school perceive nations as increasingly aware of the advantages of cooperation.[2]

Each of these positions has strong and compelling arguments to support them, but there is also evidence in both cases that would counter these proposals. Odom and others foresee a world order that lies somewhere between the two alternatives. Their theory is supported by history and the balance of power politics evidenced in all regions of the world prior to the world wars. Their position maintains that while the United States may be able to project its military power, political and economic factors preclude it from doing so in all cases. In this scenario, selected regional alliances may maintain order within their spheres of influence, much as Europe did after the Treaty of Vienna from 1815 until the outbreak of the Franco-Prussian War of 1870-71.[3] However, certain areas of the world would not fall into one of these regional arrangements. While there may be cooperation between nations within particular regions, competition would likely occur between the regions, perhaps leading to military conflicts such as those seen during the age of colonialism and imperialism.

Ultimately, we must examine military history and technology in order to recognize whether the development of weaponry may make these perspectives relevant or inadequate.

York: Random House, 1979); and John J. Mearsheimer, "Back to the Future: Instability in Europe After the Cold War", *International Security* 15 (Summer 1990), and others.

2   For example, see Robert O. Keohane, *After Hegemony: Cooperation and Discord in the World Political Economy* (Princeton: Princeton University Press, 1984); Robert Jervis, *The Logic of Images in International Relations* (New York: Columbia University Press, 1989); Stanley Hoffmann, "A New World and Its Troubles", *Foreign Affairs*, 69 (Fall 1990), among others.

3   William E. Odom, *America's Military Revolution: Strategy and Structure After the Cold War* (Washington: American University Press, 1993), 7-13.

Primitive and Classical Warfare

"Peoples in primitive societies throughout the world lived more or less in a state of perpetual warfare."[4] As a consequence, warfare became a major function in each culture from the first human communities, with consequences for many aspects of social and individual behavior. Warfare was the primitive norm rather than a state of disequilibrium as it is considered in modern societies. On the average, primitive warfare accounted for about 30 percent of the deaths in the adult male population of early societies. Such a dominant social function soon led to specialization in skills and social roles as well as to various forms of primitive military organization. Military institutions, therefore, are among the oldest developed by human society.

The societies that engaged in primitive warfare were small, territorially ill-defined, and mobile, if not nomadic. Blood revenge rather than territorial or economic motives prevailed as the reason for fighting. Other motives included wife stealing, taking of slaves, aggrandizement of food and goods, religious duty, individual prestige, sport, and, later, capture of the positions of chief or other high office in the more organized societies.

The warrior role fell to all men of the tribe who were generally trained from youth in war rituals and skills. Armed conflict became increasingly organized as technical skills - hurling spears, shooting arrows, duels with knives and swords, and so forth - became more demanding. The size of warrior bands grew. The conflicts themselves were, as classified by scholars, of several types: feuding (organized violence between bands within a village or tribal group, akin to civil war); raiding (usually by small bands of 10 to 100 men for some limited objective, such as revenge, goods, or the capture of persons for slaves or sacrifice); and open pitched battles (involving from 200 to 2,000 warriors meeting in some prescribed area, with each side usually drawing men from allied villages or tribes).

Raids and pitched battles required some degree of leadership and organization, even though most of the fighting took place on a man-to-man basis. In open pitched battles, elaborate formalities often initiated and ended battles. Warriors had to be notified, convened, and moved to the place of battle in unison. Although a principal objective may have been revenge, prisoners and booty also had to be systematically shared or carried off.

---

4   William Tulio Divale, *Warfare in Primitive Societies: A Bibliography* (Santa Barbara, CA: ABC-Clio, 1973), xvii.

Treachery, attacks on guest villagers, and alliancing required coordination and leadership, which in turn led to the emergence of a military elite.[5] Archaeological evidence suggests that the emergence of elites occurred more rapidly among the priestly caste than the military. Even in primitive society religion was a primary motivation for warfare. Prisoners were used as sacrifices or slaves. Warriors were motivated, and still are, by religious fervor. In may cases in early societies, the role of priest and warrior-leader were combined, at least initially. As both religious belief and warfare evolved and became more complex, these roles separated and became more specialized.

As primitive peoples settled in fixed territories to engage in agriculture and herding, societies began to acquire stability and hierarchical structure under the leadership of a tribal chief or a monarch. Agriculture, herding, and commerce were carried on in territories with ill-defined boundaries. Warriors became more specialized in function and training, weapons and tactics became more complex and efficient, economic and political motives gained in importance, and battle casualties increased in magnitude. Territorial boundaries were patrolled and cities were fortified. Wars were conducted for territorial acquisition, plunder, promotion of trade, or the advancement of a religion or an ideology. Military equipment such as siege engines, heavy archery, and chariots became intricate, engineered, and manufactured, thus beginning the arms industry. Horses, camels, chariots, and ships moved armies from place to place. Soldiers had to be trained in their specialized military skills. Supplies and logistics, whether from a home base or from a conquered population, became vital considerations in military strategy.

In time, armies consisted of specialized, trained, disciplined, and organized groups of men whose occasional warfare activities were carried on even as the rest of the society performed its routine affairs. Military leaders were usually chieftains, kings, or other senior nobility or public officers. Armies began to assume great size as early as 3,000-2,000 BCE

---

5   Ibid.; Quincy Wright, *A Study of War* (Chicago: University of Chicago Press, 1942); also, same author, "The Study of War", *International Encyclopedia of the Social Sciences* (New York: Macmillan, 1968), vol. 16.; John Keegan, *A History of Warfare* (New York: Vintage Books, 1993); George C. Kohn, *Dictionary of Wars* (New York: Doubleday, 1986), and R. Ernest Dupuy and Trevor N. Dupuy, *The Harper Encyclopedia of Military History: From 3500 BC to the Present* (4th ed.; New York: HarperCollins Publishers, 1993).

(Before Common Era), when battles between Egyptians and Syrians brought out contingents of 10,000-15,000 men on each side. By the eighth century BCE, the Sargon Dynasty of Assyria maintained a regular army of from 50,000 to 100,000 fighting men, with another 50,000 in auxiliary contingents.[6]

Large-scale conquest, the political consolidation of great empires, and the expansion of militant religions dominated the development of military institutions from the fourth century BCE through the fifteenth century CE (Common Era). In the fourth century BCE, Alexander (the Great) of Macedon led a force that usually consisted of 30,000-40,000 infantry and 5,000-7,000 cavalry to gather, through conquest, an empire that stretched from Egypt to India. His "secret weapons" were two innovations: the Macedonian phalanx infantry formation and the siege engine. Of equal, or even greater, importance was the establishment of a system of supply depots and logistical trains.

In Rome, from about the third century BCE to the regime of Julius Caesar in the first century BCE, the development of military organization, tactics, and military administration reached new levels of sophistication and professionalism. From the outset, each Roman tribe or clan furnished units with a certain number of horsemen (traditionally ten of the richest men) and footmen (legend sets their number at about 100 sentries); 30 of these units of horsemen and footmen comprised a legion. The king or general who led the legion rode at the head of the cavalry. The infantry, less wealthy and less skilled than the cavalry, was divided according to age into advanced troops and reserves and according to weapon skills into swordsmen, javelin throwers, engineers, and even musicians.

As the Roman Empire evolved, the citizen-soldier became the exception and his place was taken by professional soldiers who served between twenty and thirty years before retirement. The Romans perfected the logistical developments of Alexander so that their armies were no longer tied to living off the land by foraging, an art that would not be revived in Europe until the 1700s. By 216 BCE, when Hannibal engaged Varra at Cannae, a Roman legion consisted of 5,000 infantrymen. There were sixteen Roman and allied legions (80,000 men) plus 6,000 cavalry deployed against Hannibal's 40,000 infantrymen and 10,000 cavalry; Hannibal won. In 48 BCE, Caesar's 22,000-man army defeated Pompey's force of between

---

6   Oliver L. Spaulding, Jr., H. Nickerson, and J.W.Wright, *Warfare* (New York: Harcourt, Brace, 1925), 10, 25.

36,000 and 45,000. These figures indicate the approximate size of military units of that day.

As the jurisdiction of the Roman Empire spread around the Mediterranean basin from Spain to southwest Asia and from Carthage to Gaul, encompassing some 150 million people, the Empire never had less than 300,000 men under arms and required a central staff to manage this vast military enterprise.[7] Armies of similar, and even larger, size were established in China. Classics on warfare that continue to be studied today, such as Sun Tzu's *The Art of War*, were a product of Chinese warfare at this time.

Other famous large-scale military operations included: Attila, whose army of about 200,000 Huns and Germans was defeated in 451 CE; Mohammed and his successors, whose horsemen extended Islam across North Africa and Southern Europe during the years 622-732; Charlemagne, whose army of feudal knights brought together an eighth-century empire encompassing France, Germany, and Italy; the Viking Norsemen of the ninth to eleventh centuries, who left permanent political establishments in Normandy, England, and Iceland; the Christian Crusades against Islam in the eleventh to thirteenth centuries; Genghis Khan's invasion of Iran and Russia in the thirteenth century, and the English attempt to conquer France in the Hundred Years' War from 1337 to 1453.

Nor were such developments restricted to the western world. This period saw the rise of the highly militarized warrior civilizations of the Olmec and Aztec in Mexico and Central America. In China, the political society was split between "men of the pen" and "men of the sword", a division so complete that separate portions of royal staircases were set aside for each class. The Chinese moved to invade and rule areas as far afield as Korea and present day Vietnam and Malaya. An unsuccessful attempt at amphibious invasion was made against Japan, as well as a successful occupation of Taiwan. In the early 1400s, Chinese naval expeditions of over 25,000 men reached the east coast of Africa. In 1453, the forces of the emerging Ottoman Empire, using heavy siege artillery, conquered Constantinople (Istanbul), bringing an end to the Greco-Roman (Byzantine) Empire.

---

7   Ibid., 215, and *passim.* The classic discussion of the evolution of the Roman Army remains Michael Grant, *The Army of the Caesars* (New York: Charles Scribner's Sons, 1974).

Medieval Transformations

The economic structure of feudal Europe from the eighth to the thirteenth centuries altered the nature of military organization and leadership in significant ways. The essential economic relationship of feudalism was the cultivation of land by a tenant farmer who paid fixed dues, rents, or taxes to a local lord who held title to the lands of all his tenants. Over the centuries, a hierarchy of tenancy developed, with local and regional lords holding land titles or being tenants themselves under grants from or contracts with higher nobles, kings, or the Church.

Significantly, in what Europeans called the Middle East and the Far East, a different tradition emerged, based on personal loyalty and fealty, rather than on land tenure. Rule was of people, bound by religious and philosophic ties, rather than on material wealth and property. The Ottoman Empire, based on the political philosophy of Islam, counted communal loyalty as most important. Indeed, the empire was ruled through its confessional communities. In China, the philosophy of Confucianism, involving familial loyalty, tolerance, and obedience to authority developed. In both areas, as throughout much of the rest of the world, concern for land tenure and precise boundaries was of marginal import. The Ottoman and Chinese Empires have been used to illustrate the point, but similar developments were occurring in the Persian, Moghul, and other empires and countries. These differences, oversimplified here, remain a major cause of cultural conflict between European-based civilizations and large parts of the rest of the world, including their respective approaches to war and conquest.

Associated with the European system of landholding and agriculture was a tradition of military service, or vassalage. Each local lord owed military service to a more senior noble or king, in return for the rights of hereditary land tenure. At the same time, each lord, noble, and king maintained a band of armed retainers attached to his household who protected his landholdings, maintained local order, and, with him, rendered military service when called upon by the superior noble. The number, equipment, skills, and leadership of each band of armed retainers varied widely, in part dependent upon the lord's income from rents, his personal martial interests and skills, and his alliances with other nobles. In short, military officership or leadership was contingent upon noble and landholding status. While the nobility spent much of its time in individual military exercises as a source of sport and self-glorification, there was little occasion or opportunity for training large contingents of infantrymen or cavalry except during actual battle.

The practice of hiring soldiers of fortune or mercenaries developed in response to the lord's occasional need for skilled soldiers on short notice. The high cost of mercenaries' salaries and maintenance in an era of primitive tax arrangements limited the growth of this practice for some time. In contrast, China continued the development of a professional military class and maintained substantial standing armies. Several of the major European medieval military campaigns, on the other hand, were carried out by volunteer armies recruited under special circumstances. The army of 50,000 men that followed William the Conqueror to England in 1066 was motivated in large part by promises of land in that country if conquered. Religious reasons and tales of the exotic East, as well as obtaining land and property, drew volunteers for the Crusades. This was particularly true for the lesser nobles and "second sons" as estates in continental Europe grew smaller and smaller due to hereditary subdivision.

By the end of the twelfth century, Philip II of France and Henry II of England, spurred by advancing and more costly military technology and manpower specialization, had managed to organize tax structures that enabled them to hire large numbers of mercenaries on a permanent basis, thus freeing themselves substantially from dependency upon the military resources of the nobility. By 1202, Philip's professional army was estimated to consist of about 2,800 men, some 2,000 of them infantry and 800 with other skills. The force included knights, mounted sergeants, mounted crossbowmen, foot sergeants (ordinary spearmen), foot crossbowmen, and sappers.[8]

The thirteenth and fourteenth centuries saw a decline in the use of cavalry tactics in Europe. Both rider and horse had become too heavily armored for maneuverability or staying power. Together, their iron armor could weigh as much as 100-140 pounds. At the same time, the invention of the longbow, with accuracy at 250-300 yards, returned the infantry archer to a major role on the battlefield. This period also saw the development of the crossbow. Although less accurate, and with a shorter range than the longbow, the crossbow had much greater penetrating power - enough to penetrate the knight's armor. Interestingly, the crossbow generated an attempt at arms control. It was banned by the Pope as being

---

8   John Beeler, *Warfare in Fuedal Europe, 730-1200* (Ithaca: Cornell University Press, 1971), 40-43. Also, Spaulding et al., op. cit., ch. V.

too cruel for use against Christians (1139). The Papal ban had only a marginal effect, however.

The longbow, along with new forms of infantry recruitment, came into prominence during England's Hundred Years' War against France. In 1346, Edward III not only hired mercenaries, but also initiated an indenture system of recruiting. Under this system, the king contracted with a number of his subjects to raise troops for him. The contractor would command the troops he raised, keep them in the field for a fixed time, and receive a stipulated sum from the royal treasury. This system enabled Edward to gather about 7,000 men-at-arms, the squires and other attendants of the men-at-arms, 10,000 archers, 4,000 infantry, smiths, artificers, and other specialists, for a total of 35,000. This was the force he used for his first raid on France, hardly a large-scale beginning to a long-term war.[9] But such were the dimensions of military operations of that day. Edward's successes rested upon the longbow as a weapon and his return to organized and disciplined infantry. Edward's other winning weapon was the cannon.

Gunpowder had been known for centuries and used primarily for setting fire to ships and other targets. Although known to the Chinese for some time, they had never developed it for warfare, but rather used it in firecrackers and similar pyrotechnics for entertainment purposes. The first time gunpowder was used to fire a projectile was during the reign of Alfonso the Wise, King of Castile (1221-1284). Edward III, at the battle of Crecy in 1346, was the first to use a cannon. His five cannons ended an age of castle fortification and introduced an age of artillery and firearms.[10] In effect, this was the first Military Technical Revolution (MTR). While weapons had evolved substantially from the first clubs used by cavemen, the use of gunpowder allowed the development of a military technology that aimed at causing multiple casualties with a single blow. Weapons to this point, no matter how complex, were designed to inflict single casualties with each missile or blow.

---

9   Ibid., 374 ff.

10   Ludwig Renn, *Warfare* (Freeport, NY: Books for Libraries Press, reprinted 1971), 122; Spaulding et al., op. cit., 375 ff.

Renaissance Military Technology

The fifteenth and sixteenth centuries in Europe were a period of prolonged transition from medieval to modern military technology and organization. Cannons were refined, standardized, put on wheels, and drawn by horses; artillery units grew in number. Stronger fortifications were built for defense against siege engines and cannon. Ottoman influences were manifest in the development of highly disciplined, professional infantry, the Janissaries, supported by artillery. The Janissaries were highly organized and trained, and even introduced the military march musical form - which they used to maintain formation. When this system broke down due to corruption (ca 1650), the Ottoman Empire began its decline.

This variety of technology was compelling changes in the organization of battlefield units, the coordination of command, and the maintenance of supply lines. France continued to rely upon heavy cavalry formations and the mounted charge. The Swiss and Germans developed the infantry phalanx and file formations, requiring substantial discipline. French and Italian foot soldiers were usually archers, crossbowmen, swordsmen, and javelin throwers involved in less coordinated actions. Hand-firearms were available by 1500, but not widely used.

Much of the fighting of the sixteenth century was between France and Spain over control of the rich Italian states. Systems of officership - not yet a profession in Europe - began to emerge: captains led companies; groups of companies were led by colonels; the king led the army. European armies tended to range in size from 10,000 to 20,000 men. There were branches and each had a chief: supply marshal, scoutmaster general for intelligence, camp (provost) marshal, and so on. Mercenaries were the principal recruits, but their recruitment was still the privilege and responsibility of nobles. Armies were raised for specific campaigns rather than for permanent service. Attempts were made early in the seventeenth century, without success, to create officer training schools.

By this time in China, the Turco-Mongols had conquered and been absorbed by Chinese civilization. This substantially ended any military threat to the Chinese Empire, and the professional military class began to atrophy. As with gunpowder, the Chinese, with little or no external threat, also made no substantial advances in military technology, as was happening in Europe where warfare was endemic. A similar decay was occurring in the Ottoman Empire for much the same reasons.

Great strides in military organization were made under Maurice of Nassau (The Netherlands), King Gustavus Adolphus of Sweden, Cardinal Richelieu of France, and the Spanish army during the seventeenth century. Similar reforms, under different conditions, were initiated by Cromwell in England. Much of this change reflected the arrival of the musket as a hand weapon using prepared cartridges and the development of the infantry as a disciplined and mobile body. Maurice of Nassau, for example, developed highly disciplined infantry, including a detailed, illustrated manual of arms. This period also saw the initial use of field artillery.

This survey of the development of military technology and institutions emphasizes the organization of armies for the conduct of land warfare. Navies were also growing in importance, not only for troop transport and supply, but as fighting units in their own right.[11] From time to time in history, control of the seas has been the dominant organizing influence in the growth of specific military institutions. Not until the height of the Roman Empire was a naval fleet clearly distinguishable from the mercantile, although the Athenian fleet at Salamis and the Persian fleets of Darius and Xerxes approximate naval forces. At that time, navies fought each other in phalanx and other formations imitative of those used in land warfare. The Norsemen, who invented the longboat as a new type of warship, gave a new importance to piracy and land raids from the sea; there was little distinction between sailor and soldier in these operations. To promote and protect their sea-borne commerce, the Hanseatic League of north European towns developed large sailing vessels to serve both mercantile and naval purposes.

During the sixteenth century, Italians, Spaniards, Ottomans, and English began to give serious attention to matters of sea exploration, colonial trade, piracy, and naval warfare. In the Far East at this time, the Chinese developed naval forces, as did the Japanese and Koreans. The Korean "Turtle Boats" were specifically designed for naval warfare. The English defeat of the Spanish Armada in 1588 was a turning point in western naval warfare (as was the Korean defeat of the Japanese in the eastern[12]) in that

---

11   Renn, op. cit., 212-234.

12   As a result of the Korean repulse of the Japanese invasion, Japan sealed its borders and banned firearms, not to emerge again until the mid-1900s. Upon opening their country, they imitated the military technology of Europe and the United States. In less than fifty years, they became a major, modern world power, crushing first China and then Russia at the turn of the century.

it confirmed the importance of naval warfare and inaugurated a new era of British naval power. England's first military academy, in fact, was created to train naval rather than army officers. From the seventeenth century on, naval organizations were an integral part of the military institutions of most powers.

In the eighteenth century, the most significant changes in armament were the substitution of the flintlock for the matchlock musket and the introduction of the bayonet in place of the pike. These further underscored the major role of the infantryman and motivated greater attention to his training and deployment. Larger armies went hand in hand with the political integration of several states in Europe. Military organization became more hierarchical and complicated, and military leadership began to acquire a professional *esprit*.

America's Politico-Military Revolution

An unsettling development for European political and military leaders were the wars fought on the American continent, including the American War of Independence. The French and Indian War, in particular, was of some military significance. Wars in Europe were fought by semi-professional armies on an open field of battle. The Americans, Canadians, and Indians refused to fight on these terms. Instead, they initiated what would later be termed guerrilla warfare. They hid behind trees, attacked without warning, and used hit-and-run tactics. They also introduced the long rifle, vastly increasing range and accuracy.

The American War of Independence was less significant for military developments than political ones that affected the military. Here was a war in which a government, fearful of a permanent army, refused to recruit a small but well-trained and well-supplied army, as General Washington requested. Instead, the Continental Congress preferred to let recruitment go on haphazardly and for short terms of service; some 400,000 men in a population of about 3,000,000 passed through army service for short and long periods from the beginning to the end of the war. American officers were chiefly, but not exclusively, the wealthy and the politicians rather than nobles or mercenary soldiers. Infantrymen were reluctant, short-term volunteers who brought their own weapon, the musket or, in some cases, the long rifle. Above all, the War of Independence ended with a clear constitutional definition of civilian supremacy over the military and a representative democracy whose very existence was a threat to Europe's monarchies.[13] However, it must be remembered that France, Spain, and the Netherlands were at war with Britain at the same time as the Americans and thereby contributed substantially to the latter's success.

A substantial change in the political phase of warfare occurred at the beginning of the nineteenth century. For the first time, nations, particularly France, engaged in mass conscription for military service from the general populace. The French Revolution of 1789 and the rise of the Napoleonic Empire inaugurated the philosophy that citizens were obligated to perform military service for their nation. Initiated in Europe, these developments would not spread to the United States until the War Between the States. In World War I, conscription extended to Asia, including both the Ottoman and Chinese Empires. The rise of nationalism went hand in glove with the rise of mass armies. However, although the armies were made up of conscripted civilians, the weapons technology remained essentially the same.

America's Uncivil Civil War

Possibly the greatest change in the history of warfare occurred in the period 1861 to 1865. At no time in history has there been a greater conjunction of political, cultural, economic, technological, and military factors. The Military Technical Revolution (MTR) of today pales in comparison to the events of the American War Between the States. The changes we have noted thus far have been evolutionary and incremental. By 1865, the "face of war" would be forever changed, not just on the American continent, or even Europe, but throughout the world.

The American War Between the States tested whether a new form of government - representative democracy - would survive, and in what form. Do political subdivisions, having a somewhat different culture, have the right to secede from the larger political entity? Does a central government have the right to enforce its will against a regional majority of citizens? How far can the protection of minority rights go; to the extent of dissolution of the national government? Significantly, although these questions were answered for America in its Civil War, answers to these

---

13   Alfred Vagts, *A History of Militarism* (New York: Meridian Books, 1959), ch. 3.   Also see, Russell F. Weigley, *The American Way of War: A History of United States Military Strategy and Planning* (Bloomington: Indiana University Press, 1977).

same questions are still being sought throughout the world in the aftermath of the Cold War.

The years 1861-1865 saw a classic illustration of the ethnological Law of Cultural Conflict. Here were two very different cultures within a single polity whose clash was inevitable. The South represented the agrarian, decentralized, aristocratic, individualistic, paternalistic, hierarchical culture of the age of chivalry; the North, the highly centralized, evangelistic, homogenizing, capitalistic, industrial society.

Important as the foregoing may be, our concern here is with the military changes that were wrought. The American Civil War represents a massive change in warfare. It marks the end of the archaic era and begins modern "total" war. Until the American Civil War, war was the purview of kings, chieftains, and other rulers, fought by selected individuals. The impact on the rest of society occurred only in the form of taxes or if civilians "got in the way" of a battle. The War Between the States saw the entire polity mobilized to support the war, and, for the first time, saw the deliberate attack on the opponent's entire economic system, culture, and civil populace that was carried over into the period of occupation after the war.

These philosophical changes in strategy were accompanied by the introduction of technology, resulting from the Industrial Revolution, that permitted the maneuver, simultaneously, of mass armies over enormous distances, on multiple fronts, by a single headquarters. The early years of the war would mark the end of the era when generals physically led their troops into battle. Operation Anaconda[14] initiated the total destruction of an opponent's economy, political system, and even culture. Anaconda's intent was not just to blockade the opponent's government and military potential, but to wage economic war against the society and population at large. The strategic policy represented by Operation Anaconda was replicated on the tactical fronts. Most well known, perhaps, is Sherman's March to the Sea. It began with the deliberate shelling of civilian areas of Atlanta by massed artillery, the burning of the city of Atlanta, and the laying waste of a swath through Georgia about sixty miles wide from Atlanta to Savannah. Similar

---

14 Operation Anaconda was a strategy designed to split the Confederacy in half along the Mississippi and totally blockade all ports of entry, and then slowly, but steadily, squeeze the noose tighter and tighter, as its namesake does to its prey.

operations, though less well-known, occurred in other theaters of the conflict.

The War Between the States saw a massive influx of high technology, much of it dual use, that is, with both military and civilian uses. While the war began with battles fought in the European style of open-order warfare, within months the lethality of weapons caused armies to entrench and fight from behind barriers. Even so, they still suffered casualties on a scale that would not be seen again until World War I. The telegraph, which moved with the armies, allowed rapid communication between the central government and armies operating in widely separated, but coordinated, theaters. Use of the railroad facilitated the movement of armies and their equipment at speeds and in numbers unheard of before. The techniques of mass production allowed Northern armies to be rapidly equipped with standardized equipment from boots to bullets.

Naval vessels were powered by steam, and thus no longer dependent on the vagaries of weather to maneuver. These same naval vessels would no longer be made of wood, but would be clad in iron (and later steel). Breech-loading repeating rifles would be introduced on a massive scale. Machine guns would be used to produce volumes of fire formerly only possible by equally large numbers of soldiers. Cannon would be rifled, almost tripling their range and accuracy, as well as increasing their penetrating power. The sky would be introduced as a new dimension through the use of hot air balloons. This enumeration of innovations barely scratches the surface of the new technologies that would be introduced in this war. Many of these technologies, as well as the techniques of their employment, were observed, first hand, by officers of the European powers. They were adopted and used by them in subsequent wars throughout the world. If the introduction of gunpowder was the first military technical revolution, then the American Civil War was the second.

The nineteenth century was, therefore, the beginning of very large-scale wars in which great armies moved in and out of areas densely populated by civilians. Civilian casualties often exceeded the military. Light and heavy weaponry began to be mass-produced, and arms industries flourished. Political ideology became a major justification for declarations of war. Once started, wars tended to draw in large numbers of countries to maintain or restructure balances of power. The French Revolution and the Napoleonic Wars spread the ideas of liberty, equality, and fraternity among the autocracies of Europe. The Crimean War halted Russian intervention southward. Nationalism was the ideological motivation for the Italian and German wars of unification.

The principles of states rights versus federalism, slavery, and a conflict of cultures were in part responsible for the American Civil War, one of the bloodiest of that time. This was exceeded, however, by the Taiping Rebellion in China (1850-1864) which was responsible for twenty million deaths. In Paraguay, most of that country's population died in the Lopez War (1865-1870). The century saw the Russo-Turkish War in 1878 and the Spanish-American War of 1898. It also saw the Boer War at the end of the century which brought about concentration camps, an ominous development in the campaigns against civilians.

Another striking development in the evolution of military institutions in Europe during the nineteenth century was the emergence of military officership as a profession. "Prior to 1800 there was no such thing as a professional officer corps. In 1900 such bodies existed in virtually all major [western] countries."[15] No longer was officership achieved in Europe or America on the basis of aristocratic status, wealth, purchase, mercenary skills, or political connections. In Prussia in 1808, a system of open recruitment, education, and examination was initiated to assure a highly competent officer corps for that country. The United States (1802), France (1808), and Great Britain (1802) established their own military academies in the first quarter of the century. Meanwhile, the Prussians formulated a professional ethic and produced a professional literature that includes classics in military theory and philosophy.

The professional officer classes which had developed much earlier in both the Ottoman and Chinese Empires had by this time atrophied. As the threat from Europe to the Ottoman Empire grew, there were substantial reform efforts made to revive the professional officer class. The efforts would be cut short by World War I. For a variety of complex reasons, no such reform efforts occurred in China, but did, with substantial success, in Japan.

War in the Twentieth Century

The twentieth century has been a continuation of the warring nineteenth century, but on a more massive scale. World War I cost nine million

---

15   Samuel P. Huntington, *The Soldier and the State* (New York: Vintage Books, 1964), 19.

military and thirty million civilian lives. World War II cost seventeen million military and thirty-four million civilian lives. The airplane added a third dimension to military operations that had hitherto been essentially confined to land and sea. Advanced military technology, radio, and mass production industries brought entire populations into the orbit of military operations and management. Vast military bureaucracies were required to conduct wars and to maintain states of preparedness. Military leaders became increasingly pervasive influences in the political, economic, and even cultural lives of major nations.

Since the end of World War II, nuclear fission, the atom bomb, jet airplanes, intercontinental ballistic missiles, space satellites, television, and laser technology have made it militarily possible to destroy most of human civilization in a matter of hours or days. This fearsome possibility did not, as we shall see, slow the competition in military technological development or the escalation of commerce in armaments. Nor has this possibility discouraged limited wars such as those in Korea, Vietnam, Afghanistan, and the Middle East, or the countless military confrontations that have increasingly engaged United Nations peacekeeping efforts. In so hostile and warlike a world, with few global military institutions for collective security and peacekeeping, each of the more than 180 nations, large and small, has been forced to look to its own defense. The motivation for strengthening national military organizations and institutions, at whatever cost, appears to be compelling and overriding.

The record of human warfare, as quantified in 1960, was equally compelling: 14,531 wars in 5,560 years of recorded human history; only ten years of complete peace in the 185 generations covered by this period.[16]

---

16   A report on "war as a permanent condition," *Time* (September 24, 1965), 30-31. No survey of warfare can fail to refer to Quincy Wright's monumental *A Study of War* (2 vols., Chicago: University of Chicago Press, 1942) which, for the first time, provided a thorough history of war and an interdisciplinary analysis of war's characteristics. J. David Singer's Correlates of War Project at the University of Michigan has drawn together substantial quantitative data about attributes of wars: participants, length, destructiveness, etc. See J. David Singer, "The 'Correlates of War' Project", *World Politics*, 24 (January 1972) 2, 243-70. Also, J. David Singer and Melvin Small, *The Wages of War 1815-1865* (New York: John Wiley, 1972), which is a handbook of the data collected. David W. Zeigler, *War, Peace, and International Politics* (Boston: Little, Brown, 1977), provides a comprehensive introductory survey of the role

During the period of the Cold War, from 1945 to 1988, there have been almost 100 substantial wars and insurrections,[17] and this in a period of bipolar stability, when the two superpowers supposedly stalemated each other. This figure does not include the multitude of minor actions, coups, and terrorist campaigns that were occurring. Nor does it include criminal activity, such as that in Columbia or the Golden Triangle area of Southeast Asia. These could be classified as wars, given their casualty figures and impact on international relations.

Technological development is not new; it has been going on since humans discovered they could kill prey and enemies more easily with a stick than with bare hands. Then someone discovered that a stick was even more effective with a rock attached to it. The technology has never stopped advancing; the arms race was in full swing. Contributing to insecurity is the penchant in the modern world for nations, both developed and not, both pluralistic and dictatorships, to view arms purchases and development of weapons technology less by the needs of security and military utility and more as matters of prestige and full employment.

The technological search for security has, ironically, become one of the principal propellants of the qualitative *vis-a-vis* the quantitative arms race. The meaning of "qualitative" is perhaps best suggested by comparing the bow-and-arrow to nuclear weapons. The arrow is lethal to one person at a time; a nuclear device may destroy a city full of people at one time. Both weapons are human artifacts produced at different stages of technological advancement. The potential lethality of military weapons is the principal motive for developing them, and students of this morbid subject have developed a "lethality index" with which to evaluate different weapons.

A United States Army colonel, T. N. Dupuy, created such a lethality index in the early 1960s. The lethality score took into account six attributes, as noted in Table 2.1. In the table, we can see examples of Dupuy's lethality index applied to selected known weapons as of 1964. Some sixteen years later, Julian Perry Robinson of Sussex University applied the same lethality scoring procedure to weapons developed since Dupuy's evaluation.

---

of war and various approaches to peace as these relate to the conduct of international politics. On the "inevitability" of war and the views of various philosophies on the subject of war, Donald A. Wells, *The War Myth* (New York: Pegasus, 1967).

17 Patrick Brogan, *The Fighting Never Stopped* (New York: Vintage Books, 1990), app. I.

Robinson's results are included in Table 2.1. The progression in the lethality of weapons is the essence of the qualitative arms race.

Table 2.1 The Lethality Index*

Dupuy's List: 1964		Robinson's List: 1978	
Broadsword	20	Assault rifle	4,200
Longbow	34	Medium howitzer, nerve gas shell	1,400,000
Flintlock, 18th century	47	Fighter bomber with napalm firebombs	1,900,000
Breechloading rifle	230	Main battle tank	3,200,000
Machine gun, World War I	13,000	Multiple missile launcher	12,000,000
Tank, World War I	68,000	Fighter bomber, nerve gas bombs	28,000,000
Field gun, World War I	470,000	Tactical guided missile, nerve gas warhead	91,000,000
Howitzer 155mm, World War II	660,000	Heavy bomber with cluster bombs	150,000,000
Ballistic missile, high explosive warhead	860,000	Heavy bomber, high explosive load	210,000,000
Fighter bomber, World War II	3,000,000	Tactical guided missile, 20 kiloton warhead	830,000,000
Fission explosive 1-megaton airburst	666,000,000	Strategic guided missile, 1-megaton warhead	18,000,000,000

* Index values calculated on basis of known or estimated performance of six factors: effective sustained rate of fire (how many arrows, bullets, etc. can be shot in one hour); number of potential targets per strike (target referring to one person standing unprotected in mass formation each occupying four square feet of ground); relative effect of strike (the possibility of the victim being incapacitated, with a 50 per cent probability of death); effective range (using a formula based on thousands of yards); accuracy (probability of the strike hitting its target); reliability (probability that the weapon would not misfire).

SOURCE: San Francisco *Examiner* (July 4, 1978), based on Julian Perry Robinson report in *Bulletin of Atomic Scientists* (March 1978), 42-45.

While the tables above list modern "hi-tech" (high technology) weapons systems, "low-tech" (low technology) weapons have actually caused more casualties, but seem to attract the least attention from the news media, academics, and politicians. It is the same phenomenon as occurs with traffic deaths. Highway traffic fatalities are a leading cause of death and injury, but occur in ones and twos, and therefore receive minimal notice. An airplane crash that results in a number of deaths at one time gets headlines, yet air travel is four or five times safer than highway travel.

Among low-tech weapons, perhaps the deadliest weapon of modern warfare is also the cheapest: the anti-personnel (AP) mine. Manufactured AP mines cost less than $5.00 each. Modern AP mines are particularly deadly because they are made of non-ferrous materials, thus making their detection extremely difficult. They can be, and have been, disguised in all manner of ways, including as children's toys. Literally millions of these weapons have been indiscriminately spread in areas of conflict since the end of World War II.

Another low-tech weapon is the ubiquitous AK-47 assault rifle and its copies. This weapon is cheap, rugged, and readily available on the open and black markets. Like highway fatalities, these low-tech weapons receive little attention, while weapons of mass destruction and high technology conventional weapons receive a great deal of attention because of their potential to kill by the thousands or millions at one time. This difference comes at a time when traditional warfare between nations and their armies is becoming the exception, whereas insurgencies are the rule. What makes these low-tech weapons particularly pernicious is that they can be manufactured, bought, and sold outside the normal confines of arms trade between national polities. "Once thought virtually a historical anachronism, the clandestine private trade has made a comeback in the Iraq-Iran war and in other situations where combatants or isolated states have been embargoed."[18] The "other situations" include supplies to terrorists and quasi-legitimate insurgents.

Generally, in the period since these tables were compiled, the lethality, *per se*, of the various weapons, with one notable exception,[19] have not

---

18 Robert E. Harkavy and Stephanie G. Neuman, eds., *The Arms Trade: Problems and Prospects in the Post-Cold War Period* (Thousand Oaks, CA: Sage Publications, 1994), 9.

19 The notable exception is the development in the then Czechoslovakia (now the Czech Republic) of the plastic explosive "Semtex". This explosive is three to four times more powerful than other plastic explosives. Because small amounts of the explosive may be molded into various shapes, it has become a weapon of choice for criminal activity, including terrorists. Unfortunately, it is also

substantially changed. The actual explosive power encased in a warhead is still roughly equivalent to what it was when these tables were created. There has been, however, a major change in target acquisition, information processing, and the accuracy of delivery systems. The warheads of smart bombs, for example, carry the same explosive power as their "dumb bomb" equivalents. The difference lies in their accuracy and expense. During the Korean War, several flights of aircraft were required to drop their ordnance, at close range, in order to knock out the Bridges of Toko-ri. During the Falklands War and the Persian (Arabian) Gulf Conflict, a single smart bomb, launched from aircraft at medium or longer range, accomplished the same purpose.

This change in modern technology gave rise to the term Military Technical Revolution (MTR). This revolution calls for the complete revision of military organization and doctrine. Its impact on arms control and disarmament is equally revolutionary. Much of the technology that is employed to enhance everything from intelligence gathering through data processing and evaluation and communications to the final delivery of the weapon with all but unerring accuracy from intercontinental ranges, is termed dual-use technology. Dual-use technology, as noted earlier, is technology that has both military and civilian applications. As an obvious example, the computers used by the military to process target acquisition data are no different from those used by civilian industry. Some of these dual-use technologies are seemingly simple. The laser range tool used by modern surveyors in laying out highways is equally adept at finding the range and azimuth to targets. There are an almost infinite number of dual-use applications. The implications for arms control arrangements seems apparent. An artillery piece is an artillery piece and has no other purpose; a computer can serve equally well to do a health budget or target a missile. Similarly, a satellite can transmit weather data or intelligence information. A modern, fiber optic telephone system takes the concept even further. It no longer is dual use in the sense of either-or, but one that can be used simultaneously for both.

Communications and ranges have been greatly enhanced. Some experts go so far as to state that the importance of direct fire weapons will rapidly

---

readily available both on the open market and the black market even though the Czechs have agreed to limit its production.

decrease in the future.[20] Targets are now acquired through satellites that transmit the information to a command center thousands of miles away. That command center then sends firing orders by telemetry to the firing unit which itself is hundreds of miles away from both the target and the command center. Where hundreds of rounds may have had to have been fired to destroy the target in previous decades, a single missile is now fired.

Some new technologies go even further, such as the Joint Stand-Off Weapon and the Joint Direct Attack Munitions currently under development in the U.S. These combine "the best of both worlds" by being highly accurate, as are the current smart bombs, but at the same time being fire-and-forget weapons that do not require the launch crew to continuously guide them. These developments in technology will not only have a far-reaching impact on arms control and disarmament, but may well necessitate the total revision of policy and military doctrine as well as a total restructuring of military organizations. The impact may be at least as great or greater than the development of *blitzkreig* between the world wars or the development of nuclear weapons.

At the same time, some of the most lethal weapons are perhaps the most simple. All the sophisticated technology alluded to did little to assist the forces of the Soviet Union or the United States in Afghanistan and Vietnam, respectively. Both nations lacked the political will to defeat their technologically unsophisticated opponents. A motivated guerrilla force cannot be bombed into submission. Militarily, they can only be defeated by the age-old infantryman on the ground. Just as Napoleon was unable to defeat the Spanish guerrillas (where the term guerrilla originated) with the modern technology of the time, so too, modern technology cannot militarily defeat such a force. Nor was Napoleon the first to learn this lesson; the Romans faced the same problems in Britain, Germany, and the Balkans. Even the ancient Egyptians faced the problem when they attempted to conquer Nubia. Significantly, ". . . sophisticated weaponry may be useless when confronting a technologically unsophisticated, but politically astute adversary".[21]

---

20 Hirsch Goodman and W. Seth Carus, *The Future Battlefield and the Arab-Israeli Conflict* (New Brunswick: Transaction, 1990).

21 Seth Carus, "Military Technology and the Arms Trade: Changes and Their Impact" in Harkavy and Neuman, op. cit.

Military Institutions: A Dilemma of Self Governance

Our brief survey of the military side of human evolution reminds us that the motivations for organized social and political violence have for millennia been stirred by the fear and anger arising from actions ranging from wife stealing to attempted world domination. Whatever the motivation, people need not look far for a reason to fight. Such reasons are the inevitable consequence of different perceptions of reality, different value priorities, distrust of the intentions of others, and fear for one's own safety and survival. These problems have been historically compounded as populations have expanded, creating a need for more living space.

The escalation of human conflicts tends to be limited only by one adversary's capacity to overcome its opposition. The major elements of this capacity have been (a) weapons technology, (b) military organization, and (c) political will, the willingness to assume the risks and costs of violence, that is, warfare. Our brief survey points up the breathtaking quality of the human genius for developing weapons technology from spears to multi-megaton nuclear missiles, from weapons capable of killing only a single person at a strike to those able to kill several millions. Military organization, too, has grown from tiny raiding parties to massively mobilized armies, navies, and air forces. Military organization, we have seen, has responded in large measure to the changing requirements in the supply and handling of increasingly lethal weaponry. In turn, modern economies have in important ways been organized in response to the production and other requirements of military organizations and their weaponry.

What seems to remain unchanged, but profoundly in dispute today, is the willingness to assume the risks and costs of warfare. There are those who consider wars of any type to be inhumane and obsolete. Others believe that there are some values worth fighting for: the liberty-or-death type of choice. But it is clear that nuclear war could readily end both life and liberty. It is increasingly evident that limited wars, such as Vietnam and Afghanistan, are not only difficult to limit, but are also less and less predictable in their political outcomes. Concern for such spread is a major factor in the political decisions made in the context of warfare in the former Yugoslavia. Are there, therefore, risks and costs of warfare that political communities should be willing to assume? Or are there alternative human institutions for conducting serious conflicts without endeavoring to destroy the adversary?

Warfare is a form of conflict interaction between human beings. Weaponry and military organizations are *instruments for*, rather than *causes of*, this form of conflict interaction. The conflict is between people, not between weapons. Arrangements for arms control and disarmament tend to focus on matters pertaining to weaponry and military organization whereas arrangements for peacekeeping tend to be concerned with the management of conflict between people. One of the most fundamental dilemmas of human self-governance arises out of the manner in which political communities employ their weaponry and military institutions. Do the military serve as instruments of safety, security, and order, protecting the community's institutions for carrying on its inevitable disagreements and conflicts nonviolently? Or, are the military tools of oppression and aggression in the hands of self-aggrandizing, lawless, foolish, or primitive leaders? These questions have absorbed political philosophers and political leaders since ancient times.

The military organizes and controls the community's resources for physical coercion. This fact raises two issues: (1) Who controls the military? (2) Against whom do the military exercise physical coercion? With respect to the first issue, as we have seen in our brief history of warfare, in most political communities, at least historically, the principal political leaders have also been the principal leaders of the military, for example, kings and nobles, totalitarian dictators, and the like. However, in communities that are constitutional democracies, the principle of civilian ascendancy over the military has been the key to establishing and preserving the lawful and constrained exercise of physical coercion for purposes about which there is community consensus. That consensus is usually manifest in the popular, competitive, and constitutional election of the chief executives of the community, its legislators, its independent system of justice, and, most importantly, its use of political party institutions as the vehicle for carrying on its more serious value conflicts. "Ballots instead of bullets" are the preferred instruments of coercion in constitutional democracies, at least in their domestic conflicts.

What makes the emergence of "military-industrial complexes" (MIC) so worrisome for some contemporary constitutional democracies is the tendency of MICs, through their potent lobbying efforts, to weaken other civilian institutions, particularly political parties and legislatures. In dictatorships, on the other hand, accountable to no one, the military and civilian managers of the means of physical coercion are usually one and the same. They are relatively unconcerned about civilians or electoral consensus; the relationship becomes one of unrestrained military ascendancy. The consequence is almost invariably a police state and political oppression.

There are also those political halfway houses, such as the former Soviet Union and the People's Republic of China, where authoritarian regimes maintain substantial, but hardly have complete, civilian control over the military, usually through the leadership's political party. Even with the dissolution of the Soviet Union and the regime changes in China, the balance between the party overlords and the military remains delicate. The Russian military, for example, has already demonstrated its ability to defy Moscow in the Republic of Moldava. On the other hand, it demonstrated its support for Yeltsin in its shelling of the Russian parliament.

All political communities, regardless of whether constitutional or totalitarian, require resources of physical coercion, that is, a military institution, to provide protection from external enemies and attackers. Here, too, it is inevitable that political communities will have conflicting interests from time to time. But how inevitable is the exercise of military power in the conduct of these inter-communal conflicts? The world has yet to clarify its definition of the differences between "aggression" and "defense," although, as we shall see in a later chapter, the General Assembly of the United Nations, after twenty years of discussion, adopted in 1974 a definition of "aggression" as part of a code of international law.

As the technology of weapons advances, it pulls military organization along with it. In separate nations, military organization is a spur to distrust. The world has not yet constructed a constitutional system of selfgovernance wherein there exists (a) elected civilian ascendancy over the military, (b) community consensus in the selection of civilian leaders, and (c) the employment of the military as instruments for the protection of systems of orderly disagreement. Instead, the world continues to engage in warfare, seeking as best it can to prevent or ameliorate war through arms control agreements and attempts to create a climate of trust reinforced by institutions for peacekeeping and conflict management. The uncommonly difficult question is how to convert the world's many military institutions from instruments of international warfare into constitutionally controlled professional "police services" for the maintenance of collective security throughout the world.

3 The Conditions of Insecurity for the Superpowers

National security is a multi-faceted condition that depends on various forms of power working in combination. These forms include military, economic, and political elements. In some cases, economic and political power may be more important to national defense than the military. It must be stressed, however, that all elements are interdependent.

One element of national security that is frequently overlooked is political will. Power alone is insufficient if the opponent understands that there is a lack of political will to employ it. In an open, pluralistic society, political will very often depends upon public support. Policies, particularly foreign military endeavors, that do not have broad public support cannot be sustained for very long periods of time. The United States was not defeated militarily or economically in Vietnam, but the war did lack popular support, even though politicians were determined to pursue the conflict. In contrast, President Bush carefully nurtured the popular consensus needed to support the U.S. and Allied actions in the Persian Gulf. In closed, authoritarian societies, such public support is less explicit, but no less critical. This is, in part, the reason why these regimes pay particular attention to the view of reality sent forth by their ministry of information and propaganda.

The underlying cause of insecurity, whether among nations, domestically, or between individuals, is a lack of trust. Nowhere is trust more positively exemplified than in multi-ethnic nations such as the United States, Canada, Australia, and others. How trust within or between societies is exhibited is through cultural understandings. Societies that stem from a comparatively individualistic, confrontational background tend to resort to violence more readily than those rooted in a group-oriented, non-confrontational background. President Reagan's famous quotation of a Russian proverb, "trust, . . . but verify," is meaningful because, if you *really* trust another, there is no need to verify.

These considerations notwithstanding, the contemporary pursuit of national and global security is generally perceived as a hardware issue, that is, a matter of possessing sufficient weaponry, military organization, and will to use the weaponry. Hence, the propellant of the arms race is the international competition for security. Actually, there are two races, both stated in terms of hardware: the nuclear arms race and the conventional race.

During the Cold War, roughly from 1945 to 1990, two superpower coalitions - the North Atlantic Treaty Organization and the Warsaw Pact organization - held sway over much of the world, and were responsible for two thirds of the world's military expenditures. Other nations, particularly in the Middle East, were, and still are, racing along behind. The precipitous decrease in the arms trade worldwide that has been occasioned by the end of the Cold War is evidence of the influence of these two coalitions.

The other propellant of the arms race, in addition to the search for security, is technological, commonly referred to as the qualitative arms race. Huge research budgets and unbounded human ingenuity pour forth new weapon technologies. Each new weapons system upsets some nation's sense of security. Turning off human ingenuity is about as difficult as turning up a political community's sense of security. Such are the circumstances of insecurity in the world today.

This chapter examines the assumption that military resources are the best objective measure of security and introduces the subjective aspects of "sense of security". This subjectivity manifests itself in hawkish and dovish estimates regarding the amount of military strength needed to be secure. Out of the debate between Hawks and Doves comes the public budget for the security services provided by the military. These have apparently been the major considerations in the perceptions and negotiations of the two superpowers during the Cold War.

Security as Subjective Judgment

Does a gun in the home add to the safety of its occupants? Put this question to any group in the United States and it will provoke a heated debate within seconds. Perhaps not surprisingly, the sides will divide up not between those who own a gun on the one hand and those who do not on the other, but rather between those who feel that a gun will add to their security and those who feel that the gun will increase their insecurity. In short, the issue reveals itself not as a matter of weapon possession, but rather as a psychological one pertaining to the sense of security.

What is most striking about such a debate is the highly and necessarily subjective character of the views held about the sense of security. It matters not whether the individual or family actually possesses a weapon. The security (*vis-a-vis* sporting and hunting) argument of one side will be that the weapon will serve as a deterrent to violence or illegal entry into the home. The other side will argue that the presence of a weapon is likely to be unknown to an intruder and an incitement to instant escalation as soon as the intruder discovers this.[1] One side will argue that the weapon is necessary for retaliation and revenge. The other side will decry these actions as meaningless once an exchange of gunfire begins. One side will feel better about having the "protection" of a weapon; the other side will prefer to live with the risks of being weaponless. Finally, the proponent of arming is likely to take some pride in the technology and skills associated with weapons possession while the disarmer will cite the large number of accidents and intrafamily deaths resulting from the availability and/or mishandling of guns. The bottom line is that, in the United States, someone is killed with a handgun every 50 minutes.

What is the basis for feeling more safe or less safe, with or without weapons? Obviously the conclusion about one's safety is arrived at on the basis of subjective beliefs and feelings stimulated by ostensibly relevant objective conditions or events. The leaders of the two nuclear superpowers, for example, have felt relatively secure from nuclear attack because of the size of their stockpiles of nuclear warheads: 11,000 possessed by the United States and 5,000-6,000 by the Soviet Union in the 1980s. Through various treaty efforts involving substantial mechanisms for verification, the number of both warheads and their delivery systems are being reduced. Each side is to end up with 3,500 and 3,000, respectively, still more than adequate to destroy each other. Matters were complicated by the dissolution of the U.S.S.R. which created four nuclear powers (Russia, Ukraine, Belarus, and

---

1 An unintended effect of recent liberalization of gun possession laws in Florida was a decrease in robberies, and similar crimes, against Floridians. Interviews with perpetrators indicated that a major factor in shifting victims was that the perpetrators had to assume that Floridians were armed. The criminals shifted to victims who were readily identifiable as tourists or other non-Floridians who would be less likely to be armed. Unfortunately, crime did not decrease. Thus, in a perverted way, a "balance of power" of sorts was achieved. This effect - a reduction in violent crime - has been duplicated in other communities in the United States.

Kazakhstan) where there had only been one. The last of the successor states to the U.S.S.R. with nuclear weapons, the Ukraine, acceded to the START agreement and other treaties in November 1994. The Ukraine's reported reluctance to give up nuclear weapons had more to do with domestic politics and emerging relations with Russia than any real desire to be a nuclear power.

In the case of smaller nations, particularly those that are neighbors, they watch the build-up of nearby armed forces closely and suspiciously, assuming that one's own strength and security necessarily declines as the neighbor's military power increases. Security is likely to be viewed as a zero-sum game. The active search for one nation's sense of security can, under such conditions, be the principal cause of the insecurity of others. Out of this relatively simple dynamic have come history's recurrent arms races.

As significant a subjective judgment as arming or not arming oneself deserves closer examination. What is the judgmental or psychological process involved in such a choice? Behavioral scientists refer to this process as "subjective probability". In their daily lives, people must constantly estimate the probability of events. But how well do these private assessments conform to the laws of probability, that is, mathematical or objective probability?

Often not very well. One reason is that we often confuse the intensity of our wishes or hopes with the probability that some desired event will take place, a confusion that may frequently be observed in children around Christmas Eve or in political candidates trying to keep up the morale of their campaign workers. We also make subjective probability estimates on the basis of personal experience.[2]

The judgmental consequences of personal experience were revealed in an experiment comparing risk taking by beginners just starting training as bus drivers with that of trained drivers and of an experienced instructor. The test task was to drive a bus between two posts. The posts were set at various distances from each other, ranging from gaps that the bus could clear very easily to openings narrower than the bus. The experienced drivers not only performed more successfully than the inexperienced, but

---

2   Analysis and examples are based on John Cohen, "Subjective Probability", *Scientific American*, 197 (November 1957) 5, 128 ff. Also, the same author's *Chance, Skills, and Luck; The Psychology of Guessing and Gambling* (Baltimore: Penguin, 1960).

also took less risk. The beginners sometimes tried to drive the bus through an impossibly narrow gap; the trained drivers seldom did; the instructor never did. The relevant experience undoubtedly involved a subconscious measuring and counting process that improves one's judgmental accuracy as the number of assessment experiences increased. In this experiment, for example, the more experienced the driver, the less risky (inaccurate) his subjective probability estimate regarding the narrowest gap through which he could safely drive.

Improvement in subjective probability assessment resulting from cumulative experience illustrates, too, one of the rules of mathematical probability, namely, the additive theorem. This theorem states that small, independent probabilities of an event add up to a *larger* probability. For example, assume that you are drawing for a winning ticket in a lottery. Your chances of success will increase in proportion to the number of tickets you purchase. Two tickets will double your chances, three tickets will triple them, and so forth. However, ask your friends if they would prefer to draw 1 ticket from a box of 10 or 10 tickets from a box of 100, in the latter case putting back the ticket drawn before making the next draw. Most will prefer to make the single draw from the box of 10, even though the chances of drawing the winning ticket is exactly the same in both cases. They prefer a single apparently large probability (1 in 10) to what they perceive as a set of smaller probabilities (10 in 100). Their subjective probability assessment does not match the mathematical probability.

Juries and politicians are constantly having to weigh one large item of evidence (and the probabilities associated with it) against the sum of several small items (and the probabilities associated with them). For example, should one friendly summit meeting between superpower leaders be the basis for important detente policies, particularly since it is impossible to have such meetings frequently? Or should detente policies be premised upon the success or failure of many more meetings by lesser officials? Is it better to disarm in one fell swoop or in small increments over a period of time?

There is another kind of situation in which chances are multiplicative rather than additive. For example, a general may have to decide whether to stake success on a single big battle or a succession of smaller ones. Assume that he must win each of the smaller battles in order to undertake the next in the series. His chances of success are multiplicative, not additive. For example, assume that the chance of success in each battle is 50-50, that is, $1/2$. The overall chance in a series of battles is $1/2 \times 1/2 \times 1/2$. . . . On this basis, the more battles he has to win, the smaller is his chance of final success. People very often choose the series with multiple chances rather than the single chance, thinking that it is better to have more opportunities than better odds, even though mathematically the series' single chance is less risky, that is, has a greater probability of success.

These examples simply illustrate that there may be, and often is, a significant difference between mathematical probability and a person's subjective probability estimate about the prospect of an event occurring. In international relations, such estimates are made regarding the extent of a nation's security, with a number of psychological factors that tend to promote arms races. Some of these factors consist of evidence that is presumed to be objective.

One factor is the degree of perceived hostility of one nation toward another. A second is the degree of trust or distrust between the two nations. The third factor, usually thought to be the most objective, is the quantity and quality of the other's weaponry. The first two are often compounded and complicated by extraneous factors, not the least of which are two that are connected. One is cultural differences and the very real danger of "mirror imaging," that is, projecting one's own cultural values on what is predicted that the opponent will do. Connected to this is the adage that "perception is reality". It does not matter whether or not you have a gun if a mugger's belief is that you do and that you will use it; he will go elsewhere. A similar logic applies between countries.

The perception that another nation seeks to inflict destruction upon or deny resources to one's own nation may readily be based upon the behavior of posturing leaders, threats and name-calling, ideological enmity, military maneuvers, and even normal competition. It is in creating these perceptions that cultural differences can have an impact. This was amply demonstrated during the Gulf War. Especially when it is political, Arabic speech is characteristically full of bombast and flowery overstatement.[3] Euro-American languages, on the other hand, have no such traditions and, indeed, are the opposite, being based on very direct, confrontational speech. How much of Saddam Hussein's initial threats and western reaction to them were based on misinterpretations will probably never really be known, but they undoubtedly played a substantial role. When leaders of the Soviet

---

3   Until quite recently, there were contests among Arab tribal poets to outdo each other in poetic rhetoric in support of their respective rulers. On more than one occasion, these contests actually substituted for war.

Union spoke of "capitalist encirclement", "capitalist ruling circles", and "imperialist aggression" in comments about the United States, Americans are hardly about to interpret such talk as anything but hostile.[4] Conversely, when American leaders embark upon Communist witch hunts, warn against the "Red menace", call the U.S.S.R. the "Evil Empire", and threaten "massive nuclear retaliation" against any Soviet aggressions, the Russians have no difficulty identifying their principal enemy.

However, Anwar Sadat's famous trip to Jerusalem from Cairo and the ensuing peace process between Egypt and Israel suggest that inter-nation hostilities can be reversed, or at least ameliorated. Sadat gave his life in order to begin a process of building incremental trust. Without his sacrifice, neither Yassar Arafat nor Yitzhak Rabin would have received their Nobel Peace Prizes in 1994 for the steps toward resolution of the Palestinian-Israeli conflict. Indeed, such steps were only possible because persons of European-based Jewish culture slowly gained an understanding of Middle Eastern culture, and *vice versa*. Similarly, the treaty between Jordan and Israel would not have come about in 1995 had not small, incremental steps been made over a long period of time by King Hussein and Israeli leaders.

Perception and subjective probability enter the calculus in arms control negotiations in several ways. Of the two major components of distrust, the prediction regarding the future conduct of the other party, while based on some degree of hard evidence, is also tainted by subjective estimates. The judgment that the expected conduct will have negative consequences for oneself creates distrust willy-nilly. U.S. Senate discussions regarding SALT II, for example, included many predictions that the Soviet Union was likely to try to cheat and that such cheating could have profound negative consequences for the survival of the United States. In short, many senators *prima facie* distrusted (and still do) the former Soviet Union's leaders. The reverse is also true; many in Russia's leadership do not trust the United States. As a consequence, successful reductions of both nuclear and conventional arms can only be brought about as mechanisms of mutual verification are fully established.

---

4   It should be noted that some elements in the U.S.S.R. successor states still speak in these terms, albeit without the "capitalist" modifier; nor is this historically new. The Russian czars from Ivan the Terrible through Peter the Great to Alexander II spoke in the same manner.

Some will argue that it is difficult to measure with precision such factors as hostility and distrust, but there can be no mistake about the quantity and quality of an adversary's weaponry. The other's weapons stockpile is usually considered the most "objective" measure of that party's intentions and of the degree of one's own security. Weaponry can be seen, counted, and evaluated for quality. The greater the quantity and quality of the other's weapons, the more serious is the presumed threat to one's safety. But how much is "more"? Unfortunately, the answer almost invariably involves a large degree of subjective probability assessment. The search for a military balance becomes a comparison of apples and oranges (tanks *versus* neutron bombs, for example) and soon flounders on the unmeasurable, and the arms race becomes inexorable.

To this "objective" comparison must be added several other imponderables. When comparing weaponry, there must be considered not only the will to use them, but also the question of operational training. Much modern equipment is of little use if soldiers are not trained to use them. A classic, and recent, example occurred in the border war between Chad and Libya. The Libyans had large quantities of some of the latest Soviet conventional technology, yet were defeated by the more poorly equipped, but better trained, Chadians.[5] There are any number of similar examples.

The Search for Objective Sources of Security

Possibly the most costly of human endeavors is the search for objective grounds for feeling physically safe. Powerful and famous persons surround themselves with bodyguards, usually at great private or public expense. Corporations and other propertied organizations expend large sums for plant and other security systems. Communities pay taxes for expensive police forces. Nations carry the weighty burden of military budgets and expensive weapons systems. One of the most widely held of human beliefs is that "might makes right". A corollary proposition is that military might assures security. The side with the most guns is presumably the safest, a delusion reinforced by the fact that weaponry lends itself readily to quantification.

---

5   A classic example is the Turco-Mongols of Ghengis Khan. Western history describes the Mongol "hordes" that conquered much of the known world, but rarely mentions that in almost every battle they were substantially outnumbered. Much of their success can be attributed to superb training.

However, there are those who will vigorously argue, on both empirical and logical grounds, that such an assumption is not only in error, but also dangerous. This point of view usually starts from the assertion that an escalating arms race decreases rather than increases security. An additional contention is that there are many sources - objectively observable and measurable - of physical security other than or in addition to the military. The latter include a nation's economic resources, technological and educational capacities, cultural and social values and practices, and adaptive political institutions. These sources of strength are, it is argued, along with the military, highly significant for security. Even in military strength, much of combat effectiveness has to do with factors that are not quantifiable. Indeed, such factors as *esprit de corps*, leadership, training, and motivation, all imponderables from a scientific point of view, may be more important than the number of guns.

It is hardly a novel proposition that a prosperous and equitable economy is a source of strength and security. But throughout history, has not the possession of natural resources and national wealth invited attack from the predatory and the greedy? In other words, is not a prosperous economy potentially a source of insecurity? The answer depends upon a number of factors. The citizens of a society in which wealth is widely distributed are more likely than not to pay the taxes and support its defense forces. Concentrated wealth, on the other hand, is likely to be less secure among an envious or angry citizenry unwilling to protect the wealth of the few.

Another factor is the extent to which the citizenry is the principal source as well as beneficiary of the community's resources. What sense does it make to try to capture a nation of highly productive farmers if these farmers go on strike or slow down production when they fall under the military rule of some hated foreigner? To offer a more specific illustration, would the United States remain the "bread basket of the world" if its farmlands and farmers were captives of some odious conqueror? In other words, economic strength is perceived by many as a principal source of national security even in the absence of great military strength. Witness the contemporary success of Germany and Japan in the world's economy. Witness the dramatic rise in influence of the Arab oil-producing states.

Witness also the difficulties of the economy of the former Soviet Union and its successor states. The relationship of the arms race and the dedication of enormous resources to military and related spending to the overall economy was a major factor in the eventual demise of the U.S.S.R. During the 1950s, the Gross National Product of the Soviet Union was growing by about 5.8 percent annually compared to a United States rate of 3.2 percent annually. Khrushchev boasted that the Soviet economy would soon surpass the American and that the communists would "bury" the capitalists. But at about that time, U.S. growth moved up to about 4 percent and, by the early 1970s, the Soviets were down to 3.7 percent GNP growth annually.

Soviet economists placed the blame on the leveling off of Soviet capital growth (no new technologies, no new industries, too little equipment replacement in old industries), the stabilization of the labor force (very little occupational mobility, low birthrate, much manpower tied up in armed forces), rigid bureaucracy (whose elaborate rules and procedures discouraged individual enterprise), and accelerating military expenditures (growing at 4.5 percent annually). Both Soviet and American economists agree that an arms race could compel even a totalitarian economy to spend itself into a self-destructive depression. "Reducing military expenditures, however, would weaken the Soviet Union's principal claim to world power. . . [hardly acceptable to] the conservative leanings of the Soviet gerontocracy."[6] This prescient observation proved to be correct. With the build-up of military forces by the United States in the 1980s, the U.S.S.R. was financially unable to sustain the arms race.

Another frequently cited foundation of national security is the technological and educational achievements of a society. Life in a modern industrialized and civilized community requires a literate and well-educated populace. One need only look at the tribulations of the many nations in which only 1 to 5 percent of the people are literate or educated to conclude that ignorance is a major source of instability and insecurity for these communities. In contrast, the United States is clearly the technological and educational envy of the world, the nation with the greatest number of colleges and universities, the most varied educational enterprise, the greatest investment in research and human inventiveness, the producer of computers, moon landings, lasers, and other grand achievements of high technology by an educated, free, and inventive people. The U.S. has become a leading Information Society.

We may argue over the quality or quantity of these claims but, overall, the objective evidence and the world's envy tend to confirm their validity. However, technology and education are hardly an American monopoly. Witness the surprise and shock experienced in the United States when, in

---

6   An analysis by Arrige Levi, former editor of *La Stampa* of Turin, in *Atlas World Press Review* (February 1979), 35-36.

1957, the Soviet Union sent aloft its Sputnik. It immediately became a matter of American pride that the United States catch up; politicians and taxpayers were never more willing to pay out the funds necessary for education and research. Ironically, a highly educated and inventive populace is essential not only to produce high technology, but also to carry forward the qualitative arms race, that is, the contest for superiority in new and ingenious military technologies.[7]

With whom should American technological superiority be shared? This is a troublesome question. Less educated and less skilled putative allies often do not have sufficiently educated people to handle, let alone develop, advanced equipment. On the other hand, industrialized allies, for example, Japan and Germany, starting with more limited technology, often out-invent and out-produce the U.S.

Most difficult, however, is the issue of transferring United States technology and know-how to our adversaries, current or potential. For example, during summer 1979, Dresser Industries of Dallas began to design and equip a $144 million plant near the Volga River to produce oil drill bits for the Soviet oil industry. The same facility could have been quickly converted to the manufacture of projectiles capable of penetrating the armor of the latest United States tanks. This transfer of American technology could not only help increase Russian oil production, but also made available a potential military projectile plant. Was this good or bad for United States security? Could we trust the Russians?

During and after the Gulf War, it was learned that the technological base and weapons development program of Iraq were much more advanced than previously suspected. Much of this equipment and knowledge came not from Iraq's former ally, the U.S.S.R., but from the U.S. and other NATO countries, particularly Britain and Germany!

Even more complicated is the topic of dual-use technology. As will be discussed later, many advanced technologies have both a military and a civilian use - without modification. How do we differentiate? Although the Export Administration Act prohibits technology sales to Communist governments if such transfers make a "significant contribution" to their

---

7   Even more prosaically, and contrary to much popular belief, education is a major imponderable that contributes directly to military strength. It is an historical fact that better educated people are more trainable, and, as a consequence, perform better on the battlefield. Given the Military Technical Revolution (MTR), such education has never been more important.

military potential, it has become increasingly difficult to tell whether an item is a sword or a plowshare.

A further source of security, many will argue, are the cultural and social values and practices of a society. Invention and the arts flourish in those communities where basic social attitudes promote tolerance, respect for others, optimism, and freedom of association and discussion. It was the basic position of Andrei Sakharov, one of the developers of the Soviet H-bomb, that the lack of freedom in the Soviet Union was detrimental to the achievements and the very safety of that nation. Knowledge cannot grow well or spread freely in a closed and isolated society; science is an open process that malfunctions under conditions of secrecy. Not many cultures value freedom and creativity, nor do some national elites care to risk the revolutionary consequences of educating their people. Such societies are among the least stable or secure in the world.

Many of the above arguments make it easier to comprehend how a society's political institutions may be an additional objective source of security. The political community that is willing to distribute its shares of power widely among its citizenry, that has a capacity for expressing and resolving profound disagreements, and that produces leaders skilled in the discovery and pursuit of widely shared political goals is also likely to have strong and highly adaptive institutional arrangements to accomplish all this.

For Americans, many of the relevant institutions are specific and well known: a free press and academy; a competitive political party system that succeeds in harnessing dissent, insurgency, and innovation; an open bureaucracy that is fair game for the dissatisfactions of legislators and taxpayers; a judicial system and legal profession accustomed to victories, defeats, and compromises; and the most varied and numerous array of organized interest groups in the world. As a consequence, the United States has perhaps the noisiest, most transparent, and, according to some, the most revolutionary political system in the world. What may seem to be sound, fury, and confusion to some is more likely the friction of a complex society adapting to new conditions and goals. At least such were the institutions that Woodrow Wilson had in mind when he called upon his fellow-citizens to fight to keep the world "safe for democracy". He was not alone in assuming that pluralistic political institutions are a source of society's strength and security. It is also the goal of these institutions to make violence obsolete as a technique for resolving human conflict and advancing social change.

These are brief summaries of the assumptions of those who argue that safety and security is derived from sources other than military strength. Each of these other sources is objective to the extent that it may be observed and quantified: the economy in dollars and standards of living; education in terms of numbers of literate citizens and years of formal education; culture in terms of degrees of consensus about particular attitudes and practices; and politics by participation, votes, and capacity for conflict resolution.

The more psychologically sensitive will, however, continue to wonder how much of the derived sense of security comes from objective measures and how much from highly subjective probability estimates. The world is full of irrational, trigger happy, and dangerous persons, groups, and regimes that are gratified by destroying wealth, burning books and other repositories of knowledge, inflicting primitive and totalitarian values upon others, and closing down venerable political institutions. In such a world and against such forces, only clearly overwhelming military might seems to provide the best protection and the most clearly measurable sense of security. Hence, bigger armies, air forces, and navies, better weapons, and more powerful military alliance systems become the order of the day. From this point of view, Switzerland is presumably safe only because every one of its citizens is a soldier. Germany and Japan, although disarmed, are presumably safe only because they are protected by the American defense umbrella.

Such are the arguments back and forth regarding the nature of security and the objective and subjective measures upon which our sense of security is premised. Hawks tend to perceive the world as risky, specific adversaries as evil and dangerous, and the objective military sources of security as the most important. Doves, on the other hand, continue to be more willing to live with a higher degree of risk, see potential adversaries as misguided but educable, and count most sources of security, particularly the military, as only temporary assurances for what is essentially, in their view, a subjective judgment.

With such divergent points of departure, each side arrives at quite different policy conclusions regarding such practical issues as weapons development, military strategy, defense budgets, foreign policy, and, most generally, the investment of all kinds of community resources for the support of security services. The fact is that the world as a whole currently spends almost $1 trillion a year (1993 and 1994 estimates) for military purposes. The arms race has been one of the most serious preoccupations of mankind, clearly suggesting that the predominant perceptions are distrustful and the resulting policies are hawkish.

Table 3.1 U.S. Defense Expenditures, 1980-1994
As Percent of GDP and Spending (in constant 1987 dollars)

Year	Percent of GDP	Percent of Government Expenditures
1980	5.1	22.7
1983	6.3	26.0
1984	6.2	26.7
1985	6.4	26.7
1986	6.5	27.6
1987	6.3	28.1
1988	6.0	27.3
1989	5.9	26.6
1990	5.5	23.9
1991	4.8	20.6
1992	5.0	21.6
1993	4.6	20.7
1994	4.2	18.9
1995	3.7	16.9
SOURCE: U.S. Office of Management and Budget, *Budget of the United States Government*, annual.		

However, with the demise of the U.S.S.R. and the Warsaw Pact, defense budgets are being "slashed" by the former superpowers (See Table 3.1), and the arms race has seemingly been relegated to the backburner. In many cases these reductions are more apparent than real. How long they last remains to be seen. Unfortunately, regional arms races have, in large measure, accelerated. As an ancillary to this apparent arms reduction, many of the arms industries, both governmental and civilian, are seeking customers elsewhere in the world in order to sustain their livelihood.[8] They are abetted in this by the very governments that are reducing production of arms for themselves; the unit price increases when fewer are produced.

If sense of security could be objectified as a simple budgetary issue, such questions as "How much is enough for security services?" could be more easily debated as a public issue. Of course, this is not likely, given the highly subjective aspects of sense of security, not to mention the difficulty in comparing significant national budgets such as those of the United States, Russia, and China. Another challenge to statistics of this character is their validity. Many nations, even among relatively open societies, are secretive about how much they spend on defense and similar services. The United States, for example, expends substantial amounts in "black budgets".[9] How should funds spent for dual-use technologies be classified? Furthermore, comparisons of budgets of highly centralized governments such as France with decentralized governments such as the United States and Switzerland make comparisons difficult, if not impossible.

Debates occurring at the local community level usually reveal the difficulty of validly connecting cause and effect or reaching public policy conclusions. The perpetual debate about community policing and crime prevention is a classic example. When you increase the number of police officers on the street, does crime decrease? How do you measure the number of crimes that were not committed because of police presence? Quite apart from the principle that you cannot prove a negative, there are too many other factors involved for such simplistic notions.

The difficulty in comparing security expenditures is amply illustrated in the case of the reunification of the two Germanies. The weaknesses of East Germany, particularly economically, had eluded most intelligence agencies during the Cold War. It was only after German reunification in the 1990s that the full extent of these erroneous estimates became known. Similarly, during the Cold War, the Central Intelligence Agency (CIA) and

---

8   Arms sales have generally declined in 1994; of concern is the destination. However, this decline also appears to be caused as much by the economics of the Third World as by any deliberate policy of world powers. With the drawdowns in both NATO and the ex-Warsaw Pact, the arms market is saturated with surplus weapons. *Washington Times*, January 6, 1995, A15.

9   For a discussion of black, or hidden, budgets, see, for example, Tim Weiner, *Blank Check: The Pentagon's Black Budget* (New York: Warner Books, 1990).

Defense Intelligence Agency (DIA) constantly feuded about the economic status and military spending of the U.S.S.R. (Both were wrong, but the DIA was less so.) More importantly, neither recognized how far along the road to dissolution the U.S.S.R. had come. Its fall came as a major surprise to the West.

Another way of evaluating the cost of security is to compare military expenditures to gross world or gross national product. This is a debatable comparison on at least two grounds. First, the dollar value placed on the same goods or services may vary from country to country. Second, many of the more primitively produced goods and services in the developing nations of the world are omitted from censuses of economic activity in those places. However, the available but imperfect statistics do give a more concrete impression of the gross dimensions of the military costs borne by the productive societies.

We have already noted that the approximately one trillion dollar total world military expenditure represented about 4.2 percent of the gross world product. The 1991 military expenditure of the United States represents 4.9 percent of the American gross national product. In 1981, by contrast, the figure for the U.S. was 5.5 percent and, in 1986, was 6.6 percent. The comparable figures for the Soviet Union were 10.3 percent in 1991, 13.3 percent in 1981, and in 1986, 13.1 percent. Stated in terms of per capita military expenditures, these percentages represent 1991 military outlays of about $103 per capita worldwide, more than $1,110 for each U.S. citizen, and close to $887 per Soviet citizen. The largest spenders per capita in 1991 were Kuwait, Qatar, Saudi Arabia, United Arab Emirates, United States, Israel, Oman, U.S.S.R., Norway, and Singapore.[10] In 1994, the list had changed only slightly: Kuwait, Israel, United States, Brunei, Singapore, Saudi Arabia, Oman, Norway, France, and Switzerland.

The Soviet percentages remained at about the same level for more than a dozen years and was, of course, a matter of great attention and debate among American security policy makers and intelligence officers. Even though Soviet defense outlays remained about the same, it was evident that a massive buildup of their armed forces was taking place. As a result,

---

10   The expenditures in the Arab nations are largely a result of the Gulf War. In fact, this illustrates the point of perceived insecurity. Prior to Iraq's attack on Kuwait, the Gulf states felt relatively secure and their military forces were nominal at best. As a result of the Gulf War, that condition no longer obtains and these states are all creating armed forces almost from scratch.

expenditures in the U.S.S.R. grew to the point of causing an economic depression from which the successor states are still struggling to escape. Some dismissed the high Soviet outlays as a short-term effort to reach parity with the Americans (presumably with the unstated acquiescence of American policy makers). Others viewed the rate of Soviet expenditure as evidence of a Soviet drive for military superiority. The Soviet leaders kept reminding everyone that they had to worry about China and Europe as well as the United States.[11]

These kinds of data led to extensive, heated, and often arcane discussions about the relative military strengths of the United States and the Union of Soviet Socialist Republics. Fiscal and hardware comparisons inevitably fueled the arms race since these were the dimensions that best supported the views of worst-case analysts and Hawks. Since the end of the Cold War, however, military expenditures have fallen precipitously in all of the successor states of the U.S.S.R. as well as among other members of the now defunct Warsaw Pact. This decline has occurred even though several of the successor states have been engaged in both civil wars and armed conflicts among themselves. Russia, for its part, has embarked upon an aggressive arms export program, particularly in conventional arms, of limited success.

Comparing the Superpowers

The simplest, albeit probably the least valid, yardstick for comparing American and Soviet military strength is the fiscal one.[12]   Although there have been substantial changes in the balances as a result of the demise of the U.S.S.R. and the Warsaw Pact, a comparison of the two is still of more than academic interest. The process by which the demise was brought about, and more importantly for our purposes, the manner in which the superpowers reached a disarmament accord, are instructive for application

---

11   Russia continues to maintain this position, and has now added their need to modify the Conventional Forces in Europe Treaty to accommodate for the defense of the "near abroad" and internal security matters such as Chechnya.

12   We continue the comparison of the U.S. and the U.S.S.R. despite the end of the Cold War. The comparisons are the most familiar. Furthermore, Russia continues to be militarily the other superpower. Additionally, the comparisons best illustrate arms races, military expenditures, and other characteristics reflecting a wide spectrum of political systems and policies.

in such contests on a regional basis. Just as instructive is the difficulty in making the comparison and determining a trustworthy balance.

In 1991, the U.S. was spending $280.3 billion, in constant 1991 dollars, while the U.S.S.R. was spending $260 billion. Compare this with the expenditure rate of ten years earlier. In 1981, the American expenditure total was $253.6 billion while that of the U.S.S.R. was $327.8 billion.[13] What is overlooked in these figures is that the U.S. peaked at $341.3 million in 1986, the height of the 1980s arms race, while that of the U.S.S.R. peaked at $361.7 million in 1988, a rate of expenditure that was economically unsustainable. Comparative figures are reflected in Table 3.2. China, France, and the United Kingdom have been added for comparison.

Table 3.2   Comparison of Military Expenditures, USA-USSR, 1981-1991[14]

Year	USA	USSR	China	France	UK
1981	253.6	327.8	51.2	39.4	37.7
1982	276.1	334.4	51.6	40.1	39.9
1983	294.4	338.6	50.4	40.8	43.7
1984	306.5	341.0	49.5	40.7	44.3
1985	331.6	345.8	49.5	40.7	45.4
1986	341.3	349.4	48.5	40.8	44.7
1987	339.3	356.8	48.9	42.0	44.0
1988	332.3	361.7	49.7	41.9	41.3
1989	329.9	328.7	49.0	42.3	41.7
1990	318.4	303.7	52.3	42.4	42.2
1991	280.3	260.0	51.0	42.4	43.2

There was no change in the real or perceived threat to either of the superpowers during this period, other than that posed by each other. While

---

13   The figure in 1993 for the United States was $297.6 billion. In 1993, Russia, alone of the Soviet successor states, spent $113.8 billion. The apparent decrease represents the break-up of the U.S.S.R. Significantly, Russia still has the second highest military expenditure rate in the world.

14   In billions of constant 1991 dollars.

the U.S.S.R. engaged in counterinsurgency in Afghanistan in the early part of the period, there was no real change in the threat to the U.S.S.R. itself. The United States faced no change in external threats and was rebuilding after its 1975 withdrawal from Vietnam.

Note that the U.S.S.R. increased its spending relatively slowly, while the U.S. increased sharply. The U.S. increase represents at least a two-fold policy decision on the part of the Reagan administration. The first was to reinvigorate what had become the "hollow military" of the post-Vietnam period. The second was a conscious decision to engage in an arms race with the "Evil Empire". The other three nations - China, France, and the UK - saw almost no expenditure movement at all. The arms race was primarily between the two superpowers, with the others on the sidelines, or limited participants at best.

A sharper picture comes into focus when two additional indicators are used: military expenditures as a portion of the GNP and as an expenditure per capita. The former adds relative economic strength into the equation and the latter takes into account the relative size of the polities involved. Tables 3.3 and 3.4 reflect this comparison.

Table 3.3   Military Expenditures as Percent of GNP, USA-USSR, 1981-1991

Year	USA	USSR	China	France	UK
1981	5.5	13.3	8.2	4.1	4.8
1982	6.2	13.2	7.6	4.1	5.0
1983	6.3	13.0	6.8	4.1	5.2
1984	6.2	13.0	5.8	4.1	5.2
1985	6.6	13.1	5.1	4.0	5.1
1986	6.6	12.8	4.6	3.9	4.8
1987	6.3	12.9	4.2	3.9	4.6
1988	6.0	12.7	3.9	3.8	4.1
1989	5.8	11.5	3.6	3.7	4.1
1990	5.5	11.0	3.7	3.6	4.1
1991	4.9	10.3	3.3	3.6	4.3

While the U.S. GNP continued to grow from year to year in this period, the U.S.S.R. began to drop after 1989, another indicator of the effect of the arms race policies of the Reagan administration. In 1989, the GNP of the U.S.S.R. was estimated at $2,870 billion, in 1991 dollars. The comparable figure for 1991 was $2,531 billion, not much more than the 1981 figure of $2,470 billion with which the U.S.S.R. started the period.

On the other hand, the rapidly declining portion of GNP spent by China on its armed forces is an indirect consequence of the arms race between the U.S. and the U.S.S.R. China's economy grew substantially during this period, from $623,400 million in 1981 to $1,528,000 million in 1991. The major perceived military threat to China was the U.S.S.R. Whether China would have liberalized its economy in this period regardless of U.S.S.R. trends is a somewhat moot point. With the U.S.S.R. fully occupied with the U.S., China apparently felt it had less to fear from the U.S.S.R. It maintained a constant level of military expenditure while devoting the increasing resources of its economy to other sectors.

Table 3.4 Military Expenditures per Capita, USA-USSR, 1981-1991

Year	USA	USSR	China	France	UK
1981	1102	1220	51	728	669
1982	1187	1234	51	738	710
1983	1254	1238	49	748	776
1984	1293	1234	48	742	786
1985	1386	1240	47	738	802
1986	1412	1241	46	737	788
1987	1391	1256	45	757	773
1988	1349	1263	45	750	724
1989	1326	1138	44	751	729
1990	1272	1044	46	748	737
1991	1110	887	44	744	750

The U.S.S.R., at the outset of the period, was spending more per capita for defense than the U.S. The U.S. trend steadily increased until 1986, and then declined relatively slowly. The U.S.S.R. attempted to keep pace, but, during the last two years of the period, the expenditure per capita dropped sharply, ending the period spending substantially less than the U.S. The relatively constant rates for China and France reflect their essential non-involvement in the U.S.-Soviet arms race. In the case of the UK, at least a part of the increase in spending per capita is attributable to pressure from, and support for, U.S. efforts. A substantial amount, however, was devoted to countering the bitter internal terrorist threat posed by the Irish Republican Army (IRA).

A look further back helps elucidate the superpower arms race. When we examine military expenditures for the period from 1960 to 1975, the United States spent more that $1 trillion on its military budgets while the Soviet Union spent about $860 billion. Together, these two giants spent about two-thirds of all the military outlays worldwide for this period. These vast sums excluded costs for domestic security forces. During this period, the United States was engaged in a war in Southeast Asia. On the other hand, the U.S.S.R. had no such military engagements.

Table 3.5 Comparison of Military Forces, 1994[15]

	USA	**Russia**	**China**
General Purpose Forces			
Personnel	1,650,500	1,714,000	2,930,000
Tanks	14,800	19,500	8,000
Warplanes	3,400	5,200	5,900
Surface Combat Ships	137	161	55
Submarines	104	185	50
Strategic Nuclear Forces			
ICBM	705	1,161	14
SLBM	384	700	12
Bombers	200	158	60

Returning to the comparison of American and Russian military strength, another traditional yardstick is military hardware. A few of the rapidly

---

15 From International Institute for Strategic Studies, *The Military Balance, 1994-1995* (London: Brassey's, 1994). Data is as of June 1, 1994.

changing manpower and weapons statistics are summarized in Table 3.5. Since China is a large concern for Russia, recent data for it are also presented.

The ten largest militaries, by number of personnel, in 1991 were China, U.S.S.R., United States, India, North Korea, Vietnam, Turkey, Pakistan, South Korea, and France. Political events such as the end of the Cold War and the break-up of the U.S.S.R. into its constituent republics modified this list somewhat. In 1994, the ten largest militaries, by number of personnel, were China, United States, Russia, India, North Korea, Vietnam, South Korea, Turkey, Pakistan, and Iran.

A more revealing list, one that reflects perceived threats and instability, is the number of military personnel in relationship to size of the population. In this category, for 1994, the U.S. falls to a rank of 53 in the world, Russia to 30, and China to 113, placing all three well down in the pack. The top ten in this category were, in order for 1994, North Korea, Israel, Jordan, Albania, Bosnia, Sao Tomè, United Arab Emirates, Syria, Iraq, and Greece. Of every thousand citizens of North Korea, 53 are in the military. In Greece, of every thousand people, slightly more than twenty are in uniform. By contrast, the rate per thousand for the U.S. is 7.0, Russia, 15.1, and China only 2.6.

Even a cursory interpretation of these figures will reveal how difficult it is to determine the military balance between the superpowers. The Soviet Union had a far greater number of troops in its military services. It was also a landlocked country with borders many thousands of miles longer than those of the United States, with presumably hostile neighbors at its eastern border (the People's Republic of China), and NATO just beyond its former Warsaw Pact allies' western border.

Although this is rarely mentioned, the Soviet Union also had some internal policing problems not experienced by the United States, namely, several hostile nationality groups among its constituent republics. How critical this situation has been is being amply demonstrated with its demise. There have been ethnic conflicts in every one of the successor republics to the U.S.S.R. In several of the republics, including Russia itself, these conflicts have engendered armed conflict, with substantial casualties. Conflicts have also troubled Warsaw Pact countries. The former Czechoslovakia, for example, has been sundered (albeit peacefully) into two new states, the Czech Republic and Slovakia. There is conflict between Russia and Romania concerning the Republic of Moldava. Within the former U.S.S.R., a particularly brutal repression of the breakaway area of

Chechnya has been witnessed. The Republic of Georgia all but ceased to exist for a time due to internal conflict. Millions have been made refugees and thousands killed in the disputes between Armenia and Azerbaijan, to select but a few.

A similar difficulty of comparison applies in connection with tanks. Again, the Soviet Union was a landlocked country, largely dependent upon land mobility for its troops. However, an American analyst could easily wonder about the need for such an overwhelming superiority in tanks (which Russia continues to have). Since tanks are usually considered offensive [attack] weapons, there must have been other factors involved in this imbalance. Adding data about the balance of tanks between NATO and the Warsaw Pact led to an even less encouraging interpretation. Before its dissolution, the Warsaw Pact had 20,500 tanks (including those east of the Urals) to NATO's 7,000. Why so many Pact tanks if their intentions were defensive rather than offensive?

The American-Soviet balance in tactical aircraft seemed close enough, but Soviet superiority in surface combat ships and submarines surely reflected a desire to compensate for being landlocked. It is an old issue in Russian military affairs for that nation to seek warm water ports and sea outlets to the rest of the world. It may also be true that the Soviet Union built a substantial naval force - 243 combat ships and 243 submarines - in order to extend its political and diplomatic influence into regions and nations far beyond its immediate borders. At least, such is the American Hawk view of Soviet naval forces, particularly when one takes into account the 1,015 Soviet submarine-launched ballistic missiles (SLBM).

The balance in superpower strategic nuclear forces is an entirely separate ball game and the principal concern of SALT I, SALT II, and START negotiators. Here the United States, creator of the nuclear bomb, was clearly the dominant force in number of deliverable nuclear warheads: 9,200 to the Soviet's 5,000, in 1979. With the agreement to implement START, bilateral and unilateral declarations by the United States and Russia, the latter speaking as the Commonwealth of Independent States (CIS), not only launch vehicles, but also warheads, are being destroyed or rendered inert. By about 2003, the CIS and the U.S. will have reduced their nuclear arsenals to 3,500 and 3,000 warheads, respectively. While the warheads have different explosive power, or megatonnage, the United States was still out in front during the Cold War. However, the Soviet Union, and now Russia, tend to prefer a bigger megatonnage bang for its nuclear warhead buck.

It is with respect to strategic delivery vehicles that SALT negotiations and verification techniques became pertinent. While it is extremely difficult to measure from a distance the size and explosive power of a nuclear warhead, it is quite possible to verify the number and placement of delivery vehicles. The latter were the principal subjects of SALT negotiations. As part of their drive to overtake the American nuclear force during past decades, the Soviet Union had actually passed the Americans in numbers of intercontinental ballistic missiles (ICBMs) and submarine-launched ballistic missiles (SLBMs). On the other hand, the United States continued to be ahead in number of bombers, accuracy in reaching targets, and, number of warheads. These three components of the American strategic nuclear force - ICBMs, SLBMs, and bombers - are usually referred to as the Triad.

The achievement of a rough balance in American and Russian (CIS) strategic nuclear forces was the purpose of the policy of "essential equivalency", that is, a rough but sufficient balance in the size of the forces such that neither side may expect or claim an overriding superiority. One of the flaws (among several) of both SALT I and SALT II was its reliance on reducing delivery vehicles to the exclusion of warheads, particularly in light of the advances made in technology. The START talks attempted to deal with this error by eliminating warheads and adding on-site investigations. As a part of the disarmament agreements, launch vehicles and warheads are being physically destroyed by each party. The destruction is being mutually witnessed.

Military strategists consider the comparisons, such as those in Table 3.6, relatively meaningless unless one also takes into account such factors as (a) long-term trends in force size and (b) changes in hardware technology and effectiveness. A comparison between alliance systems - NATO *versus* Warsaw Pact - rather than the two superpowers alone was also of importance during the Cold War. In considering similar figures today, such alliance systems must be weighed in the balance.

Perhaps the most visible and awesome trend to follow was the race in strategic weaponry described in Table 3.6. Soviet "catch-up" is vividly presented by these figures. On the other hand, should we have added in the number of Soviet tanks, aircraft, etc., that were located east of the Urals? China and the U.S.S.R., after all, have repeatedly engaged in "hot" conflicts over borders, so the Soviets (and now the Russians) had to protect themselves against China. Even so, Soviet forces stationed east of the Urals represented a substantial replacement and reinforcement potential.

The most striking comparison in Table 3.6 is the long-run stability in the number of American strategic nuclear delivery vehicles in contrast to the manifold increase in numbers of Soviet vehicles from 550 to a peak of 2,523 in 1975. The United States policy makers apparently made a determination in the mid-1960s that about 2,200 delivery vehicles would be more than enough to deter a Soviet attack or devastate most Soviet cities, industrial centers, and population in a counter-attack. In fact, such a number of delivery vehicles is considered from five to ten times as many as needed, that is, sufficient to provide substantial overkill. The Soviet Union, on the other hand, was determined to demonstrate that it was equal to the United States as a nuclear superpower on the one hand and capable of carrying on a two-front nuclear war on the other hand, that is, the Soviet argument that they have more potential enemies than does the United States.

Table 3.6 The Strategic Weapons Race

	1965		1972		1975		1982		1991	
	USA	USSR	USA	USSR	USA	USSR	USA	USSR	USA	USSR
Delivery Systems:										
ICBM	854	270	1054	1618	1054	1599	1054	1350	1000	1244
SLBM	496	120	656	740	656	784	800	950	624	924
Bombers	936	160	457	140	465	140	546	100	306	185
Total	2286	550	2167	2498	2175	2523	2400[16]	2400	1930	2497
Warheads	4480	870	5880	2220	10312	3083	17478	9330	9680	10996
Megatonnage	4547	2700			3415	9385	6480	5925	6200	

The other terrifying data in Table 3.6 are the number of deliverable warheads and their respective total megatonnages. A single megaton is the equivalent of one million tons of TNT. As of 1975, the Soviets had 3,083

---

16 Based on numbers agreed to in SALT II.

warheads with a total megatonnage of 9,385 whereas the United States, with as many of 10,312 warheads, had a lower total megatonnage of 3,415. The greater Soviet megatonnage, in fact, subsequently became a source of American dissatisfaction with the course of the SALT II negotiations.

The Table 3.6 projections for 1982 show the two superpowers with a joint stockpile of 26,808 warheads and a total explosive capacity of 12,405 megatons (or 12,405 million tons of TNT). The atomic bombs that destroyed Hiroshima and Nagasaki had explosive yields equivalent to 14,000 and 20,000 tons of TNT, respectively. Little wonder that all who understood the implications of these stockpiles were so certain that any superpower nuclear exchange would end life and civilization on earth. This prospect has now been compounded because there are a larger number of nations with nuclear capability. Also of great concern has been control over nuclear weapons in the successor states of the former Soviet Union, and, just as importantly, the number of Soviet scientists and technicians with extensive knowledge of weapons production who have become redundant and, often, freelancers.[17]

In addition to the trends in escalating nuclear stockpiles, there are technological features that make it difficult to measure the equivalency of various military forces. Continuing with the U.S.-U.S.S.R. example, the United States has always been more advanced with respect to the accuracy with which its nuclear vehicles reach their designated targets. Because an ICBM force is literally fixed in concrete, it is the most vulnerable component of the Triad. Hence, both sides planned to introduce mobile missile systems, known in the United States as the MX missile. The MX plan was to build trenches or underground tunnels about thirteen miles in length in which the missiles were to be kept moving around. The enemy would have greater difficulty making a direct hit, unless, of course, new devices are invented for detecting and locking onto the moving missile targets. Submarines are the leg of the Triad most difficult to detect, but both sides worked determinedly to improve submarine detection and

---

17   For an excellent summary of the challenges caused by the break-up of the U.S.S.R. in this area, see U.S. Congress, Office of Technology Assessment, *Proliferation and the Former Soviet Union* (Washington: U.S. Government Printing Office, 1994). For a broader look world-wide, see U.S. Congress, Office of Technology Assessment, *Proliferation of Weapons of Mass Destruction: Assessing the Risks* (Washington: U.S. Government Printing Office, 1993).

antisubmarine weapons systems. Nevertheless, one vigorously espoused and presumably cheaper alternative to the land-based shuttle concept of MX called for substantially augmenting the submarine leg of the Triad, that is, increasing the number of submarine-launched ballistic missiles (SLBMs).

The bomber leg of the Triad also underwent rapid technological change. The Russian Backfire bomber is capable of completing a one-way flight from Russia to Cuba. This raised questions about efforts to exclude it from classification as a strategic bomber (which are considered capable of completing an attack and returning to home base). On the American side, the F-111 fighter-bombers then stationed in Western Europe were able to complete round trips to the Soviet Union; they raised similar questions regarding their strategic classification.

Although production is now suspended, development of the U.S. B-2 bomber added something new to the equation: stealth technology. Stealth technology permits the low-flying B-2 to reach its targets with little chance of detection and interception. The effectiveness of stealth technology was demonstrated by the F-117 using it during the Gulf War. The radars and other aircraft detection equipment used by the Iraqis were Russian.

The development of cruise missiles with a capacity for delivering nuclear bombs has also been the subject of debate. A cruise missile is an unmanned, self-propelled, guided missile that is small enough to be launched from aircraft, submarines, or ground platforms. The effectiveness of cruise missiles was also demonstrated during the Gulf War. Missiles such as the Tomahawk were launched from naval vessels over a thousand miles from their targets. Television allowed the world at large to witness the devastating accuracy of this technology. While the missiles used in the Gulf War contained conventional warheads, they could just as easily have carried nuclear ones.

The more one gets into the subject of military hardware and comparisons of military forces, the more one realizes the impossibility of achieving precisely measurable balances or an objective military measure of security. In other words, if arms control negotiators pay attention only to the military hardware and military forces, it is a certainty that they would never arrive at a quantitatively and psychologically satisfying security arrangement. The ingredients for imbalance and destabilization are permanently built into this limited definition of security.

But the problem gets magnified even more as we move on to a third aspect of comparison, namely, alliance systems. Alliancing is an ancient and standard approach to augmenting one's military capacity as a counterforce or deterrent to a potential enemy. During World War I, the Allies (Russia, France, England, Italy, the United States, Japan, and others) were aligned against the Central powers (Germany, Austria-Hungary, the Ottoman Empire, and Bulgaria). In World War II, it was the Allies (the United States, United Kingdom, most of western Europe, the U.S.S.R., and others) against the Axis (Germany, Italy, and Japan, and others). Even the United Nations, when created at the end of World War II, was generally conceived as a collective security alliance system of the former Allies intent upon preventing further aggressions by the defeated Axis powers. The two Germanies, Italy, and Japan were disarmed and, for varying periods of time, excluded from the United Nations. The UN collective security arrangement, particularly in the Security Council, lost its effectiveness as soon as the former allies became adversaries during the Cold War era. Nor are alliance systems, such as NATO and the Warsaw Pact, new. The oldest written records of international politics, and even ancient history, include records and references to such alliances. The Trojan War, for example, was fought between two coalitions.

For its part, following World War II, the United States pursued a policy of collective defense agreements and alliances that reached into every corner of the world. The Rio Treaty of 1947 was a multilateral extension of the Monroe Doctrine wherein the United States and the twenty-one nations of Latin America agreed that an armed attack against any American state "shall be considered as an attack against all the American states and . . . each . . . one undertakes to assist in meeting the attack". In 1949, the United States and eleven other nations[18] established the North Atlantic Treaty Organization (NATO) with the understanding that "an armed attack against one or more of them in Europe or North America shall be considered an attack against them all". The ANZUS Treaty among Australia, New Zealand, and the United States in 1951 and the bilateral Philippine Treaty of the same year concluded similar mutual defense arrangements. Bilateral mutual defense treaties were also signed at different times with Japan and South Korea.

A more complicated alliance was the Southeast Asia Treaty Organization (SEATO) among seven nations: United States, United

---

18   Belgium, Canada, Denmark, France, Great Britain, Iceland, Italy, Luxembourg, the Netherlands, Norway, Portugal and the United States. Turkey and Greece were admitted in 1952. West Germany was admitted in 1955. Spain was admitted in 1982.

Kingdom, France, New Zealand, Australia, Philippines, and Thailand. The war in Vietnam and the changing structure of power in southeast Asia led to the disbandment of SEATO in 1977. The containment of the U.S.S.R. - from the Soviet view, encirclement - was completed by the signing of a mutual defense treaty among Turkey, the United Kingdom, Iran, Pakistan, Iraq, with the United States as an observer, in 1955. Turkey and the United Kingdom are NATO members, while Pakistan provided the link with SEATO. The agreement went through several name changes after the withdrawal of Iraq in 1959, but ended at the time of its demise in 1979 as the Central Treaty Organization (CENTO).

Although the United States was the militarily most powerful member of each of these defense alliances, the American national security was also well served in each case, providing the United States with strategic outposts and military friends in many corners of the world. These alliance obligations explain why slightly over 500,000 U.S. troops were based in overseas locations at the end of 1980. Although the end of the Cold War, and the ending of several of these alliances, has brought about a reduction in the number of U.S. troops stationed permanently overseas, the number still remains substantial (about 260,000 in 1993).

The Soviet Union was not dormant in its own search for allies. The eight-nation Warsaw Pact, created in 1955 as a counter to NATO, was the most substantial of the Soviet alliances, although here, too, the superpower was clearly the dominant member. The U.S.S.R. also concluded a large number of bilateral agreements, many only marginally short of mutual defense agreements, with many nations around the world. Several of these agreements included the permanent assignment of Soviet forces or the use of facilities and ports.

Just how to weigh the contribution of an alliance system to one's national security again reduces itself to criteria that turn out to be highly subjective. What does seem objectively indisputable was that in the Cold War world the two most powerful alliance systems were NATO and the Warsaw Pact. Atop each of these was, of course, one of the two superpowers. As though the rest of the world hardly existed, most military analysts leapt to make a hardware comparison between the two alliance systems, as in Table 3.7. These comparisons for 1978-1979 and others for subsequent years tend to be of dubious accuracy and offered incomplete statements of the military realities. For example, as noted, in 1978, Warsaw Pact tanks, some of them quite old, were said to number 20,500 compared to NATO's 7,000. These figures, however, did not recognize that NATO possessed nearly 200,000 highly accurate antitank missiles. Other comparisons were similarly misleading.

After centuries of warfare in the "cockpit of Europe", NATO and the Warsaw Pact existed on the assumption that yet another war might take place on the continent. The victim of several invasions from Western Europe, the Russians left (and leave) no doubt that they wished to protect their European borders and those of their satellite states with a preponderance of military manpower and hardware. However, NATO insisted upon parity and sought to balance the Pact's 20,500 tanks by maintaining a preponderance of tactical nuclear missiles: 7,000. This was a very expensive military standoff and led to initiation in 1972 of East-West talks about Mutual Balanced Force Reductions (MBFR). Although both sides seemed eager to achieve a lower and less costly balance of military forces, the negotiation quickly became one of comparing apples and oranges as each side indicated its requirements for having a sufficient sense of security.

Table 3.7 Comparison of NATO and Warsaw Pact Military Forces, 1978-1979

	NATO	Warsaw Pact
Combat Troops	790,000	960,000
Tanks	7,000	20,500
Tactical Aircraft	1,000	2,800
Tactical Nuclear Missiles	7,000	3,500
Artillery Pieces	2,700	10,000
Sources: *Newsweek* (April 7, 1978); U.S. Arms Control and Disarmament Agency, *Annual Report 1979*.		

The MBFR talks evolved into the Conventional Armed Forces in Europe (CFE) Treaty which came into force in July 1992. While the Warsaw Pact and the Soviet Union no longer existed, their various successor states had continued the negotiations. They are now referred to as the Budapest/Tashkent Group, but to facilitate discussion we will continue to call them the Warsaw Pact.

Signatories of the CFE agreed to specific limits of conventional weapons systems (called TLE - Treaty Limited Equipment) that were to be deployed between the Atlantic Ocean and the Ural Mountains (ATTU), i.e., Europe. TLE major categories include the groups noted in Table 3.8. The treaty limits are specific to each nation, but for ease of reference and comparison with some of the preceding tables, we have consolidated them into the two major groups. The limits apply only to the area covered by the treaty. Nations, such as the United States, Canada, Russia, and Turkey, which lie all or in part outside the ATTU, have no limits on their overall forces, only those within the ATTU. The holdings are those declared, in compliance with the CFE, as of December 1993.

Table 3.8 CFE Treaty Comparisons, 1993[19]

Category	NATO		Ex-Warsaw Pact	
	Holding	Treaty Limited Equipment	Holding	Treaty Limited Equipment
Manpower	2,410,498	2,790,281	2,619,213	2,970,930
Tanks	20,085	19,142	27,225	20,000
Armored Vehicles	28,625	29,822	36,271	30,000
Artillery	18,061	18,286	23,166	19,970
Attack Helicopters	1,592	2,000	1,545	2,000
Combat Aircraft	4,708	6,662	7,509	6,800

The CFE Treaty limits were in large measure negotiated prior to the collapse of the Warsaw Pact and the break-up of the U.S.S.R. As a result of these political changes, Russia has been requesting an early review of the treaty limitations. The other signatories oppose this suggestion. Basically, the Russians perceive a greater potential threat on their northern and southern flanks than previously existed. When the treaty was negotiated, these areas were internal to the U.S.S.R.

---

19 Adapted from International Institute for Strategic Studies, *The Military Balance, 1994-1995* (London: Brassey's, 1994), 267.

Although the various forms of the balance of terror during the Cold War gave the appearance of stability, at least in Europe, the competition between the two rival pacts bred great political distrust throughout the world, not least between the superpowers themselves. Although major strides have been made since 1990 in alleviating some of that distrust, the habits and attitudes of over four decades die only slowly.

4 The Conditions of Insecurity for the Developing Nations

Throughout the Cold War, the two superpowers never engaged each other in direct military contest. However, neither missed an opportunity to engage in the multitude of armed conflicts that occurred throughout the world during the period. While the bulk of the arms trade, at least in dollar value, was conducted by the two superpowers, lesser powers were also engaged in providing weapons to the rest of the world.

Of even greater significance than the dollar value was the type of weapons sold. The bulk of the arms sales by both the United States and the former Soviet Union dealt with high value, sophisticated major end items, such things as high performance jet aircraft, advanced main battle tanks, and major warships. A large proportion of these items were transferred to allies of the superpowers. On the other hand, the smaller powers engaged in the arms trade were supplying much less costly end items such as rifles, artillery pieces, mortars, land mines, and light aircraft. The unit cost of these items could be measured in thousands, in some cases hundreds, of dollars rather than the multi-million dollar items transferred by the superpowers. The price of one F-16 will buy thousands of AK-47 assault rifles, including millions of rounds of ammunition. The significance of the difference is that these smaller weapons systems are the ones that did the bulk of the killing in the post-World War II era.

The World's Military Outlays

World military expenditures are thoroughly and authoritatively reported elsewhere in great detail and on an annual basis.[1] The purpose of citing

---

1   The most authoritative sources include: United Nations; Stockholm International Peace Research Institute; United States Arms Control and Disarmament Agency; International Institute for Strategic Studies in London; North Atlantic Treaty Organization; United States Central Intelligence Agency;

some of the data specifically is to provide a relatively concrete impression of the size, content, and scope of the financial outlays that the world seemed willing to expend for its security services. There are, of course, other costs of a nonfiscal kind: social and psychological consequences, such as collective fear or collective sense of insecurity; possible alternative uses of funds; and the crisis climate generated by a world of garrison states.

Before proceeding with a discussion of defense expenditures in its various forms, a note of caution is in order. Just as with all objective factors, and with statistics in general, the various factors are indicators only. In arriving at any analysis, whether for policy or academic purposes, the various factors must be evaluated within their political, social, economic, and cultural contexts as well as in concert with each other.

Indicators such as spending are particularly subject to a number of distortions. There is the difficulty in obtaining reliable data; many countries are reluctant, to say the least, to provide information. Information that is provided is distorted, often honestly, because of the manner in which defense expenditures are counted. In some countries, portions of the defense budget are located in places other than in the defense area; some information is classified; some military forces are used for purposes other than defense, such as law enforcement, domestic construction, health services, and any number of other duties. With these and similar caveats, let us examine some of the expenditures for the world's military forces.

In 1978, the 142 largest nations of the world were spending about $480 billion annually (in 1978 dollars) for the support of military forces and the purchase of weapons and military equipment. This contrasted with the 1967 world military expenditure of $201 billion, that is, 7.1 percent of Gross World Product (GWP). By 1987, military expenditures had reached $1,215 billion (in 1991 dollars[2]), an all time high. With the demise of the Warsaw Pact and the dissolution of the U.S.S.R., expenditures dropped some 14.5 percent in 1991 to $1,038, which represented 4.2 percent of GWP and about $192 per capita. By 1994, world military spending had fallen below

---

and the United States Agency for International Development. Two particularly relevant and available sources are: Ruth Leger Sivard, *World Military and Social Expenditures* (Washington: World Priorities, published annually); U.S. Arms Control and Disarmament Agency, *World Military Expenditures and Arms Transfers* (annual).

2   Unless otherwise specified, dollar values throughout the remainder of this chapter are in 1991 dollars.

the trillion dollar mark to $840 billion (in 1991 dollars); roughly equivalent to spending levels in 1968, that is, roughly 3 percent of the GWP and $157 per capita.

An average of 10 percent of central government expenditures were devoted to military expenditures in 1991 dollars. This continued a downward trend that began in 1988. Significantly, the 28 most advanced nations' share of that spending decreased from 80 percent of the total in 1981 to 77 percent in 1991 and to 74 percent in 1993. However, the "developing" world's share increased to make up the difference. The most significant decreases occurred in Eastern Europe, where military spending decreased by 70 percent between 1988 and 1993. The world share of spending for this region dropped from 35 percent in 1983 to 15 percent in 1993. In contrast, for the five year period from 1988 to 1993, growth in military spending occurred in four regions of the world: Subsaharan Africa (1.1 percent), East Asia (2.3 percent), South Asia (2.9 percent), and Oceania (4.2 percent). Even with the build-up associated with the 1990-1991 Gulf War, spending in the Middle East declined by 0.2 percent.

Who were the Big Spenders? Throughout the period from 1945 to 1991, the biggest spenders were the United States and the U.S.S.R., and their respective coalitions. Of the total world expenditures, the North Atlantic Treaty Organization (NATO) countries accounted for 41.4 percent of the total in 1981 and 46.2 percent in 1991. The Warsaw Pact countries accounted for 36.3 percent of the total in 1981 and 26.6 percent in 1991.[3]

If the 28 developed countries are examined as a group, spending followed similar trends, declining by about 19.8 percent from a peak in 1987 to a low in 1991. Spending declined some 11 percent in this group in the year 1991 alone, and their overall share of total spending declined from 80 percent to 77 percent.

---

3   Unless otherwise noted, figures for the balance of this chapter are from U.S. Arms Control and Disarmament Agency, *World Military Expenditures and Arms Transfers, 1991-1992* (Washington: U.S. Government Printing Office, March 1994), ibid., *World Military Expenditures and Arms Transfers, 1993-1994* (February 1995), and ibid, *World Military Expenditures and Arms Transfers, 1994-1995* (April 1996).

Table 4.1 Military Expenditures, 1993

Country	Amount[4]	Ranked by	
		Expenditure	Armed Forces Size
United States	297.6	1	3
Russia	113.8	2	2
China	56.2	3	1
France	42.6	4	12
Japan	41.7	5	24
Germany	36.7	6	18
United Kingdom	34.0	7	22
Italy	20.6	8	13
Saudi Arabia	20.5	9	32
South Korea	11.9	10	8
The only difference in 1994 was that France and Japan exchanged places in the ranking.			

However, in the rest of the world, spending took a generally upward trend, rising some 12 percent in 1990 to a new high of $242 billion by 1991. The top five spenders in 1991, as noted in Table 3.2, were, in order, the United States ($280.3 billion), the U.S.S.R. ($260 billion), China ($51 billion),[5] United Kingdom ($43.2 billion), and France ($42.4 billion). In 1993, the top rankings, even with the break-up of the U.S.S.R., had not changed substantially. The last column in Table 4.1 represents the rank of these spenders based on the numbers of military personnel.

---

4   Amount is shown in billions of U.S. dollars.

5   Note the large gap between the United States and the U.S.S.R. as compared to the totals for the next three.

For what was the $1 trillion spent? There were wages to be paid to the 24.65 million persons (23/5 million in 1994) who made up all the world's regular military forces, the 9 million others who comprised paramilitary forces, the 24 million employed in civilian support work for the military, and the 19 million in the ready reserves. Research and development consumed another large amount, that is, to support human inventiveness and adaptiveness, a remarkable spur to the qualitative arms race. Yet another portion constituted the annual procurement expenditure for weapons and military equipment.

Of particular interest was the relationships between the developed and the developing countries. In a world population of over 5 billion, more than 24 million persons were in armed forces, and more than half (17,570,000) of these were in the service of developing nations that can least afford it. However, military expenditure for each soldier in the developing world was substantially less ($57 per capita) than for a soldier in the developed world ($678). It costs a great deal less to maintain and equip a soldier in Bangladesh than it does in the United States.

Trade in Conventional Arms

Over the 1960-1975 period, the United States exported $41 billion worth of arms to other countries. Much of this went to support the Republic of Vietnam and other forces engaged in the war in Vietnam, such as Thailand, Korea, Australia, and New Zealand. By 1978, the United States was supplying some 32 percent of all of the arms transferred from one country to another. The Soviet Union was a close second, exporting $27 billion worth of arms to other countries during the 1960-1975 period and supplying 34 percent of the arms transfers of 1978. The U.S.S.R. did not engage its own forces directly in conflicts until 1979, when Soviet forces were moved into Afghanistan. During the fifteen years covered, other suppliers were significant, but to a far lesser degree: France exporting $3.8 billion, followed by China, West Germany, Czechoslovakia, Poland, Canada, and others in decreasing amounts. By 1978, France was supplying 7 percent of the world total in arms transfers and the United Kingdom and West Germany 5 percent each.

Table 4.2   Top Ten Arms Exporters, 1994

Exporter	Amount (in $ millions)
U.S.A.	12,400
United Kingdom	3,400
Russia	1,300
China	800
France	800
Germany	700
Israel	470
Czech Republic	300
Spain	280
Canada	230

By 1991, the world arms trade picture changed only slightly. During the period 1987 to 1991, $227.2 billion worth of arms transfers were made. Of that total, the U.S.S.R. was responsible for $84.3 billion, or about 37 percent. The United States accounted for $58.8 billion, or about 26 percent. Between these two superpowers, they accounted for 63 percent of the total. This arms trade was almost totally in conventional arms; both superpowers refused to export nuclear, chemical, and biological weapons as a matter of policy. Additionally, almost all of the latest technology was kept at home, depending on the recipient. Recall that of the more than 23 million deaths that occurred in warfare since 1946, almost all was caused by conventional weapons. Note, too, that the above figures do not account for many items of dual-use technology that were transferred as a part of normal commercial trade.

In addition to the two superpowers, who were the other major exporters of war material, and where was it going? Table 4.2 summarizes data for the top ten in each category for 1994. Given the social, educational, and economic circumstances of developing countries, the overall trend of arms exports was downward. In the decade from 1981 to 1991, exports fell about 7 percent, with the most precipitous drop coming in the latter half of the decade. Despite the scramble of major defense industries to compensate for declines in sales, the trend down is apparently continuing.

Table 4.3 Top Ten Arms Importers, 1994

Importer	Amount (in $ millions)	Major Supplier*
Saudi Arabia	5,200	Varied
Egypt	1,500	U.S.
United States	1,100	Varied
Israel	1,000	U.S.
South Korea	1,000	Varied
Turkey	950	U.S.
Taiwan	775	U.S.
Japam	650	U.S.
Angola	600	Russia
Spain	525	U.S.

*   A major supplier is a nation that provides more than 50 percent of the total arms imports to a given polity.

Tables 4.2 and 4.3 list the ten largest exporters and importers. Almost all of this consisted of conventional weapons systems. Who imports these arms? The developing countries of the world - despite their great need to improve the education, health, and prosperity of their people - imported arms at the rate of $17 billion in 1994. This reflected a decline from previous years. Arms exports to the developing world peaked in 1984 at a record high of $58 billion. Even so, the economic and political motivations and consequences for such arms buying must be substantial.

There are aberrations in the foregoing chart, particularly in the first two countries listed. Saudi Arabia, recovering from the Iraqi threat, has essentially been creating a military organization from almost nothing. Almost all the U.S. imports were from a wide variety of sources within the western bloc, although some procurements were of former Soviet equipment for U.S. training purposes.

There are those nations whose sole or predominant source of weapons is a specific country. Substantial leverage can be obtained over the recipient when most of its weapons systems are provided by a single supplier. The United States was the *sole* source, i.e., more than 60 percent, in the period 1987-1991, for Barbados, El Salvador, Guyana, Honduras, Jamaica, Malta, Tunisia, Luxembourg, and the United Kingdom. During the same period, the U.S. was the *predominant* source of imports by Australia, Bahrain, Belgium, Botswana, Canada, Dominican Republic, France, Germany, Guatemala, Israel, Italy, Japan, South Korea, Lebanon, Mexico, Netherlands, New Zealand, Niger, Philippines, Portugal, Singapore, Spain, Taiwan, and Turkey.

For its part, the U.S.S.R. was the *sole* source in that same period for Afghanistan, Benin, Cape Verde, Congo, Cuba, Equatorial Guinea, Guinea, Guinea-Bissau, Laos, Madagascar, Mauritius, Sao Tome, Tanzania, Vietnam, and South Yemen. The U.S.S.R. was the *predominant* source for imports to Bulgaria, Burkina Faso, Cambodia, Czechoslovakia, Ethiopia, East Germany (before unification), Hungary, North Korea, Mozambique, Nicaragua, Poland, Romania, and Syria, with most of the balance coming from other Warsaw Pact nations. China was the *sole* source in this period for Rwanda, Sierra Leone, and Zimbabwe, as was France for Ivory Coast and the UK for Malawi during this same period.

These five states (U.S., U.S.S.R., China, France, and UK) are the only polities that qualify as being sole-source countries. Even when the limit is lowered to cover the predominant-source category, the exporters remain the same. Economics alone is an insufficient reason for membership in this exclusive club. This group of five remained pretty much unchanged throughout the Cold War; it does not appear that it will change in the foreseeable future, other than that Russia has replaced the U.S.S.R. Other major suppliers include France, West Germany, the United Kingdom, and, in more recent years, smaller producing nations such as Brazil and Israel. Even North Korea has occasionally been one of the top ten exporters. That South Africa may enter this group is a strong possibility.

Conventional Weaponry and Its Sale

As already observed, the Soviet Union in 1978 was the world's largest supplier (34 percent) of arms to other countries and the United States (32 percent) a close second. The two superpowers frequently exchanged this distinction. With the demise of the U.S.S.R., the U.S. has assumed the uncontested role as world's leading arms supplier, a role it has maintained with few exceptions since the turn of the century. Although, with the end of the Cold War, the absolute amounts of weapons have dramatically decreased, what is of most concern is the type of military systems that is being supplied, and to whom.

Conventional weapons are everything other than nuclear systems.[6] The most costly part of the world's arms race is in the export and import of nonnuclear weapons systems. Table 4.4 provides an overview of this arms trade, particularly between developed and developing nations.

Perhaps the most striking data in the table are the figures for conventional arms exports and imports, confirming that the suppliers are the developed nations and the purchasers the developing nations. According to the U.S. Department of State, during the 1950-1976 period, the United States alone transferred abroad over $110 billion in arms and related military services. During 1978, United States sales totaled over $6.7 billion to 68 countries. Most of this weaponry went to countries in the Middle East, specifically Israel, Iran, and Saudi Arabia, while about one-third went to NATO, South Korea, and Japan. Only about 3 percent of United States arms sales were made to countries in Latin America.

Shipments to particular countries can reach astronomical figures. For example, between 1968 and 1977, the United States shipped to Israel a total of at least $4.2 billion worth of arms. This particular flow of arms was at a low figure of $28.6 million in 1968, reached $303.2 million in 1971, shot up to $977.9 million in 1974 immediately after the 1973 Arab-Israeli war, and dropped to $875.3 million through 1977. Between 1950 and 1975, American military sales to Iran totaled $9.5 billion and to Saudi Arabia $2.4 billion.[7] While the individual recipients and gross amounts change from year to year based on the perceived security needs of the United States, the proportions have not materially changed.

There has been a drastic drop in both exports and imports of arms with the end of the Cold War. In 1983, arms imports and exports represented 2.7 percent of all the world's trade. By 1987, the proportion had fallen slightly to 2.4 percent. However, by 1993, the arms trade represented only 0.6 percent of all world trade.

While Russia continues to try to obtain hard currency through arms sales, often at prices well below cost, the United States remains the premier exporter of arms. By 1994, the U.S. was also the world's largest importer,

---

6   Chemical and biological weapons are included as conventional in this discussion because their technological development was such that they had only a peripheral impact on the arms race between the two superpowers and the balance of power in the Cold War.

7   U.S. Department of Defense figures for Israel reported in *Newsweek* (March 20, 1978), 28.

Table 4.4 World Arms Transfers, 1981, 1987, 1991 and 1993

	Year	World	Developed States*	Developing States*
Population (in millions)	1981	4537.9	1094.0	3443.9
	1987	5037.3	1141.9	3895.4
	1991	5398.6	1174.8	4332.8
	1993	5534.4	1028.5	4505.9
Armed Forces (in thousands)	1981	27320	10140	17180
	1987	28750	10430	18320
	1991	26020	8667	17350
	1993	24610	7041	17570
GNP per Capita	1981	4320	14510	1084
	1987	4562	16080	1186
	1991	4619	16630	1279
	1993	4729	18540	1576
Military Expenditures Per Capita	1981	232	769	62
	1987	241	870	57
	1991	192	678	57
	1993	157	630	49
Arms Exports ($ millions)	1981	66610	61780	4889
	1987	68710	61450	7301
	1991	25530	23540	1880
	1993	21960	20220	1755
Arms Imports ($ millions)	1981	66610	14090	52370
	1987	68710	14000	54650
	1991	25530	6325	19390
	1993	21960	4810	17190

* As defined by the U.S. Arms Control and Disarmament Agency.
SOURCE: U.S. Arms Control and Disarmament Agency, *World Military Expenditures and Arms Transfers, 1991-1992* (1994), 47, 89, and *World Military Expenditures and Arms Transfers, 1993-1994* (1995), 49, 97.

reflecting the growth of multinational corporations in the defense sector. An important factor has been the unintended consequence of advertisement through use of weaponry on the battlefield. After the Gulf War, U.S.

military equipment was, and for the nonce remains, in great demand because of its demonstrated capability. Arms purchasers also noticed that the equipment that was defeated on the deserts of Iraq and Kuwait was primarily of Russian manufacture. This phenomena has been replicated repeatedly, e.g., after the various Arab-Israeli Wars.

What motivates such a costly arms trade? Despite their tremendous need for economic and social development, the developing countries that are big arms purchasers have relatively clear motivations, namely, defense against external attack, maintenance of internal order, and increased diplomatic prestige. Nothing stimulates arms purchases as quickly as the acquisition of weapons by one's neighbors, particularly if the neighbors have been enemies in the recent past. A nation's substantial military strength presumably deters what it perceives as its more trigger-happy neighbors. If India arms, Pakistan is driven to do so as well; if Israel arms, Syria feels compelled to follow a similar course.

A less visible motivation is internal security. American weapons sent to Nicaragua, for example, may have had more to do with maintaining the incumbent regime there than with the defense of that country against predatory neighbors. The presence of Soviet troops in or near East European satellite countries, in Afghanistan, or in the so-called "near abroad" served more to discourage internal disorder than external attack. The international arms trade may have more to do with the discouragement of domestic revolutions and civil wars than with the maintenance of peace in the international arena. A review of armed conflicts that have taken place since 1946 reveals that only a very few were inter-state wars in the traditional definition.[8] In 1996, of the 33 active armed conflicts in the world, none was an inter-state conflict. Rather, they have been internal wars, insurgencies, and revolutions, usually supported by one or both of the superpowers. However, excessively sophisticated weapons may prove to be utterly useless for maintaining internal order. Possession of sophisticated weaponry did not protect the Shah of Iran and U.S. interests in that country. Indeed, the expenditure for such weapons and the U.S. influence it brought with it was a major reason for the Shah's downfall.

---

8   See, for example, Patrick Brogan, *The Fighting Never Stopped* (New York: Vintage Books, 1990), George C. Kohn, *Dictionary of Wars* (New York: Doubleday, 1986), or John Keegan, *A History of Warfare* (New York: Vintage Books, 1994).

A third motivation that spurs the purchaser of arms is international prestige. Only nuclear Big Shots (pun intended) are admitted to the Nuclear Club, and this is a major consideration in the pressure for nuclear proliferation. Nuclear weapons are a great equalizer in the power politics of the world. To a lesser degree this also motivates the purchase of sophisticated conventional weaponry.

With the demise of the U.S.S.R., nuclear proliferation has become a matter of great concern. As demonstrated in the aftermath of the Gulf War, even states such as Iraq that are signatories to the Nuclear Non-Proliferation Treaty (NPT) may hide the development of nuclear weapons. Would North Korea have attempted a nuclear program if it did not believe that U.S. nuclear weapons were at least available to South Korea; or Pakistan, if such weapons were not in the possession of India. On the other hand, it should be noted that since August 9, 1946, no one has been killed by a nuclear weapon fired in anger; however, upwards of 23 million people have died primarily through the use of conventional weapons, most of which were neither sophisticated nor expensive.

From the point of view of suppliers, the motivations to sell are equally compelling. The fourth motivation - wages and profit - are a major inducement for arms production and sales. At the peak of the Cold War, of the United States labor force of some 80 million, more than 700,000 jobs were defense-related.[9] This rose to 1.4 million by 1991 and then began a decline to about 800,000 in 1994, and still dropping. While this number has decreased substantially with the end of the Cold War, defense industries are still a major component of the American economy. This number grows substantially larger, but indefinably, in the wake of the Military Technical Revolution. More and more industries provide dual-use technology, items that only their purchaser knows for sure whether they will be put to military use or not.

Another factor affecting this statistic is the globalization of the arms industry. While the United States is somewhat behind its European and Japanese competitors in this field, more and more weaponry, not to mention weapon components, are being produced under license, through international consortiums and similar arrangements. This is a factor that future arms control negotiators will have to deal with. Supplier nations are also interested in improving their balance of payments, for example,

---

9   As more and more defense technology becomes dual use, it becomes difficult to identify the "defense industry" and who is employed by it.

exchanging high technology weapons for oil, or more recently, hard currency. Finally, selling weapons abroad reduces the per unit production cost of military equipment, a savings in the price of purchases for the supplier's own armed services.

A fifth motivation relates to the management of relations among one's allies. For example, if a supplier wishes to constrain military conflict between two allies, as the United States has in the case of Greece and Turkey over Cyprus, it becomes possible to do so by cutting off the supply of equipment and spare replacement parts to one or both allies. As a result of such actions by the U.S., many smaller nations have taken to obtaining arms from multiple sources, even at the expense of denying themselves more advanced technology or reduced costs. To continue with the example of Cyprus, prior to the 1970s, the United States would have been listed as the sole source for Turkey's weaponry. In 1994, the United States is no longer even the predominant source, although it remains the major supplier. Ironically, Greece, who did not suffer the indignity of an arms embargo as did Turkey, nevertheless observed what had happened and moved even more quickly to diversify its sources of arms. A similar pattern has taken place throughout the world.

In general, conventional arms transfers encourage local arms races, aggravate regional tensions, and lead to the misallocation of scarce resources within developing countries. In 1977, President Carter initiated a policy that would consider arms transfers as "exceptional" foreign policy actions, placing the burden of persuasion upon those who wish to purchase particular items. Conventional arms transfers were no longer to be considered useful foreign policy instruments. This first small step toward reducing the role of the United States as the major conventional arms supplier, however, had little impact.

United States policy has remained seemingly contradictory. Under the Clinton administration in 1994, arms control negotiators and the State Department attempted to negotiate conventional arms control treaties while the Secretary of Commerce and Secretary of Defense were traveling around the world advocating the purchase of American weaponry. Until such time as all major suppliers adopt collective criteria for determining when such transfers should or should not be made, the Carter policy is likely to continue to have little effect. The Coordinating Committee on Export Control (COCOM) was a relatively successful effort among allies for regulating the export of high technology. Some similar mechanism, with a broader charter, would be required if it is to control the globalization of the conventional arms industries.

In the post-Cold War world, and with the reduction in forces of the major protagonists, the arms market has become saturated. Arms merchants have become more aggressive as the purchases for "own use" decline. This situation becomes further aggravated by those technologies that are dual use.

Technological Advances and the Qualitative Race

The world spends $32 billion or more annually for weapons research and development (R&D). This is a tremendous investment in human ingenuity and inventiveness and, as has been amply demonstrated, produces some remarkable results. The investment is aimed at producing and improving military hardware. However, it may be a kind of global derangement to have so much ingenuity and inventiveness motivated by fear for national security. Much fewer resources are directed toward figuring out how the world can be made safer at less cost, possibly through new institutional arrangements. For our purposes here, the qualitative arms race helps us make sharper the distinction between developed and developing nations.

In its broadest sense, the qualitative arms race extends to every facet of military equipment development. This may range from improved vehicles for delivering nuclear weapons to improved surgical instruments intended to repair wounded bodies. So comprehensive are the concerns of military research and development that it becomes well-nigh impossible to distinguish the military from the civilian uses of much of the improved technology and discoveries. In fact, among the positive arguments often used in support of large budgets for military R&D are the peacetime civilian payoffs. In the ordinary course of civilian research, according to military R&D people, civilian technological advances would be far less likely without the pressures of military need. Furthermore, it is argued, Congress is less likely to appropriate funds for civilian research as readily as for military purposes.

From another point of view, the question arises whether and how to halt or slow the qualitative arms race. It may have taken a few million years to advance from throwing rocks to throwing nuclear bombs, but, even if military R&D did not receive another penny, could this policy achieve a halt to human inquiry, discovery, invention, creativity, and competitiveness? Perhaps the question about halting the technological race is the wrong question. Perhaps the more fundamental question is: "How do we make it unnecessary and undesirable for human beings to throw anything at each other?" Meanwhile, human discovery and technological progress are clearly here to stay.

Controlling the relationship between advancing technology and global security is becoming increasingly complex and difficult, even for those with the most laudable intentions. The line between military and peaceful uses of technology seems to be disappearing. Efforts to control the growth and dissemination of currently available weaponry are undermined by wholly new technologies that make the existing weapons systems obsolete. Two examples may be drawn from developments in laser and satellite technology.

Particle-beam weaponry (PBW) is one of the current technologies in rapid development. PBW is based on lasers (light amplification through stimulated emission of radiation). Lasers are directed beams of electrons, protons, or neutrons that have been concentrated together to produce high levels of energy emission. In recent years laser technology has demonstrated its usefulness in fields as wide-ranging as metallurgy and surgery. It is also well known that the United States, Russia, and other nations are engaged in a race to develop military applications, that is, PBW. Theoretically, PBW would be capable of instantaneous transfer of energy to a target at essentially 100 percent efficiency. The ability to hit and destroy any and all targets is, of course, every military strategist's dream.

The practical applications of a PBW system appears to be in the future. However, it is only a matter of time before the theoretical propositions of, for example, the Strategic Defense Initiative (aka Star Wars) to be made practical. How effective and devastating this technology can be was demonstrated during the Gulf War. The battle of 73 Easting (named for a map location) in the Gulf War was a graphic illustration of the difference between a qualitative arms race and a quantitative one.[10] During this battle, a single troop of American armor engaged an Iraqi brigade, roughly three times it size, and destroyed it without suffering a casualty. This American victory was brought about by a combination of various technologies, not the

---

10 It also provided another demonstration of the difference between a *well-trained* combat force and one that is not. The most advanced technology in the world is useless to armies and navies not highly trained to employ it. Indeed, the technological advances have made training more critical than at any time in history.

least of which was the use of lasers for sighting and ranging. The mind boggles at the mass devastation that could take place between two equally equipped and trained forces.

What are some of the military uses of PBW? PBW could hit incoming missiles almost without fail, attack enemy satellites, serve as a ship-borne anti-cruise-missile weapon, carry out successful air-to-air attacks, and, ultimately, in strategic missions, destroy an enemy entirely. Although difficult to imagine, PBW could make nuclear weapons - today's "ultimate" weapon - obsolete. Conceivably, the laborious efforts to achieve SALT and START arms control agreements may simply turn out to be a discussion of an outmoded weapons system.

In the research for the Strategic Defense Initiative, PBW has thus far proven infeasible, at least in a practical way. However, the research has led to many other civilian and military uses of lasers, ranging from CDs for music to delicate surgery to targeting guidance systems. Research on its use in weapons continues, and its practical application as a weapon is in the foreseeable future.

Among the great achievements of modern science and technology are the satellites that orbit the earth. They enhance communications and provide a wealth of information about both earth and space. The peaceful uses of satellite technology, including instantaneous communication to all parts of the world, have only begun to be discovered and applied. The same is true of their military uses. In order to keep dangerous nuclear and other weaponry out of the skies, the superpowers agreed in 1967 to a Treaty on the Peaceful Uses of Outer Space and Celestial Bodies. The object was to keep the moon's surface and outer space free of weapons of mass destruction and other objects that could be orbited and possibly dropped unexpectedly out of the sky. One nuclear-powered Soviet Cosmos satellite, for example, did fall out of the sky in northern Canada in January 1978. Cosmos 954 was a reconnaissance satellite, not a weapon. Its nuclear reactor was used simply to power an ocean-scanning radar. On its side, the United States Skylab fell out of the sky on July 11, 1979. Both sides have kept to this agreement. However, space technology, because it is "civilianized", is available to many, if not most, nations. The primary barrier to having weapons in space is the technology, and, if the history of warfare proves nothing else, overcoming this barrier is only a matter of time, circumstance, and motivation.

Another example of the qualitative arms race involved the "hunter-killer" satellites tested by the former Soviet Union. The satellite was designed to destroy orbiting reconnaissance, communications, and navigational satellites at will. The Soviet Union began testing hunter-killers in 1976. Two days before he left office, President Ford approved an American program to develop and deploy a similar weapon. President Carter rescinded the deployment order, but allowed the Pentagon to continue development of several other antisatellite systems. He was persuaded by proponents who argued that American forces are "critically reliant on space for surveillance, reconnaissance, early warning, navigation, meteorology, mapping, communications, and command and control".[11]

Because of the development of this technology for civilian use, many developing nations have within their capability the use of satellites for military applications that were once restricted to the superpowers. Witness the civilian news media's use of satellites during the Gulf War to bring the "bad guys" side of the war into the world's living room. French commercial networks have provided satellite photographs of Libyan chemical facilities to news organizations. The point here is that these technologies are available to non-governmental agencies. It requires no great leap of imagination to realize that all but the poorest nations can now obtain what was once highly classified information. Brazil, India, and Israel all have satellites in orbit. Among the advantages is, perhaps, the increased global visibility of the horrors of war. Satellites also make it more difficult for governments to lie or cover up things that they do not want their own people to know.

Finally, yet another example of the profound difficulty of disentangling peaceful from military uses of advancing technology is the problem of using nuclear fuel to produce energy without also producing the plutonium byproduct that is necessary for building nuclear weapons. Both nuclear fuel and atom bombs are made from uranium that comes out of the ground. There are two types of atoms in natural uranium, U-238 and U-235. Only U-235 splits naturally, resulting in energy that may be converted into electric power or used as an explosive. Less than 1 percent of the atoms of natural uranium are U-235.

Through an expensive diffusion process, manufacturers are able to "enrich" the natural uranium by separating and discarding some of the U-238 so that the remaining uranium has a greater or more enriched percentage of U-235. If natural uranium is enriched beyond a certain degree

---

11 Statement by Robert Kirk, President of Vought Corporation, reported in *Newsweek* (February 13, 1978), 53.

(20 percent), the uranium can be used to make bombs. Current commercial nuclear reactors, called light water reactors (LWR), require uranium fuel that is enriched only to 3 percent of U-235 and therefore cannot be used for bombs. This low level of enrichment requires 1,200 stages and a very great amount of electrical power. Thus, it is possible to sell nuclear reactors and uranium fuel without danger of their being easily or quickly diverted to the manufacture of nuclear bombs. But a determined purchaser could, with difficulty (4,000 stages and enormous amounts of electricity) and time, make bombs. In this context, "with difficulty", is, of course, relative. Nations may bypass part of the process, as was done by Iraq, and obtain plutonium and enriched uranium from elsewhere. Israel accomplished the same thing when it initiated its nuclear weapons program.

Bombs can be manufactured from highly enriched uranium and also from plutonium, a man-made element that does not exist in nature. Plutonium is created in a nuclear reactor when some of the "useless" U-238 captures neutrons set free in the fission process, an event that transforms U-238 into plutonium-239. Once plutonium is separated from the spent fuel that is discharged from a reactor, the plutonium can readily be shaped into an explosive. A dozen pounds or so of plutonium can make a bomb of the 20-kiloton capacity dropped on Nagasaki. The separation of plutonium from the spent nuclear fuel is called reprocessing.

Plutonium can also be used as a fuel for reactors. Separated plutonium can be recycled back into light water reactors. It can also fuel another type of reactor called a breeder reactor. A breeder reactor, by transforming U-238 into plutonium, can create more fuel than it uses and thereby increase the energy output from uranium fiftyfold. The commercial success of breeder reactors, because of their projected high capital costs, is still undemonstrated. Many nations with little fossil fuel or uranium resources are, of course, eager to achieve energy independence through the development of breeder reactors. This raises all the hazards of making available a plutonium stockpile.

Military and peaceful motivations for acquiring nuclear fuel and facilities are likely to be overwhelming in the absence of some system of stringent international controls. Plutonium in the hands of terrorists or an unstable national leadership could become a potent instrument of international blackmail. The excessive stockpiling of plutonium can be dangerous to the community around it. The availability of plutonium could facilitate the proliferation of nuclear weapons.

Some steps have been taken to hold back the nuclear floodgates. The International Atomic Energy Agency (IAEA) has developed and been given responsibility for a safeguard system under which countries must file regular reports about their civilian nuclear activities. They must allow international inspectors - now numbering between 200 and 300 - to visit their nuclear facilities to verify the reports and ensure that there has been no diversion of materials from civilian to military purposes.

The difficulties in implementing such a program are legion, as has been demonstrated in both the aftermath of the Gulf War and in the case of North Korea. Additionally, some states, such as Israel, refuse to participate in the regime. These difficulties generate distrust and, in turn, the Arab states, in particular Egypt, have used this as justification for arms build-ups. This is compounded when one of the superpowers gives at least tacit, if not explicit, approval to non-participation.[12]

In sum, rapidly advancing technologies in stealth weapons, information acquisition and processing, lasers, satellites, and communications, to mention only the better known examples, are introducing security risks and problems about which it is increasingly difficult for policy makers, military strategists, and arms controllers to keep abreast. Theoretical definitions that try to distinguish between offensive and defensive weaponry, strategic and tactical forces, and civilian and military uses are falling by the wayside as a consequence of accelerating technological change. Even the hypothetical distinction between developed and developing countries is being extinguished now that almost any country can produce a nuclear bomb.

The consequences of pervasive distrust for the security problem are profound. There is again the question of what constitutes a balance of military forces sufficient to assure security. There is simply no way to arrive at an answer quantitatively or technologically. How much should a nation or the world spend for security services? Much depends on whether the security expenditure is a collective one in which all share equitably or a competitive one that assumes a direct connection between size of military forces and sense of security. A third dilemma arises from the propensity to make hypothetical worst-case analyses of security situations. The principle here is to assume the worst that a potential enemy can do to you and then prepare thoroughly to overcome such an eventuality. Worst-case analysis often leads to political demands by Hawks for zero-risk preparation; it is

---

12 See, for example, Seymour M. Hersh, *The Sampson Option* (New York: Random House, 1991).

also contingent upon the human imagination's boundless capacity to hypothesize worst-case scenarios. (This differs from the military use of the concept where worst-case analysis usually means "acceptable risk".)

There may be an unintended consequence as a result of the qualitative arms race. The Gulf War and subsequent computer simulations at Fort Knox, Kentucky, have demonstrated the extreme effectiveness of modern technology on the battlefield. If two or more forces of roughly equivalent technology and training were to engage each other on the field of battle, this would result in mutual annihilation, the extreme phase of the strategy of MAD (mutually assured destruction). In short, the demonstrations show that major powers are unable to engage in warfare.

One resulting challenge of such a stalemate would be to keep the less technically endowed countries from ever assuming that the risks of war with a less developed neighbor is worth the cost. Of greater concern is the danger of advanced technology falling into the hands of insurgents and terrorists. A demonstration of this danger was the devastating use of the chemical agent sarin in the Tokyo subway system in March 1995.

The sources of low technology conventional weapons are the same as those that provide high technology; developing nations rarely manufacture their own small arms. Much more attention is bound to be paid to conventional arms control. An antecedent requirement, however, seems to be the elimination of political distrust among the developing nations.

5   Sources of Distrust Among Nations

We have seen how weapons, the trade in weapons, and the competitive stockpiling of weapons can be a source of distrust and insecurity among nations. The irony is that they can, under certain circumstances, also be a source of security - but not trust. Built into politics among nations are elements that create and perpetuate political distrust. A brief examination of some of these elements may enable us to better understand additional causes of the arms race and some institutional and behavioral hurdles that must be surmounted if collective security is to be achieved.

There are several features of relationships among nations that, sometimes clearly, often imperceptibly, affect the extent of distrust and conflict among them. Some of the factors that are usually presumed to *reduce* distrust and conflict include: common culture, common language, similar racial characteristics, and similar social, political, and economic institutions. Conversely, when these factors are neither common nor similar, the occasions for fear, distrust, and conflict seem to multiply. There are a number of the latter factors that bear upon questions of security and military strength. These include: competition among world political leaderships or elites; the concept and practices of national sovereignty; the inexorable march of technological advancement; and the widespread practice of military and political secrecy.

There are two "laws" to be kept in mind as we review these causes of distrust and insecurity. One, the "law of cultural conflict", really a hypothesis, impacts on some of the causes of multi-ethnic conflict. The second is the "law", really an old cliche, that "perception is reality".

The law of cultural conflict was developed originally by ethnographers and anthropologists to explain the almost constant conflict among primitive groups. The law holds that when two cultures that are based on dissimilar societal foundations come into contact, they will be in conflict, and, more often than not, that conflict will be violent. The corollary to this is that similarly based cultures are more likely to cooperate for mutual benefit. The law is presumed to explain conflicts, for instance, between nomads and city dwellers and between hunter-gatherers and agrarian societies.

Designed for primitive cultures, the law is equally applicable to modern society. The nineteenth century, for example, witnessed the all but inevitable conflict between the industrial, heavily populated northern U.S. and the agrarian, sparsely populated South. Equally, the European age of discovery and imperialism also illustrates this law in both political and economic contexts. The Cold War of the twentieth century provides yet another example.

"Don't confuse me with facts" is a half frivolous statement used when we confuse perception with reality. The same set of facts may be the basis for completely different conclusions by different individuals. Regardless of the conclusions, for the individual or for society, their distinct interpretation of the facts becomes *their* reality. People, governments, and societies tend to respond to perceptions rather than to empirical reality or logical rationality. Consequently, differences in perception can lead to disastrous consequences between polities. An important corollary is that the perception that certain nations and/or ethnic groups have of each other may predispose them to settle differences through military action rather than through diplomacy.

Competing Elites

One of the pitfalls in analyzing and trying to resolve the problems of security and arms control is the almost exclusive focus upon their military hardware aspects. A familiar analogy may be drawn from medicine where, very often, for lack of well-confirmed knowledge about the *causes* of a disease, practitioners spend a great deal of time and effort diagnosing and treating *symptoms*. In E.B. White's more felicitous language, "I am afraid that blaming armaments for war is like blaming fever for disease".[1]

Symptomatic relief may make the disease more tolerable for the patient, but it almost never cures the disease that causes the symptoms. Similarly, to focus on the diagnosis and treatment of military hardware issues may bring "symptomatic relief" through the treatment we call "arms control". However, this approach fails to deal with causes. The cause of the arms race is to be found in the beliefs and behaviors of the human beings who feel that their sense of security requires that they mobilize weapons and military forces. The particular individuals who tend to pursue this mode of treatment are the competing elites of the world community.

---

1   *Essays of E.B. White* (New York: Harper & Row, 1977), 102.

Who comprise these elites? Are they a finite and identifiable group of persons? The answer to the latter question is "yes". In fact, several well-known reference works provide a current compilation of Who's Who among the leaders of the world community: *Worldwide Government Directory, Profiles of Worldwide Government Leaders, Current World Leaders*, and *Political Handbook of the World*, to mention a few. The first two offer profiles of more than 26,000 governmental and nongovernmental leaders in or related to 195 governments. In addition, it is a major duty of the various national intelligence agencies to keep abreast of just such compilations, and more. It is the members of this world elite who decide its policies, including those related to war and peace.

Not all of these leading persons compete politically or on a worldwide basis, nor are most of them concerned with problems of national or world security. However, close examination of these world leaders would probably reveal that those who are most concerned with security and safety are the very ones who are most competitive with respect to control and management of the world's wealth, policies, and institutional arrangements. These are familiar concerns of politicians and businessmen. These are the types of leaders who would most often be included in any roster of actively competing elites.

These men and women have different conceptions of reality and the human condition, conceptions that are steeped in their respective cultural traditions. They have different notions about how the economic resources of the world should be developed and distributed, notions that have such names as capitalism, communism, socialism, and so on. These competing elites have fundamentally different attitudes towards religion, education, and the goals that human society should seek. Historically, too, these elites have often had painful experiences dealing with each other, usually as the result of wars, religious or racial bigotry, or economic exploitation. As a consequence, elite factions perceive each other as serious adversaries.

The forms that elite conflicts take in actual practice tend to fuel political distrust. For example, Soviet and American political leaders were keenly aware that their respective nuclear stockpiles were excessive, well beyond the overkill range. Further, they were also fully cognizant of the fact that their respective nuclear delivery systems were aimed directly at each other. Each recognized their own vulnerability to attack. Under such conditions of fear and distrust, the Anti-Ballistic Missile Treaty was negotiated between the superpowers to ensure that *each remained vulnerable*, resulting in mutually assured destruction (MAD). The subsequent START process and treaties took these discernible conditions into account.

Why, then, did the nuclear superpowers insist upon pursuing the nuclear arms race, even after that race had been slowed to a walk? What change brought about the agreements for unilateral and bilateral reduction in nuclear weapons between the former U.S.S.R. and its successors, and the United States after almost fifty years of competition?

If we consider that these were (and still are) sophisticated competing political elites for whom weaponry is only one of several instruments of power, we may discover that the nuclear arms "walk" may have had much to do with the prestige and influence each superpower wished to maintain or promote for itself among the less mighty nations, organizations, and movements. SALT, START, and the reduction of the strategic nuclear balance may simply reflect an implicit agreement between superpower leaders that the time had come to stabilize the nuclear instruments of influence, particularly since other instruments of competition - international tradee, regional organizations, transnational political parties, and so forth - were beginning to emerge as alternatives to military modes of superpower ascendancy in world affairs.

Although the negotiations concerning reduction of nuclear arms began prior to the end of the Cold War, they were accelerated after the U.S.S.R., now Russia, was perceived as a much reduced threat and competitor to the United States. Therefore, if the superpowers could slow down their nuclear competition, they could better demand that others - Israel, China, Pakistan, India, and North Korea, for example - do so as well in their respective arenas. In short, the environment of world elite competition was subtly being transformed from military to other means of contest. Whatever the two superpowers saved in military expenditures could better be used in their worldwide competition with such economic giants as Japan, West Germany, China, and others. In the end, the fall of the U.S.S.R. was in large measure due to the increased pressures of the costs, both economic and societal, placed on it by the leadership of the United States, particularly during the Reagan administration.[2]

---

2 For an opposing minority viewpoint of the reasons for the fall of the USSR, see Raymond L. Garthoff, *The Great Transition: American-Soviet Relations and the End of the Cold War* (Washington: Brookings Institution, 1994). The difference of opinion is in reality one of emphasis on the external factors *vis-a-vis* the internal factors and their relative impact. Each school of thought

At the risk of oversimplification, therefore, one can argue that the principal sources of distrust, arms races, and war are embedded in the perceptions of and relationships among competing world elites. These sources of distrust are equally applicable to a major world power such as the United States and to the smallest nations such as Sao Tome or San Marino; only the scope changes. The sources include different subjective senses of security, ideologies, "political missionaryism",[3] and a reliance upon military hardware as an objective measure of safety and power.

In short, world security and the arms race can be better understood and possibly controlled if we investigate, in addition to the symptoms that appear in the form of military hardware, elite relationships. Mishaps, such as wars, occur because of the failure or inability to build alternative relationships in the institutions of competition, e.g., world party systems, regional forums, and international marketplaces, to serve as arenas other than the battlefield for the competitive relationships.

National Sovereignty

Nationalism and national sovereignty are primarily a European concept, but one which, in modified form, has spread to the rest of the world. Some of the differences are rather substantial. The very root of the word nationalism - nation - is in dispute among academics as well as in the popular press and may carry substantially different meanings for different people.[4] For our purposes here, nationalism and national sovereignty will be limited to the state system that has emerged and evolved in the last two centuries.

---

maintains that both were involved, but places greater or lesser emphasis on the different factors.

3   Political missionaryism is the attempt, through politics and economics, to cause other polities to adopt the political system of the "missionary" because it is "the best system", etc. Thus, the United States, quite apart from any national security interests and altruistic concerns, attempts through political persuasion to cause other polities to adopt "democracy". Such missionaryism is also evidenced in the attempts by the former U.S.S.R. to spread their doctrine; or that of Iran in attempts to spread Shiite fundamentalism.

4   For a discussion of the varying interpretations of nation, state, and similar terms, see Walker Conner, *Ethnonationalism: The Quest for Understanding* (Princeton: Princeton University Press, 1994).

In Europe, whether one inquires of language, ethnic identity, or nationality, usually the response represents a homogenous population: French, German, Swedish, etc. In many of the second and third tier of states, however, state or polity only occasionally equates with ethnic or national identity. In sub-Saharan Africa, for example, the response may be any one of three kinds. The genocides in Rwanda and Burundi in 1994-95 bear witness to the lack of identity with the state; instead, it is with an ethnic identity. In the Middle East, a quite different response may be obtained: Arab rather than Syrian or Egyptian; Jew rather than Israeli. When religion becomes a factor, as in India, yet another response is made. A similar process occurs elsewhere in the world, modified for cultural differences. A major challenge lies in dealing with the difference between state identity and ethnic, linguistic, or religious ones.

Historically and literally, in Europe, the king was sovereign in his realm. By definition, the king or queen had the "final say" in matters of public or governmental policy and presumably in the resolution of conflicting interests within their realm. Political philosophers and institution-builders have since expanded and refined in theoretical as well as practical detail many meanings of the concept sovereignty. Sovereignty today commonly refers to prerogative, that is, the capacity to make ultimate, final, decisive political choices to the extent that any human choices can be ultimate, final, and decisive.

In the course of time, monarchs and their non-European equivalents came to delegate or share, or have taken away, their sovereign prerogatives. This was done over time by royal ministers, houses of parliament, cabinets, political parties, and popular electorates. As the system of feudal relationships that prevailed for many centuries in Europe was transformed into the modern state, the attributes of sovereignty that once adhered to royal persons came to be the principal characteristic of organized nations.

These characteristics, in large measure, and with local variation, have been adopted by the rest of the world.[5] As the state system and the ideologies of European-style nationalism began to dominate the structure of world politics over the last two or three centuries, the symbols and

---

5   Nationalism, in its political sense, is essentially a European concept and only reached much of the rest of the world in the twentieth century where it has gained at least nominal adherence. Of greater importance is the more basic adherence to ethnic rather than national, identity. Much ethnic identity is currently cloaked in the trappings of nationalism.

practices of national sovereignty acquired paramount importance. The essential trait of the nation is assumed to be its capacity and freedom to choose for itself, that is, to be its own ultimate sovereign in matters of conduct, internal organization, self-defense, and relationships with others.

The separation of sovereign national organizations from sovereign royal persons proved to be a great convenience for politicians. The distinction varied in non-European parts of the world, but, generally, arrived at a similar formulation. The effect of the concept of nationhood was substantial. However, because these were alien concepts for much of the world, local traditions of tribe or caste were often just below the surface.

Even within the western world there are varying manifestations of nationality. For example, the United States, Canada, Australia, and similar countries' political evolution is different from that of Europe. These former colonies have a history of *delegating* power from the bottom (local government) to the top (federal government), whereas most European nations developed by taking power from the top, the sovereign. In Islamic political theory, sovereignty and national power is understood to be part of a worldwide political community of the *umma* and the belief that political sovereignty rests with God, not man. Similar variations occurred in Asia, often heavily influenced by the Chinese doctrine of Confucianism.

Modern politicians, particularly in egalitarian and democratic societies, prefer to depersonalize the exercise of power. Rather than claim prerogatives for themselves as persons, they prefer to exercise those prerogatives on behalf of some constituency or organization. This claim of agency is what makes governments representative. In many parts of the world, however, while actual power remains in the hands of individuals or family-associational groups, its exercise is often given a facade of democracy and depersonalization.

The formal relations among sovereign nations are far more ponderous than the informal relations among world leaders. The exercise of private policy or preference, particularly in the facilitation of friendships, proceeds more easily on the informal side of inter-nation affairs. It is when inter-nation leadership relationships are hostile and distrustful that the barrier of national sovereignty is quickly erected. A vivid example of this following World War II was the former Soviet Union's refusal to agree to inspection of its nuclear facilities as would have been required under the Baruch Plan. This plan called for turning over the United States' nuclear monopoly to an international agency on condition that all nations open their facilities to inspection. The former Soviet Union considered such inspections a flagrant breach of its national sovereignty and, in a sense, an invasion of its national right to privacy. What this posture, premised upon national sovereignty, reflected was a profound distrust of Americans, capitalists, and the UN majority by the Communist leaders and their certainty that their own scientists would shortly break the American monopoly by producing a Soviet atom bomb.

Since the end of World War II, the number of sovereign nations has increased from approximately 50 to more than 180.[6] As empires built during the eighteenth and nineteenth centuries continued to disintegrate, postwar nationalist leaders decried the evils of imperialism. These local leaders struggled, with more or less success, to put together the symbols and organizations necessary to advance their new nationalisms, achieve the full status of sovereign nation-states, and join the world community of nations as equals. For its part, the world community, as structured by the United Nations system, treated these newcomer nations as sovereign equals. Thus, the one-nation, one-vote principle prevailed in the United Nations General Assembly as well as other United Nations agencies. In these settings, the voice and vote of tiny San Tome is equal to the voice and vote of any superpower. The major powers, however, have retained more than a modicum of control by having permanent seats and veto power in the Security Council.

Many of these new nation-states are creations of the former colonial powers. As such, entire ethnic groups have been either split apart or mixed together with others within their colonial boundaries. There is no common sense of cultural identity or commonality among their peoples. This has all too often led to violence among the leaderships of the various ethnic groups, including those of the former Czarist-Soviet Empire.

All this notwithstanding, in less than two generations, the membership of the world community, in the form of nation-states, has almost quadrupled. Nationalism and national sovereignty, as major features of their domestic integration, have served as well to incorporate them into the world community. To facilitate their becoming integrated nations, their leaders chose anti-imperialist and anti-superpower slogans and policies. This was a motivation for creating the organization of nonaligned states as a working

---

6   The number varies depending on what is counted as a sovereign nation. As of July 1996, there were 185 members of the United Nations. The Vatican City and Switzerland are not members of the UN, but do have observer status, as does the Palestine Liberation Organization.

coalition in world affairs. This also explains the emergence of a North-South debate over the distribution of the world's economic resources. Here again political distrust continues to be generated by the memory of unhappy past relationships, the pervasiveness of cultural and economic differences, and the need to use national sovereignty as a shield in the struggle for international power and influence.

Even as new nations advocate nationalism, older nations also defend themselves by standing behind their national sovereignty. Meanwhile, the evolution of supranational organizations and worldwide treaty relationships proceeds on its course. As soon as nations become members of a supranatural organization, their national sovereignty and freedom to behave without constraint are diluted by the obligations and advantages of membership in these organizations. The Security Council veto, for example, is a major manifestation of sovereignty, yet it has a history of dilution. Initially, the former Soviet Union exercised its veto with great frequency. That defensive practice has since declined significantly: 77 vetoes in the first decade of its UN membership; 26 vetoes in the second decade; only 17 vetoes in the third. Since the founding of the United Nations, the U.S. has used the veto about 70 times. In more recent years, the United States, finding itself in an increasingly defensive situation, exercised its veto from zero in the first two decades to 21 vetoes between 1966 and 1977.[7] On May 17, 1995, the United States cast its first veto in five years to block a Security Council resolution concerning Jerusalem. Its last previous veto was on May 30, 1990. Russia's last use of the veto was in December 1994 against a resolution concerning Bosnia.

Of even greater importance, not only has Russia used its veto in a very limited manner, it now often cooperates with the U.S. and other Security Council members in peacekeeping missions and similar joint activities. It has become a willing partner with its former adversaries in attempts to reduce international tensions and build trust. This has manifest itself in ways ranging from Russia's tacit concurrence in the coalition formed to defend Kuwait against Russia's erstwhile ally, Iraq, to active participation in UN peacekeeping efforts in the former Yugoslavia. Like it or not, these cooperative involvements are illustrative of reductions in Russian national sovereignty.

---

7   The United States did not exercise its first veto until March 17, 1970, over Rhodesia. However, it had used the threat of the veto, sometimes even more effective than an actual veto, on previous occasions.

Within the broad sweep of history, the move of humankind toward larger and more comprehensive associations is inexorable. Nationalism and national sovereignty, which is only about 300 years old in its place of origin (Europe) and literally yesterday in many new states, nevertheless remain potent forces. However, a new specter has arisen called ethno-nationalism. Many of the new states, created as colonies, are dealing with demands for adjusted boundaries and territory to re-establish the integrity of particular ethno-national groups. This phenomenon is not limited to former colonies. Ethno-nationalists are well established in several of the older nations of the world, including those in Europe. Meanwhile, regionalism continues to gain momentum, with the European Union leading the way. The result of ethnonationalism is many-sided conflict on the one hand whereas regional movements push for supranational integration on the other hand.

Just as membership in supranational organizations constrains the exercise of national sovereignty, other forms of international collaboration also nibble away at the sovereign prerogatives of states. The growth of regional organizations such as NATO and the former Warsaw Pact, the European Union, the Organization of American States, the Arab League, and the Organization of African Unity, as we have noted, tends to diminish the freedom of action of member states. A concomitant development is the growth in numbers of multilateral treaties, each of which creates a national commitment to a transnational process that, bit by bit, diminishes the sovereign prerogatives of national leaders. Although 1995 saw the addition of Sweden, Austria, and Finland to the European Union, Norway rejected membership primarily on grounds that it would lose its national sovereignty. Much of the debate that preceded U.S. ratification of the GATT-WTO Treaty and NAFTA revolved around the potential loss of national sovereignty to invasive transnational agencies.[8]

Another sovereignty-diluting development has been the phenomenal proliferation of multinational corporations (MNCs). Since the end of World War II, literally thousands of corporate enterprises have come into being to conduct manufacturing and other economic functions in two or more nations. As of 1978, corporations, not countries, comprised nearly 40

---

8 GATT-WTO is the General Agreement on Trade and Tariffs, which was succeeded in January 1995 by the World Trade Organization. NAFTA is the North American Free Trade Area, consisting of Canada, Mexico, and the United States.

percent of the 100 largest organized economic units in the world. Thus, for example, in 1993, General Motors Corporation, with sales of almost $134 billion, was the world's largest corporate economic unit. There were only 21 nations that were larger economic units. GM ranked ahead of Denmark, whose gross national product was slightly over $133 billion.

In 1978, the ten largest corporations in the world and their country of origin included: General Motors (U.S.) , Exxon (U.S.), Royal Dutch Shell (U.K.-Netherlands), Ford (U.S.), Mobil (U.S.), Texaco (U.S.), British Petroleum (U.K.), Standard Oil of California (U.S.), National Iranian Oil (Iran), and International Business Machines (U.S.). In 1993, the ten largest corporations and their nominal nation of origin were General Motors (U.S.), Ford Motor Company (U.S.), Exxon (U.S.), Royal Dutch Shell (U.K./Netherlands), Toyota Motors (Japan), Hitachi (Japan), IBM (U.S.), Matsushita Electric (Japan), General Electric (U.S.), and Daimler-Benz (Germany). In 1992, U.S.-owned MNCs, not including banks, had assets of over seven trillion dollars and employed some 24 million workers. The changes in the list reflect the growth of non-U.S. economies.

The decisions of these corporate enterprises regarding the extraction of mineral and other natural resources, the location of plants and other labor-intensive units, the setting of prices and wages, the disbursement of dividends on stocks and bonds, and so on, have far-reaching strategic as well as economic consequences. Officers of corporations and officers of governments have only begun to become accustomed to dealing with each other on matters that affect national security and world peace. There are those business enthusiasts who claim that the world will eventually have an end to war largely because it is "bad for business".

Until the 1980s, the defense industry itself was generally considered a national asset. With increasing frequency, not only have many of these companies become multinational and in many cases privatized, but they have been subject to mergers and takeovers. Even where the arms companies are still state enterprises, they have engaged more and more in international joint ventures.[9] With the United States leading the way as the largest exporter of arms (as of 1993) and the world's fourth largest importer, other countries have followed this pattern. Just as an American-made automobile may well have components, including major assemblies, from over thirty different countries, many weapons systems now have

---

9   Organization for Economic Cooperation and Development, *Globilization of Industrial Activities* (Paris: OECD, 1992).

components of both private and public manufacture from several different countries. Part of this trend is driven by the facts of economic interdependence and part by the fact that most countries can no longer afford the costs of producing their own brand-name major weapons systems. Furthermore, companies are less and less identified as strictly defense industries. In 1993, the top ten U.S. defense contractors were McDonnell Douglas, Lockheed, Martin Marietta, General Motors, Raytheon, United Technologies, Northrop, General Dynamics, Loral, and Grumman. All of them are multinational and all of them produce substantial non-defense related products. With the increase in dual-use technologies, identification of strictly defense industries has become difficult.

Notwithstanding these several tendencies in the weakening of national sovereignty, the nation is bound to be with us for generations to come. The requirements and manifestations of national sovereignty will continue to generate political distrust. Many nations will continue to insist upon their national privacy in resisting arrangements for international inspection and verification of their military or other resources.

Even where the United States and Russia have established an inspection regimen to conduct verifications, the arrangement remains the exception rather than the rule. It involves only one specific category of weapons. The general rule of resistance to inspections, due at least in part to national sovereignty, is evident from the magnitude of the failures of the UN inspection organization formed under the Nuclear Non-Proliferation Treaty (NPT), in Korea, Iraq, and elsewhere, as well as the refusal of nations such as Israel to even participate.

Another device for preserving a nation's sovereignty is attaching codicils to treaties and agreements, as did the United States in the GATT Treaty and several members of the European Union, notably Britain.

Even as the mass media of communications become increasingly capable of reaching into every corner of the world to observe and report events, national leaders, in the name of national sovereignty, will undoubtedly continue to insist that only their own versions of reality be communicated. National censorship will continue to reduce the flow and shape the bias of information going across borders. However, as shown by the Gulf War and with the debates in Asia over satellite television, such barriers are being broken down at a geometrically increasing rate. Technology, particularly computers, has caused a quantum leap in this breakdown through such things as the Internet, which, ironically, was originally created by the U.S. Defense Department to facilitate military research and development.

National sovereignty will also continue to be the basis for claims to equality in forums such as the United Nations, despite the unequal contribution of support that most nations make. Further, for some time to come, sovereign states, rather than transnational political parties or international organized interest groups, will compose international coalitions, alliance systems, and voting blocs. Above all, national sovereignty will continue to stimulate, as it always has in the past, the search for the military resources that national leaders consider vital for their influence in international affairs and for the safety of their regimes and populations against predatory neighbors. In sum, national sovereignty and ethnonationalism are bound to be major sources of political distrust among nations for the foreseeable future.[10]

A major part of the infrastructure of political insecurity and sovereignty is territoriality - the fear of losing the territory that is "home". Wars are fought and arms races are run either to protect the territory of home or to find more territory for an expanding population. For all their differences, the various forms of sovereignty and nationalism rest on territoriality. What is the Law of the Sea Treaty about? What are arms control treaties about - territory and its protection. What are the conflicts in Northern Ireland and Bosnia about? What is the Arab-Israeli conflict about? Ad nauseum.

The issue of territoriality must not be confused with sovereignty, although the two are closely associated. Territoriality is not restricted to humankind. It is common throughout the animal kingdom. It is critical to our discussion because territoriality, when combined with the more recent concept of ethnonationalism, is a potent mix that has led to much of world conflict over the past three or four thousand years. Territoriality is the motivator, to a large degree, for political, economic, and military institutions. Sovereignty in turn is based on territoriality; the ruler must have a place over which to be sovereign.

Governments were originally formed to defend and administer territory. The borders of the territory were often rather nebulous, but there was a home base into which intruders entered at great risk. Internally, governments were created in large measure to establish rules about territory

---

10 For a discussion of the external-internal paradigm in developing nations, see Norman A. Graham, ed., *Seeking Security and Development: The Impact of Military Spending and Arms Transfers* (London: Lynne Rienner, 1994).

and property. The UN Charter contains provisions that state that a nation's territory is inviolate, as, presumably, is its sovereignty.

Technological Development

The 1990-91 Gulf War has been hailed as advancing the Military Technical Revolution.[11] The technology displayed, some of it still in the latter stages of development, during the Gulf conflict was truly awesome in its accuracy, speed, and firepower. In the exuberance for this new technology, what was overlooked was the "most feared" weapon by Iraqi soldiers: the aging B-52 bomber armed with conventional "dumb" bombs.[12] The B-52 appears to have broken the back of what fighting spirit they may have had and was the same that was used in the Vietnam War. Technology also had limited success in finding and destroying Scud ballistic missiles. U.S. intelligence could confirm no kills on the ground.[13] Ironically, the tactics and methods used to intercept the Scuds were practically identical to the tactics and methods employed to defend against the V-2 in World War II. That said, however, much of the technology demonstrated was truly amazing.

Table 2.1 of Chapter 2 summarized the tremendous advances in the lethality of weapons. The more of an adversary's persons and property a military device can destroy or injure, the more powerful the "rock-thrower" presumably is. As long as unthinkable nuclear exchanges remained theoretically "thinkable", it was feasible for military strategists to plan and produce nuclear weaponry as though these could be used for the most part like any other bomb in traditional wars. Nuclear bombs were, according to this view, simply another phase in the advancing qualitative arms race. Consider the United States Emergency War Plan known as Halfmoon, prepared in 1948, which called for "a main offensive effort" by dropping

---

11 Michael J. Mazaar, Jeffrey Shaffer, and Benjamin Ederington, *The Military Technical Revolution* (Final Report of the CSIS Study Group on the MTR, Center for Strategic and International Studies, March 1993).

12 It is also interesting to note, as an aside dealing with technology, that these planes were older than most of the air crew flying them.

13 Michael R. Gordon and General Bernard E. Trainor, *The Generals' War: The Inside Story of the Conflict in the Gulf* (New York: Little, Brown and Company, 1995), 247.

50 atomic bombs on targets in 20 Soviet cities.[14] Or, as long ago as 1977, one leading but hawkish American strategic analyst could still write a magazine article entitled "Why the Soviet Union Thinks It Could Fight and Win a Nuclear War".[15]

The "thinkability" of nuclear war stayed with political and military strategists for a long time. By the 1980s, respected members of academia would propose that the world could be made safer if more nations, rather than fewer, had nuclear weapons. The assumption was that fear would be widespread enough to motivate the creation of effective constraining rules.[16] Once nuclear weapons were employed, Pandora's box would be open. This made it clearly evident that attention should be given to eliminating the real causes of insecurity, rather than its symptoms.

In fairness, military officers who failed to plan for the employment of and defense against nuclear weapons would have been derelict in their duty. As the nuclear powers, through research and development, learned more about the force that had been unleashed, a great deal of what was, in the 1940s and 1950s, irrational fear began to dissipate, replaced by more realistic understanding and pragmatism. The absurd air raid drills in schools of the 1950s ceased, as did the designation of fallout shelters, backyard bomb shelters, and the like. Greater knowledge spread among a much broader spectrum of people. The veil of secrecy was lifted. Since the military in all five nuclear powers were under the control of civilians, civilian and military joined forces to find realistic approaches.

Another realization was that there is a substantial difference between tactical and strategic nuclear weapons. A danger arises from any escalation from tactical to strategic levels of engagement. From the 1960s on, U.S. tactical forces were no longer organized to fight a nuclear war. The pentomic division became obsolete quite rapidly. Almost all major training exercises assumed away the nuclear threat. Nevertheless, personnel were still trained in separate exercises on nuclear, biological, and chemical

---

14 David Alan Rosenberg, "American Atomic Strategy and the Hydrogen Bomb Decision", *Journal of American History*, 66 (1979), 68.

15 Richard Pipes, in *Commentary* (July 1977), 21-34.

16 Kenneth N. Waltz, *The Spread of Nuclear Weapons: More May Be Better*, Adelphi Paper No. 171 (London: International Institute for Strategic Studies, 1981).

(NBC) defense. This training included reporting fallout and other nuclear effects.

An unintended consequence of these fearsome weapons was to create a bipolar stalemate between the superpowers. This stalemate permitted the superpowers to talk to each other and build a degree of mutual trust. Another unintended consequence, of greater importance for world peace, was that each of the superpowers had to pause and consider consequences before confronting each other. Most wars in this century, including the two global conflicts, began as limited wars between minor world actors. As these brush fire wars grew, the major powers were drawn into the fray. This has not occurred in the nuclear age. Imagine the outcome of the 1962 Cuban missile crisis *without* the specter of MAD looming over the shoulders of the superpowers. Would President Kennedy have acted differently during the Bay of Pigs if only the U.S. had nuclear weapons? What would have been the consequences of the building of the Berlin Wall? Or the 1973 Arab-Israeli War? Would Israel have risked war with Syria in the 1982 invasion of Lebanon without a veiled nuclear threat?[17]

Since Hiroshima (and, proportionately, since the start of history), insecurity and multibillion dollar research and development (R&D) budgets - usually 10 percent of major-power military budgets—have spurred the search for military knowledge and the exercise of human inventiveness on behalf of an accelerating qualitative arms race. The $32 billion world R&D current annual expenditure for military research reports only the governmental part of expenditures. The figure does not include the military-related R&D outlays of private corporations or backyard inventors. It is the kind of investment that produced the atom bomb and all of its successor technologies and also placed men on the moon. Similar R&D resources, unfortunately, are not available to those seeking remedies for the pathology of international war.

Given these military security priorities and enormous R&D resources, advancing military technology has constantly fueled the arms competition, destabilized military balances, unsettled almost everyone's sense of security, and, above all, sustained attitudes of political distrust. A short chronology

---

17   Unfortunately, smaller powers involved in post-World War II conflicts have been used as surrogates by the major powers, often to test new, conventional technology.

of major military technological developments since World War II provides some details supporting the above contention.

In July 1945, when it detonated the first A-bomb experimentally, the United States became the possessor of a nuclear monopoly that would last only a few short years. A month later, it dropped a 14-kiloton (equivalent to 14,000 tons of TNT) A-bomb on Hiroshima causing 135,000 casualties. Shortly thereafter, a 20-kiloton bomb on Nagasaki resulted in 64,000 casualties. These city-destroying bombs were measured in kilotons at that time; they are now measured in megatons (each equivalent to one million tons of TNT). In technological terms, we reached the point where one bomb could cause the equivalent devastation that had previously required massive air raids. Equally as ominous, but often overlooked, was the development in Germany of the V-2 rocket - a ballistic missile. This eventually would provide the essential delivery system for nuclear weapons.[18]

In August 1949, Soviet scientists detonated that nation's first A-bomb. The British followed in November 1952, the French in 1960, China in 1964, and India in 1973. The technological monopoly had become nuclear proliferation, with about ten other nations presently in the wings at the point of producing, or already having, their own nuclear weapon capability.[19] Israel is estimated to have between 200 and 300 nuclear weapons. Pakistan and North Korea are believed to be developing nuclear weapons. On the positive side, the Republic of South Africa unilaterally gave up its six bombs in 1992. Brazil and Argentina, both well along in their developmental programs, mutually decided to end them and allow for inspection and verification on a bilateral basis.

Fusion bombs came next after the earlier fission type. The United States detonated its first hydrogen bomb with a 10 megaton yield in November

---

18   The Scud missile that created so much problem in the Persian Gulf War has characteristics not very different from the original V-2.

19   In its broadest sense, almost any developed or "near developed" nation could produce a nuclear weapon.

1952.[20] The Soviet Union followed suit in 1955, and China did the same in 1967.

Table 5.1   Circular Error Probable (CEP)[21]
      (in meters)

Time Period	CEP	Bombs Required
World War II (B-17)	3300	9070
Korea & Vietnam (F104/105)	400	176
Gulf War		
F-16	200	30
F-117 (Stealth)	10	1

The technological contest and escalation has taken place for other weapons systems. It was one thing to create bombs that could destroy entire cities but another to deliver these bombs directly to cities halfway around the earth. In August 1957, the Soviet Union tested an intercontinental ballistic missile (ICBM) that traveled the length of Siberia. In August 1958, the United States fired a test ICBM, the Atlas, with a range of 6,000 miles. The era of intercontinental ballistic missiles had begun. The R&D engineers of nuclear delivery systems concerned themselves with range, throw-weight (the megatonnage of nuclear explosive force carried in the warhead), and CEP (Circular Error Probable). CEP is the distance from the target within which, on the average, half of the nuclear warheads would most probably fall. At first, CEPs were five miles or less. Now they are as low as 10 meters.

---

20   For the story of the American decision to go ahead with the super bomb program, see Herbert F. York, *The Advisors: Oppenheimer, Teller and The Superbomb* (San Francisco: W.H. Freeman, 1976), James E. Dougherty, and Robert L. Pfaltzgraff, *American Foreign Policy, FDR to Reagan* (New York: Harper & Row, 1986), Marintvan Creveld, *Technology and War: From 2000 B.C. to the Present* (New York: The Free Press, 1989), David Halberstam, *The Fifties* (New York: Ballantine Books, 1993), ch. 2.

21   Adapted from Gordon and Trainor, op. cit., 189-190.

A comparison of these developments and the accuracy involved for non-nuclear systems is demonstrated in Table 5.1 above. The CEP for nuclear weapons is on the same order of magnitude. Given the accuracy of modern technology, CEP for nuclear weapons almost becomes irrelevant. The conflict and type of aircraft are depicted in the first column, the CEP in the second, and the number of bombs it takes to ensure target destruction are in the third.

During the Gulf War, CNN and ABC, among other media, treated the world to pictures of Tomahawk cruise missiles steering down the streets of Baghdad to their targets like flying carpets. Although they carried conventional warheads, they were capable of carrying nuclear ones as well. The difference in technology of delivery systems can be assessed by realizing that in World War II, the target was an entire ship or factory; today, the target may be the bridge of the ship or a specific smokestack of the factory. In World War II, a 33 percent strike rate was considered good; in the Gulf War, the Tomahawks achieved a 66 percent on-target rate. And this does not even consider the range at which they were fired!

By 1960, the notion of multiple warheads entered the technology. Multiple reentry vehicles (MRVs) were developed to land in a specific pattern around the same target. The next technological leap was MIRV (multiple, independently-targetable reentry vehicles), which could be aimed at different targets after being fired and conveyed by the same missile "bus". Development of MIRVs has proceeded so rapidly that the SALT II Treaty would have placed a limit of ten to fourteen warheads on any single missile. The START treaties, now being implemented, place similar restrictions on MIRVs, but provide for inspection and verification of *both* the warheads and the delivery systems. Failure to verify the delivery systems was one of the objections to the SALT treaties. Nuclear warheads are useless without the "bus", but the bus is not useless without the warhead. Over 5,000 ballistic missiles have been fired in anger since World War II. They have been used in four of the last six wars in Southwest Asia.[22] Ballistic missiles are now in the hands of over thirty of the states of the developing world.

Development of the U.S. anti-ballistic missile (ABM) began in 1954. Ways were needed to identify and destroy enemy missiles before they could inflict damage. Relatively little was expended on the program until the

---

22   Mark Hewish and Barbara Starr, "Catching the Bullet: Theater Ballistic Missile Defense Faces Realities", *International Defense Review*, 27 (June 1994), 31.

Sentinel program was funded in August 1969. Significantly, the U.S.S.R. had declined any attempts at arms control negotiations dealing with ABMs until this funding was made.[23] Within weeks, they agreed to negotiations that eventually led to the ABM Treaty. For mutually assured destruction to work, there had to be mutually assured vulnerability. Although negotiations began, development of these weapons continued until the actual signing of the treaty.

The U.S.S.R. successfully intercepted a ballistic missile during tests in 1961. They then began construction of the Galosh ABM system around Moscow in 1965. U.S. R&D on these weapons ceased until President Reagan introduced the much broader concept of the Strategic Defense Initiative (SDI) in 1983. After attempts to intercept Scuds in the Gulf War failed, technology from the SDI was applied to the development of tactical anti-ballistic missiles. (The ABM Treaty deals with strategic interceptions.) In May 1993, President Clinton closed the SDI Office in the Pentagon, but replaced it with the Ballistic Missile Defense Office. Not only is the United States conducting R&D in this area, but so are other nations such as Israel.

The advancing nuclear weapon and delivery system technology is matched by developments in other areas. High-resolution photo reconnaissance systems have been developed that are capable of observing human individuals on the ground from orbiting satellites more than 100 miles up. These flying cameras are essential for military intelligence and verification of arms control agreements. Such systems are now in the hands of civilian corporations. For example, French SPOT satellites circle the earth at slightly over 500 miles up. The three currently in orbit have photographic and infrared equipment that can take pictures of the earth's surface with a resolution of about 50 feet. Military equipment currently in space can reputedly read individual automobile license plates. Iraq and Libya have used this system to obtain military information about their neighbors.[24]

This technology is also being used to locate scarce water in the Empty Quarter of Saudi Arabia, to monitor environmental pollution, and to perform a host of other beneficial activities. There are at least 78 such

---

23 Simon P. Worden, *SDI and the Alternatives* (Washington: National Defense University Press, 1991), 105.

24 For example, the Iraqis ordered SPOT satellite photos of Kuwait and northern Saudi Arabia prior to their 1990 invasion of Kuwait. Gordon and Trainor, op. cit., 16.

civilian remote sensing programs under way. Even the military is getting into the act, using both satellite intelligence gathering and underwater sonar arrays, originally designed to track Soviet submarines, to provide data on fish and whale populations and movements. As yet, these sensors have only a limited capability of penetrating such common phenomena as weather, clouds, dust storms, and the like. Yet, even as the technological capacity to observe and gather intelligence improves, the technology of concealment advances as well. Cruise missiles with diameters as small as 21 inches are now available for delivering nuclear weapons over a distance of up to 2,000 miles. Cruise missiles are small enough to be hidden underground, in submarines, or in aircraft, and launched from any of these.

All the advancement is not reserved to the field of nuclear weaponry. As noted, the age of lasers is upon us. It is difficult to contemplate that the same technology that permits extremely delicate eye surgery also has the potential to destroy buildings. The more immediate use of laser technology is in guiding other weapon systems to their target.

The advancing technology in conventional weapons is also impressive. The roster of military marvels is overwhelming:

(a) "Smart" bombs or precision guided munitions (PGMs) capable of seeking out and striking targets with almost infallible accuracy through the use of television cameras, radar, laser beams, and similar electronic technology.

(b) Planes carrying airborne warning and control systems (AWACS) capable of detecting low-flying planes up to 250 miles away and with sufficient military command and communication equipment to serve as key command headquarters.

(c) Night vision devices and other equipment that create electronic battlefield sensors capable of detecting, day or night, the presence and movement of troops or equipment.

(d) Ships that are able to speed over water at 90 miles per hour on a cushion of air.

The list of ingenious devices goes on and so does their lethality. For example, in World War II, an estimated 300,000 bullets were required to kill a single infantryman. In 1967, during the Mideast War, a Russian Styx surface-to-surface "smart" PGM-type missile (cost: $20,000) sank the Israeli destroyer *Elath* (cost: $150 million). In the 1973 Middle East War, similar Soviet-made surface-to-air missiles (SAMs) brought down 90 Israeli fighters in 2 days, and a 20-pound, infantry-fired, wire-guided Soviet

Sagger missile destroyed 130 Israeli tanks in several hours.[25] The Afghani Freedom Fighters were barely holding their own against Soviet gunships until supplied with U.S.-made Stinger man-portable SAM missiles, which all but ended the Soviet helicopter gunship threat. The classic demonstration of advanced technology, both military and civilian, was, of course, the 1990-1991 Gulf War that brought an awareness of this technology into the living rooms of people all over the world in real time.

Lest one get carried away with technology, however, it is well to remember once again that more people have been killed since 1945 by inexpensive assault rifles, SEMTEX explosives,[26] and $5.00 or less land mines than have ever been killed by all the high technology. It must also be remembered that high technology still has some severe limitations. Satellite cameras cannot see through clouds or under ground. A soldier, figuratively at least, has to be on the ground to designate a target. Only the United States is capable of all-weather, around-the-clock carrier operations. Technology, nevertheless, moves onward toward higher accuracy, miniaturization, improved penetration of targets, and lower cost per weapon unit.

The U.S. Army has switched from emphasis on the soldier to emphasis on technology in its advertising campaign for "Force XXI". The Army envisions itself a completely digital force that electronically connects every part of the system, human and non-human, on the battlefield. By the year 2000, the Army will have as many computers as people.[27] By the year 2020, the Army will field a combat efficient system with integrated technology that does not miss targets or become lost. It will have fewer

---

25 Paul F. Walker, "New Weapons and the Changing Nature of Warfare", *Arms Control Today*, 9 (April 1979) 4, 1, 5-6; Richard Burt, "Nuclear Proliferation and the Spread of New Conventional Weapons Technology", *International Security* (Winter 1977), 119-139.

26 SEMTEX is a brand name of plastic explosive that is more powerful per gram than other plastic explosives. It is essentially odorless and almost impossible to detect. It is the ideal weapon for terrorists. The Czech Republic, where it was originally developed and manufactured, has agreed to place trace chemical markers in newly manufactured SEMTEX.

27 Kevin Goldman, "Army Launches New TV Ad Campaign", *Wall Street Journal*, March 7, 1995, 9B.

people in harm's way, but they will employ more equipment.[28] Technology of the future will seek to make each individual soldier a weapons system unto himself or herself, more potent that an entire company of predecessors in World War II.

The momentum of the qualitative arms race is difficult to analyze, negotiate, or halt. In contemporary industrial societies, it is something of a sacrilege to suggest that technological progress of any kind be slowed down or stopped. It would be as though Alexander Graham Bell, Thomas Edison, Henry Ford, and Jonas Salk were being required to put an end to their creativity at risk of going to jail. In an open and technologically sophisticated society, it is well-nigh impossible to constrain human inventiveness. Even in closed societies such as the former Soviet Union, China, or Iraq, the inevitable pressures of military competition, consumer demand, and imitation of the living styles of other societies conspire to promote technological change. How else can a society cope with the persistent fear that some adversary will create the Ultimate Weapon, the certainty that technological progress will continue unabated, and the likelihood that adverse developments in the military field may weaken one's own security.

Precisely because it is the most creative and technologically advanced society in the world, the United States is, unfortunately, the principal source of this type of technological destabilization and distrust. Some proud and chauvinistic policy makers have even proposed that the United States concentrate its military chiefly on research and development, creating new hardware wonders at such a pace as to make previous wonders obsolete even before they go into full production. At such a pace, the Russians and others presumably could never catch up and the United States would be forever secure. This argument is both gratifying and terrifying. Indeed, the implementation of this hypothesis is partly responsible for the demise of the U.S.S.R. and the Cold War.

As we look toward the 21st century, we should probably be less concerned with the technology and more with who controls it. Just as world economies have become internationally interdependent, so too have weapons development and manufacture. For a given technology to be restricted from export to a renegade nation requires the cooperation of several governments and civilian manufacturers who, if restricted in one

---

28   William Mathews, "STAR 21, Strategic Technologies for the Army of the 21st Century", *Army Times*, November 21, 1994.

country, simply transfer that part of their operation elsewhere. Although one of the reasons the U.S. government made Global Positioning Satellite technology available worldwide was altruistic, the U.S. also faced the fact that there was no way to restrict it. It could only impose some limitations, at best temporary.

Military and Political Secrecy

Secrecy and spying are forms of informational warfare. As such, their practitioners assume that a situation of conflict or potential conflict exists, enemies or potential enemies may be specified, and suspicion is the order of the day. Indeed, the basic rule of international relations is to trust completely no other nation. Because of this, there are limited intelligence operations going on even between ostensible allies. This is illustrated by Israel spying on the United States, even though it has more access to U.S. secrets than almost any other country; or the United States spying on France, as another of any number of examples. As a consequence, vast sums of money and effort are expended throughout the world (a) to keep military technologies and strategies secret and (b) to carry on the intelligence operations aimed at ferreting out each other's secrets.[29] This secrecy-intelligence circle is probably the most enduring manifestation of political distrust:

---

29   The literature on espionage, the Central Intelligence Agency, and military and political intelligence generally is vast. A useful bibliography is Ronald M. Devore, *Spies and All That . . .; Intelligence Agencies and Operations,* Political Issues Series, vol. 4, no. 3, Center for the Study of Armament and Disarmament, California State University Los Angeles, Los Angeles CA. 90032, 1977. An authoritative history and organizational analysis is Tyrus G. Fain, ed., *The Intelligence Community: History, Organization, and Issues* (New York: R. R. Bowker, 1977). For a more popular overview of the issues, Tom Braden, "What's Wrong with the CIA?", *Saturday Review* (April 5, 1975), 14-18, and the special issue of *Society* (March/April 1975) on "Espionage/USA". Additional references are Jeffrey T. Richelson, *Foreign Intelligence Organizations* (Cambridge, MA: Ballinger Publishing, 1988); Jeffrey T. Richelson, *The U.S. Intelligence Community* (New York: Harper Business Publishing, 1989); James Bamford, *The Puzzle Palace* (New York: Penguin Books, 1983); and Roy Godson, *Intelligence Requirements for the 1990s* (Lexington, MA: Lexington Books, 1989).

One of the strongest arguments in support of the functions of national intelligence agencies may be found in Georg Simmel's paradox: "The most effective prerequisite for preventing struggle, the exact knowledge of the comparative strength of the two parties, is very often attainable only by the actual fighting out of the conflict".[30] As witnessed in the Gulf War of 1990-91, the Arab-Israeli Wars, and any number of others, even fighting the war does not reveal all the surprises. However, the greater the knowledge, the less likely miscalculations on the part of national leaderships. In more contemporary strategic language, the most effective deterrent to war is exact knowledge of the relative military capabilities and political intent of the most likely adversaries.

Historically, there are many tragic examples of misperception of the strength of the other side - either as underestimates or overestimates - that have contributed to gross policy errors. In 1914, the Germans overestimated the size of the French army by 121,000. The French overestimated German strength by 134,000. The actual strength of each side became evident only in the event of military combat. In later years, the world overestimated Hitler's military resources after the German occupation of Czechoslovakia, and later Hitler underestimated the strength and the resolve of England and the Soviet Union. Here again the final and decisive measurements came on the battlefield.

Along these same lines, a substantial case can be made that the Korean War could have been ended in one year.[31] MacArthur was so positive, and had that feeling reinforced by his intelligence officer, that the Chinese

---

30   Georg Simmel, "The Sociology of Conflict", *American Journal of Sociology*, 9 (January 1904), 501, quoted and discussed by Lewis A. Coser, *Continuities in the Study of Social Conflict* (New York: Free Press, 1967), ch. 12 on the dysfunctions of military secrecy. Stanton K. Tefft, ed., *Secrecy; A Cross-Cultural Perspective* (New York: Human Sciences Press, 1980), offers a broad-ranging examination of secrecy as a feature of social and political interaction from the perspectives of anthropology, political science, and sociology. Using the Prisoners' Dilemma as an analytical model of the arms race, Brams and colleagues endeavor to demonstrate the wisdom, under certain circumstances, of the superpowers sharing intelligence data in order to achieve conditional cooperation. Steven J. Brams, Morton D. Davis, and Philip D. Straffin, Jr., "The Geometry of the Arms Race", *International Studies Quarterly*, 23 (December 1979), 567-600.

31   Halberstam, op. cit., ch. 7.

would not enter the conflict that direct and clear evidence to the contrary was ignored. As United Nations forces approached the Yalu River, Chinese soldiers almost willingly gave themselves up and, in response to questioning, said that there were many of them moving into Korea. MacArthur nevertheless continued the offensive, whereupon the Chinese decimated the 8th U.S. Cavalry. The Chinese then pulled back, sending a strong signal that, if the UN continued northward, they would intervene again. The warning was ignored. Both tactical and strategic errors were committed as the U.S. bombed the Korean end of the few bridges over the Yalu.[32] Even after the presence of the Chinese was recognized, their numbers were underestimated on the order of magnitude of ten.

More modern examples are the intelligence failures during the Gulf War. The size and capability of the Iraqi forces were grossly overestimated. The employment of Scud missiles by the Iraqis was underestimated. Political intentions on both sides were misread. The Iraqis completely misunderstood the lethality of modern air power and the employment of missile technology to gain dominance over the battlefield.

Notwithstanding these errors in judgment, the multibillion dollar intelligence activities of the United States Central Intelligence Agency, the former Soviet KGB and its successors, and the intelligence communities of other nations throughout the world continue to be considered essential for the prevention of errors in strategic decisions by national leaders. However, intelligence activities are conducted in secret and their findings are treated as national secrets. In turn, these secrets aggravate the distrust dilemma and escalate the arms race.

If we probe more deeply into the management of secrets and spies, other substantial risks are revealed. Secrecy may be and has been a cover for political, bureaucratic, and military misjudgments or breaches of the law. Secrecy can also be a tool of power, a barrier between those who have a "need to know" and those who do not. This barrier may determine who is a member of the more influential political in-group and who must remain in the out-group. As investigations of the CIA and the FBI in the 1970s revealed, spying may carry substantial risks for civil liberties. In the case

---

32   It was a strategic error in that it was a direct threat to the Chinese on the other side of the Yalu, almost as if the schoolyard bully had said, "I dare you to cross this line". It was a tactical error in that the Yalu froze over within a matter of weeks, as it does almost every year, and therefore the bridges were no longer needed anyway.

of the FBI, one has only to recall the massive personal files maintained in secret by J. Edgar Hoover. The McCarthy investigations of the early 1950s and the Watergate scandal indicate how spying on foreigners may easily flow over into spying against one's own citizens.

Nor are such operations limited to the traditional intelligence agencies. Federal police agencies have repeatedly engaged in intelligence work against political dissidents in the United States and elsewhere. Secret police are the main force used to control the population in totalitarian regimes. Gestapo, for example, is the German abbreviation for Secret State Police. Civil liberties and human rights thus endangered may create a climate of suspicion and fear that spreads all too rapidly among the citizenry. Another qualm about bureaucratic spying is that the validity and reliability of the information gathered may be questionable, yet, because of secrecy, occasionally remains unchallenged. Worst of all, the function of information gathering by spies may readily slip into forms of political coercion and violence domestically and internationally.

Secrecy may also work to the detriment of the public image of intelligence, security agencies, and their legitimate activities. Failures are broadcast far and wide; successes almost always remain secret.

Among the principal motivations and justifications for political, commercial, and military secrecy is the maintenance of technological advantage over others. Governments, corporations, and even individual scientists keep secrets for as long as possible in order to deny a competitor some perceived advantage. It took the former Soviet Union four years to break the American A-bomb monopoly. Meanwhile, American military and political ascendancy in world affairs was unchallenged. Soviet development of the fission bomb owed a great deal to the spying of Klaus Fuchs. On the other hand, with regard to the intelligence provided to the Soviets about the hydrogen bomb, in the words of Andrei Sakharov, "We got the same kind of help you (the U.S.) did. It was all the wrong information".[33] This was not because the information was invalid, but because the American scientists did not have the right information until a last minute breakthrough.

Spying and secrecy are not limited to governmental organizations. Corporations spend millions of dollars in the development of new inventions and products, an investment that they try to protect with secrecy

---

33   Halberstam, ibid., 92.

until their discoveries can be patented.[34] As for the scientists themselves, the glory of being first to discover new knowledge is unquestionably a major motivation for the inquiries they pursue.

Another motivation for secrecy is the opportunity it presents for bluff and surprise. By leaking partial or incorrect information about a secret weapon, one side can keep the other uncertain and anxious about what the latter might be up against in a military confrontation. Another sort of bluff is opaqueness. A nation "allows" its new weapons to be discovered, but continues vaguely to deny their existence. This tactic has been used by Israel, for example, with regard to its nuclear weapons program.

Surprise requires that a secret be well kept so that an adversary is overwhelmed when discovering it during a military confrontation. This was exemplified by the devastating and surprising accuracy of Soviet-supplied antitank missiles used by the Arabs against Israeli tanks in the 1973 October War. Similarly, the devastation wrought by the advanced technology employed by the United States and its allies in 1990-1991 against Iraq came as a shock and surprise not only to the Iraqis, but to the rest of the world as well, including many Americans.

Yet another motivation for secrecy is the rarely acknowledged political need for mystery and conspiracy as instruments of national cohesion. Few attitudes unite a nation as quickly as fear of some perceived enemy. The question that often ends any debate between Hawks and Doves is the hawkish equivalent of "but can you trust the Russians?" This question, together with the recurrent and inevitable discovery of spying by the other side, paves the way for witch hunts and spy scares. The Palmer raids against suspected communists after World War I and the McCarthy "Red" hunt following World War II, both stimulated by official and popular fear, were prime examples of this kind of secrecy, spying, and fear.

In general, then, secrecy, spying, and bluffing reinforce political distrust, accelerate the arms race, encourage public investment in costly intelligence organizations, and may obstruct the advancement of knowledge generally.

There is also the risk of nuclear war, as the Cuban missile crisis of 1962 demonstrated. Given the large intelligence budgets for the CIA and the KGB, each of the superpowers was presumably well-informed about the disposition of the other's forces. Any major changes in these dispositions

---

34 For a popular survey and discussion of corporate espionage, *U.S. New & World Report* (March 4, 1996), 45-48.

are usually signaled publicly and in advance by one side, as was the case of the CENTO (Central Treaty Organization) treaty permitting the placement of American missiles in Turkey within range of the Soviet Union. One of the most disturbing aspects of the Cuban missile crisis for American leaders was that the Soviet Union was secretly making a major change in the disposition of its strategic weapons. Not only was the placement of Soviet missiles in Cuba a flagrant challenge to the Monroe Doctrine and a real military threat to American security, the move also raised profound questions about the Soviet leadership's effort to accomplish all this in secret.

The trends, fortunately, have not all been in favor of secrecy, spying, and suspicion. Much has been accomplished since World War II with respect to unilateral reporting, arrangements for "hot lines", verification techniques (particularly by observation satellites), and on-site inspection. In other words, there is a growing number of arrangements for sharing "exact knowledge", as suggested by Simmel. A fundamental byproduct of this tendency is the promotion of trust among nations and competing elites.

Unilateral reporting of one's military resources is an inescapable part of politics in open societies where priorities and budgets are debated publicly and where most military research, development, and procurement contracts must be made part of the public record. Although bureaucracies tend to proliferate the secret classification of documents and other information, this tendency is not likely to go unchallenged or persist forever. The press is always eager to disclose and expose. Opposition political parties are curious to learn if secrecy has been a cover for policy blunders on the part of the incumbents. Taxpayers are extremely reluctant to pay for the high cost of document classification programs, miscarriages of civil rights that are often associated with such programs, or intelligence agencies preoccupied with keeping or discovering secrets. The latter, for example, prompted an extensive post-Cold War debate about the role and mission of the CIA.

Such tendencies in an open society make it easier for intelligence operatives of totalitarian regimes to ascertain much about the types, quantities, and uses of the military hardware of these societies. Totalitarian operatives need do no more than make a trip to an American local library, a request to the U.S. Government Printing Office for a copy of the secretary of defense's latest annual report, a subscription to the New York Times, an examination of the Federal Register, and so on. While many programs are kept secret even in an open society, a great deal more is found on the public record than would be conceivable in closed societies. Even "black budgets"[35] are open to some degree of speculation in the public media.

The former Soviet Union was surely the champion secret-keeper of the world for decades. It was a remarkable feature of most arms control negotiations between the United States and the Soviet Union that the weapon names and stockpile quantities data used by both sides were those presented by the United States. Soviet negotiating practice accepted the American names and figures as the basis for negotiations. From the Soviet point of view, this practice was a cheap way of checking the competency of American intelligence operations while at the same time playing their own military cards close to the chest. From the American point of view, the practice has been multipurpose: a proud demonstration of American intelligence competency; a deterrent to Soviet trickery; but, above all, a policy designed to compile exact knowledge and promote trust between the two nuclear giants.

As noted earlier, in keeping with *perestroika* and as a good faith gesture, the Soviet leadership announced a willingness to publish data about their nuclear inventories as part of the Soviet contribution to the continuation of the SALT and, subsequently, the START process. Also in the interest of trust, on March 24, 1992, the nations of NATO and the former Warsaw Pact signed the Treaty on Open Skies in Helsinki. Using a complex formula that allocates flights and other matters, each of the former opponents was allowed to overfly the other with designated intelligence gathering equipment.

The day may come when all nations, as a procedure for promoting global trust and preventing war, unilaterally and regularly report their weapons inventories to some international agency such as the Military Staff Committee of the United Nations Security Council. Initial steps have been made in this direction, but the reporting to the United Nations of international arms sales remains essentially voluntary; there are no means

---

35 "Black budgets" are for highly classified and secret government programs. They are known only to a select few and are buried in the allocations of money to other agencies with innocuous names. A classic example is what is now known as the National Security Agency. Not only its existence, but its very name was classified for over thirty years and its very large budget was buried as a black budget. Even today, much of its budget is hidden and most Americans do not know it even exists.

for enforcement or inspection. The Security Council established a Register of Conventional Arms in 1991 for seven categories of equipment and weapons systems. In addition to being voluntary and non-binding, it is *ex post facto*. In other words, arms transfers are reported after they have been accomplished rather than before when such transfers can be influenced. The Register does, however, contribute to greater openness and communications. Encouragingly, by 1994, 81 nations had made reports, albeit of varying degrees of validity and completeness.

A "hot line" is a direct and constantly open communication system between the leaders of the United States and the former Soviet Union for use in emergencies. Russia, as the agent of the CIS, continues the practice. The original hot-line system consisted of underseas cables, one line following a northern route between Washington and Moscow and a second line on a southern route across North Africa. The first hot-line agreement between the superpowers was signed in 1963. A modernization treaty, aimed at bringing the communication technology up to date, was completed in 1971 and has been repeatedly updated. The modern "hot line" is no longer a line at all, but satellite communications that travel with the respective leaders wherever they go.

The importance of these ostensibly simple arrangements should not be underestimated. When two powerful parties, ordinarily described as "enemies," make arrangements to communicate with each other instantaneously in emergencies, there must exist a substantial stake and shared interest that surpasses any gain that may be served by their enmity. In this case, any one of a number of simple human or mechanical errors could unleash a nuclear exchange that is unintended and unwanted. Even in less urgent situations, a hot-line system may permit the nuclear superpowers to avoid the kind of face-off that occurred in the Cuban missile crisis or, as it actually did, in the 1973 Middle East war. The practice of using the hot line for direct communication between superpower leaders is a profoundly positive measure aimed at sharing exact knowledge as well as responsibility for preventing major wars triggered by errors of information or failings of judgment, as happened in World War I and World War II.

Exact knowledge through verification has been a tale of reconnaissance technology. The Mata Haris have been for the most part replaced by less scintillating national technical means (NTM) of data gathering about weaponry: U-2 and SR-71 planes, orbiting satellites, over-the-horizon radar stations, a variety of airborne, ground-based, and undersea sensors, high resolution cameras capable of providing a clear photograph of an object one foot across from an altitude of 500 miles, and a cafeteria of computer-generated analytical systems that produce maps, interpret photographs, and analyze many forms of evidence. Rumor and hearsay have been replaced by direct visual or electronic observation. In the words of then congressman, later secretary of defense, Les Aspin:

> In short, the "national technical means" of surveillance available to this country for observing Russian missile tests are multiple, redundant and complementary. They enable the U.S. to detect all long-range missiles fired from the U.S.S.R. They are, in fact, far more reliable than most human intelligence gathering (that is, spying), which may yield secondhand, dated information or even false, slanted information.[36]

The technical means to which Aspin referred have become even more effective since his statement was made. However, his statements about human intelligence were at best misguided, as any number of disasters and surprises subsequently demonstrated. Over-reliance on NTM, for example, left the U.S. surprised when the Shah of Iran fell in 1979. NTM also caused the CIA estimates of the viability of the Soviet economy and political system to be seriously overstated. Had the U.S. and its allies faced a somewhat better trained and motivated opponent in the Gulf War, the lack of intelligence would have led to a disaster.

NTM was unable to locate Iraq's Scud-B missiles and grossly underestimated their number. The Iraqis used decoys for Scuds that could not be distinguished from the real thing farther away than 25 meters. Other examples could be cited.[37] NTM are unable to penetrate certain weather phenomenon, cannot see under ground, and have only a limited capability under water. In the case of nuclear weapons, they cannot "see" inside the nose cone of a missile. Most importantly, they cannot sense the feelings and thoughts of the political elite that makes the decisions; they cannot

---

36   Les Aspin, "The Verification of the Salt II Agreement", *Scientific American* (February 1979) 2, 38.

37   For a discussion of how evaluation of human capabilities, training, and tactics were gathered and evaluated by human intelligence rather than NTM prior to the Gulf War, see Gordon and Trainor, op. cit., ch. 5. Without this HUMINT evaluation, the success of the air phase of the war would have been problematical at best.

determine political will. If there is to be secrecy, human intelligence remains a key element. NTM can only supplement it. Each has its advantages and disadvantages and must be employed together if they are to be effective. The most effective and ideal means, however, is to establish political trust and openness, thereby obviating the necessity for intelligence gathering.

The technological revolution in reconnaissance, however, has had a profound impact on the negotiation of arms control agreements. It is now possible for arms control negotiators to claim that all agreements may be sufficiently verified by national technical means so that the risk of cheating is substantially reduced. Distrust is simply assumed, and verification is arranged. Theoretically and practically, there is always some possibility for cheating.

Improved verification capabilities have, in turn, encouraged arms controllers to broaden the scope of their negotiations and agreements, including the specification of a growing number of ground rules for noninterference with each other's national technical means of verification. As the number, scope, and verifiability of arms control agreements increase, the scope of trust also expands.

Perhaps the touchiest approach to the reduction and elimination of military secrecy is inspection. Proposals for direct, on-site inspection of national military forces by some international agency often elicit all of the negative responses that a family experiences when presented with a warrant to search its home. For the family, searches and inspections are generally perceived as annoying and demeaning invasions of privacy. The same is true for nations, particularly for closed societies. Most nations continue to see this as an insult to their national sovereignty. The trend in the 1990s is to diminish sensitivity when inspections are mutual, at least among the major powers.

Inspection usually requires that qualified observers, representing either an international agency or one of the parties to an arms control agreement, be permitted to examine personally and directly the weapons and/or military personnel of the nation being inspected or be allowed on-site during weapons tests and similar exercises. Theoretically, the process of inspection could put an end to all military secrecy. It hardly follows, though, that an end to military secrecy means an end to military strength. What would decline in importance and cost, however, would be high-risk bluffing and the expensive intelligence operations presently associated with political and military secrecy.

The notion of inspection had an unpromising beginning with the Soviet rejection of the on-site inspection requirement of the Baruch Plan of 1946. The United States would have agreed to place all atomic resources under the control of an international agency, the United Nations Atomic Energy Commission (AEC). As a condition of this grant of its nuclear monopoly, the United States required that all national territories be open to AEC inspection teams. Preoccupied with its own A-bomb development program and conservative about its national sovereignty, the Soviet Union rejected the proposal. During the course of the discussions, however, the concept of inspection was thoroughly aired and produced a substantial literature. The 1950s and early 1960s witnessed the advancement of reconnaissance and verification technology, as noted. In some respects, the Cuban missile crisis was a Soviet test of United States capacity for unilateral reconnaissance. The high-resolution U-2 photographs of the Cuban missile launcher sites were a dramatic demonstration of that capacity.

During the 1960s and 1970s, the acceptability and legitimacy of inspection advanced considerably. The International Atomic Energy Agency (IAEA) has been charged with responsibility for keeping careful account of all fissionable materials transferred from one country to another for nuclear energy purposes. This responsibility includes the inspection of security systems for nuclear power plants, accounting procedures (to detect the diversion of plutonium for explosive uses), and safety provisions for the handling of fissionable materials. However, the inspection force of the IAEA is understaffed and overworked. Its limited effectiveness was demonstrated in North Korea and Iraq, both signatories of the NPT.

Russia's attitude toward inspection has also been changing. In the Peaceful Nuclear Explosions (PNE) Treaty of 1976, wherein a 150 kiloton limit was placed on PNEs for projects such as extraction of underground energy sources, the Soviets agreed for the first time to a provision for on-site inspection. These inspections by American observers are scheduled whenever a PNE takes place. This treaty also calls for the mandatory exchange of relevant technical data. The PNE Treaty was a companion to the Threshold Test Ban Treaty, signed in 1976, which limited Soviet and American underground nuclear tests to a maximum yield of 150 kilotons.

The Comprehensive Test Ban Treaty was a further step in confidence building measures. Although such a comprehensive treaty has only recently been adopted (September 10, 1996), the United States, the United Kingdom, and the Soviet Union agreed earlier, through memoranda, not to test nuclear weapons. This has been a measure of confidence-building progress. France and China demurred, and have tested; NTM provided verification. The nuclear test by China in May 1995 introduced a somewhat ominous note, particularly since it came the day after signers agreed that the Non-Proliferation Treaty be renewed and remain in effect for an indefinite period.

In another approach to openness, President Reagan and General Secretary Gorbachev agreed during November 1985 in principle to the establishment of Nuclear Risk Reduction Centers. After a period of exploratory talks, formal talks began in 1987 and resulted in a bilateral agreement signed in November 1987. The centers, with special facsimile communications, became operational in 1988. These centers permit communications between the governmental *staffs* of Russia and the United States, an expansion of the "hot line" which is reserved for the heads of government.

These treaties were followed by a plethora of agreements culminating with the START treaties, each a step along the way in reducing political distrust. Although SALT II was never ratified by the United States Senate, each nation agreed to abide by its terms as long as the other did. The SALT II Agreement provided the basis for the subsequent START negotiations which began in 1982. These negotiations did not proceed smoothly. There was a series of walkouts, starts, and stops. Nevertheless, in 1985, Gorbachev unilaterally announced that the U.S.S.R. would cease deployment of intermediate-range ballistic missiles. This was followed in 1986 by a call for a ban on nuclear weapons worldwide by the year 2000. In 1987, there were agreements to eliminate intermediate-range nuclear forces. In 1988, there was an agreement on ballistic missile launch notification.

In the 1990s, with the advent of the START treaties, on-site inspection had become accepted by the major powers. This included short-notice inspections as well as verification and inspection of both delivery means and warheads. Inspectors actually witness the destruction of many of these items. The success of Russian-American efforts set an example for the rest of the world, and even grew to include conventional weaponry.

In the conventional weapons arena, in 1990, NATO and the then still extant Warsaw Pact signed the Conventional Forces in Europe (CFE) Treaty which limited the number of tanks, artillery pieces, armored vehicles, combat aircraft, and attack helicopters in each alliance. Although each alliance retained significant numbers of combat equipment, it was less than before the treaty. With the Tashkent Declaration in 1992, the twelve successor republics to the U.S.S.R. announced their accession to the CFE Treaty and agreed to an allocation of forces among themselves that divided up the commitments of the U.S.S.R.

The 1996 Wassenaar agreement on conventional weapons trade was another forward step in the conventional weapons field. This was an agreement among more than 30 nations designed to control the trade in conventional weapons and dual-use technology. Intended to go into operation in September 1996 on a voluntary basis, experts predicted that the exchanges of information would become compulsory soon after.

Overall, the sources of political distrust among nations - competing elites, national sovereignty, technological developments, and military secrecy - continue to be potent. However, substantial progress has been made, at least among the major powers. Progress is likely to be slower among the lesser powers where most of the military conflicts have occurred. The sources of distrust are being challenged and constrained as the world grows smaller and its capacity for self-destruction grows larger. World elites are beginning to find the military levers of power either awkward or obsolescent, often playing second fiddle to economic considerations or to nonmilitary political coalitions within supranational organizations. National sovereignty, which will hardly ever be declared obsolete, continues, like old soldiers, to fade away slowly, exacerbated by the numerous ethno-religious conflicts. Military technology advances almost unabated, but increasingly in competition for tax dollars and consumer needs. Secrecy and spying also continue to have a substantial place in world affairs, but here, too, the principles of disclosure and publicly shared information seem to be gaining ground in the interest of minimizing international distrust.

6   Sources of Distrust from within Nations

More often than most politicians and statesmen would be willing to acknowledge, foreign policy is made more for the folks back home than for any international motivation. Patriotism and national chauvinism still refer to powerful popular attitudes within nations. Furthermore, like all public policy, foreign policy touches and affects different domestic interests in different ways, benefiting some and disadvantaging others. In the United States, there are Democrats and Republicans, factions within each major party, thousands of organized interest groups, a national government of divided powers and separate branches, a federal system with fifty states, and many other sources of political division that in some way relate to the conduct of foreign affairs. In Russia, a similar complexity exists: parties, bureaucracy, the military, regions, and nationality groups function actively, each with its own interest and perspective.

Hawks versus Doves

Cutting across the domestic political diversity within all nations are Hawks and Doves. Their differences are fundamental and pervasive in the conduct of foreign policy.

As we have already noted, Hawks tend to be nationalistic, deeply committed to national security, and suspicious of all past or potential foreign enemies. Hawks rely heavily on military approaches to international influence and national security. They tend to emphasize the previous betrayals and foibles of an adversary. They also tend to be most demanding regarding the terms of treaties and other international agreements.

Doves tend to be internationalists, humanists, more inclined to see parties to a conflict rather than enemies, promotive of nonmilitary techniques of conflict management such as arbitration and international law, interested in economic and social approaches to international influence, inclined to trust their opposite parties in the negotiating process, and often more interested in concluding agreements *per se* than in the fine details of their specific terms.

141

Hawks suspect whereas Doves trust, usually on the basis of the same empirical evidence. Doves call Hawks paranoid; Hawks call Doves foolish. The simple fact that both perspectives exist in every country and set the tone of every domestic foreign policy debate is itself sufficient to keep alive the problem of political distrust among nations. If Hawks and Doves need an enemy or adversary about whom to disagree, they had their answer in the 70-year hostility between the capitalist West and the communist East. With the end of the Cold War, new candidates for the role of enemy are being sought. Meanwhile, certain nations in the Islamic world and certain remnants of the communist world appear to be in the running for enemy status.

Regardless of the identity of the enemy, the postures of Hawks and Doves flow logically from their respective assumptions about an adversary's intentions and their interpretations of their own self-interest, the very issues that created a dilemma for our hypothetical prisoners. In fact, the postures are built into the professional responsibilities of particular offices. What president of the United States or other national leader and what citizenry would want a military high command that fails to speculate about worst-case scenarios? It is the professional responsibility of the military to engage in such exercises and to provide appropriate advice. Whether or not the advice is accepted is another matter. Similarly, what president and citizenry would want economic advisers who fail to point out that economic ruin could be brought on by excessive military spending and may be worse than some degree of military insecurity or some kinds of military defeat?

The Hawk and Dove assumptions, interpretations, and debates are illustrated by the following instances drawn from the post-World War II era.

There is, once again, the case of the 1948 Emergency War Plan Halfmoon prepared by the Joint Chiefs of Staff. Recall the historical setting. In 1945, at the end of World War II, the United States, as it had in every previous war, began a rapid demobilization of its armed forces, returning millions of soldiers and sailors home, and disposing of weapons and equipment it had sent to all corners of the world. However, the Soviet Union only partially demobilized despite its cruel losses suffered during the war.

As early as 1946, American military strategists began advising President Truman, as it was their responsibility to do, that the Soviet army was capable of taking Western Europe (except for Great Britain), Turkey, Iran, the Persian Gulf, Manchuria, Korea, and North China in a matter of weeks or months.[1] The United States, they reported, had left itself only enough forces to defend the Western Hemisphere. Recalling some of the wartime difficulties in cooperating with the Communists against the Axis and observing the Soviet postwar threats to occupied Berlin (the Berlin Crisis came in the summer of 1948), Greece, Turkey, Iran, and other countries on its periphery, American military and political leaders became deeply suspicious of the intentions of dictator Stalin and the Soviet leadership. Soviet unwillingness to negotiate about the Baruch Plan for turning the U.S. nuclear monopoly over to an international agency, along with other evidence, convinced American leaders that the Soviets were striving to develop their own nuclear capability. Lubricated by mutual distrust, Soviet-American competition over the future of Europe and other strategic areas of the world, worst-case military analyses on both sides, and the professional obligation of military planners to take such cases into account, the wheel of the Soviet-American arms competition began rolling faster and faster and, it seemed, irreversibly.

Preparedness to counter Soviet conventional forces became the prime concern of American military planners between 1945 and 1949. Concern for Soviet nuclear capacity came later. Between 1946 and 1948, it is estimated that only about a dozen A-bombs were available. This fact was not reported to President Truman until April 1947! Truman was shocked to learn how small the stockpile was. Further, only about 27 to 32 B-29 bombers capable of delivering A-bombs were on hand. Many of the A-bombs were unassembled and would require twenty-four specially trained men about two days to prepare each bomb for action. In order to develop a feasible nuclear attack force, in October 1947, the Joint Chiefs of Staff informed the chairman of the U.S. Atomic Energy Commission that there existed a military requirement for approximately 400 atomic bombs (20 kilotons). Soon after, in May 1948, came the plan for Halfmoon under which fifty atomic bombs (probably the entire stockpile at that time) would be dropped on targets in twenty Soviet cities.

President Truman rejected the Halfmoon proposal and requested an alternate plan using conventional forces. By September 1948, however, following the nasty Berlin Crisis and airlift, Truman found that he had to assure his defense officials that he would be willing to use atomic weapons

---

1   The following account is based on David Alan Rosenberg, "American Atomic Energy and the Hydrogen Bomb Decision", *Journal of American History*, 66 (1979).

if it became necessary. Henceforth, and anticipating the massive retaliation doctrine of President Eisenhower's secretary of state, John Foster Dulles, United States military strategists, reinforced by new nuclear technologies, became absorbed in discussions about the number of A-bombs needed, the specific Soviet cities to be destroyed, and the procedures for giving the fatal command. Not many Communist spies were needed, if any at all, to communicate all this to the already paranoid Soviet leadership. By the early 1950s, with the United States embroiled in Korea and the Soviet Union vetoing all collective security moves at the United Nations, fear and distrust were rampant.

Leaping ahead to the mid-1970s - thousands of nuclear bombs and megatons later - we find that the American strategic debate had also escalated to keep abreast of the weaponry. The issue had become whether a nuclear war was any longer thinkable, survivable, and winnable. The issue is stated by Professor Richard Pipes of Harvard, who at one time was director of the Russian Research Center at that university.

> The classic dictum of Clausewitz, that war is politics pursued by other means, is widely believed in the United States to have lost its validity after Hiroshima and Nagasaki. Soviet doctrine, by contrast, emphatically asserts that while all-out nuclear war would indeed prove extremely destructive to both parties, its outcome would not be mutual suicide: the country better prepared for it and in possession of a superior strategy could win and emerge a viable society. "There is profound erroneousness and harm in the disorienting claims of bourgeois ideologies that there will be no victor in a thermonuclear world war", thunders an authoritative Soviet publication. The theme is mandatory in the current Soviet military literature. Clausewitz, buried in the United States, seems to be alive and prospering in the Soviet Union.[2]

What should the United States do? "It is high time to start paying heed to Soviet strategic doctrine", advised Professor Pipes. Scientists and accountants have been too influential in the formulation of current United States strategic theory; it is important that the military be given a central role. Pipes then cites analyses of Soviet military literature as evidence that the Soviet ruling elite regards conflict and violence as natural regulators of all human affairs: "War between nations, in its view, represent only a

---

2   Richard Pipes in *Commentary* (July 1977), 21.

variant of wars between classes. . . ".[3] Because they think a nuclear war can be won and may be willing to make a preemptive nuclear strike in order to win it, we must "make it impossible for them to succeed".[4]

In 1978, Professor Pipes criticized the war plans of both Republican and Democratic administrations because ". . . deeply embedded in all our plans is the notion of punishing the aggressor rather than defeating him".[5] With the election of Ronald Reagan, Professor Pipes, one of the nation's leading experts on the Soviet Union, was given the opportunity to influence the implementation of his position when he was appointed as the senior Soviet specialist for the National Security Council.

In the summer of 1982, President Reagan issued a National Security Decision Document that revised American nuclear strategy. Ancillary documents outlined a campaign to pursue aggressively the internal reform of the U.S.S.R. and cause its retreat from world empire. The plan called for a buildup of the military to eradicate the "hollow" military that had evolved under the Carter administration. The new military effort would equal or surpass that of the Soviets and be capable of fighting and winning a war. In conjunction with this, an information campaign was to be initiated that consistently and constantly called attention to the human rights violations of the Soviet Union and its persecution of minorities, most especially Russian Jews. The third part of the program, seemingly contradictory, was to continue to pressure the U.S.S.R. for arms control agreements, particularly in the nuclear arena. The plan was further supported by bringing pressure on putative allies to increase their defense capabilities - to "pay their share".

The campaign's effectiveness is evident. When combined with the former Soviet Union's domestic political and economic difficulties, the Berlin Wall came down in 1989 and the Soviet Union ceased to exist in 1991. Under the Bush administration, this was accompanied by an increasing number of arms control agreements, many of which were initiated as unilateral declarations by the leaders of the two respective superpowers.

---

3   Ibid., 26.

4   Ibid., p. 34. Pipes' analysis is a model of the Hawk position and logic.

5   Speech printed in *Aviation Week and Space Technology*, November 6, 1978.

The Reagan-Bush perceptions and policies were not without their critics.[6] When we hear from the Doves, we learn that Professor Pipes may have been selective in the evidence he offered regarding Soviet strategic doctrine and intentions. Actually, Pipes was proven correct when classified Soviet documents later became available. Worst-case analysis feeds on worst-case analysis, however, and gets to be nerve-wracking for the reader of these analyses. Robert L. Arnett, a Soviet specialist at the Library of Congress, responded to Pipes and, looking at the Soviet literature, concluded that Pipes's inferences were incorrect.[7] Arnett then quotes the writings of a Soviet defense minister, a leading Soviet military text writer, and others, in which all agree that the rejection of nuclear war is dictated by the realities of the era. Although it was unpopular and even ideologically incorrect to speak of Communist defeat under any circumstances, a number of Soviet strategic thinkers had, publicly at least, expressed doubts about Soviet chances for survival and meaningful victory in a nuclear war.

Domestic Order and Domestic Oppression

A second source of international political distrust originating from within domestic politics is the question of domestic order. One of the principal traits of government is its monopoly of the basic instruments of organized violence within its community. The government that does not have such a monopoly, or near monopoly, cannot long maintain domestic order or itself in power. As history amply demonstrates, it is not a very long road from domestic law-and-order to domestic political oppression. Hence, the importance of the American Constitution's provisions placing civilians in control of the military, the separation of civilian from military leadership, and the practice of legislating military appropriations for the short periods of one or two years.

Even more important than civilian control is a competitive party system and an independent, functioning judiciary based on the rule of law. Civilian control over the military is not, in itself, a guarantee of good order and respect for human rights. It is not coincidental, or historically unusual, that

---

6   For an extensive critique of the policy, see Robert Scheer, *With Enough Shovels: Reagan, Bush and Nuclear War* (New York: Random House, 1982).

7   "Soviet Views on Nuclear War", in William H. Kincade and Jeffrey D. Porro, *Negotiating Security* (Washington, D.C.: Carnegie Endowment for International Peace, 1979), 115-120.

it was the civilian leaders who were anxious to go to war in the Persian Gulf, and the uniformed military who urged restraint. Many of the most egregious violators of human rights have been regimes dominated by civilian oligarchies, e.g., the Soviet Union, Nazi Germany, Fascist Italy, Iraq, Iran, and China. These oligarchies, of course, did not have to deal with a truly competitive party system. Civilian control over the means of organized violence is not, in and of itself, sufficient, if accountability within an open party system, legislature, and electorate is lacking.

Whether called police or armies, weapons and militarily trained personnel are indispensable elements in any system of domestic order.[8] Revolution, civil war, terrorism, subversion, riots, and crime are very real and ever-present threats to societies and governments no matter how long established. As a consequence of these possibilities in domestic politics, governments necessarily become the principal producers, purchasers, and users of military equipment.

But the more a government arms itself for domestic purposes, the greater it appears to be a military threat to the security of its neighboring countries or traditional international adversaries: the security dilemma. In this way, the maintenance of domestic order may become a significant stimulator of the arms race. For example, when Syria armed itself in the 1960s and 1970s, primarily for domestic reasons (unrest caused by the Moslem Brotherhood and others), Iraq felt threatened and armed itself. Both were supplied weapons primarily by the Soviet Union. Iran, in turn, felt threatened by Iraq and armed itself. Iran's major supplier was the United States, which was seeking to balance the growing influence of the Soviet Union in the region. Not surprisingly, all three have had revolutions; Iran and Iraq eventually went to war with each other.

In these and other examples, the role of arms changes with the occasion and the possessor. A well-armed central government is difficult to overthrow without the aid of outside suppliers to the revolutionaries, except

---

8   There is another security dilemma here.   There is the Anglo-American experience and tradition that maintain that one of the greatest dangers to a regime, democratic or authoritarian, is a professional standing army that has a tendency to become separated from the mainstream population.   Universal military service provides a non-military population with training to counter-balance the professional cadre.   Additionally, it provides a constant infusion of the values of society at large.   Like so many political theories, however, examples may be cited on both sides of the issue.

by internal coup d'etats. Without strong pluralistic, differentiated institutions, a well armed regime may become oppressive to its citizens, thereby giving cause for discontent and revolution. However, if it is poorly armed, a regime quickly finds it difficult to maintain order or defend itself in a civil war. The cycle of arming, oppressing, and rebelling becomes circular within the nation. Unfortunate side effects of this internal process are the undermining of international confidence in the regime and the escalation of the arms race in the neighboring region.

An interesting special case is that of the Shah of Iran. Spurred by the billions of dollars earned by his oil-rich country and ambitious to become the leading military power in the Middle East and counter the growing threat of Iraq, the Shah indulged himself in the purchase of highly sophisticated weaponry, mainly from the United States. He was also able to equip a small and loyal royal guard and secret police, both of which enabled him to maintain an oppressive regime for many years. However, when the Shiite Muslim ayatollahs led by Khomeini united to challenge the Shah, the latter found to his dismay that the weapons he had purchased were too sophisticated for domestic purposes and his royal guard and secret police too small to deal with the mass demonstrations against his regime. What the Shah lacked was a citizen militia loyal to a central government in which the citizens had a vested interest. This was a case where the resources for a powerful international military organization were available, but grossly mismanaged. The purchase of inappropriate weapons and the inadequacy of training for the troops meant disaster for domestic purposes. The Shah's military build-up, of course, disturbed his neighbors, generated distrust of his intentions and judgment, and generally strained international relations in that region.

Multiple Functions of Military Establishments

Armies do more than fight wars. There is substantial validity to some of the claims in the U.S. military recruitment advertising: learn an important skill while you serve; see the world at Uncle Sam's expense; get yourself a patriotic job; reap the benefits of employment in one of the world's largest organizations; be all you can be, and so on. The hard fact is that military institutions throughout the world serve many functions in addition to those of defense, security, and the maintenance of order. If armies were no longer needed for security and order, new institutions would undoubtedly have to be created or old ones adapted and expanded to fulfill some of these other functions.

If we were to examine the military institutions of every nation and society, we might be surprised to realize that the military in most nations have been *the most organized and stabilizing influence in the community*. This has been true historically and continues to be so in large measure today. There are, of course, societies in which churches are the principal organization, or a close second to the military. In modern times, civil governments were created to manage and advance the community's common interests. In the last two or three centuries, corporate enterprises and political parties have also become significant mobilizers of communities.

In the American experience prior to the Civil War, governments and political parties were the predominant organizers. The two became so intertwined that the failure of one - the political parties - led to the failure of the other, and to the Civil War. In the latter half of the nineteenth century, American parties were revived, but corporate enterprise became strong until harnessed during the Wilsonian and New Deal eras. It was not until World War II and the Cold War that followed that United States military institutions became a major organizing influence in American life. When President Eisenhower warned about the influence of "the military-industrial complex", he was reporting on a new fact of American political life, namely, the emerging economic coalition between military and selected corporate organizations.

Of increasing importance was the influence of various corporations on political office-holders. For example, the top ten defense contractors in the United States contributed about $2.2 million to congressional campaigns in 1994.[9] The results can be disturbing. The military can be required to purchase certain weapons systems, on occasion, even though they have testified they had no need for them. Base closure becomes another contentious issue. For decades, the military has advocated the closure of many facilities as excess to its needs. Congressmen were unable to pass the appropriate legislation until the late 1980s, when they set up a separate commission under legislation that required an up or down vote on its *total* recommended list of closures.

In sum, what is new for Americans - standing army and military-industrial complex - has been "old hat" for many other societies, that is, the

---

9   Center for Defense Information, *The Defense Monitor*, vol. XXIII (1994) 7, 4.

predominance of military institutions as the major organizing influence in the community.

Armies, particularly the more successful ones, have also traditionally performed important *educational functions*. One often hears the claim that the U.S. Department of Defense supports probably the largest educational budget in the world. The raw youth recruited for most armies in the world often become literate through military training programs. For example, this was a major factor (along with the revision of the alphabet) in Turkey, which went from a society of less than ten percent literacy to one of ninety percent literacy in a period of less than two generations.

The requirements of even the simplest military technology lead to training for a large range of occupations. Soldiers learn to be mechanics, for example, and then open automobile repair shops when they return to civilian life. This skill training is more relevant in the sophisticatedly equipped armies of the developed nations. However, it may be proportional in developing countries. In many developing countries, they must learn to read and write before they can be trained to handle some of the most elementary modern military equipment. Literacy is an essential skill for the military as well as for a pluralistic and economically progressive society.

It costs tens of thousands of dollars to train an airplane pilot. The desired skills are worth an annual civilian income of between $50,000 and $175,000 in the United States for pilots. The United States military also provides a variety of scholarships and fellowships through assignments to various military academies and through such programs as ROTC (Reserve Officers Training Corps). For those American soldiers and sailors who became veterans of World War II and later wars, the GI Bill has afforded further civilian education and opportunity to more than 10 million individuals, nearly all of whom also became taxpayers.

In yet another direction, the military is a principal *socializing force* in the community. A young person's experience in the military services comes at a highly formative period of his or her life. The socialization that takes place during this period and under these circumstances tends to endure. Habits of personal care and hygiene, particularly in developing countries, are acquired as a result of military instruction and pressures. A variety of experiences in group living are acquired under different circumstances of tension, various mixes of races and nationalities, and different degrees of social preparation. Respect for authority on the basis of organizational necessity, individual merit, and similar criteria are explicitly communicated. The successful army also knows how to make the ordinary citizen into a proud patriot. Although there may be disagreement regarding the merits of the military socialization process, the fact remains that the military does socialize its troops. The individual who goes into the services as a raw recruit comes out a veteran and very often a different person.

An ancillary product of the socialization process, at least in those countries whose military is made up of large numbers of draftees, is to create a pool of persons with military backgrounds in the use of force. This tends to dilute a government's control over the use of force, without obviating its law and order role. It is not coincidental that the leaders of insurgencies have, more often than not, come from the ranks of the country's army, navy, or air force. Coups d'etats staged against governments of all stripes have almost invariably been staged by professional military persons. Dictators are well aware of this risk. Where they feel it necessary to maintain a draft system, they have taken great care to isolate draftees in separate organizations with different loyalties. In addition, dictators surround themselves with a substantial elite guard.

Yet another function of the military is *employment*. In many societies the financial resources are simply not available for paying full-time employees to perform certain public functions, for example, emergency disaster relief, road building, fire fighting, the distribution of food and medicine, and so on. Yet, the necessary manpower to perform these functions may be readily available and unemployed. Enlistment into the armed forces has been a traditional, cheap, and convenient way of putting together the unemployed manpower to serve the common need.

We have noted elsewhere that some 1.4 million civilian jobs (1993) in the United States labor force are defense-related. In awarding defense contracts, the Department of Defense is careful to take into consideration the employment consequences of the contract, and is particularly concerned that the resulting employment is widely distributed around the country, although perhaps a bit more so in the districts of friendly and influential congressmen. This has become even more crucial as bases are closed and the Defense Department budget reduced. Interestingly, a similar process is occurring in Europe where military contracts are also being reduced. Communities that are neglected are quickly heard from. Labor unions, whose members' employment depends upon such contracts, tend to support military budgets that result in high employment in defense industries.

Nowhere was this more evident than in the post-Cold War environment. Under the Clinton administration, substantial emphasis has been placed on the export of military equipment in order to at least partially compensate for the domestic reductions. For example, it was argued that a proposed Export Administration Act would ". . . liberalize export controls and redesign export control procedures and processes in light of the dramatic changes in the world, and keep controls focused only on weapons of mass destruction, missiles, dangerous conventional arms, and other threatening military capabilities. . . ".[10] In other words, liberalize the export of those weapons that do not challenge U.S. dominance. On the other hand, a DoD study on *World-Wide Conventional Arms Trade, 1994-2000* forecasts that arms exports will drop from the $625 billion in the period 1981-91 to approximately $291-330 billion in the 1991-2000 period and has maintained that general position since. They also estimate that the U.S. arms industry will retain 53-59 percent of market share.[11] It is of passing interest that as long ago as 1920 the United States accounted for almost half of the world arms trade. In February 1995, the Clinton administration reinforced its policy of assisting and facilitating the arms trade by directing embassies to provide special assistance to U.S. companies in marketing and bidding on foreign defense contracts.[12]

This relationship between the military and employment often is the basis for a rebuttal to the argument that military spending is noneconomic and a waste of human and natural resources. The rebuttal usually points to all of the economic payoffs that flow from high employment in the defense industries: expendable income in the hands of 1.4 million workers and their families; the development of skills and products that may be used for both defense and nonmilitary purposes; the stimulation of employment and production in other parts of the economy as a consequence of spending by defense employees and contractors. Further, the argument goes, the production of military equipment is no more wasteful than the production of cosmetics, smoking, and alcoholic products, most patent medicines, and

---

10   Lynn Davis, "Export Controls and Non-proliferation Regimes in the Post-Cold War World", *The DISAM Journal*, 16 (Spring 1994) 3, 65.

11   "Global Arms Sales to Drop, Predicts Study", *Janes Defence Weekly*, 11 March 1995, 9.

12   "U.S. Allows Arms Sales to 10 in Ex-East Bloc", *Washington Post*, February 18, 1995, 1 (by Dana Preist and Daniel Williams). See also, John G. Roos, "DoD Support at International Exhibitions is Key Element in National Export Strategy", *Armed Forces Journal International* (April 1994), 2.

countless other wholly unnecessary and even harmful consumption goods of contemporary life.

We must conclude that the multipurpose military establishment performs a sufficient number of functions for the community to warrant keeping it around for a long time. The acceptance of the military as a normal feature of community life also assures that the military will be at hand to make substantial claims upon the public budget. Their presence, their claims, the public support given, and the political and economic influence that results all combine to make the military a highly significant element in the domestic politics of most nations. However, the acceptance and success of military institutions at home may well generate distrust and insecurity abroad.

The Destabilizing Behavior of Public Bureaucracies

Another source of political distrust originating from the dynamics within nations is the role and behavior of national governmental bureaucracies. Competition for resources and competing career ambitions occur within these administrative agencies and tend to have consequences that inflate military budgets. In addition, administrators in different agencies come to the problems of security and arms control from different perspectives with different perceptions and modes of analysis and diverse procedures for arriving at public policy.

One of the difficulties in analyzing bureaucracies is that their mission, organization, and function vary widely from nation to nation. Much has been written about the American bureaucracy and its decision making process.[13] Less has been written about the bureaucracies of other parts of the world. It is tempting and human to "mirror-image" in these instances and transfer the characteristics of one bureaucracy to those of another. The results are not always accurate.

In Europe and European-style governments only the most senior policy making positions are held by political appointees. Other senior positions are held by professional civil servants. This practice has been termed the

---

13 See, for example, Graham T. Allison, *Essence of Decision* (Boston: Little, Brown & Co., 1971); "Conceptual Models and the Cuban Missile Crisis", *American Political Science Review*, 58 (September 1969); Allison and Morton H. Halperin, *Bureaucratic Politics And Foreign Policy* (Washington: Brookings Institution, 1974).

Westminster Model.[14] These professional civil servants are often much more involved in the decision and policy making process than are their American civil servant counterparts. In large measure, they, too, are protected from arbitrary dismissal. European civil servants, like their American counterparts, rarely take part in partisan political activity.[15] Unlike their American counterparts, however, they are in a position to provide advice and assistance, and, to a greater degree than the Americans, affect the political decision making process at a much higher level. A notable exception is France, where a small group of civil servants are graduates of the *Ecole Nationale d'Administration.* This elite is not only a source of senior civil servants, but also party politicians, including presidents of France.

In current and past communist states, essentially everyone is employed directly or indirectly by the government, hence all are bureaucrats. Party loyalty is the key to individual advancement. All of the post-Stalin leaders of the former Soviet Union rose to their positions through either the government or the party bureaucracy.

Modern authoritarian states of various types are similar in structure. They often use the political party to consolidate their power, usually reinforced by personal followings and loyalties. Bureaucrats owe their positions to persons in the seats of power and serve at those persons' pleasure. This may involve their lives as well as simply a job. Their conduct, motivations, and loyalty could not be more different from the American model.

In many developing countries, there are often not enough literate people to staff a meaningful bureaucracy nor enough money to pay them, and the two factors combine to produce inefficiency and corruption. Nor do these nations, many of which are former colonies, have a traditional professional bureaucracy. They manifest all the evils of the "spoils system" and see their positions as a form of sinecure or source of enrichment. Rather than providing continuity and stability, they are often one of the causes of domestic instability.

---

14 See Kim Richard Nossal, "Bureaucratic Politics and the Westminster Model" in Robert O. Matthews, Arthur G. Rubinoff, and Janice Gross Stein, eds., *International Conflict and Conflict Management* (Scarborough, Ontario: Prentice-Hall of Canada, 1984).

15 In fact, civil servants in the United States are prohibited from political activity, by law.

The sheer number of agencies centrally concerned with the making of foreign policy in any sizable nation can be breathtaking. Under the Constitution of the United States, the president is responsible for the conduct of foreign affairs, but the Congress appropriates the funds for these matters. Congress also holds the prerogative of declaring war. Within Congress, the two houses and a number of their respective powerful committees, not to mention factions within the major political parties, play a vital role in shaping foreign policy. Lobbies and other special interests have particular access to members of Congress, although they also reach into the federal bureaucracy as well. The Department of State is a major instrument of foreign policy, but this status hardly diminishes the influence of the Department of Defense, the Central Intelligence Agency, the Arms Control and Disarmament Agency, and, increasingly, such departments as Agriculture, Labor, Energy, Commerce, and Treasury.

Outside the government, but very influential in its policy making, are such consulting organizations ("think tanks") as the RAND Corporation, the Heritage Foundation, the Carnegie Endowment for International Peace, the Institute of Defense Analysis, and the Hudson Institute, to mention a few. Then there are also the experts at universities. Last in this listing, but often first in influence, is the press, where the manner in which events are reported may predetermine the course of foreign policy. Needless to say, the array of foreign policy agencies within Russia, the People's Republic of China, the United Kingdom, France, and nearly every other major nation compound the problem of bureaucratic competency and consensus.

Like any other group in society, agencies within a bureaucracy compete for limited resources. One approach to claiming and obtaining additional resources is to acquire or create additional functions. Questions of function and mission involve not only the *esprit de corps* of the competing agencies, but also the funds, personnel, and technology necessary to implement the functions. The stakes, from a bureaucratic point of view, are usually substantial.

In the United States, financial resources in the form of congressional appropriations are a major bone of contention among agencies. The defense budget, now (1996) $250 billion,[16] is presented to Congress after passing through an elaborate Defense Department system for program and budget development. This system presumably strengthens civilian control over the services and moderates the intensity of interservice bargaining. Over fifty

---

16   Statement of U.S. Secretary of Defense, Press Conference, December 12, 1996.

days of hearings are conducted by House and Senate Armed Service Committees and Appropriations Committees, listening to 200-400 witnesses, mainly from the Pentagon. Approximately 10,000 pages of testimony are printed as a result, not including the reports of the committees themselves. Reports and commentary are received from the Congressional Budget Office (CBO) and the General Accounting Office (GAO).

While each of the services within the Department of Defense and each of the agencies within the separate military services has presumably had a full opportunity to present and defend its budget requests, it has happened that a bureaucratic faction within the Defense Department, in collusion with friendly congressmen on the respective legislative committees, has objected during hearings to the amount of money requested by the secretary of defense for its agency. The protest is usually made in terms of some strategic doctrine or some technological considerations, but the bottom line is the question of more or less resources for the particular agency. Coincidentally, a particular congressional district may be the greatest beneficiary of contracts, installations, and other military expenditures. Similarly, it is not uncommon for members of Congress to insist on the purchase of equipment for which the service has stated it does not need, or items in excess of that requested by the services. Motivations in this process are generated within the congressional bureaucracy and reflect their desire to further their own interests.

Similar struggles over agency resources arise in connection with issues of personnel. For example, should two or more agencies be consolidated and the staffing for each reduced? Or should the staffs remain separated despite duplication of duties by some? How many troops should different branches of the Army, Air Force, or Navy be allocated? The impulse of every bureaucratic agency is, of course, to retain staff and add more.

Even in the negotiation of arms control agreements, competing agency interests must be represented. It is not unusual for an arms control negotiating delegation to include officials from the National Security Council, the Department of Defense, the Department of State, the Arms Control and Disarmament Agency, NASA, Commerce, Energy, and possibly a personal representative of the president. Each agency has a point of view to present, a function to perform, possibly some responsibility for the implementation of treaty provisions, and a budget to request after the arms control agreement is signed. In addition, there is the usual bureaucratic concern for recognition and influence, that is, for being present "where the action is" and "having a say" about the action taken.[17]

Even when they are not struggling for resources, bureaucratic agencies, as others groups in society, approach problems and decisions with biases in perception and modes of analysis. Bureaucrats are popularly assumed to be informed, objective, rational, and neutral: hence, most working administrators would probably be reluctant to acknowledge the presence of bias, the subjectivity of their judgments, and the network of bureaucratic friendships that characterize their actual working conditions. Or, if they do acknowledge these less-than-ideal characteristics, they might be inclined to argue that most of the shortcomings are dealt with in "the cauldron" of bureaucratic consultation and decision-making procedure.

Differences in the training of administrators in various agencies may have important consequences for their approaches to data gathering, analysis, and interpretation of findings. Military, strategic, and technological functions and programs are particularly subject to such differences in professional skills. Natural scientists, mathematicians, engineers, and professionals trained in related disciplines are among the principal makers of defense, security, and arms control policy. They are trained in logical and linear thinking. As a consequence, much security and military doctrine is based upon systems analysis, game theory, and similar rigorous but, in some cases, incomplete or inappropriate modes of thought. Among these bureaucrats there often is little place for the less tidy intellectual approaches of historians, psychologists, political scientists, anthropologists, and other social scientists. The differences in the consequent policies may be profound, as different as increasing weapons based on conclusions drawn

---

17 Although the process has been modified in some details, for a succinct description of the handling of the defense budget by Congress, Nancy J. Bearg and Edwin A. Deagle, Jr., "Congress and the Defense Budget", in John E. Endicott and Roy W. Stafford, Jr., eds., *American Defense Policy* (4th ed.; Baltimore: Johns Hopkins University Press, 1977), 335-354. For another view and criticism of the same process, Congressman Les Aspin, "The Defense Budget and Foreign Policy: The Role of Congress", op. cit., 321-334. Aspin expresses his disenchantment with the Armed Services Committees and the Defense Appropriations Subcommittees "as molders and disposers of the defense budget". A more recent analysis is contained in Dennis S. Ippolito, *Blunting the Sword: Budget Policy and the Future of Defense* (Washington: National Defense University, 1994).

from one kind of thinking or reducing them on the basis of conclusions derived from an entirely different intellectual perspective. These differences occur primarily from differences in intellectual training, not differences of perception and ideology as we find between Hawks and Doves. Nevertheless, the differences are often coincident with those of Hawks and Doves.

The importance of theories and analytical viewpoint for how a bureaucratic analyst arrives at his explanations, predictions, and public policy decisions has been elucidated by Graham Allison in his still valid study.[18] Allison identified three conceptual models which, when applied to the analysis of policy problems created by the Cuban missile crisis, led not only to different perceptions of events, but also to several different policy recommendations.

Allison's first model of decision making assumes that national policy is made by a single actor through a rational thought process. Applied to the Cuban missile crisis, this simply identifies the primary American objective (removing the missiles), considers the alternatives available (do nothing, employ diplomacy, invade, blockade), and concludes that the final choice (blockade, or "quarantine", as it was called) was the only rational choice for the United States. The conclusion was theoretically that of a single national actor.

Allison's second model focuses on organizational process. It views policy decisions as the outputs of large organizations rather than as rational choices by single actors. Thus, different bureaucratic organizations initially structure the situation-of-choice by raising the problem and gathering the information upon which action is to be taken. From this perspective, the decision in the Cuban missile crisis requires an understanding of the CIA-Air Force disagreement about intelligence data (a disagreement that determined the day of the discovery of the Soviet missiles), the response options of various organizations, and the priority of organizational implementation (in this case, the Navy's traditional desire for autonomy, which altered the plan for the blockade). This model sees the policy decisions as the outputs of a mosaic of organizations.

---

18   Graham T. Allison, op. cit. Allison's models have since been pushed and pulled, criticized, modified and supported in a wide body of literature. However, they still remain a leading basis for the analysis of bureaucratic decision making in the United States.

The third model sees policy as the consequence of bureaucratic politics, that is, a series of bargaining negotiations. Policy decisions are the result of a bargaining process in which all aspects of information, analysis, and choice are subject to the skills and influence of the negotiators, or players. Thus, the choices made in the Cuban missile crisis were the bargains concluded by the president and representatives of the State Department, the CIA, the Defense Department, the Navy, and others.

Irving Janis describes yet another way of arriving at policy decisions.[19] Bureaucrats and political leaders, he notes, are reluctant to be wrong, different, or the object of peer disapproval. Thus, when a group or committee of them considers a policy decision, the small-group dynamics operate in such a way as to produce concurrence as a defense of self-esteem and as a demonstration of humanitarian impulses. This usually occurs at the expense of critical thinking and leads to decisions at the lowest common denominator, that is, the choice of that option which is least resisted by most of the members of the decision-making group and is the most conservative of the policies available. Insight, innovation, and risk taking are not the forte of bureaucratic committees.

Further examination of the destabilizing bureaucratic processes leads us into the realm of bureaucratic procedure, the pursuit of bureaucratic careers, and the personal ambitions of some key administrators. Briefly, bureaucratic procedures usually involve the collection of information, the analysis of evidence, the identification of policy options, and the search for a consensus regarding an option to be chosen. Bureaucratic procedures may also serve as a method for concealing bias and subjectivity as well as for sheltering bureaucrats from personal responsibility for their choices. It is one thing when a decision is the deed of a person, quite another when it is the "output" of a blameless procedure.

Then there are the usual career concerns of employees in large organizations. In this respect, a public administrator is no different from any other employee interested in pleasing his boss, holding on to a job, and possibly earning a promotion from time to time. The hierarchical character of bureaucratic organizations may tend to discourage independence and innovation, which in turn promotes the bureaucratically "safe" and escalatory choices noted above.

---

19 Irving L. Janis, *Victims of Groupthink: A Psychological Study of Foreign-Policy Decisions and Fiascoes* (Boston: Houghton Mifflin, 1972).

Thus far we have seen how the struggle for agency resources and the differences of perception and analysis within different parts of a bureaucracy tend to lead to "safe" security decisions. Usually a safe choice leads to expansion of military functions, increase in military budgets, acquisition of new technologies, and emphasis upon primarily military objectives, namely, being stronger than or defeating an enemy. As these behaviors are conducted within the bureaucracies and within the nation, the consequence for relations *among* nations tends to be escalatory. Of course, bureaucracies throughout the world are organized and employed differently. Nevertheless, the different patterns of bureaucratic interaction within nations are likely to be among the factors that contribute to the environment of distrust, fear, and growing stockpiles of weaponry.

Usually the factors surveyed here - the Hawk-Dove debates, the connection between domestic order and domestic oppression, the nonmilitary functions of the military, and the behavior of public bureaucracies - are considered far afield of the problems of security and arms control. We have made the case that they are indeed relevant and influential. They are to be taken into account.

Part II

SOURCES OF TRUST

7 Confidence Building: The Promotion of Political Trust

If a major cause of insecurity and arms races lies in the distrust among the world's competing elites, then remedial steps should include creating the conditions of political trust among them in a realistic and lasting way. "Confidence building" is the popular rubric for such policies and actions.

Perhaps the most difficult and elusive confidence-building measure at this time in human history is the development of systems of institutionalized trust. Peacekeeping, as practiced by the United Nations and certain regional organizations, is another increasingly important approach to confidence building. At a practical level, for example, peacekeeping has thus far saved untold millions of dollars and countless lives.

The arms control process itself has confidence-building consequences that transcend the treaties and agreements that purport to match weapons systems, maintain verification programs, or creaste credible nuclear strategies. As we survey confidence-building policies and actions, we may conclude that the "secret cure" for insecurity, arms races, and wars may involve nothing more than reducing and eliminating political distrust among the world's leaders.

What principles can we learn from the experience of banks that provide mortgages and car loans for building institutions of political trust? What kinds of negotiations have succeeded in replacing civil amd international wars with such trust-promoting, conflict-managing institutions as systems of representation and party politics? On the economic side, we do know that the institutionalized trust associated with mortgages stimulates the economy and increases citizen happiness by facilitating the purchase of homes. On the political side, we suspect that the trust derived from successful negotiations within systems of representation and party politics enable elites to engage each other seriously in conflicts, yet pursue justice and freedom without resorting to violence. Are such institutional developments pertinent and possible on an international scale?

Political institutions rarely, if ever, come into existence full grown or from innovative actions taken around a conference table. Rather, they evolve because they have proven themselves functional. Even the classic cases of the Federal Convention that wrote the Constitution of the United States and the San Francisco Conference that produced the Charter of the United Nations recorded in contractual form many of the political institutional developments that had occurred previously. Today, there are a number of evolving world institutions that hold promise of being promotive of international political trust. However, these confidence-building institutions continue to have many policies, programs, practices, and political transactions that require additional nurturance.

Our concern for the evolution of political institutions warrants a brief definition of the concept "institution". Karl W. Deutsch offers one. "An *institution* is an orderly and more or less formal collection of human habits and *roles*, that is, of interlocking expectations of behavior that result in a stable organization or practice whose performance can be predicted with some reliability." Examples of such institutions are governments, corporations, legislatures, courts, and the family. Buying in marketplaces, voting in elections, getting married, and holding property are types of practices performed within institutions. "To *institutionalize* a practice, process, or service is to transform it from a poorly organized and informal activity into a highly organized and formal one."[1]

David B. Truman characterizes an institution as a human group whose patterns of membership and interaction have become formal, uniform, stable, and general.[2]

Formality refers to the relatively highly organized character of institutions. Positions are designated and persons are chosen to fill the roles called for by these positions. Rules are written to help verify behavioral expectations and to expose those who depart from these expectations.[3] *Uniformity* refers to the similarity of patterns of role behavior within particular types of institutions, for example, the nurturant behavior of parents in the family or the bargaining behavior of transactors in the marketplace. *Stability* alludes

---

1   Karl W. Deutsch, *Politics and Government* (Boston: Houghton Mifflin, 1980), 175.

2   David B. Truman, *The Governmental Process* (New York: Knopf, 1951), ch. 2.

3   The importance of language in prescribing rules and behavioral expectations is made clear, in all its complexity, in Sue E.S. Crawford and Elinor Ostrom, "A Grammar of Institutions", *American Political Science Review*, 89 (September 1995)3, 582-600.

to the tendency for members and behaviors to revert to a prior pattern or equilibrium following a disturbance. Stability also refers to the durability of institutional behavior patterns, for example, the process of voting for a representative in Congress in 1996 is not much different from voting in 1896. Finally, *generality* is that similarity of basic attributes that certain institutions have regardless of the society or place in which they may be found, for example, a family is recognizable as such in every society, a legislature is a legislature wherever one is found, and so forth.[4]

Once the attributes of institutions are specified, it is relatively simple to recognize how they contribute to the development of trust. The qualities of formality, uniformity, and stability contribute to the predictability of most patterns of behavior within an institutional framework. Predictable behavior is one of the elements in the development of an attitude of trust. Another element is the judgment that the behavior will have positive or negative consequences for oneself. Any institutionalized group is, by definition, a cooperative system in which shared goals are pursued by common effort. Thus, any appropriate behavior within the institution is highly likely to be aimed at achieving the shared goal, that is, to have positive consequences for individual members. "Institutionalized trust" is nothing more than the attitude of trust that results from and is reinforced by the predictable behaviors of the members of an institution.

Negotiating Profitable Transactions

One of the important lessons of behavioral research is that *successful* communication, negotiation, and transaction between parties, whether adversary or not, tend to reduce the conflict aspects of their relationship and eventually lead to attitudes of trust and inclinations to cooperate.[5]

---

4   This same definition of institutions may be applied regardless of the evolutionary position of a society or group. In primitive cultures the only difference is that the process is not written, but is established in ritual and custom. Modern advanced societies retain a great deal of such "ritualization", particularly as it applies to international law.

5   For surveys of relevant theories, Ralph M. Goldman, *Contemporary Perspectives on Politics* (New Brunswick, NJ: Transaction Books, 1976), Bernard Barber, *The Logic and Limits of Trust* (New Brunswick, NJ: Rutgers University Press, 1983), and Roderick M. Kramer and Tom R. Tyler, *Trust in Organizations: Frontiers of Theory and Research* (Thousand Oaks, CA: Sage

Successful communication leads the parties to shared meanings regarding language and symbols, to common perceptions of reality as described in the content of the communication, to better understanding of each other's value preferences, to mutually profitable transactions between them, and, in time, to more trusting predispositions toward each other. Even though the communication process may start out negatively, and even angrily, the interactions slowly, and often imperceptibly, tend to co-orient the parties to similar realities and values.

The *political currencies* available for these transactions have been categorized as *incumbencies* in office, *shares* of political prerogative, and political *commodities* such as goods (including armaments), services, and funds. Political institutionalization is a consequence of successful transactions among political leaders exchanging these currencies. Political trust follows from successful transactions. In the most general sense, arms control is, according to this conception, the mutually profitable end product of a process that awards *incumbents* in governmental offices with *shares* in the control and management of military *commodities* (armaments).

Such, of course, is one of the fundamental merits of the United Nations as a world communication center. Analysis of the content of former Soviet Union statements in that forum over the past fifty years revealed a sharp decrease in the invective directed at the United States as well as a decrease in the use of the veto in the Security Council. This decrease reflected not only a growth in Soviet strength and self-confidence since the days when strong language was their leaders' principal counter to the American nuclear giant, but also the success of Soviet-American transactions in many areas that have led the parties out of the Cold War into an era of detente. The growth in communicative activity between the superpowers and among all the nations of the world within the UN context is, therefore, to be applauded.

Advancing technology also promotes communication. Television and radio sets may be found in the most remote corners of the world and in the

---

Publications, 1996). For an explanation how negotiations contribute to social order, Anselm Strauss, *Negotiations* (San Francisco: Jossey-Bass, 1978). Also, Robert Jervis, "Cooperation Under the Security Dilemma", *World Politics* (January 1978). For a typology of political currencies pertinent to transactions leading to political trust and arms control, Ralph M. Goldman, "A Transactional Theory of Political Integration and Arms Control", *American Political Science Review*, 62 (September 1969), 719-733.

most authoritarian of societies. Satellites bring into the home pictures of events in every part of the globe. The world press is numerous and competitive, particularly in open societies. Local events may acquire worldwide significance instantaneously. Disclosure and publicity have been extended and converted into a potent weaponry. The world is able to follow events such as the Gulf War - from both sides - as it unfolds. The world was able to watch the Berlin Wall fall, as it happened, through satellite communications. Private news organizations publish compelling satellite photographs, e.g., Libya's chemical plants and the damage wrought by the subsequent U.S. air strikes. The new communication technology will eventually lay secrecy, military or any other kind, to rest and assure the world of one of the effective instruments for promoting political trust, namely, a free amd competitive press.

International communication is advancing along other fronts: social, cultural, economic, political, and even military. Tourism and other forms of international travel have become major industries. For some communities and countries, tourism has become a major source of income. Peoples and cultures previously unfamiliar with and fearful of each other have begun to become familiar and less threatening. Some tourists can hardly wait until a peace treaty has been signed between former enemy states in order to be able to travel to the other's land, e.g., Israeli tours of Egypt and Jordan.

Cultural exchanges are a well-established means of reaching out and communicating. Such exchanges are often a first step in the improvement of relations between two hostile powers. Ballet companies and symphony orchestras are permitted to perform and tour in the "enemy" country, much to the delight of appreciative audiences. Artists and art collections are sent on loan and leave the impression that "any culture that produces such beautiful art can't be all that bad". Athletic events are arranged, suggesting that there may be more civilized forms of competition than warfare, for example, the Olympics and the memorable ping pong matches that led to the opening between the People's Republic of China and the United States. Scientists, physicians, and academic specialists are permitted to visit, heightening the common ground from which the search for knowledge and the good life may be pursued together. As familiarity with other cultures increases, trust and the sense of human brotherhood tends to deepen.[6]

---

6   For a cross-cultural discussion of exchange programs and the mass media, Ralph M. Goldman and Alexander P. Potemkin, "The Politics of Cultural Exchanges", *International Studies Notes*, 19 (Winter 1994), 37-41.

Readers of "the bottom line" often believe that *real* payoffs are those of an economic and material character. What brings in the bucks is what counts. For promoting the growth of international political trust, few processes pave the way as assuredly as international trade. In the eighteenth and nineteenth centuries, this was a fundamental precept of free trade doctrine, namely, that trade, even though competitive, leads to friendly and mutually dependent relations and prevents war. Although often leading to nonviolent conflict, trade discussions between the superpowers, the Third World's demands for a "new international economic order", and the consultations among OPEC nations that set world oil prices are, in truth, communicative activities aimed at defining and coping with unprecedented international trade problems and opportunities. The resulting negotiations and transactions among such nations are likely to be profitable, even in a nonmonetary sense, for all concerned and, hence, help build an environment of trust.

Multinational corporations have grown in number and in share of international trade activity in recent decades. It is the contention of free traders that, as the proportion of multinational corporations producing and distributing *nonmilitary* goods increases, corporations involved in *military* products will become a diminishing minority within the total framework of international trade. In time, slowly but surely, war would become "bad for business". What is bad for business is likely to be vigorously discouraged by business and the governments they influence. Selling Pepsi Cola rather than tanks to China may have more than symbolic significance in the promotion of international political trust and the maintenance of peace.

Just such a tendency seems confirmed by the declining demand for arms in the post-Cold War. This trend has led to consolidations in the American defense industry. Many, if not most, of the defense-oriented corporations are currently increasing their production of dual-use products. Fewer corporations are strictly defense industries. Thus, for example, General Motors, the world's largest multinational corporation, was in 1994 also the fourth largest U.S. defense contractor. However, it is better known for its civilian output whose production is expanding multinationally.

Blurring the lines between civilian and defense production seems to reinforce the free trade assumption that war hurts business. All this is confirmed by the formation in 1995 of the World Trade Organization (WTO). WTO is designed to institutionalize free trade by urging countries to remove their national barriers. At the same time, WTO provides yet another forum for nations to iron out their differences without resorting to force.

In sum, political communication and exchanges promote trust. This is evident in the following trends: the growing frequency of summit conferences among world leaders; the widening scope of bilateral, multilateral, and universal negotiations dealing with political, economic, social, environmental, and military issues; and the intensifying participation of nations in supranational organizations, including the United Nations. The frequency and significance of these communicative interactions have increased from year to year and have received growing attention from the world press. Rather than brandish weapons and diatribe at each other, world politicians are more and more inclined to turn to the United Nations and to regional organizations to make their case and solicit support.

In retrospect, then, it appears that the volume, pace, and significance of international communication, negotiation, and related transactions are increasing and, in many respects, becoming institutionalized. Tourism, cultural exchange, international trade, and treaties among nations are likely to be difficult to turn off or discard as the years pass. The trend is positive: toward intensification and institutionalization.

Raising the Cost of Betrayal

From our description of the Prisoners' Dilemma we learned that the most self-interested behavior of a nation is to exploit rather than cooperate with another nation, particularly if the other nation is inclined to act cooperatively. Such exploitation may be interpreted as stark betrayal of trust. But this would be true only if the two parties had an agreement to cooperate and expectations arising out of this cooperation. The Prisoners' Dilemma model makes no such assumption. On the contrary, the model creates a paradox that tests whether trust or distrust exists in the minds of one or both parties. In the real world of international politics, such gross betrayals of trust are rare simply because the working assumption of most national leaders is that their adversaries, and, often enough, their friends *cannot* be trusted. Suspicion is the working hypothesis.

However, there does exist a substantial body of international law that brings some order and reasonable expectations to international relations. This is not a legislated body of law, nor does the world have a judicial system for applying laws or enforcing them. International law consists of traditional practices in the conduct of affairs among nations but, more precisely and explicitly, it is made up of a large body of contractual agreements for the most part enforceable only by an aggrieved party to the contract itself. From this point of view, technically the Charter of the United Nations is a multilateral contract among sovereign nations; it is *not* a constitution for an integrated system of government.

More and more treaties and agreements are including mechanisms for enforcement, often by a third party or supranational institution. Examples include enforcement measures put in place in the European Union as a part of the Maastricht Agreement and as part of the establishment of the World Trade Organization. One of the few encouraging things to come out of the conflict in the former Yugoslavia is the establishment of an independent international judicial process for investigating and prosecuting war crimes. This is not a court established by victors to judge losers.

Each of the traditional practices and all of the provisions of treaties and similar formal agreements, like any contract between two or more parties, are designed to specify with some clarity the conduct that the parties may expect of each other (the empirical aspect of trust) and prescribe only such conduct that in given situations would bring positive advantage to all the parties (the normative aspect of trust). Clearly understood traditional practices and well-written treaties thereby serve as features of institutionalized trust which, bit by bit, are likely to promote enduring political trust among participating nations. However, if agreements are misunderstood or rejected, it becomes necessary to devise ways of raising the cost of betrayal.

Several ways of raising the cost of betrayal are employed with varying degrees of effectiveness. *Publicity* is one punitive tactic that is frequently used. One nation describes the breach of trust incurred by another and points the finger of guilt. The accused nation replies with denials, a different version of events, and levies charges against the accusing nation. These exchanges get nowhere until such time as the intelligence agencies of neutral countries, the press, or some supranational organization independently investigates what happened and makes a public report of its findings. International monitoring of elections is an example. As we shall see in our discussion of United Nations peacekeeping, publicity may be extremely influential in identifying the offending parties, bringing pressure for better conduct, and perhaps leading to a nonviolent and equitable resolution of the conflict. In the absence of publicity, world leaders and world opinion flounder in misinformation and doubt about the circumstances of a conflict and the account of it that should be believed.

With neutral and authoritative publicity of the facts of the case, events can be understood, sides can be taken, and pressures brought to bear.

It is not often that nations *censure* one of their number, but when they do, the censure resolution either may or may not function as a weighty fact of international politics. When the League of Nations condemned the Japanese for invading Manchuria in 1931 and Italy for attacking Ethiopia in 1936, the censures were ignored. Instead, the incapacity of the League of Nations to prevent aggression and, later, World War II, became evident. On the other hand, the United Nations censure of South Africa for its apartheid policies was admittedly a source of discomfiture for that nation. The purpose of a censure resolution may be more symbolic than practical, as in the case of the Arab-sponsored United Nations resolution condemning Zionism as a form of racism. Another form of censure is diplomatic isolation, in which a nation refuses to recognize another, and actively asks the world community to refrain from doing so. Examples would include the Clinton administration's efforts to isolate selected "rogue" nations such as Libya.

A *boycott* or *sanction* is a punitive technique that may be more successful because it increases the cost of exploitative behavior. The boycott may be economic, that is, refusal to engage in general trade with or to sell or buy specific products of the boycotted nation. A military boycott is a refusal to sell weapons to the exploiter. A boycott is rarely 100 percent effective. Some countries, for example, will side with the boycotted nation and serve as its supplier or as a channel through which supplies from elsewhere may flow. These difficulties notwithstanding, boycotts do serve as a means for raising the monetary cost of betrayal. Economic sanctions and political and diplomatic isolation were used to substantial effect in bringing about the end of apartheid in South Africa and a cease-fire in the Bosnian conflict. Sanctions by the United Nations have increased. In 1988, the UN was engaged in only one; in 1992, it was involved in two; by 1994, it was engaged in seven boycotts.

A more serious action against nations that embark upon major breaches of political trust is *military*. When the North Koreans attacked the South Koreans, the United Nations, under the requirements of Chapter VII of its Charter, declared the former an "aggressor" and responded militarily with what President Truman called "a police action". In the Cuban missile crisis, President Kennedy ordered a naval quarantine, a military action that fell short of war when the Soviet Union backed off. President Johnson's escalation of American involvement in the Vietnam War was, in his words, intended to discourage further North Vietnamese incursions upon the South and to demonstrate to the North Vietnamese that it would be cheaper for all concerned if they came to the negotiating table. The recurrent Arab-Israeli wars in the Middle East have in part been tests of American resolve in supporting the existence of Israel as a sovereign nation. The most recent example, of course, is the restoration of the independence of Kuwait following the Iraqi invasion. In each of these cases, the military objective of total victory has been forestalled and given way to diplomatic negotiations. Where successful, the cost of breaches of international trust have been raised to a level that discourages or punishes exploiters.

Systematizing Conflict Resolution

Conflict is an inevitable part of human social life. Conflict arises out of scarcity of resources, different perceptions of reality, and different value priorities. If constrained adequately, social and political conflict may actually advance human progress.

Serious conflicts are those in which the parties either consider the stakes high or are determined to eliminate each other entirely. The conflicts that occur among leaders in world affairs usually involve high stakes and often a desire to eliminate the adversary - precisely the motivation for arming. Weapons provide a way of influencing the distribution of high stakes, eliminating an adversary, or preventing an adversary from eliminating oneself. A confidence-building program seeks to reduce the perceived value of the stakes, end the capacity of any one nation to destroy another, and develop techniques of conflict resolution that help the parties find their way to a transaction that can at least partially satisfy both.

Conflict management is a rapidly growing field of study and practice.[7] International conflicts are increasingly mediated by third-party

---

7   For a thorough bibliography of major works from the 1960s to the present, James H. Laue, "Contributions of the Emerging Field of Conflict Resolution", in W. Scott Thompson and Kenneth M. Jensen, eds., *Approaches to Peace: An Intellectual Map* (Washington, DC: United States Institute of Peace, 1991), ch. 12. A closely related literature on negotiation has also become prolific. For earlier influential works, see Anselm Strauss, *Negotiations* (San Francisco: Jossey-Bass, 1978); I. William Zartman, *The 50% Solution* (Garden City, N.Y.: Anchor Press/Doubleday, 1976); I. William Zartman, ed., *The Negotiation Process* (Beverly Hills: Sage, 1978).

interventions. The busiest of these mediators are the officers, particularly the secretary-general, of the United Nations. Friendly, interested, or neutral superpowers may perform a similar function, as has the United States in the Middle East and the former Soviet Union in the Indian-Pakistan dispute over Kashmir. Relatively successful efforts are those in Mozambique in 1994 and Angola in 1995. Although parties to a conflict rarely choose to do so, they may, if they wish, turn to the International Court of Justice in search of a more or less binding settlement of their dispute. In such instances, ICJ acts as an authoritative interpreter of existing international law if applicable to the case. Unlike judicial systems within nations, ICJ has no enforceable statutory law to interpret or means by which to enforce its decisions.

In a comprehensive survey of international conflicts during the period 1945 to 1974, Robert L. Butterworth analyzed 310 conflict cases. He found third-party conflict management interventions numbering as follows: 122 by the United Nations; 26 by the Organization of American States; 16 by the Arab League; 13 by the Organization of African Unity; 7 by the Council of Europe; 10 by the United States; 2 by the Soviet Union; 4 by the United Kingdom; 5 by NATO; 2 by the Warsaw Pact; and 12 by the International Court of Justice. Miscellaneous third parties intervened in many of the remaining cases, but as many as 55 conflicts had no third-party involvement whatsoever.[8]

The increasing involvement of the United Nations is reflected in a variety of ways. In 1988, the UN played a role in 11 disputes involving peacemaking; in 1994 it was participating in 28 such efforts. In 1988, the UN had deployed some 11,120 military and civilian personnel from 26 countries. In 1992, the UN had 13,800 personnel from 56 countries deployed. In 1994, there were 77,700 military and civilian personnel from 76 countries deployed in seventeen different UN peacekeeping operations. While the UN had observed no electoral contests in 1988, in 1994, it was involved in 21 election observations.

Within the short span of three decades (1945-1979), then, the world experienced more than 400 international conflicts of sufficient seriousness to engage or nearly engage military forces. Given such a high frequency of conflict, it is indeed impressive that a catastrophic world war has been

---

8   Robert L. Butterworth, *Managing Interstate Conflict, 1945-74; Data with Synopses* (Pittsburgh: University of Pittsburgh Center for International Studies, 1976).

avoided. The batting average of the conflict-managing parties, particularly the United Nations, has been better than usually recognized.

As international conflict resolution continues successfully, as third-party conflict managers sharpen their skills, and as institutions of conflict resolution become more available, systematic, and stable, the world can look forward to a significant advance in international trust. The stakes will be lowered because the *survival* of parties will no longer be at issue. The need for military solutions will appear too costly and, possibly, even unnecessary.

Developing Systems of Institutionalized Trust

Political distrust, as we have argued, is the principal generator of the arms race and is a major obstacle to the resolution of serious conflicts among the world's political elites. If this argument is valid, then political trust must develop before a system of global security can be achieved and before conflicts can be resolved by regular rather than crisis procedures.

However, trust is not a gift that can be given, nor is it a condition that can be willed. Trust is an attitude that, as behavioral scientists explain, is an outcome of successive mutually beneficial (profitable) transactions between two or more parties. Once again we cite the typical commercial transaction. Person A pays money for a product being sold by Person B. If the product satisfies A's needs and if the money is sufficient to give B a profit from which he derives his livelihood, then both transactors will be happy with the exchange, consider the deal profitable according to their respective criteria, and be sufficiently trusting of each other to be predisposed to future favorable transactions with each other.

Social and political transactions differ somewhat from economic ones in that the things exchanged (currencies) are less explicit, less specific, and usually less quantifiable. For example, in a social exchange, Person A may give advice to Person B in exchange for the latter's deference. This is a real social transaction, but one that is difficult to describe in quantifiable units. A familiar political example is legislative "logrolling" wherein Legislator A gives his vote to Legislator B's bill in exchange for B's vote favoring one of A's projects. Similarly, international treaties are little more than contracts recording political currencies that have been exchanged between participating nations.

The simplest transactions are those in which two parties simultaneously transfer currencies between themselves, for example, money to a cashier in exchange for a bag of groceries. However, when the transfers take place at different times, anticipation and trust become significant attitudes in the situation. If your grocer knows and trusts you on the basis of good longstanding relations, he will be inclined to extend credit to you, that is, trust you to pay later for goods that you purchase now. You have the convenience of paying your food bill in a single monthly sum; he has the profit that comes from the sale.

Remembering that transactions are occasions for twofold evaluations - (1) an empirical evaluation based upon the predictability of the other's behavior and (2) a normative evaluation regarding the positive or negative consequences of that behavior for oneself. The more predictable the other's behavior and the more positive the consequences for ourselves seem, the stronger is our attitude of trust toward that other person. Nations that fulfill treaty obligations to each other over time tend to become staunch allies and engage each other in cooperative activities beyond those prescribed in their treaties. In the relationship between the United States and Canada, the two countries have gone so far as to integrate elements of their armed forces (North American Air Defense Command) and civilian services such as the Saint Lawrence Seaway and NAFTA (North American Free Trade Agreement) to their mutual benefit. Despite occasional disagreements, each finds the other's behavior predictable and anticipates mutually beneficial consequences from their collaborations.

Institutionalized trust prescribes ways of organizing for social, economic, and political transactions so as to maximize the predictability of each party's behavior and to facilitate favorable evaluations of mutual benefit. Predictability usually requires reliable information about previous patterns of conduct, e.g., the regular payment of bills, the adherence to treaties, and the like. In our daily lives we observe many forms of institutionalized trust. Turning again to our mortgage loan example, banks and credit agencies will trust almost anyone under clearly defined conditions. The bank bears almost no predictable risk precisely because the borrower's past and present behavior show him or her to be a good credit risk who would stand to lose a valuable equity in a home if he or she were to default on the mortgage payments. The bank extends its trust on the basis of the borrower's empirically observed past behavior: regular employment and income; faithful repayment of other loans or credit; willingness to have home repossessed by the bank if mortgage payments are defaulted.

This commercial relationship of trust is so well organized that millions of mortgages are outstanding, millions of homes have been built, and society has prospered as a consequence. Foreclosures are few in relation to the volume. Refinancing is possible for those who are temporarily unable to meet the conditions of the loan. It all seems so reasonable. Yet, the institution of mortgage lending like all systems of institutionalized trust, evolved slowly.

Politics has its examples of institutionalized trust. When a political party in control of a government willingly gives up public office to a challenging party that has won an election, the expectation, usually based upon observed past behavior, is that the newly incumbent party would do the same if it were defeated in the next election. The normative judgment is that such peaceful changes of regime are in the best interest of the entire political community. Similar attitudes of trust may be found in legislative and judicial situations. Again, logrolling is the most familiar example. Plea bargaining and other forms of pretrial negotiation have recently become highly institutionalized transactions calling for trust among the parties to a judicial proceeding.

Which, then, are the institutions that promote political trust and could serve as nonviolent alternatives to revolution, civil war, or international war? The answer is at hand in every textbook about human self-governance:

- court systems, wherein disputes and breaches of civic trust are dealt with in a public fashion according to principles consistent with the mores of the community;
- representative assemblies, to which significant persons, groups, and other constituencies send agents to articulate their interests and achieve public policies that presumably bring the greatest profit to the greatest number;
- political party systems, which serve as the vehicles for mobilizing ballots rather than bullets, establish priorities among community values, and through which competing elites may conduct their drive for public office.

These are political institutions that function as arenas of political conflict. When they are poorly designed or when they malfunction, the community is likely to become irreparably divided and may even cease to exist. When they are well designed or evolve adaptively, the community flourishes, its competing elites come to trust each other, and the diverse interests in the community carry on their conflicts with less intensity and a greater sense of security.

Such political institutions and the institutionalized trust that they generate are present in today's world in primitive form. The outline of a world court system is perceptible in the existence of an International Court of Justice and a difficult-to-enforce body of international law and practice. The Security Council and the General Assembly of the United Nations are representative bodies, representative of nations rather than electoral constituencies. The European Parliament, a regional body, is based on electoral constituencies as well as nations. Present, too, are components of a world party system that is likely to flow from the recent growth of transnational political parties, namely, the Socialist, Christian Democrat, Liberal, Conservative, Green, and other partisan internationals. It remains to be seen whether these institutions develop to a degree that enables them to promote and sustain international institutionalized trust.

To better understand how certain political institutions promote trust and security, we need to separate out the development of these institutions from the establishment of governments. We also need to look at historical cases in which the long process of institutional development has successfully resulted in trusting elites, enduring governments, integrated political communities, arms control, and an end to warfare. Examples are not hard to come by. We need only review the strife-torn histories of some of the world's older nations to discover the nature of the process.[9]

Before doing so, we need to add an observation regarding the military. Military institutions do not resolve conflicts. Rather, military organizations and their weapons are instrumental in the conduct of conflicts and, coincidentally, in the protection of institutions. On the one hand, the military may serve hostile leaderships engaged in serious conflicts. As such, military organizations become a source of fear, distrust, arms races, and war. On the other hand, the more civilized function of the military is to preserve safety, enforce constitutional and legal decisions, and maintain order so that the conflicts of hostile leaderships may be carried on in non-destructive ways. With this distinction in mind, it becomes an empirical matter to determine how military institutions have historically related to other institutional arenas of conflict, that is, representative assemblies, the courts, and political parties.

---

9   Ralph M. Goldman, *From Warfare to Party Politics* (Syracuse: Syracuse University Press, 1990).

The British experience is a well-recognized example. That community was ostensibly an established nation as early as the sixth century. Yet, for a full millennium, until the Glorious Revolution of 1688-1689, England endured civil war after civil war. Whether over the royal succession or landed property or personal prerogative, the English nobility took up arms against each other with deadly regularity. Political insight as well as dramatic artistry led William Shakespeare to immortalize many of these struggles by focusing his audiences' attention upon the relationships among the competing nobles. When peace did prevail in England, it was usually during the reign of a monarch who understood how to deal with the nation's principal leaders, interests, and representatives as they manifest themselves in Parliament. The king or queen who dealt skillfully with this representative assembly and managed well the conflicts there was also facilitating the development of a conflict-resolving, trust promoting political institution.

The English nobility were also the military leaders of the land. Each had his personal guard or feudal army. The monarch, as liege lord, and absolute until the Magna Carta, could call up these "private" armies only under specific circumstances, for example, invasion or with the consent of the relevant noble. The ability of a monarch to maintain nationwide domestic order depended a great deal upon whether or not he was supported by a substantial coalition of nobles. When royal coalitions fell apart or were challenged, civil war ensued. In contrast, military forces for expeditions to foreign lands were usually made up of volunteers and financed in a variety of ways, only one of which was appropriation by Parliament. Additionally, the nobility and local sheriffs (Shire Reeves) performed functions related to maintaining domestic order.

During the seventeenth century, the revival of the principle of the divine right of kings and the low regard in which the Stuarts held Parliament led to century-long civil wars that moved back and forth from battlefield to Parliament. The settlement of the Glorious Revolution established a new relationship between the monarchy and the representative assembly, with the latter assuming dominant control of the nation's military institutions.[10]

---

10   It should be noted that Parliament was not truly representative until the beginning of the twentieth century. Membership in Parliament, the political parties, and electoral participation was based on property ownership and gender. It took the British almost 700 years to develop their Parliamentary

Several institutions converged in their development during this period. The outcome was a critical transition from civil war to governmental stability. The numerous armies of the nobility were incorporated into a centralized military organization which, in turn, ended up under the civilian control of Parliament. It was declared incompatible for a person to have active military status and parliamentary membership at the same time, thereby legally separating the personnel of the two institutions. Biennial parliamentary appropriations for the military kept the latter on a short leash.

More significant was the emergence of parliamentary political parties during the latter half of the seventeenth century and the beginning of the eighteenth. The parties were initially coalitions of personal factions in Parliament, with noble and military allies backing them up. Over the years, the personal coalitions became fairly stable in composition, that is, factions and political parties. As party leaders became increasingly interested in dominating parliamentary votes on public policy, they took up the task of electing as many of their fellow-partisans to Parliament as possible. This carried the parties outside the halls of Parliament into electoral constituencies. Over a period of about half a century, the British party system emerged, stabilized, and became a meaningful and effective vehicle for elite competition; in short, a nonmilitary alternative to civil war. The Glorious Revolution was England's last internal war.

Remarkably, a similar process of institutional development occurred in a very different political culture: Mexico. There, internal wars, carried on by the semiprivate armies of competing caudillos, were common from the time of independence from Spain in 1821 to the selection in 1929 of a successor to President Plutarco Calles. Mexico's critical transition to governmental stability took place between the Revolution of 1910 and the last attempted civil war in 1929. During these two decades, the difficult task of centralizing the nation's military institutions was carried forward by succeeding Mexican presidents. The principal arena of nonviolent conflict was the national party system which emerged during this transition; the single party in its various formations proved even more representative than the Mexican Congress. Whereas in Great Britain, Parliament had become the conflict-resolving political institution, in Mexico, the dominant party performed this function. In both cases, the broad outlines of governmental

---

institutions, a fact that should be kept in mind in assessing similar institutions of newly emerging nations today.

structures existed long before particular political institutions enabled those structures to stabilize and become effective.

We see a similar experience in the United States. The Founding Fathers wrote the Articles of Confederation and revised them into the Constitution, but it was the political parties and Congress that eventually provided the conflict-resolving, trust-promoting functions. When the American party system collapsed in 1861, so did Congress. A brutal Civil War left the country deeply scarred. Stability returned only after the Reconstruction Period was liquidated, and the party system again achieved strength and balance.

As a congenital self-disarmer, the United States failed to develop centralized military institutions until the beginning of the twentieth century. Volunteer armies and state militia reflected the highly decentralized character of the American military system prior to World War I; the Civil War was essentially a conflict between Northern and Southern state militias. During and after World War II, the United States experienced the first large scale centralization of a permanent military establishment.

In the American case, there is a long standing tradition of civilian dominance over the military, born of the experience of England's Glorious Revolution. Even in times of greatest crisis, from the American Revolution through the Civil War to Vietnam and the Gulf War, the American military institution has evolved in a subordinate role and has never threatened civilian dominance. The conflict resolving roles of the political parties, state legislatures, Congress, and the independent judicial system have made it unnecessary - demonstrations and riots excepted - to call on the military. The nation has undoubtedly had the last of its civil wars. It has successfully passed through a critical transition that reestablished Congress and the party system as the central institutions of political conflict.

What lessons can be learned from these thumbnail case histories of institutional development?

1. Competing elites require an alternative to the battlefield for the vigorous and serious pursuit of their inevitable disagreements. A competitive political party system serves as the most effective alternative.

2. The community's military can be converted from competing armies into institutions of internal order and safety. This transition requires that the military be centralized under civilian control. Civilian control should be widely shared. In the broadest sense, shared civilian control is a special kind of domestic arms control. The sharing is best

accomplished through the organization of an efficient representative assembly; efficiency refers to representation of all significant political interests in the community.

3. Stable government follows rather than precedes the development of mature and effective political parties and representative assemblies. It is in the parties and the assemblies that negotiate the most critical rules for conflict resolution and institutionalized trust.

How does all this apply to international arms control and global security? The history of the development of political institutions within nations strongly suggests analogies for similar developments at the international level. Although there may be debate about the stage, pace, and future consequences of the international institutional developments, they are undeniably already in progress.

At the regional level, for example, the European Union, made up of nations that formerly were at war with each other time and again over the centuries, has begun to centralize its military institutions. One of the key purposes of the Maastricht Agreement of 1991 is for the member nations to work toward common defense and foreign policies. Meanwhile, in the multilayered structure of the European Union, the European Parliament, thought to be the weakest component, has been expanding gradually from a membership of nine countries and 190 representatives originally to fifteen countries and 626 representatives in 1996. Even more significant is the fact that the Parliament currently conducts direct popular elections of its representatives, a first among supranational bodies. Previously, members were appointed from nations. Now members represent a popular electoral constituency and run for office as party nominees. The transnational parties that have been increasingly active in Europe (and the world) include Social Democrats, Christian Democrats, Liberals, Conservatives, and others.

Thus, in little over a single generation, despite their disagreements, Europeans have been centralizing their military institutions, assigning greater responsibilities to their representative assembly, and developing transnational parties as instruments of elite competition. Formerly hostile national leaderships are now trusting collaborators for the advancement of Western Europe's prosperity, the improvement of their collective security, and the maintenance of internal order and peace. The model is bound to be imitated in other regions. e.g., Central America, Africa, and South America.

Similar institutional developments are occurring, less visibly, in and around the United Nations system. Despite the strong mandate of Chapter VII of the UN Charter for a collective security system, such a system is still relatively nonexistent. Yet, the United Nations' military experience with peacekeeping must be counted as a significant, albeit unapplauded, beginning. With the end of the Cold War, the role of the United Nations in peacekeeping - and peacemaking - has grown. There have been both successes and failures. Perhaps even more significant for the future has been the United Nation's role in supervising elections. With the assistance of the UN, civil wars have been resolved in Mozambique, Namibia, and Angola, among others.

As an arena for conflict management and conflict resolution, both the Security Council and the General Assembly, representative assemblies of a special kind, have a respectable record of achievement. Again, it may be generations before the representatives to one or both of these bodies are directly elected by the peoples of the world, but the general structure and the conflict-resolving, trust-promoting functions are already being performed.

What is perhaps lacking is an influential transnational political party system. The granddaddy of transnational parties is the now-defunct Communist International (Comintern), which, at its height, claimed 90 Communist parties as members with a total individual membership of 60 million, not including some 40 million voters in capitalist countries. The Socialist International has reported some 100 affiliated national parties, 24 consultative parties, and three fraternal organizations such as the International Union of Socialist Youth. Christian Democrats have regional organizations in Europe and Latin America, with 64 member parties and 17 observer groups. The Liberal International claims 40 national parties as members and 22 observer groups. The International Democrat Union, the latest arrival to the transnational party system, also known as the Conservative International, has 57 national parties as members and claims to represent more than 170 million voters. These transnational parties operate openly and compete with each other in various supranational agencies such as the European Union. Their influence is informal and limited, but promotive of the institutional growth of supranational governing bodies.

Thus, even with the prospects for world government well into the future, the most relevant institutional developments for promoting international political trust, increasing collective security, and moderating the arms race are presently in existence.

Returning to Collective Security

When the League of Nations and the United Nations were created, the political leaders of the world were in effect acknowledging that unilateral national security could no longer provide the full measure of safety that it had in previous times. Weapons had become too destructive and alliance systems too unreliable. Collective security became a significant concept following World War I. It was written into the United Nations Charter with a degree of explicitness never before achieved in an international agreement. However, a working system of international collective security has yet to become operational and reliable. The Cold War, nuclear weapons, the emergence of a Third World from disintegrating colonial empires, and other factors put the collective security concept "on hold". Peacekeeping, with its special contemporary meanings, became the replacement concept.

The political leader who speaks of national security usually refers to the assumption that his nation has the primary responsibility for its self-defense. Self-defense includes the protection of the nation's territory, citizens, social and political institutions, economic interests, and all else that a predator nation might destroy or take away. Self-reliance is the basic posture. The only limit to defense preparations, he would insist, is the perceived weakness or strength of the suspected enemy. With such postures and policies, national security, unfortunately, rests upon and promotes international political distrust and arms races.

Collective security, on the other hand, is best described as a mutual insurance contract among states. Under the terms of the contract, each state agrees to guarantee the safety of all the others in exchange for a similar commitment by the others. Collective security assumes that the maintenance of security and order is a fundamental and legitimate common interest meriting shared responsibilities. It also assumes that an international conflict may have an "aggressor" and a "victim" and that the identity of the aggressor may be determined by a collective judgment. It further assumes that the collective military forces will be sufficient to punish or discourage the aggressor. In addition to this capacity for collective sanctions, the concept of collective security would presumably supplant the balance-of-power as a system for maintaining the peace. Finally, collective security assumes universality of membership in the system, that is, all members of the world community are part of the security contract.

With these assumptions in mind, the official collective security system for the world was prescribed in Chapter VII of the Charter of the United Nations, part of which is quoted below. The brief comments in brackets are the authors'. The title of Chapter VII is "Action with Respect to Threats to the Peace, Breaches of the Peace, and Acts of Aggression".

Article 39. The Security Council shall determine the existence of any threat to the peace, breach of the peace, or act of aggression.

[The Cold War soon made such determinations almost impossible because of the veto power of the Permanent Members. This development prompted the General Assembly's Uniting for Peace Resolution of 1950. The ethno-nationalist conflicts of the 1990s have made such a determination even more difficult. The end of the Cold War, however, has also brought about increasing cooperation among the major powers and a substantial decrease in the use of the veto.]

Article 40. In order to prevent an aggravation of the situation, the Security Council may . . . call upon the parties concerned to comply with such provisional measures as it deems necessary or desirable.

[The Security Council was to be the United Nations' principal agency for deterring aggression and resolving conflicts.]

Article 41. The Security Council may decide what measures not involving the use of armed forces are to be employed to give effect to its decision. . . .

[This is the authorization for boycotts and similar collective pressures, although the Security Council abdicated this responsibility to the General Assembly during the height of the Cold War.]

Article 42. Should the Security Council consider that measures provided for in Article 41 would be inadequate or have proved to be inadequate, it may take such action by air, sea, or land forces as may be necessary to maintain or restore international peace and security. Such action may include demonstrations, blockades, and other operations by air, sea, or land forces of Members of the United Nations.

[This is the ultimate authority for the United Nations "police action" against North Korea described by President Truman. Military sanctions are recognized here as the ultimate response to an act of aggression.]

Article 43. All members of the United Nations . . . undertake to make available to the Security Council, on its call and in accordance with a special agreement or agreements, armed forces . . . necessary for the purpose of maintaining international peace and security. Such agreement or agreements shall govern the numbers and types of forces, their degree of readiness and general locations, and the nature of the facilities and assistance to be provided.

[Neither the Security Council nor the General Assembly has yet determined how these special agreements are to be accomplished on a regular basis nor what their provisions about the disposition of forces should be. Instead, forces are created on an ad hoc basis for each contingency as it arises. A recent step has been the informal institution of a policy of regional balance among such forces. On the encouraging side, several smaller nations (e.g., Canada, Ireland, Sweden) have established specific training programs for peacekeeping forces to prepare them for their unusual military role. The United States Department of Defense is also considering how best to incorporate this requirement of UN peacekeeping among its several functions.]

Article 44. [Any Member providing peacekeeping forces may participate in Security Council decisions regarding their employment.]

Article 45. In order to enable the United Nations to take urgent military measures, Members shall hold immediately available national air-force contingents for combined international enforcement action.

[This Article, as does Article 43, raises fundamental issues about the nature of national standby forces. Significantly, it deals with air forces, which are usually the least effective in this role.]

Article 46. Plans for the application of armed force shall be made by the Security Council with the assistance of the Military Staff Committee.

Article 47. There shall be established a Military Staff Committee to advise and assist the Security Council on all questions relating to the Security Council's military requirements for the maintenance of international peace and security, the employment and command of forces placed at its disposal, the regulation of armaments, and possible disarmament. The Military Staff Committee shall consist of the Chiefs of Staff of the Permanent Members of the Security Council or their representatives. . . . The Military Staff Committee . . . may establish regional subcommittees.

[The Military Staff Committee was to be the beginning of the world's "Department of Defense", that is, the central military bureaucracy responsible, on the one hand, for peacekeeping planning and operations and, on the other, for arms control. Article 47 fits the historical experience about the necessity for centralizing the military institutions of the community. This Article has yet to be put fully into effect. The MSC meets periodically at the United Nations, and a small permanent staff has been established. Meanwhile, as we have noted, peacekeeping has become a major concern and activity of the General Assembly and the secretary-general. As for arms control, this MSC responsibility has been dispersed among numerous other agencies and forums, on the premise that arms control is a problem separable from peacekeeping. The provision for regional subcommittees was particularly prescient, recognizing that most armed conflicts are likely to be relatively local in character and best handled by a local "police force".][11]

Articles 48-51. [T]he members of the United Nations shall join in affording mutual assistance in carrying out the measures decided upon by the Security Council. . . . Nothing in the present Charter shall impair the inherent right of individual or collective self-defense if an armed attack occurs against a Member of the United Nations, until the Security Council has taken measures necessary to maintain international peace and security.

Chapter VII thus establishes a world collective security system that, when implemented, could be a major step toward the centralization of global military institutions. This process of military centralization at some time in the future could be a phase in a critical transition similar to that described earlier for Great Britain, Mexico, and the United States. At such time, the world's representative assemblies (presumably successors of the General Assembly and the Security Council) and its transnational political party system could converge to share civilian control of the global military.

Unfortunately, the leaders of the world are not yet prepared to fully implement the provisions of Chapter VII. The hurdles, institutional and other, have been several, and, in many respects, understandable. Each of the hurdles has been further heightened by the pervasiveness of international political distrust. Yet, one by one, the hurdles are apparently being surmounted.

Rousseau's parable of the stag hunt illustrates the problem of universality. In the parable, all members of a hunt are required to remain at their assigned positions to prevent the stag from escaping and to thereby completely assure that all hunters will share in the delicious venison that is the purpose of the hunt. If any one of the hunters is distracted or defects (presumably because he is misinformed, disloyal, or simply chases a more

---

11 Ralph M. Goldman, *Is It Time to Revive the UN Military Staff Committee?*, No. 19, Occasional Paper Series, Center for the Study of Armament and Disarmament, California State University, Los Angeles (Los Angeles: Regina Books, 1990).

available passing rabbit), the stag will escape and none will enjoy venison. This requirement of universal participation means that any one member of the cooperating group may deny the collective goal to all the members.

Universality is difficult to achieve in any human system. For example, recognition of the People's Republic of China rather than the Republic of China on Taiwan as the proper representative of China at the United Nations in 1971 was a "great leap forward" for the principle of universality, yet left Taiwan out. In general, however, the problem of universality of membership has been overcome. The size of the United Nations has more than quadrupled since its founding. China, with one-fourth of the world's population, could hardly have been excluded for long. Nevertheless, Taiwan, one of the world's leading economies, is still without representation. The failure of the United Nations to recognize the government of Kampuchea (Cambodia) led to bloodshed until recently. A more positive policy has included almost all other nations, e.g., North and South Korea in 1991 and the reinstatement of South Africa in 1994.

The second hurdle relates to the problem of identifying an aggressor. The United Nations' effort to brand North Korea and the People's Republic of China as aggressors in 1950 was the first and last serious attempt to apply this principle of collective security, until the Iraqi invasion of Kuwait. Even in the latter case, although Iraq was branded the aggressor, the forces that restored Kuwaiti independence were not UN forces, but a coalition led by the United States.

The Korean War demonstrated that the United Nations did not have adequate criteria for making a judgment about aggression by one sovereign nation against another. While there could be *parties* to an international conflict, it was not certain that there needed to be an *aggressor*. Further, it became clear that the United Nations did not have the means to enforce collective sanctions against an aggressor, particularly, as in the case of Korea, when only one superpower provided the military forces while the other (in this case, the Soviet Union) objected.

The question of defining aggression has nonetheless troubled the United Nations, particularly the General Assembly. A definition of aggression capable of commanding general acceptance by the international community has been sought without success for nearly 200 years. It was attempted at the Congress of Vienna (1815), at the Hague peace conference of 1899, at the Versailles peace conference of 1919, and by the League of Nations. The San Francisco conference of 1945 decided not to try to include a definition in the United Nations Charter, noting that "the progress of modern warfare renders very difficult the definition of all cases". In 1951, the General Assembly referred the tasks of drafting a Code of Offenses Against the Peace and Security of Mankind as well as the Question of Defining Aggression to its International Law Commission consisting of twenty-five law experts. In 1954, the General Assembly appointed a special committee of thirty-five members to speed along the process.

Not until April 1974, more than twenty years later, did the General Assembly adopt a definition of aggression in eight articles. The UN definition of aggression alluded to many types of acts: invasion, bombardment of territory, blockade of ports, attacks on the armed forces of one state by those of another, and sending terrorists into another state. The definition also acknowledges that its list of acts was not exhaustive, leaving it to the Security Council to expand the list or apply it to specific acts as it saw fit.

Another hurdle has been the veto. The veto power held by the five permanent members has the political and military capacity to challenge or halt any action of the United Nations, even to the point of war. From the outset, the Security Council's efforts to exercise its collective security functions were frustrated frequently by the Soviet Union's use of its veto power. With the end of the Cold War, however, the exercise of the veto has become rare. It must be remembered, of course, that in the years immediately following World War II, the United Nations was largely dominated by the United States, with the Communist bloc a distinct minority. While the United States openly supported its friends and allies with military and economic aid as well as favorable votes in the United Nations, the Soviet Union was also actively supporting Communist parties and revolutionary guerrillas, aided by the exercise of the veto whenever necessary.

Finally, perhaps the most serious hurdle on the road to a feasible collective security system are the requirements for large collective military forces sufficient to deal with military conflicts of all sizes and types. Two or three hypothetical scenarios will suggest how difficult it is to conceive of a practical system. Practical examples may be found in the cases of Somalia and Bosnia.

The most elementary scenario puts the nuclear superpowers in an all-out nuclear exchange. Since such a catastrophic exchange could have taken place within a matter of an hour or two at the most, it is difficult to conceive of a military role for the United Nations at all. Place such a scenario on a regional basis, where one of the non-declared nuclear powers employs its weapons. Even if it had its own stockpile of nuclear weapons, the United Nations could hardly step in to threaten or punish an "aggressor" or both parties. Nor is the day close when all nuclear powers would be willing to turn over their entire nuclear arsenals to the United Nations, giving that body a monopoly of the world's most powerful instruments of violence. Meanwhile, rapidly advancing technology may make these weapons obsolete. The ideal, but unrealistic solution, would be total nuclear disarmament, as proposed by General Lee Butler and some 60 senior officers from some 37 countries.[12] This would require a very great deal more and better institutionalized trust among nations than currently, or foreseeably, exists.

A second scenario relates to possible conflicts between middle-sized nonnuclear powers. Here, too, it would be extremely difficult to put together sufficient military forces to implement a collective security determination. The Middle East wars have been examples of this type of conflict. Iraq, Iran, North and South Korea, while still nonnuclear states, possess some of the largest armies in the world. The military force that a United Nations collective security system would require to break up a fight between powers of this size would have to be substantial indeed: several hundred thousand if not millions of troops, substantial air force contingents, and so forth. The price tag for such a military organization would be many, many times the entire budget of the present United Nations system, with current ad hoc expenditures for peacekeeping forces thrown in for good measure. This, too, is likely to remain a distant goal. This scenario was amply demonstrated during the Gulf War.

A third hypothetical scenario is one in which the world's security forces serve the kind of peacekeeping missions now performed by the United Nations, NATO, the U.S., or the Organization of African Unity. From the perspective of the UN in these situations, either the Security Council or the General Assembly serves as a third party with sufficient influence to convince most nonnuclear states in conflict with each other to accept a standstill cease-fire and allow a United Nations peacekeeping force to police the voluntary truce until the conflict can be resolved at the negotiating table. In such a scenario, the United Nations peacekeeping force remains relatively small, is financed for short periods, remains on duty at the pleasure of both parties to the conflict, and carries a minimum of weaponry. As we shall see, such peacekeeping missions are the current

---

12   *New York Times* (December 6, 1996), p. A8.

concept of collective security and a practical response to the political and military realities of conflicts between small nonnuclear states.

An International Police Force?

One confidence-building proposal that has been constantly reiterated is the creation of an international peacekeeping-peacemaking police force based in an international organization such as the United Nations. Issues of sovereignty, control, and cost have once again been grounds for principal objections to this proposal.

As of January 31, 1994, the United Nations had 73,400 military, 2,100 police, and 2,200 civilian personnel from 76 different countries deployed on peacekeeping missions of various types. This cost, apart from lives lost, some $3.6 billion. Given the limited success of many of these forces, the time has apparently arrived to reassess their role and function. The original UN peacekeeping missions, of which only five remained in progress as of January 31, 1988, were designed to separate two state antagonists, police truce lines, and the like. However, most conflicts since 1946 have not been inter-state wars. Rather, they have been insurgencies and ethnic conflicts, often as clients of external state actors. As we shall see, this complicated the UN peacekeeping missions,

National sovereignty has been the principal objection to an international police force. The American experience with its own federalism is perhaps a good analogy. When the Constitution was written, national defense was made a federal function. However, the states retained the right to maintain their own military forces, that is, state militia. The American Civil War was fought essentially by opposing state militia. Much of the fight was over the issue of states' rights – the sovereignty of the states versus those powers ceded to a sovereign federal government. The dispute continues, albeit far less violently. Even in recent times, state governors have tried to withhold their state troops (National Guard) from deployment outside the U.S. in support of national policies with which the state administration disagreed, e.g., support of the Contras in Nicaragua. Similarly, the nations of the world perceive a prospective UN police force as interference in their internal affairs and a breach of sovereignty that is in direct violation of the UN Charter.

The sovereignty issue extends into matters of command and control of the military forces employed in peacekeeping. Should the troops of one peacekeeping nation be subject to the control of the commanders of another nation? The implications are still being sorted out. Part of the problem is military resources and competence. Bosnia is the current example. The U.S. presumably has the best military hardware. The Russians have the principal access to one of the warring parties, that is, the Serbs. NATO has a commitment to keep the peace in Europe. And so on. It requires a long negotiation to figure out how to respect national sensitivities and yet establish a clear line of command. It would be no easier for an international police force.

How would the proposed police force be funded? It appears that the major and near-major military powers throughout the world spend between 4 percent and 5 percent of GNP, on average, for their military forces. If only a small portion of that amount of the world GNP were devoted to the support of world security services, the issue of sufficient funds would disappear. In fact, there would presumably be savings for all. However, cost is an issue with underlying non-fiscal motives: the fairness of membership dues, the efficiency of UN administrative activities, disagreements over peacekeeping policies, etc. So long as dues are used as leverage to obtain political objectives, there never will be "enough money" to finance a police force. Many opponents of this concept are quick to point out the great difficulty the United Nations has in funding its current limited operations.

There is also the contradiction in tactics. Both war-making and peacekeeping may resort to the use of violence, but for different reasons and different methods. Most world military forces are trained and equipped for the primary war-making mission to defend their national borders. If the defense forces are prepared to meet the assault from a neighbor on their borders, this should presumably deter such threats. Military forces are trained to bring the *maximum* available firepower to bear on the enemy. Their mission is to "close with, kill or destroy the enemy by fire and maneuver". If one bomb will "probably" do the job, but three are available, use all three. In stark contrast, peacekeeping missions, like police forces, are trained to employ the *minimum* force necessary, even at risk to self. Are forces designed to employ maximum force competent for accomplishing a peacekeeping mission that requires finesse, tact, and judgment? It is asking a great deal of a soldier who has been trained and equipped to destroy the enemy to assume the roles of diplomat and humanitarian. This is a contradiction that is currently under study by the U.S. military.

Perhaps what is needed in not another army, but a police force with limited duties, such as peacekeeping and counterinsurgency. Significantly, many of the all too few police officers currently deployed in support of UN peacekeeping missions are provided not because of their training, but because national constitutions prohibit the deployment of military forces outside their own borders. Yet, even a cursory review of counterinsurgencies and peacekeeping operations shows that police-led operations have all but invariably been successful, e.g., Kenya and Malaya, while military ones have a disproportionate number of spectacular failures, e.g., French Algeria, modern Algeria, Vietnam, Afghanistan, and Somalia.

Although nation-building is not directly within the purview of this text, the subject is certainly a major consideration in analyzing the sources of political trust, both domestically and internationally. A professional international police force could materially assist in nation-building. Policemen generally are not perceived as threatening or challenging as is the case with a military occupation force. Because they are trained to operate selectively, with minimum force, they do not cause the resentment or damage in the population that a military force does. Additionally, police forces are not seen as a threat to national sovereignty in the manner that military forces are regardless of the color of the helmets they wear.

Perhaps the arms race is not a race at all, but rather an institutionalized process that responds to an inability to redefine the essential elements of the problems of distrust, security, and safety. The security problem may have less to do with technology, weapons, balance of military forces, and all the hardware issues that are now the focus of attention and more to do with social and psychological relationships, attitudes, and institutions that influence the subjective as well as the objective aspects of peoples' sense of security and trust. An international police force may well contribute to the necessary trust and security.

8 Security Services of the Trusted Peacekeepers: Founding Circumstances

Although peacekeeping is a time-honored pursuit of statesmen and diplomats in international politics, the concept has acquired special meaning since the passage of the General Assembly's Uniting for Peace Resolution in 1950. Many view current peacekeeping practice as the most feasible response to the real world of power politics. Civil and international wars are seen as normal consequences of the institutional rigidity of conflict and change processes in most parts of the world. Thus, the end of the Cold War has exacerbated long dormant ethno-nationalist conflicts both within states and between states.[1] It also has become increasingly evident that arms control treaties in a world without conflict-resolving and military peacekeeping institutions are reduced to mere hardware contracts. Attention goes to symptoms rather than causes.

A brief survey and interpretation of selected early instances of peacekeeping by the United Nations leads to the conclusion that this function has been expanding in scope and significance and that it may well be, incrementally speaking, one of the major trust-promoting activities in contemporary international politics. Peacekeeping may still be a weak enterprise, but so are the early activities of all institutions.

Historical Background of Peacekeeping

During different periods of history, the major conflicts of the world were in one way or another resolved by some peacekeeping process or by a predominant power. What follows is a brief account of that experience.

In classical times, one way of keeping the peace was to conquer the enemy or subdue "troublemakers" militarily. As the wealth and commercial

---

1   Walker Conner, *Ethnonationalism: The Quest for Understanding* (Princeton: Princeton University Press, 1994), passim; David Hooson, *Geography and National Identity* (Oxford: Blackwell Publishers, 1994).

traffic of the Mediterranean Sea increased, the warrior-leaders of ancient empires and city-states had various motives for embarking upon military adventures and conquests: personal ambition; aggrandizement of territory and riches; destruction of a hated adversary; and, not insignificantly, the protection of commerce and maintenance of the order and peace that enables commerce to thrive. In the latter regard, the Roman Empire was the principal peacekeeper of the Mediterranean world for several generations. A similar development could be observed along the main rivers of China, where nobles fought over the control of waterways, commerce, and territory from the twelfth century B.C.E. to the founding of the Sung dynasty in 960 C.E. Nonetheless, years of order and peace were the accomplishment of skillful peacekeepers, particularly under the Han dynasty (202 B.C.E. to 221 C.E.) when China at times surpassed Rome in size, wealth, and power.

Despite countless local wars among ambitious nobles, the medieval Catholic Church, the Holy Roman Empire, and the feudal structure of society brought a sometimes unappreciated degree of order and political stability to an otherwise crude, primitive, and contentious Western world. At a later time, the concepts of territoriality, nationhood, Protestant roads to salvation, and divine origins of royal power began to emerge. These were accompanied by the breakup of feudal military coalitions that had supported papal supremacy. As a consequence, Europe became a war-torn place whose devastation was limited only by the volunteer character of its tiny armies and its primitive weaponry.

These conflicts spread distrust among political leaders and spurred the development of new military technologies, even in that untechnological age. From the fifteenth to the seventeenth centuries, mankind created cannons, muskets, armed warships, guerrilla warfare, and other unfortunate products of human ingenuity. Militarily, periods of European peace came only when royal alliances sustained them, economic empire-building preoccupied the elites, and English control of the seas deterred wars. It was also during these centuries that scholars and jurists such as Hugo van Groot, or Grotius, and Richard Zouche - in 1625 and 1650, respectively - wrote their first treatises on international law and international relations in the hope that careful analysis and wise prescription would provide international leaders with the understanding and guidelines needed for resolving their conflicts in the interest of all.

In Asia, developments were somewhat different, and provide a marked contrast to the developments in Europe. In essence, there was a Pax Chinensis in what is now called the Far East. The Chinese dynasties had to contend with periodic attacks from technologically inferior nomads on the periphery of the empire and occasional civil wars, but they were essentially unchallenged. As a result, there was little incentive to advance military technology, in contrast to the incentives that Europe was experiencing. However, there was significant development of commerce. While the Chinese Empire itself often did not expand, its "sphere of influence" encompassed an area from southeast Asia, including Burma and Thailand, to northwest Asia, including Manchuria, Korea, and Japan.

With the end of the Napoleonic wars at the advent of the nineteenth century, the modern era of international relations and peacekeeping began. In 1815, the Congress of Vienna inaugurated the first systematic multilateral approach to the settlement of European disputes through international conferences. During the remainder of the nineteenth century, the Congress system conducted thirty such conferences, with mixed results, and, in many ways, was similar to the post-Cold War era of today. Since so much of the non-European world was possessed or controlled by the imperial powers of Europe, the Congress system, in effect, evolved a set of rules of imperial competition. When the Congress of Berlin established the first international secretariat in 1878, this institutionalization of a new bureaucracy was another indication of the importance that the major powers attributed to the peacekeeping work of the Congress system.

World War I was a consequence of the inadequacies of the Congress system. Intense distrust among European leaders, escalating alliance systems, and rigid, automatic military doctrines led to the collapse of the fragile peacekeeping system. However, European leaders did build on the experience, encouraged in part by the Wilsonian enthusiasm for constitutionalism and world order. They created the League of Nations. The League legitimized and facilitated much of European conduct, and Europe continued to be the center of world politics. The capture and dismemberment of losers' empires was carried on through a League mandate system. New rules for peacekeeping were designed.

The League of Nations consisted of two bodies: the Assembly, made up of all forty-four members, and the Council, reserved for the major powers. The League and its secretariat were dominated by the French and the British. Two of the largest nations in the world were not members during the 1920s: the United States, as a consequence of isolationism at home, and the Soviet Union, the fearsome Red Menace of the day.[2] The League acted on the basis of the existing substantial body of international law. An assumption was that the resources of a collective security system were available. The League system included the main features of two other institutions of conflict resolution: a Permanent Court of International Justice and a Court of Arbitration.

By the end of its first decade, the inadequacies of the League of Nations were starkly evident. The Soviet Union joined, but was xenophobic in its relations with other members and the organization as a whole. In 1931, the League found that it was unable to deal with the Japanese invasion of Manchuria. Japan withdrew in 1933 when the League condemned its invasion of China, effectively the start of World War II. Nor could it halt the devastating but almost forgotten war between Bolivia and Paraguay in 1933. The major powers simply ignored the League when it suited them, as evidenced by France's occupation of the Ruhr in 1923. The remnants of this approach continues today.

The League did have its minor successes. It settled a dispute between Sweden and Finland over the Aaland Islands in 1921 and a border dispute between Greece and Bulgaria in 1925. By 1935, however, the fascist ambitions of Mussolini led to a savage attack upon Ethiopia. In his historic address to the League, Emperor Haile Selassie warned that the League's incapacity to halt aggression could only lead to its demise. Hitler's invasion of Austria in 1938 was the final blow. All of the techniques of collective security - censure, condemnation, economic sanctions, and so on - had proven ineffectual. The Axis powers were unconstrainable predators. In 1941, the League's offices were reduced to a skeleton staff. In 1946, the League officially disbanded. Most of its assets were transferred to the United Nations.

The United Nations picked up the collective security legacy of the League of Nations and presumably gave it teeth in the provisions of Chapter VII of its Charter. In effect, the UN was created as the policing system for a victorious coalition. The defeated Axis was disarmed and excluded. A trusteeship system replaced the mandate system for dismantling former empires. An International Court of Justice replaced the defunct Permanent Court of International Justice. An International Law Commission

---

2   The Soviet Union became a member in 1934, but was expelled in 1939 because of its invasion of Finland.

was created to promote the development of this ambiguous body of law and its codification.

The General Assembly was to deal with matters of membership, budget, and, through its deliberations and recommendations, promote (not legislate) international cooperation for the maintenance of peace and security, the development of international law, and the advancement of the economic, social, cultural, educational, health, human rights, and political goals of all mankind. The Security Council, with its powerful five permanent members, was assigned primary responsibility for the maintenance of international peace and security and the settlement of international disputes. The secretariat, whose secretary-general is appointed by the General Assembly upon the recommendation of the Security Council, was to build the bureaucracy that would serve and implement the policies of all agencies of the United Nations system. Article 99 of the Charter also gave the secretary-general an unprecedented prerogative: the right to bring to the attention of the Security Council any matter that, in his opinion, may threaten the maintenance of international peace and security.

Although so many components of a collective security system were theoretically in place, from the outset the United Nations was buffeted about by international conflicts and forces greater than itself. Initially, nationalist leaders and movements in the territories of former empires impatiently demanded independence from their war-weary European possessors, and so the next quarter century witnessed the birth pangs of over one hundred new states joining the original fifty members of the United Nations, reaching its current membership of 185 in 1995. At the same time, the Cold War created a bipolar Soviet-American world that, after the passage of three decades, was succeeded by a multipolar world that included the People's Republic of China, Japan, and the European Union.

The end of the Cold War between 1989 and 1991 left one superpower and a large number of medium powers. At this time many ethno-nationalist movements bubbled up and may well portend the birth of new nations and the adjustment of colonial borders in others. The post-Cold War era is also witnessing the growth of regionalism and regional organizations. The community of nations today is very different from the one that established the United Nations, with even more dramatic differences anticipated for the future.

More than 600 international conflicts have taken place since the founding of the UN.[3] In a century of dangerous military technology and rapid change in the social and political structure of the world, it is indeed a miracle that the world has not yet destroyed itself. Perhaps the real miracle is the restraint and caution inspired by shared fear. Perhaps the world's leaders have learned how vital it is to build, incrementally, the structure of institutionalized trust.

The first steps, however, were hardly auspicious. Between 1946 and 1950, collective security meant little more than United Nations troops and observation missions trying to discourage major-power interventions into domestic civil wars and wars of independence from former empires. In 1950, the Korean "police action" inspired the General Assembly's Uniting for Peace Resolution, which put the General Assembly and the secretary-general into the business of peacekeeping whenever the Security Council failed at it. This was, as we have noted, the turning point for a new style of United Nations peacekeeping.

Arab-Israeli wars since 1948, the Suez Crisis in 1956, the Congo from 1960 to 1964, Somalia from 1992 to 1995, and Yugoslavia and Bosnia-Herzgovina since 1992[4] have been the largest, the most expensive, and the most militarily difficult of the peacekeeping missions.[5] These and other missions have raised profoundly difficult questions of peacekeeping procedure, the structure of the military component, the method of financing, and a host of other issues.

On the functional side, the new style of peacekeeping has come to mean investigation, observation, mediation between willing and "non-guilty" equal

---

3   The actual number depends on how international wars are defined. Many of these conflicts were internal civil wars in which foreign powers supported, directly or indirectly, one side or the other. See, for example, Patrick Brogan, *The Fighting Never Stopped* (New York: Vintage Books, 1990) and R. Ernest Dupuy and Trevor N. Dupuy, *The Harper Encyclopedia of Military History: From 3500 B.C. to the Present* (4th ed.; New York: HarperCollins Publishers, 1993).

4   Although the Gulf War is not listed because the war itself was not a United Nations' operation, the UN has been heavily involved in monitoring the aftermath.

5   A detailed listing of United Nations, NATO, CSCE, and European Union operations can be found for a given current year in International Institute for Strategic Studies, *The Military Balance* (London: Brassey's, annual).

parties to a conflict, attempts at nation building, election monitoring, and truce maintenance. The participation to date has seen the emergence of a middle-power peacekeeping constituency, ready and willing to provide standby forces for peacekeeping missions: Sweden, Canada, Denmark, Norway, Ireland, Finland, the Netherlands, Pakistan, Bangladesh, New Zealand, Italy, India, and, more recently, such former communist countries as Russia, Ukraine, and Poland.[6] The major military powers, such as the United States, United Kingdom, and France, have, with some exceptions, primarily contributed logistical and transportation support as well as some technology.

With the end of the Arab-Israeli War of 1973, the United Nations has become increasingly involved in various peacekeeping efforts. The pace of involvement in these operations has become even greater with the end of the Cold War. Additionally, regional organizations, such as the European Union, the Organization of African Unity, the Economic Community of West African States, the Organization for Security and Cooperation in Europe (OSCE), and NATO, have become increasingly involved. The rising tempo of these operations is indicated by Table 8.1. Institutionalization of the peacekeeping process has also been incremental and significant.

Selected Cases Since 1945

The United Nations has been a direct agent of conflict-resolution in well over 200 cases since 1945. By broadening the definition of "conflict case", we could include occasions of UN "quiet diplomacy" and "good offices" that would easily double the number. Some cases have been more salient than others because of the importance of the parties, the degree of violence involved, difficulties of resolution, implications for politics of the United

---

6   For evaluative analyses, Larry L. Fabian, *Soldiers Without Enemies: Preparing the United Nations for Peacekeeping* (Washington, D.C.: Brookings Institution, 1971), Indar Jit Rikhye et al., *The Thin Blue Line* (New Haven: Yale University Press, 1974), A.B. Fetherston, *Towards a Theory of United Nations Peacekeeping* (London: Macmillan, 1994), George L. Sherry, *The United Nations Reborn: Conflict Control in the Post-Cold War* (Critical Issues No. 2; New York: Council on Foreign Relations, 1990), and Lori Fisler Damrosch, ed., *Enforcing Restraint: Collective Intervention in Internal Conflicts* (New York: Council on Foreign Relations, 1993).

Nations, or the nature of the precedents, failures, and successes coming out of the peacekeeping mission.

Table 8.1 United Nations Peacekeeping Operations[7]

Activity	1988	1992	1994
Preventive Diplomacy/Peacemaking	11	13	28
Active Peacekeeping Operations	5	11	17
Military Personnel Deployed	9,570	11,495	73,393
Civilian Police Deployed	35	115	2,130
Other Civilian Personnel Deployed	1,516	2,206	2,206
Countries Contributing Forces	26	56	76
UN Peacekeeping Budget ($US millions)	230	1,690	3,610
Countries with UN-Assisted Elections	0	6	21
NOTE: Numbers are as of the end of the indicated year.			

The survey that follows will give special attention to the accretion of *institutional arrangements* resulting from the missions, and the military-political implications of the experience.[8] An understanding of

---

7   Adapted from *New York Times International*, January 6, 1995.

8   Data for each case are drawn from several sources: M. D. Donelan and M. J. Grieve, *International Disputes: Case Histories 1945-1970* (New York: St. Martin's Press, 1973); Robert L. Butterworth, *Managing Interstate Conflict, 1945-74: Data with Synopses* (Pittsburgh: University of Pittsburgh Center for International Studies, 1976); John G. Stoessinger, *Why Nations Go To War* (2nd ed. New York: St. Martin's Press, 1978); UNITAR News, 5, (1973) 1; United Nations case materials collected by Ralph M. Goldman in connection with a National Science Foundation grant; International Institute for Strategic Studies, *The Military Balance 1994-1995* (London: Brassey's, 1994), 268-277; and R. Ernest Dupuy and Trevor N. Dupuy, *The Harper Encyclopedia of Military History: From 3500 B.C. to the Present*, (4th ed.; New York: HarperCollins Publishers, 1993).

these seminal peacekeeping efforts is essential to the development of trust, not only between states, but among ethnic groups as well. These efforts provide the foundation not only for United Nations' efforts, but also for regional and multilateral attempts at collective security.

Greece: UN Special Committee on the Balkans (UNSCOB)

A civil war in Greece began with the departure in 1945 of the German occupiers. Two underground resistance organizations, the National Liberation Front and the National People's Liberation Army, both dominated by the Greek Communist Party, established a provisional government to challenge the returning Royalist Party and the king. When Great Britain terminated its assistance to the king's government, the Truman Doctrine was promulgated (March 1947) and the United States undertook responsibility for assistance to Greece and Turkey.[9]

With the collusion of the Soviet Union, arms and supplies were shipped to the Communist guerrillas through Yugoslavia, Albania, and Bulgaria. The Greek guerrillas also used these countries as sanctuaries and training areas. More than 150,000 lives were lost in the civil war and some 25,000 Greek children were evacuated (some said kidnapped) by the guerrillas from border communities and relocated in the surrounding countries.

The Greek civil war engaged the United Nations in its first peacekeeping mission. Although the Security Council promptly sent a mission to investigate the frontier incidents, a number of Soviet vetoes prevented meaningful action by that body. The United States urged the General Assembly to take up the matter. In September and October 1947, the General Assembly called on Greece's neighboring states to cease aiding the guerrillas and created the Special Committee on the Balkans (UNSCOB) to investigate and report on the situation.

On the basis of UNSCOB reports submitted from 1948 to 1951. the General Assembly issued a series of recommendations: that Greece renew diplomatic relations with its neighbors; that the 25,000 Greek children be returned; that Albania and Bulgaria cease assistance to the guerrillas;[10] and

---

9　Turkey at that time was the object of diplomatic and military threats from the Soviet Union over provinces in the east along the Georgian-Armenian-Azeri border and over the Turkish Straits.

10　Tito broke with the Soviet Union in 1949 and withdrew Yugoslav aid at that time.

that Greek army soldiers held captive in Balkan states be repatriated. In 1951, UNSCOB was replaced by a UN Peace Observation Commission, hostilities declined, and the civil war ended through attrition.

This first peacekeeping mission revealed important difficulties, enjoyed limited successes, and set some significant institutional precedents. The most serious difficulty was the stalemate in the Security Council. A disagreement among the permanent members, more specifically, the United States and the Soviet Union, meant that the Council could not act as a conflict-managing agency. The immobilization of the Security Council led to the important precedent of having the General Assembly become involved in a nonmilitary fashion.

A further difficulty, to recur frequently, was the impracticality of thorough field investigations in a conflict of this character: long and open borders over which guerrillas and their supplies could pass readily; guerrilla warfare as a difficult kind of military operation to investigate; poor coordination of observation teams functioning under many different commands. Many of these difficulties continue to arise in UN operations today.

Despite these difficulties, UNSCOB did succeed in casting the light of authoritative information and publicity upon a conflict that otherwise might have been obscured from world view. The General Assembly persisted in making recommendations that eventually constrained the parties. In sum, the Greek case set the tone of Soviet-American relationships in the incipient Cold War, put the General Assembly into peacekeeping, and demonstrated that investigation and observation could be significant sources of institutional pressure for ending a conflict.

Palestine: UN Truce Supervision Organization (UNTSO)

Palestine has had a special religious, emotional, and territorial significance for Jews, Christians, and Moslems throughout the world. In 1897, the World Zionist Congress was established with the prime objective of making Palestine the "Jewish National Home". At that time, Palestine was part of the Ottoman Empire. At the end of World War I, control of much of the Middle East was seized by the British and the French. The British occupied Palestine. In 1917, British Foreign Secretary Balfour announced his government's willingness to help the Jewish people establish a national home in Palestine provided that "nothing shall be done which may prejudice the civil and religious rights of existing non-Jewish communities in Palestine".

After the war, the British, responsible for Palestine under a League of Nations mandate, were obligated to both Jews and Palestinians for the development of their respective homelands in the area.[11] The situation in the Middle East was aggravated in the 1930s by the exodus of Jews from Germany and other parts of Europe to escape Nazi persecution and concentration camps and repeated pogroms in the Soviet Union. Jewish immigration and land purchases in Palestine reached major proportions and were strenuously resisted by the leaders of the Palestinian and other Arab nationalist movements. In 1937, the Peel Commission, a British royal commission, recommended partitioning Palestine between Jews and Arabs, a proposal that was rejected by the Palestinians. In 1939, the British announced that Jewish immigration into Palestine would be limited to 75,000 over a period of five years, at which time it would be ended. Further, the sale of land to the Jews would be restricted. At the end of a ten-year period, Palestine would be given its independence under a special treaty relationship with Britain.

In 1947, two years before they expected to establish an independent Palestine, the British, weakened by the economic, political, and social costs of World War II, turned to the United Nations for a solution to the growing conflict in the area. A United Nations Special Committee on Palestine came up with a plan to partition Palestine into two independent states, one Jewish and the other Palestinian, and to form a federation of these two as one independent nation. The Palestinians and other Arabs opposed partition; the Jews favored it with some changes. Hostilities broke out in Palestine. The Security Council called for a truce. On May 14, 1948, the British mandate ended, and the Jews unilaterally proclaimed the State of Israel. Within hours, both the USSR and the United States recognized the new nation. The following morning Arab troops from Egypt, Jordan, Syria, and Lebanon invaded Palestine to prevent the new state from coming into existence. At the United Nations, both the United States and the Soviet Union condemned the Arab action.

---

11 An excellent examination of the Palestinian question can be found in David Fromkin, *A Peace to End All Peace: Creating the Modern Middle East 1914-1922* (New York: Henry Holt and Company, 1989) and Colbert C. Held, *Middle East Patterns: Places, People, and Politics* (Boulder, CO: Westview Press, 1989).

During the next eight months, fighting was sporadic, halted from time to time by temporary cease-fires and truces. The General Assembly sent Dr. Ralph Bunche as its mediator. By February 1949, he succeeded in negotiating an armistice agreement between Egypt and Israel, followed shortly by similar agreements with Jordan, Lebanon, and Syria. The agreements established Mixed Armistice Commissions, under which a United Nations Truce Supervision Organization (UNTSO) would supervise their implementation. These arrangements were underwritten by the Security Council. UNTSO has been on duty ever since.

UNTSO's main task has been to observe and report on compliance with the armistice agreements of 1949 and, subsequently, the cease-fire arrangements following the Suez crisis of 1956, the Six-Day War of 1967, and the October War of 1973. In performing these duties, UNTSO cooperated with subsequent United Nations Emergency Forces (UNEF), the United Nations Disengagement Observer Force (UNDOF), and the United Nations Interim Force in Lebanon (UNIFIL).

UNTSO brought the fledgling United Nations directly to the center of one of the most stubborn conflicts of modern times. Both the General Assembly and the Security Council had roles to play. The General Assembly sent mediators who succeeded in bringing the parties to the negotiating table. The Security Council gave its support to a small, nonmilitary observation mission that has been performing its task far longer than anyone could have predicted. The neutrality of United Nations agencies was painstakingly established by excluding the superpowers from the mission and bringing in a large number of participating middle powers.

Indonesia: UN Commission for Indonesia (UNCI)

Following World War I, both the indigenous population and the Dutch settlers of the Netherlands Indies sought a new relationship with the Netherlands. Some preferred greater self-government within the existing constitution, others a federal union with the Netherlands, and still others complete independence for a new United States of Indonesia. Strong economic ties existed between the colony and the mother country.

When the Japanese won control of the country in 1942, they encouraged the formation of an Indonesian Volunteer Army and cooperated with nationalist leaders in the preparation of a constitution. When the Japanese surrendered in August 1945, these nationalist leaders, led by Sukarno, unilaterally proclaimed the independent Republic of Indonesia in the Dutch East Indies. The Republic of Indonesia was recognized in all but West Irian in 1949 after almost four years of warfare.

The transition was not an easy one. The Dutch suspected leaders who had been sponsored by the Japanese. The Indonesian leaders were divided among themselves about the degree of independence that the new country should seek and the amount of force that should be used in doing so. Further, it was difficult for the new government to organize itself administratively in many areas that were presumably to be included in the Republic: Java, Sumatra, Borneo, East Indonesia, the Malino States, West Irian (Western New Guinea), and other islands.

The British assumed responsibility for disarming the surrendering Japanese in 1945 and, almost immediately, found themselves trying to end fighting between Republican forces and the returning Dutch army. In January 1946, the Ukrainian S.S.R. and the Soviet Union charged in the Security Council that British troops and Japanese armed forces were collaborating in military actions against the local population and interfering with the national liberation movement in Indonesia. The Security Council refrained from taking action because direct negotiations between the Indonesian independence movement and the Netherlands were to begin in a matter of days. Late in 1946, the British withdrew their troops, but assigned a mediator to assist in direct negotiations. Meanwhile, in the Netherlands, a national election brought leaders to office who were interested in early settlement of the dispute.

The negotiations proceeded through 1947. However, midyear, Dutch troops occupied Dutch East Indies-Republic of Indonesia territories in what came to be known as the First Police Action. On August 1, 1947, the Security Council called upon the parties to cease hostilities and urged them to settle their dispute peacefully. As fighting continued, the Security Council established a three-member Good Offices Committee consisting of Australia, Belgium, and the United States. By January 1948, the Good Offices Committee achieved a truce agreement between the parties, only to have the Netherlands denounce the agreement eleven months later and embark upon a Second Police Action.

The Security Council now recommended the formation of a federal, independent United States of Indonesia and converted the Good Offices Committee into a United Nations Commission for Indonesia (UNCI), with instructions to assist the parties in implementing this resolution. In a unilateral action designed to elicit greater Dutch cooperation, the United States partially suspended Marshall Plan aid to that country. Under UNCI direction, negotiations proceeded toward a final settlement. Dutch forces were withdrawn, Indonesia agreed to respect Dutch economic rights, including fair compensation for any nationalization of property, and the Republic of the United States of Indonesia was recognized as an independent and sovereign state. The transfer of sovereignty took place on December 27, 1949. Indonesia became a member of the United Nations on September 28, 1950. UNCI maintained its contingent of military observers until early 1951, at which time it was disbanded.

The peacekeeping lessons of the Indonesian independence conflict were several. Resolution of the conflict was undoubtedly facilitated because it was not an issue loaded with East-West implications. In fact, the Communist members rather enjoyed watching Western powers trying to dismember the former empire of one of their number. The Security Council made several substantial third-party moves: attempting arbitration; providing a good-offices channel of communication that succeeded in bringing the parties to direct negotiations; and even going so far as to condemn one of the parties (the Dutch) and subjecting it to economic pressure. A facilitating factor was the military weakness of the Netherlands at the end of World War II and its inability to escalate the conflict beyond a certain point.

One substantial difficulty for the United Nations, and one that would appear again as former colonies became new nations, was the question of UN jurisdictional competency in the case. The Indonesian independence problem was perceived as a domestic matter by the Dutch, hence its two police actions against the Indonesians and its reluctance to admit third parties to mediate the dispute. The UN's role in an arguably domestic conflict set an important precedent.

Kashmir: UN Military Observer Group in India and Pakistan (UNMOGIP)

During British rule, conflict between the Hindu majority and the Moslem minority of colonial India was suppressed in order to allow some degree of cooperation between them against the colonial power. However, as the time for British withdrawal approached, cooperative efforts deteriorated. There was substantial sectarian conflict, particularly in the Punjab. This inter-communal violence continued after independence, leading to thousands of deaths and resulting in mass population exchanges. As a result, the Moslems insisted upon having a separate sovereign community.

The British statute that established Indian independence in 1947 created two independent nations, India and Pakistan.[12] The two parts of Moslem Pakistan were separated from each other by nearly 1,000 miles of Indian territory. East Pakistan would eventually become the independent nation of Bangladesh. There were also 565 princely states to which the British gave the choice of joining India, Pakistan, or remaining independent. Only three chose independence, one of which was Kashmir, a highly strategic area of approximately 85,000 square miles. Both India and Pakistan viewed Kashmir as a significant element for their national security, particularly against each other.

Some three million Moslems and about 800,000 Hindus comprised the population of Kashmir. The Maharajah, Hari Sing, was himself a Hindu. While Kashmiri Moslems resented having a Hindu as their leader, they were also reluctant to be incorporated into Pakistan. Rather than make a choice between India and Pakistan, the Maharajah arranged a "standstill agreement" postponing a decision until internal strife had subsided.

Moslems in southwest Kashmir began a revolt against the Maharajah and set up a provisional government. As the Maharajah attempted to cope with this situation, the Pakistan government protested that Hindu attacks were being made on Moslem villages. Afridi and Mahsud tribesmen began crossing the border from Pakistan into Kashmir on the pretext of aiding their ethnic kin and co-religionists. The Maharajah turned to India for military aid and offered to accede, which he did in October 1947. Pakistan promptly denounced the accession as a fraud.

Indian troops were sent to Kashmir in time to halt Moslem tribesmen as they approached the capital. At this point, Pakistan sent its own troops into the fray. An undeclared war ensued between India and Pakistan, and the respective Kashmiri communities, that lasted from 1947 until 1949. In February 1948, Pathan tribesmen also rose in revolt and were brutally suppressed by Indian forces.

On January 1, 1948, India asked the Security Council to take action against Pakistan. The Council called for a cease-fire and established a United Nations Commission for India and Pakistan (UNCIP). The commission's five members included Argentina, Belgium, Colombia,

---

12 Although generally perceived as a religious dispute, the underpinnings include very substantial ethnic divisions, including language and history, between, and even more importantly, within each of the two communities. These ethnic divisions continue to plague both nations.

Czechoslovakia, and the United States. UNCIP recommended a truce agreement under which Pakistan would withdraw its troops at once, the Indian forces would withdraw in stages, and the local Kashmiri authorities would govern the evacuated territories until a solution was reached. UNCIP also recommended a plebiscite to determine the future of Kashmir. The cease-fire came into effect on January 1, 1949, A UN Military Observer Group (UNMOGIP) was stationed along the cease-fire line by Security Council Resolution 39 (1949).

UNMOGIP consisted of 30 to 65 observers recruited from about a dozen contributing countries. The mission's principal responsibility was to report on compliance with the cease-fire agreement and provide general surveillance of the cease-fire line. So few officers supervising a cease-fire line extending thousands of miles was asking too much. Subsequent fighting in the area and recurring crises in Kashmir underscored this difficulty. On the other hand, Kashmir peacekeepers did attempt to arrange a plebiscite and both sides accepted mediation and a cease-fire. Unfortunately, between 1949 and 1953, the efforts of the UN mediators came to naught. In 1953, a plebiscite in the Jammu portion of Kashmir was agreed to by the prime ministers of Kashmir and India. India then withdrew its agreement and imprisoned the prime minister of Kashmir.[13] In 1954, Pakistan, protesting what was perceived as the rigged accession to India, appealed to the Security Council.

Discussion of the Kashmir conflict returned to the Security Council in January 1957 as a result of India's unilateral annexation of Kashmir. The UN condemned the Indian action and again called for a plebiscite. A resolution was offered calling for the demilitarization of Kashmir and the use of United Nations forces to provide appropriate conditions for a plebiscite. This was vetoed by the Soviet Union.

The Kashmir question came up again in the Security Council in 1962 when hundreds of cease-fire violations were noted. Meanwhile, a campaign for the liberation of Kashmir began to gather momentum in Pakistan. Suggestions from the United States and the United Kingdom regarding internationalizing the Kashmir Valley and the disposition of the waters of the Indus River system were rejected.

---

13 Kashmiri prime minister, Sheik Mohammed Abdullah, "the Lion of Kashmir", would not be released and reinstated until February 1975.

By August 1965, Pakistan and India began infiltrating large numbers of regular and irregular armed forces across the cease-fire line. On August 24, 1965, substantial numbers of Indian troops crossed the cease-fire line. Heavy fighting was brought to a temporary halt by members of UNMOGIP. In September, Pakistani regular forces, in retaliation for the Indian raid, crossed the cease-fire line in force. The fighting, especially air raids, spilled into neighboring Punjab. The conflict rapidly escalated into a major undeclared war between India and Pakistan that involved air raids on each others' capital cities as well as large scale tank battles. Both sides' actions bogged down and a stalemate ensued. After initially refusing, both sides agreed to a Security Council demand for a cease-fire in late September 1965 and withdrew to lines held prior to August 5.

A second UN observer force, the UN India-Pakistan Observer Mission, was established alongside UNMOGIP to monitor the cease-fire in neighboring Punjab. With the withdrawal of troops in 1966, UNIPOM was terminated. In 1971, during the Pakistani civil war, Pakistan invaded Kashmir as a diversion in an attempt to draw off Indian support for what would become Bangladesh. By agreement, Pakistan and India withdrew their troops in 1972. In another agreement, the cease-fire line established in 1949 was slightly modified. However, because of these modifications, India argued that the mandate of UNMOGIP had expired because it was established to monitor the 1949 line. UNMOGIP has stayed in place, however, on grounds that the operation could only be terminated by the Security Council, according to the UN Secretary-General.[14] Pakistan has continued to lodge complaints of cease-fire violations with the observer force. India, however, no longer recognizes UNMOGIP officially and therefore has lodged no complaints since January 1972. They have, however, continued to provide support and accommodation to UNMOGIP.

The plebiscite was not held because of Indian objections. The cease-fire was hardly maintained. Mediation efforts failed. However, third party interventions, negotiations, and suggestions for resolution succeeded in postponing the war that simmered just beneath the surface. Kashmir and its status continue to be a source of conflict between India and Pakistan. There have been substantial demonstrations for independence and for joining with Pakistan. India and Pakistan continually trade accusations of clandestine

---

14 Contrast this position with that taken by the Secretary-General in 1967 when Egypt demanded the withdrawal of UNEF I.

support for their respective sides to the conflict. UNMOGIP continues in existence.

In 1994, UNMOGIP had a strength of 40 personnel from eight countries and an annual budget of $8 million from the regular budget of the UN. UNMOGIP and events in Kashmir substantiate the intractability of some ethnic and border conflicts. From a peacekeeping point of view, however, they reinforce the lessons of UNICYP in providing an outlet for complaints and providing time for other confidence-building measures to be pursued. Institutionally, they provide a vital source of information for the Secretary-General's office and the Security Council in a highly volatile area. This is of particular importance in a place where one of the parties has tested a nuclear weapon and the other side is widely believed to have a nuclear capability. Harnessing distrust under such circumstances is essential.

Korea: A Police Action

This is the classic case in which the United Nations endeavored to implement the provisions of Chapter VII of the Charter calling for collective military measures against an aggressor. The Korean War also cast the United States in the unhappy role of "policeman for the world". When it was over, the collective security action cost South Korea, the United States, and other United Nations forces some 438,000 battle casualties and approximately 500,000 other South Korean deaths from war-related events. On the North Korean and Chinese side, there were approximately 2 million battle and civilian casualties. The war ended any hope that the Security Council could serve as the world's collective security agency, at the same time shelving the concept of collective security itself. The principal institutional development was that it brought the General Assembly into peacekeeping through its Uniting for Peace Resolution.

Before World War II, Korea had been a Japanese colony. During the war, the Allies agreed to divide Korea at the 38th parallel for the purpose of accepting the Japanese surrender. The North was to be in the Soviet zone of occupation and the South under American military government. From 1945 to 1947, a U.S.-U.S.S.R. commission attempted to form a provisional government, but without success. In 1947, the United States asked the United Nations to take up the problem.

The General Assembly established a nine-nation United Nations Temporary Commission on Korea (UNTCOK) to observe elections for a

Korean national assembly and to arrange for the withdrawal of the occupying powers. The Soviet Union refused to go along with the plan. The Soviet commander refused to admit UNTCOK into North Korea. Instead, UNTCOK verified elections held in the American zone in May 1948 and observed the convening of the South Korean National Assembly, in which one-third of the seats were left vacant for future North Korean representatives. The Soviet Union repeatedly vetoed the Republic of Korea's (ROK) application for membership in the United Nations.

Meanwhile, the Democratic People's Republic of Korea (DPRK) was established in September 1948 in North Korea. A Supreme People's Council was elected. In September 1948, the Soviet Union announced the withdrawal of its troops. North Korea applied for admission to the United Nations in 1949, but the application was not considered on grounds that the ROK was the only legal government in Korea. In May 1949, the United States began withdrawing its forces from South Korea. Within eight months, in June 1950, North Korea attempted to reunify that country militarily by invading South Korea. The United Nations Commission for Korea, UNCOK, which had replaced UNTCOK, immediately reported the invasion to the Secretary-General.

That the Security Council was able to act at all in response to the North Korean attack on South Korea in June 1950 was the result of a fortuitous set of circumstances. Three months earlier, in March, the Soviet Union began a boycott of the Security Council in protest over the Council's unwillingness to seat the representative from Beijing in place of the one from Taiwan as the legitimate Chinese delegate. In the absence of the Soviet representative, the Council was able to pass unanimously resolutions calling for a cease-fire, the withdrawal of North Korean forces, and a call to all United Nations members to help the Republic of Korea.

On July 7, 1950, the Security Council[15] established a unified military command under the direction of the United States General Douglas MacArthur. MacArthur proceeded with the apparent goal of conquering North Korea and thereby reunifying that country. In August, however, the Soviet representative returned to the Security Council and began to use the veto to end that body's participation in the conflict. At the instigation of the United States, a Uniting for Peace Resolution was adopted by the General Assembly on November 3, 1950. The resolution stated that if the Security Council failed to act in a serious conflict because of a permanent member's

---

15   United Nations. Security Council Resolution 84 (1950), 7 July 1950.

veto, the issue could then be transferred to the General Assembly for consideration. A two-thirds majority of the General Assembly could then recommend, but not require, collective action. The resolution thus circumvented the veto and brought the General Assembly directly into the global security process. At this same time, the General Assembly also created the United Nations Commission for the Unification and the Rehabilitation of Korea (UNCURK) to supervise reconstruction once North Korea had been defeated.

The United Nations forces, from seventeen countries, led by the United States, not only drove back the North Koreans, but seemed on the verge of conquering them. In October, General Douglas MacArthur's forces crossed the 38th parallel and advanced almost to the Chinese border. Despite warnings from the People's Republic of China (PRC), MacArthur insisted upon continuing his advance. By the end of November, PRC forces launched major attacks against MacArthur's forces. The PRC eventually captured Seoul, the ROK capital. Not until March 1951 did the opposing armies stabilize their positions close to the 38th parallel.

In June, the United States suggested that it might agree to a restoration of the pre-June 1950 territorial lines. The Soviet ambassador to the United Nations indicated that the terms might be acceptable to the other side. Cease-fire and armistice negotiations began on July 10, 1951. Not until Stalin's death in March 1953 did the negotiations accomplish very much. Thereafter, with India serving as a third party on the issue of prisoner repatriation, negotiations proceeded rapidly. In July, an armistice agreement was signed.

As a part of the armistice agreement, a Neutral Nations Supervisory Commission (NNSC) was established to monitor the truce. The NNSC is still in existence and provides an effective means of communication between the two sides. Until April 1993, its members were from Sweden, Switzerland, Poland, and Czechoslovakia. With the split of Czechoslovakia into two nations, its delegation was withdrawn and, as of February 1995, had not been replaced. In February 1995, North Korea withdrew its support from the Polish delegation, effectively eliminating it from participation.

Such was the first and only attempt by the United Nations to implement the theory of collective security and establish a unified military command, which still exists. It was a costly and tragic test from the point of view of human suffering and wasted resources. However, the Korean experience was not without its important institutional consequences for peacekeeping. Under the Uniting for Peace Resolution, the General Assembly and the

Secretary-General would henceforth be regularly and significantly involved in the United Nations' peacekeeping functions. The Security Council veto would frequently be circumvented. Although handicapped by the *ad hoc* character of most peacekeeping missions, their limited budgets, and the necessity of using temporary military advisers for their management, the Secretary-General and the United Nations bureaucracy could expect to and did accumulate a substantial body of experience regarding the administration of peacekeeping missions.

Korea, like the Berlin airlift in 1948, was another instance in which the United States made explicit its determination, even at great cost, to draw the line against breaches of trust and the peace. Korea, in many respects, tested the mettle and resolve of the post-World War II new international leadership and produced a stalemate. The battlefield reflected the conditions in the Security Council. New approaches to keeping peace now had to be found.

Suez: UN Emergency Force (UNEF-I)

In 1952, a coup led by Egyptian officers overthrew the regime of King Farouk and eventually installed Gamal Abdel Nasser as president. Nasser vowed to lead the cause of Pan-Arab nationalism and return the million Palestinians who had been displaced by the Arab-Israeli war to their homeland.

Under an agreement that came into effect in 1954, the British evacuated the Suez Canal Zone. From 1953 until 1956, there were intermittent raids and counter-raids along Israel's borders by both sides. Arab-supported raids by Palestinian guerrillas and terrorists were met with stern punitive reprisals by the Israelis, targeted primarily against Egyptian, Syrian, and Jordanian border posts. The Arab states protested to the United Nations, with support from the U.S.S.R., with little result. By 1955, Israeli-Egyptian relations were at the point of explosion.

In July 1956, the United States withdrew promised aid for the construction of the Aswan Dam, leaving Egypt to turn to the Soviet Union for assistance. Nasser nationalized the Suez Canal on July 26, 1956, in retaliation. The revenues from the canal were to be used to construct the Aswan Dam. Because the Suez Canal had been their lifeline to the Far East, the British led a protest by maritime nations, but to no avail. France, former co-administrator of the Canal, was also perturbed by Nasser on grounds that he was providing aid to Algerian revolutionaries. The increasing number of armed actions along the Egyptian and Jordanian borders with Israel resulted in a debate in the Security Council in October 1956 over the situation in the Middle East.

Leaders of the three nations - Israel, France, and the United Kingdom - concluded a secret arrangement on October 24, 1956, that called for an Israeli attack against Egypt to be followed by a Franco-British intervention for "peacekeeping" purposes. On October 29, 1956, Israel launched its attack in the Sinai. An Anglo-French ultimatum called for a cease-fire and a pullback of forces. When the United States introduced a similar resolution in the Security Council, however, the British and French representatives vetoed its passage.

The Soviet Union, even as its tanks entered Budapest to crush a Hungarian rebellion, sided with Nasser and threatened England and France with atomic bombs, a threat to which the United States had to respond in kind. Then, with American and Soviet acquiescence, Yugoslavia submitted a resolution in the General Assembly calling for a peacekeeping mission under the Uniting for Peace Resolution. The Assembly created the United Nations Emergency Force (UNEF) on November 5, 1956, and instructed it to separate Egyptian and Israeli forces and supervise a truce. Meanwhile, chagrined by the discovery of their secret strategy for overthrowing Nasser and disappointed by President Eisenhower's failure to support their objectives in the Middle East, the British and French withdrew and, in effect, turned over that sphere of influence to the Americans.

A UN force was created and placed between the opposing forces as the Israelis conducted a slow withdrawal to the Negev, reaching the cease-fire line in March 1957. The UN force also occupied Sharm-al-Sheik. Israel refused to permit UN operations on its side of the border. UNEF-I eventually reached a maximum of 6,000 troops, the largest peacekeeping force put together by the United Nations up to that time. UNEF-I was to oversee compliance with the cease-fire and armistice, supervise the withdrawal of British, French, and Israeli forces, and patrol the border and Sharm-el-Sheik. Peacekeeping contingents were sent by Brazil, Canada, Colombia, Denmark, Finland, India, Indonesia, Norway, Sweden, and Yugoslavia. For the next ten years, UNEF performed commendably, although there were periodic skirmishes along the cease-fire line.

In 1962, the United States agreed to provide substantial military equipment to Israel, including missiles, to counter the flow of arms from the Warsaw Pact to Egypt and Syria. In 1965, West Germany recognized the State of Israel and began to export arms to Israel as well. The Arab states broke diplomatic relations with Germany and threatened to recognize East Germany. German military aid to Israel stopped, but tensions had been heightened considerably. The United States stepped in to fill the gap. Raids and counter-raids continued.

In an almost Byzantine set of circumstances, Saudi Arabia and Iraq agreed to station forces in Jordan to bolster the defenses against Israeli raids against Palestinians based in Jordan. However, Jordan stated that the agreement was contingent upon UN forces in the Sinai and Gaza being replaced by United Arab Republic troops.[16] To accomplish this, the U.A.R. would have to withdraw its forces from Yemen where they were supporting an insurrection. This was, of course, the ultimate objective desired by Jordan and its allies because they supported the opposition side in the Yemen civil war. Finally, on May 16, 1967, President Nasser formally requested that UNEF be withdrawn. Secretary General U Thant saw no alternative but to accede to the request of the host state. At the same time, Egyptian troops and large amounts of Soviet-made military equipment were moved into the Sinai. Nasser next closed the Gulf of Aqaba to Israel.

The Suez crisis added much to the stature of United Nations peacekeeping operations. Despite brandishing their nuclear arsenals, the two superpowers had cooperated in forcing two major powers, the United Kingdom and France, to end their unilateral military intervention and step aside in favor of a United Nations Emergency Force. The size of the peacekeeping mission was substantial and the mission was carried off successfully for a decade. Secretary-General Dag Hammarskjold took the example of UNEF to offer a general proposal for the creation of standby units for future peacekeeping missions. In his proposed system, Hammarskjold made no mention of the Military Staff Committee of the Security Council, but, rather, placed the secretariat at the center of preparedness and peacekeeping operations. In fact, the secretariat was thereafter, and still is, at the center of all United Nations peacekeeping missions. Similar proposals for standby forces would continue to be suggested, most recently by Boutros Boutros-Ghali in his *Agenda for Peace* (17 June 1992) and its supplement (3 January 1995).[17]

---

16 A short-lived union of Egypt and Syria as a part of Nasser's pan-Arab philosophy.

17 United Nations, "An Agenda for Peace" (A/47/277-S/24111) and "Supplement to an Agenda for Peace" (A50/60-S/1995/1).

UNEF not only focused the debate about United Nations preparedness, but also placed substantial strain on the financial arrangements supporting peacekeeping missions. The United Nations has two methods of financing its operations: an assessment upon each member proportionate to that member's capacity to pay, and a system of voluntary contributions that any member can make for whatever purpose it designates. Under Article 19 of the Charter, members who fall in arrears in payment of assessed dues may be denied their vote in the General Assembly. Financial support of UNEF, with its 6,000 troops, became a difficult issue. How much support should come from the general budget and how much from voluntary contributions? What was to be done if a country, specifically the Soviet Union, disapproved of the peacekeeping mission; could it be forced to help finance it?

Finally, the UNEF mission was the first to be terminated abruptly at the request of a host country, raising numerous questions about the manner in which this was done. The request came unilaterally from Egypt and was implemented immediately by Secretary-General U Thant. Should not such a request receive special emergency attention by the Security Council or General Assembly? Should not the United Nations pressure the reneging party to reconsider its request? As already noted, when a similar situation arose later in Kashmir, the Secretary-General would act otherwise.

Possibly the most important lesson of UNEF-I was that the United Nations could be trusted to organize and sustain a significant peacekeeping operation. Awkwardly and suspiciously, the superpower leaders cooperated to make this possible and, not coincidentally, to alter the balance of power in the Middle East.

Lebanon: UN Observation Group in Lebanon (UNOGIL)

During the mid-1950s, President Chamoun of Lebanon, only a decade and a half after Lebanese independence, assumed a strong pro-Western posture, received military aid from the United States, and generally opposed the Pan-Arab nationalism represented by Egyptian President Nasser. Pro-Nasser opponents of Chamoun were substantially aided in their cause when Egypt and Syria merged to form the United Arab Republic (U.A.R.) on February 1, 1958. Anti-Chamoun forces united during the spring of that year, issued a call for a national strike, and embarked upon civil war. The rebels won control of the Lebanese-Syrian border. They received arms and munitions from the Syrians and propaganda support from the media of the United Arab Republic.[18]

On May 13, 1958, President Chamoun asked the United States for assistance. Units of the United States Sixth Fleet were ordered to the vicinity of Lebanon. The United States also expressed its willingness to send tanks and troops into Lebanon if requested. Chamoun next appealed to the Arab League and to the Security Council of the United Nations. On June 6, the Council established the United Nations Observation Group in Lebanon (UNOGIL) to serve as an observer mission investigating the Lebanese charges of military infiltration from Syria.

As the civil war approached a stalemate, Nasser suggested that Chamoun step down upon completion of his term of office, allow General Chehab, commander of the Lebanese army, to succeed him, and declare amnesty for all rebels. In July, however, a revolt against the king of Iraq, who had offered to assist Chamoun, complicated the picture. The Iraqi coup was interpreted by United States policy makers as a Communist move. Therefore, when Chamoun again asked for aid, the United States landed 14,000 troops and the British 2,000 in Lebanon. On July 15, the United States requested an emergency session of the United Nations Security Council. This meeting was predictably deadlocked. Secretary-General Hammarskjold, exercising an unprecedented prerogative, asserted that he discerned an "implicit consensus" for expanding UNOGIL and that he would proceed to do so, subject to review by the Security Council.

The crisis subsided when, on July 31, General Chehab was elected to succeed Chamoun. Several days later, Chehab requested that American troops leave Lebanon. On August 8, the General Assembly passed a resolution instructing the Secretary-General to have UNOGIL facilitate the United States withdrawal. UNOGIL never exceeded 214 officer-observers supplied by 21 nations. Its presence in the area did serve as a constraining influence upon the parties, but, as in the Kashmir case, the number of observers was extremely small for so extended a border.

The Lebanese crisis was particularly interesting in that at least five "conflict managers" became involved. The Security Council took notice of the conflict, but remained immobile for all practical purposes. The General Assembly was actively concerned, creating UNOGIL, but held back while

---

18 Syria and many citizens of Lebanon at this time perceived of themselves as a part of Syria. They viewed Lebanon as an artificial creation of the French, a situation that still obtains today.

other peacekeeping moves were taking place. The Secretary-General assumed an unusual administrative prerogative by undertaking to expand UNOGIL upon his own initiative. The United States and the United Kingdom sent troops, upon the request of the Lebanese president, to maintain order. However, the final solution originated with the fifth conflict manager, Nasser and the Arab League. The concept of regional peacekeeping was importantly implemented in this case and would be again in the future. Regional peacekeeping assumes that the members of a regional organization such as the Arab League prefer to handle their own conflicts without outside intervention. This motivation was particularly strong in the Lebanese case because of Nasser's claim to leadership of the cause of Pan-Arab nationalism.

The Congo: UN Operation in the Congo (UNOC)

For a decade following World War II, Belgian policy in the Congo was primarily concerned with economic and social programs. Political change was expected to come at some unspecified future time. The Congo was peaceful until 1955 when various nationalist movements demanded independence. Riots broke out in January 1959. The Belgians, hoping to avoid the kind of costly struggle the French had experienced in Algeria, set June 30, 1960, as the date of independence.

The Congo consisted of six provinces, each inhabited by numerous tribes. Various nationalist political parties were essentially coalitions of tribes. Joseph Kasavubu's party was based in the Leopoldville province and preferred a loose federation of the provinces. Patrice Lumumba's party sought a centralized governmental system and was extremely critical of tribalism. The dominant party in Katanga province was led by Moise Tshombe, whose principal aim was to prevent the exploitation of the province's vast mineral wealth by the rest of the Congo. Belgian mining companies were also extremely interested in protecting their large investment in Katanga's extractive industry.

At independence, Kasavubu became president and Lumumba prime minister. However, the army continued to be led by Belgian officers. This arrangement provoked a mutiny within a week of independence. Disorder spread, Belgian residents began to leave the country, and the Belgians sent in paratroops to reinforce their bases in Leopoldville and Katanga provinces. The second week after independence, Tshombe declared Katanga's secession from the new nation.

On July 12, 1960, Kasavubu and Lumumba requested aid from the United Nations. The Security Council passed a resolution asking Belgium to withdraw its troops and authorizing the Secretary-General to provide military assistance until such time as the Congolese government could restore internal order with its own security forces. Secretary-General Hammarskjold established the Organization des Nations Unis au Congo (ONUC), whose troops eventually numbered 20,000 drawn from twenty-five nations. Equipment and weapons for ONUC were almost entirely supplied by the United States and the United Kingdom.

ONUC found a difficult situation. The Belgians were refusing to withdraw. Tshombe said that UN troops would not be permitted in Katanga. The Soviet Union had begun to send arms and equipment to the Lumumba faction. Kasavubu dismissed Lumumba. Lumumba charged Kasavubu with high treason. By September 14, Joseph Mobutu, commander of the Congolese army, announced that the army had taken over the government.

At the United Nations, the Soviet Union vigorously opposed the entire Congolese operation, hoping thereby to place itself on the side of African nationalist movements, of which Lumumba's party was a leading exemplar. It was also a Soviet intention to disrupt the Belgian, British, and French effort to protect their economic interests in Katanga. Tshombe had considerable resources with which to resist Soviet and Lumumba maneuvers: substantial revenues from mining taxes; Belgian and other foreign mercenaries in large numbers to lead his troops; considerable support in Europe and the United States; and support from international business interests.

On August 24, 1961, the Kasavubu-Mobutu government of the Congo ordered the expulsion of non-Congolese from Katanga's security forces and, for this, asked for the assistance of ONUC. Within a few days, ONUC began to arrest and evacuate the mercenaries. On September 17, Secretary-General Hammarskjold was killed in a plane crash en route to negotiate with Tshombe. Soon after, a cease-fire was concluded between ONUC and the Katanga government. However, attacks on ONUC forces continued, and the Security Council, with Britain and France abstaining, authorized Acting Secretary-General U Thant "to take vigorous action, including the use of requisite measures of force, if necessary", to arrest and deport the mercenaries. After heavy fighting, the United States ambassador and the United Nations Special Representative, Dr. Ralph Bunche, succeeded in bringing Congolese Prime Minister Adoula and Katanga's Tshombe together on an eight-point unity agreement. Fighting broke out once again, however. ONUC, with American backing and Soviet withdrawal, finally brought the Katanga secession to an end in January 1963. ONUC forces remained on duty, at the request of the Congolese central government, until June 30, 1964.

ONUC was the largest peacekeeping force to that date and the most expensive, costing the United Nations $402 million. The mission precipitated the first serious financial crisis at the United Nations. On January 1, 1964, the Soviet Union became legally delinquent because of its refusal to pay assessed peacekeeping dues. Ten other nations were also in arrears, and France soon became an eleventh. Under Article 19, the penalty for nonpayment of dues was loss of vote in the General Assembly. The American position was that Article 19 should be imposed at the opening of the next General Assembly session. The Soviet Union threatened to withdraw from the United Nations. Most members of the General Assembly sought to avoid a confrontation.

The United States wanted peacekeeping costs to be widely shared. The Soviet Union was pressing for the return of all peacekeeping functions to the exclusive authority of the Security Council where its veto could carry decisive weight. As a way out of the stalemate, the General Assembly created in February 1965 the Special Committee on Peacekeeping Operations, better known as the Committee of 33. The 33 members were widely representative politically and geographically. Their charge was to examine the entire question of peacekeeping operations. In time, the Committee of 33 became the forum in which the superpowers addressed themselves directly to a large range of peacekeeping issues. The Committee of 33 provided an acceptable place in which to set down systematically the issues in dispute. In the drawn-out process of institutionalizing a function such as peacekeeping, the Committee of 33 must be viewed as an undramatic but important facilitator of international political trust.

Because of the veto and mutual distrust, the Military Staff Committee of the Security Council failed to provide such a forum two decades earlier, or since. It is also ironic that in 1995, the nation most in arrears to the UN was the United States, followed by Russia.

Cyprus: UN Force in Cyprus (UNFICYP)

The island of Cyprus in the Mediterranean Sea has had strategic significance for Turkey, Greece, and Great Britain over many centuries. In 1878, the Ottoman Empire ceded the island to Britain for administrative purposes. The British annexed Cyprus in 1914 and established it as a Crown Colony in 1925. The population of the island is approximately four-fifths Greek and one-fifth Turkish, with recently intense ethnic hatreds dominating the relationship between the two.[19]

The Greek majority, particularly since 1960, has tended to favor union with Greece, *enosis*. This movement has been encouraged by the Greek government, the Greek Orthodox Church hierarchy, and, at times, the international community. In 1950, Archbishop Mikhail Makarios became the spokesman for Greek Cypriots. Turkish Cypriots, considering themselves a persecuted minority, have opposed *enosis* and rely upon the government of Turkey for the protection of their interests. Turkey has been particularly concerned about the strategic importance of Cyprus for its national defense. It blocks Turkey's outlet to the Mediterranean and its second largest port. The British also have opposed *enosis* on grounds that it would aggravate the already serious ethnic divisions. Further, Cyprus was British headquarters for their Middle East military forces and an important part of the British line of communication to the Middle and Far East. As time passed, these five parties to the Cyprus conflict were joined by the leadership of NATO, of which both Greece and Turkey are members. The United States, whose responsibilities in the Middle East were increasing, was concerned as was the Soviet Union, whose interest lay in support of anti-imperial nationalist movements generally and, specifically, the possibility that its Greek and Turkish neighbors might go to war.

In 1954, the Greek government asked the UN General Assembly to consider the Cyprus problem. In 1955, Greek-led Greek Cypriots began attacking British buildings and residences in a terrorist campaign. The British, unsuccessfully, tried to confer with Greece and Turkey. As the conflict progressed, the Greeks continued to seek self-determination, the Turks preferred partition, and the British eventually expressed a willingness to abandon their sovereignty over the island on condition that they could maintain a military base there.

---

19   The intense ethnic hatred is a relatively new development on Cyprus (since the late 1950s). Until the mid- to late-1950s, ethnic Greeks and Turks lived intermixed throughout the island. When EOKA-B began terrorist operations against the British, it stirred up ethnic hatred by portraying the Turkish minority as being allied with the British. Only after that did the two communities begin to separate.

In 1957, the secretary-general of NATO made an unsuccessful offer to mediate. The Greeks remained adamant about achieving *enosis*. But, in 1958, Archbishop Makarios indicated that he would settle for independence. A London Agreement was negotiated in 1959 that included a constitution and three treaties. The Treaty of Alliance involved Cyprus, Greece, and Turkey and provided for 950 Greek troops and 650 Turkish troops to be stationed on the island to train the Cypriot army. The Treaty of Guarantee permitted Britain, Greece, or Turkey to act singly or collectively to maintain the independent status of the island, that is, prevent either *enosis* or partition. The Treaty of Establishment created a sovereign Cypriot republic, with the exception of two military bases to be kept under British rule. The constitution established a Cypriot president who was to be a Greek and a Cypriot vice president who was to be Turkish, each with veto power. The agreement came into effect on August 16, 1960.

Soon after, severe disagreements emerged. By December 1963, there was an outbreak of violence between the two Cypriot communities. With the acquiescence of Archbishop Makarios, the British formed a joint British-Turkish-Greek peacekeeping force and subsequently proposed a NATO peacekeeping force. Makarios preferred to involve the United Nations. When the temporary truce was broken, Turkey threatened to intervene. The British agreed to take the Cyprus matter to the Security Council on February 15, 1964. On March 4, the Council established a United Nations Force in Cyprus (UNFICYP), whose mission was to help prevent communal fighting. UNFICYP at various times ranged from 4,500 to 7,000 troops. Its mandate was extended every three to six months.

Meanwhile, both Greece and Turkey began sending arms and soldiers to the island. There was serious fighting during August 1964. A military coup in Greece in April 1967 brought in a regime strongly in favor of *enosis*. Greek Cypriot forces attacked. Turkey countered with a show of force at sea and in the air and threatened a large-scale military intervention. Eventually, UNFICYP was able to separate the conflicting forces.

· In time, Greek and Greek Cypriot extremists, impatient with Makarios' conciliatory efforts and abandonment of *enosis*, tried to assassinate him. In June 1974, Makarios began to remove army officers who were supporters of *enosis*. When he tried to remove as many as 600 Greek officers from the Cypriot National Guard, a military coup sent him into exile. On July 19, 1974, Makarios addressed the Security Council in an appeal for assistance. The British, at Turkey's request, arranged talks between Turkish and Greek representatives, but with little result. On July 30, Turkey landed more than 6,000 soldiers on Cyprus.

The failure of the military regime in Greece to accomplish *enosis*, its sponsorship of the coup, and its inability to respond militarily to Turkish intervention, led to its resignation and the restoration of civilian government. Turkish forces meanwhile extended their occupation to the entire northern section of Cyprus, citing the 1960 Treaty of Guarantee. In August 1974, the Security Council expanded UNFICYP's responsibility in an effort to put an end to the fighting. The Turkish Cypriot zone had, in effect, partitioned the island. On February 24, 1975, a Turkish Cypriot Constituent Assembly was convened to establish the Turkish Cypriot Federated State.

Early in 1977, Makarios, reinstated as president, and Turkish Cypriot leader Denktash agreed on principles for a settlement. Cyprus was to become a sovereign, bizonal, bicommunal federal republic, with appropriate territorial adjustments to be negotiated. Under United Nations auspices and with United States encouragement, negotiations continue to this day, with first one side and then the other blocking progress.

UN peacekeeping in Cyprus, as in the Lebanese crisis, was the occasion for involvement of representatives of a regional organization, in this case, NATO. The presence of UNFICYP contributed substantially over the years to the maintenance of internal order on the island. The mission rarely used force, except in self-defense, and developed a substantial intelligence network designed to discover and head off imminent violence. Its evenhandedness and overall professionalism have earned it the respect of both Cypriot communities as well as of Greece and Turkey. The peacekeeping task has been substantially complicated by the lack of a formal armistice agreement between the factions.

In more recent years, both Greece and Turkey have become increasingly solicitous of their relationships with NATO and the European Union and have been more predisposed toward settlement. The United States, as a supplier of weapons to both Greece and Turkey, has applied pressure to both sides by refraining or threatening to refrain from delivering arms. The most active center for proposals and negotiations to resolve the conflict has been the secretariat of the United Nations. Despite obstructions from one side or the other, the forces of moderation and improved political trust continue to grow and the prospects for settlement improve. At the same time, the longer the dispute continues, the more permanently institutionalized the communal separation becomes.

Original financing for UNICYP was based on contributions of the force members and voluntary contributions from other states, with services in kind provided by the government of Cyprus. This created a serious shortfall by 1992. After several nations withdrew their contingents, the Security Council determined that financing beyond voluntary contributions would come from the UN budget. In 1994, UNICYP had a strength of 1,218 personnel from nine nations, including civil police detachments from Australia and Ireland.

India-Pakistan: UN India-Pakistan Observation Mission (UNIPOM)

With the status of Kashmir among the factors still unresolved, relations between India and Pakistan worsened during 1964 and 1965. This was in part a consequence of a boundary agreement reached by China and Pakistan in which the latter claimed to represent Kashmir and in part a consequence of a renewed boundary dispute over the Rann of Kutch. Kutch was one of the princely states that had acceded to India at the time of independence. The Rann was an area of about 3,500 square miles with an ill-defined boundary claimed by Pakistan.

During 1959-1960, the two countries conducted a series of talks about this border problem. A border clash between the two occurred in the Rann of Kutch in April 1965, but was ended with the onset of the monsoons. The United Kingdom immediately offered to serve as a third party in the dispute and suggested a cease-fire. The British succeeded in bringing the parties together in the Kutch Agreement on June 30, which called for a cease-fire, troop withdrawals, and further negotiations before an *ad hoc* Indo-Pakistani Western Boundary Case Tribunal. Although the conflict over Kashmir was resumed at about this same time, the Tribunal began hearings on the Kutch issue. By February 1968, it awarded 90 percent of the Rann to India and about 10 percent to Pakistan.

Tensions between the two heightened over the Ladakh area of Kashmir, part of which was also claimed by China. India strongly objected to a part of a Treaty of Friendship between China and Pakistan that referred to the border in this area. In August 1965, both Pakistan and India sent infiltrators across the cease-fire line in Kashmir in a series of escalating border raids. A major operation occurred on September 6, 1965, when India launched a three pronged offensive toward Lahore with some 900,000 troops.

Secretary-General U Thant traveled to the scene to try to initiate talks. He learned officially of the cease-fire line violations from UNMOGIP

(United Nations Military Observer Group in India and Pakistan) reports. The permanent members of the Security Council agreed that the cease-fire had to be reestablished. U.N. efforts were successful, with both armies withdrawing to their pre-August positions. UNMOGIP forces were enlarged. A new United Nations India-Pakistan Observer Mission (UNIPOM) was established to supervise troop withdrawals. However, U Thant's efforts to initiate wider talks were unsuccessful.

The initiative for third-party mediation passed to the Soviet Union, which had offered its good offices. This was followed by a conference at Tashkent, arranged by Soviet Premier Kosygin, during January 1966. The resulting Tashkent Declaration provided for troop withdrawals and repatriation of prisoners of war, as well as for a Kashmiri plebiscite. UNIPOM, consisting of about 100 observers, assisted in the troop withdrawals and reestablishment of the cease-fire line. Observation of the cease-fire line was resumed by UNMOGIP when UNIPOM was terminated.

The 1965 India-Pakistan disputes once again demonstrated the usefulness of observation teams as the "eyes" of the United Nations. In this instance, the Security Council was able to intervene on the basis of the UNMOGIP report in the absence of any other complaint or information. It was, of course, impossible for the small mission to patrol the entire border. Nor could it identify an aggressor, which was unnecessary under the principal assumption of contemporary peacekeeping, that is, there are no aggressors, only equal parties to a dispute. This conflict also demonstrated the usefulness of having the United Nations in the background as others attempt mediation. In a sense, the Indians and Pakistanis were thereby encouraged to "settle out of court". This led to the Western Boundary Tribunal and acceptance of the good-offices intervention of a nearby superpower, the Soviet Union. Given the territorial ambiguities, the strategic importance, and the ethnic emotions surrounding the India-Pakistan disputes, it was no small achievement to have the Security Council so effectively bring the parties together.

Middle East: UN Emergency Force (UNEF-II)

Middle East tensions never ended with UNEF-I. By early 1967, Palestine guerrilla units, under the command of El Fatah and the Palestine Liberation Organization, began to escalate border attacks against Israel and step up their call for Arab unity in a war of liberation. Syria provided the principal base from which El Fatah made its forays and was itself the most radical

Arab voice in the campaign against Israel. King Faysal of Saudi Arabia and King Hussein of Jordan assumed a more conservative and cautious approach. In April 1967, a major skirmish between Israel and Syria occurred. President Nasser immediately proclaimed a state of emergency for the Egyptian armed forces and consummated a defense agreement with the Syrians. As demonstrations against Israel mounted throughout the Arab world, Nasser requested that the United Nations Emergency Force, which had been stationed on the Egyptian side of the border with Israel, be withdrawn.

Secretary-General U Thant acknowledged Egypt's right, as the host country, to demand the withdrawal, but referred the problem to the UNEF Advisory Committee. India and Yugoslavia, whose contingents were the largest in UNEF, expressed their desire to withdraw their contingents, which left little choice but to end the mission. The matter was bitterly debated at the United Nations as Israel and Egypt mobilized troops along their borders.

On May 22, 1967, Nasser closed the Straits of Tiran at the entrance of the Gulf of Aqaba, which in effect was a blockade of the strategic Israeli port of Elath. Israel had previously withdrawn her forces from the Straits of Tiran on condition that the Western powers would guarantee freedom of passage for Israeli shipping. Israeli appeals to Paris, London, and Washington, however, brought little response. On May 26, Nasser, in a public address, defined the issue as greater than one of territorial water; the problem was the very existence of Israel.

On June 1, General Moshe Dayan, the hero of the 1956 Sinai campaign, was appointed Israeli minister of defense. On June 2, the leader of the Palestine Liberation Organization called for a holy war to liberate Palestine. On June 5, Israel embarked upon a preemptive attack on Egyptian airfields. Within the week, Israeli forces occupied the Sinai Peninsula, the Gaza Strip, the West Bank of the Jordan River, the City of Jerusalem, and the Golan Heights. The Arabs suffered the destruction or loss of 430 planes and 800 tanks, 15,000 troop fatalities, and the capture of 5,500 prisoners. Israel suffered about 700 dead and 40 aircraft lost. The Six Day War was a stunning defeat for the Arab states and a costly investment for the Soviet Union, whose large aid in military equipment had been either destroyed or captured by the Israelis. The outcome of the war altered the balance of power in the Middle East.

The Six Day War also demonstrated the weakness of a United Nations role when its responds to a crisis hesitantly. The Israelis ignored United

Nations calls for a cease-fire until they had accomplished their military objectives. On June 9 and 10, Egypt and Syria agreed to a cease-fire to which the Israelis were now ready to subscribe. With UNEF gone, supervision of the ensuing cease-fire was placed in the hands of the United Nations Truce Supervision Organization (UNTSO). The United Nations did little more than adopt principles for reconciling the Middle East conflict. The single resolution, 242, passed on November 22, 1967, called for secure and recognized boundaries for Israel in exchange for her withdrawal from occupied territories.

Meanwhile, cease-fire violations were frequent. Israel began to plan for the establishment of Jewish settlements in the occupied territories. The Soviet Union replaced the lost Arab military hardware. The United States replaced and upgraded Israel's. Egyptian and Syrian military forces engaged in strenuous training programs. The Palestine Liberation Organization stepped up its harassments, and most especially, embarked on a terrorist campaign. Palestinians and the Arab states continued to demand Israeli withdrawal from the occupied territories. Equally as insistent, Israel demanded recognition of its territorial boundaries.

When Nasser died in 1970, he was succeeded by General Anwar Sadat as Egypt's president. Sadat worked assiduously to repair and coordinate Egyptian and Arab military capacity. On Yom Kippur, the Jewish Day of Atonement, that is, October 6, 1973, and during Islam's highest holy days, Ramadan, Egypt and Syria began a surprise attack across the Suez Canal and against the Golan Heights. Israelis literally rushed from their synagogues to the battlefield to fend off the attack. The Israelis, anticipating some early Arab military action, believed that it could be more or less readily contained. This time, the Israelis did not want to put themselves in an unfavorable political light by preempting. What was surprising, in fact, shocking, at least to the Israelis and the United States, was the competency of the Arab troops and the deadly accuracy of the Soviet-supplied ground-to-air and other missiles. The Israelis lost a near-fatal number of tanks, planes, and lives.

As casualties grew, the Soviet Union began to pour in weapons and supplies for their Arab clients. Simultaneously, the United States airlifted similar materials to Israel, actually stripping its own forces and depots in Europe. The Soviet Union then began to supply tanks and planes, and this was matched by the United States. By the second week, Israeli forces had advanced to within twenty miles of the Syrian capital and had encircled some 100,000 Egyptian troops on the East Bank in the Sinai. Egyptian troops, however, remained across the Suez in Sinai.

On October 21, Soviet and American leaders put together a cease-fire resolution which they jointly sponsored in the Security Council. Two such calls for a cease-fire failed to end the fighting, whereupon the Soviet Union proposed that a joint Soviet-American peacekeeping force be dispatched to the area. This proposal promptly sank in the sea of distrust that surrounded superpower relations. When the United States rejected the plan, the Soviet Union announced that it would unilaterally move its own troops in as a peacekeeping mission. President Nixon responded by placing American armed forces worldwide on military alert. The pace of escalation was fearsome.

The nonaligned nations in the Security Council offered a resolution authorizing the Secretary-General to dispatch a new United Nations Emergency Force to the area. Permanent members were excluded from providing troops for the peacekeeping force, but were allowed to send a few observers. The first of the 7,000-contingent UNEF-II began to arrive on October 27.

The Israelis were deeply chastened by their "victory" whereas President Sadat made the most of the "restored honor" of his nation. Secretary of State Henry Kissinger, who had been the key figure in the timing and conditions of the cease-fire, undertook intensive negotiations with all parties in an effort to use the new balance of power as the basis for peace negotiations. He shuttled back and forth between Jerusalem and Cairo in one of the most dramatic diplomatic missions of modern times.

In addition to UNTSO (the United Nations Truce Supervision Organization) and UNEF-II, the United Nations also put into the field a Disengagement Observer Force (UNDOF). This mission's assignment, begun in May 1974, was to observe Israeli and Syrian compliance with the disengagement agreement pertaining to the Golan Heights. UNDOF was the force that policed the demilitarized zone in that area. In addition, the United States provided 200 American civilian technicians to man the sophisticated early warning technology that was placed in the Sinai between Israeli and Egyptian forces. Distrustful of United Nations peacekeeping missions, the Israelis were comforted by this American trip-wire arrangement.

A peace process had indeed begun. By 1977, Menachem Begin, a former Zionist terrorist and hard-liner, had become prime minister of Israel. Jimmy Carter had just become president of the United States. Then, in November, President Sadat made a sudden and spectacular visit to

Jerusalem and addressed the Israeli Knesset. The deed itself recognized Israeli sovereignty and initiated the long and difficult face-to-face negotiations that followed. In 1978, President Carter brought Sadat and Begin together at Camp David for an unprecedented round of summit negotiations. In 1979, a peace treaty between Egypt and Israel was signed over the objections of most Arab states and mounting threats from the Palestine Liberation Organization. With the signing of the Peace Treaty and other arrangements, the mission of UNEF-II was terminated. UNDOF remains active in supervising the cease-fire line between Syria and Israel. In 1995, it consisted of about 1,300 personnel from Austria, Canada, and Poland and had a budget of $35 million. Finland withdrew its 300- man contingent in 1993.

In retrospect, the Security Council peacekeeping resolutions of October 1973 were extremely important from a number of perspectives. With superpower agreement, the resolutions once again returned the peacekeeping function to the Security Council. However, the command of UNEF-II was vested in the Secretary-General rather than the Military Staff Committee. Whereas the Soviet Union and its allies had previously been excluded from peacekeeping operations, Poland was now incorporated into the mission as a representative of the Communist bloc. Possibly of greatest significance was the Council's decision that UNEF-II, unlike other peacekeeping operations, would be supported financially as a regular expense of the United Nations to be borne by the membership in accordance with Article 17, Paragraph 2. These provisions represented a significant demonstration of political trust and cooperation and a major step forward in the evolution of United Nations peacekeeping.

Lebanon: UN Interim Force in Lebanon (UNIFIL)

If Israel has been battered by external attack, Lebanon has almost equally been torn by internal strife during most of its existence. The Lebanese political structure was created in 1943 when it received its independence from France. A small country with about two million population, in contrast to most of its Arab neighbors, Lebanon has a heterogeneous people consisting primarily of Maronite Christians, Shi'ite Moslems, Druze, and Sunni Moslems, with substantial Syrian Orthodox and Armenian minorities. Reflecting the population balance of the 1940s, the Chamber of Deputies distributed representation on a six-to-five basis between Christians and Moslems, respectively. The custom also developed that the presidency should go to a Maronite Christian, the premiership to a Sunni Moslem, and the speakership of the Chamber of Deputies to a Shi'ite Moslem. The Lebanese armed forces were carefully balanced for ethnic and religious considerations. The Druze were generally accommodated through a share of the Shi'ite community.

After the expulsion of Palestinian guerrilla units from Jordan in September 1970, southern Lebanon became the primary military base for the Palestine Liberation Organization. PLO units were large and heavily armed. In time, the Palestinian troops exceeded the total strength of the Lebanese army and remained free of Lebanese governmental control. The situation was further aggravated by the simultaneous arrival of some 400,000 Palestinian refugees, adding to the large Palestinian refugee community there since 1948, bringing yet another dimension to the religious and ethnic tensions within the country.

By the mid-1970s, the situation in Lebanon was almost entirely out of control. Palestinian troops were actively using southern Lebanon for artillery attacks and frequent raids into Israeli territory. This brought Israeli reprisals. The Palestinians had essentially set up a state within a state, particularly in the south. In the rest of the country, what had been a Maronite Christian majority was now a minority as a consequence of a dramatic growth in the Shi'ite Moslem population. On April 13, 1976, a Christian Phalangist attack on a bus carrying Palestinian civilians killed twenty-two of them. This ignited a civil war in which Christian forces fought Moslem elements. The civil war was very complex. Various warlords and ethnic groups fought each other and shifted alliances constantly, with sometimes incongruous results. The Palestinian commandos, containing both Moslems and Christians, attempted to moderate the conflict in order to concentrate on Israel. By 1977, Christians were attacking Palestinian refugee camps, and war atrocities were common.

Syria became involved in order to prevent the partition of Lebanon and for other reasons, not the least of which were irredentist concerns for a "Greater Syria". There were economic concerns; Syria made extensive use of Lebanese ports. Close relationships between families and ethnic groups in Lebanon and Syria were made difficult by the border. Some feared that a Phalangist-dominated state would provide Israel with an ally on Syria's flank. Syria was also interested in curbing the influence of the Palestine Liberation Organization in a region of vital interest to itself. In this context, it must be remembered that Syria and many in the population of Lebanon never accepted the French creation of Lebanon. Meanwhile, Israel was beginning to provide military assistance to the Christian Phalangists.

In 1977, the Arab League assigned Syria responsibility for imposing a cease-fire in Lebanon. This brought Syrian troops dangerously close to the Israeli border along southern Lebanon. Israel stepped up aid to the Maronite Christian forces, their client troops in the area. As this aid escalated, the Syrians permitted the Palestinians to launch counteroffensives. By early 1978, Israel had become a *de facto* participant in the Lebanese civil war.

Elsewhere, President Sadat of Egypt was embarking upon his peace moves with Israel. In an attempt to block these developments, the PLO committed a series of terrorist acts. On March 12, 1978, one of these attacks was made on a bus in Tel Aviv, killing over twenty persons. On March 19, the Israelis made a large-scale attack upon Palestinian bases, landing forces in southern Lebanon and preparing to remain there as long as necessary.

Condemnation of the Israeli action came quickly at the United Nations. An American resolution, passed on March 21, asserted that Lebanese sovereignty must be respected; the Israeli military action must cease. A United Nations Interim Force in Lebanon (UNIFIL) was created to maintain peace. Thus, the Arabs were able to achieve an early Israeli withdrawal through political means at the UN. The Lebanese were able to retain their sovereignty. The Israelis, although appearing to be set back by the United Nations action, succeeded in having a UN peacekeeping force provide yet another buffer at its most exposed border in the north.

On March 23, 1978, the first units of a 4,000-man UNIFIL force arrived in Lebanon. From the outset, UNIFIL troops were greeted as targets to be shot at by virtually all parties to the conflict. After all, no one ever promised that United Nations peacekeeping would take place in a rose garden. They were the smallest, least armed, and most politically constrained military unit in the area. Nevertheless, in time, UNIFIL was able to defuse much of the fighting.

The Israeli-Palestinian conflict continued in spite of the best efforts of UNIFIL. This occurred in the midst of an extremely bitter civil war with constantly shifting alliances among the various communities in Lebanon and their outside supporters, including Israel, Syria, and, increasingly, Iran. As PLO forces, particularly in southern Lebanon, continued to grow, there were continual cross-border raids and artillery attacks on Israel, in conjunction with a worldwide terrorist campaign. Both were met in kind by Israel. The situation continued to escalate until Israel invaded southern

Lebanon in 1982. This included air, naval, and artillery bombardments of the Moslem sectors of the open city of Beirut.

U.S. envoy Philip Habib and King Fahd of Saudi Arabia were able to bring about a cease-fire. Palestinian forces were withdrawn, primarily to Syria and Tunisia, with assurances that their families and other refugees left behind would be protected. However, over 400 unarmed Palestinian men, women, and children were massacred at the refugee camps of Sabra and Shatilla by the Phalangists, with indirect Israeli connivance. A multinational force from the United States, France, and Italy was deployed to supervise the withdrawal of the Palestinians, Syrians, and Israelis. This force was withdrawn in September, but later reintroduced and then withdrawn again in March 1984. An agreement between Israel and Lebanon in 1983 essentially brought the war to a close. UNIFIL moved into new positions when Israel established a security zone, manned primarily by an Israeli-controlled Lebanese militia.

The civil war in Lebanon continued, unabated, until ended by massive Syrian intervention in 1990. UNIFIL now deals with Iranian sponsored militias that conduct periodic attacks across the Israeli border and with the consequent Israeli reprisals and preemptive strikes. UNIFIL continues in operation and in 1995 consisted of about 5,200 personnel from Fiji, Finland, France, Ghana, Ireland, Italy, Nepal, Norway, Poland, and Sweden, and a budget of $138 million. UNIFIL's efforts, although commendable, again demonstrate that there is a substantial difference between peacemaking and peacekeeping. They have been repeatedly brushed aside or ignored by both Israel and its opponents in South Lebanon whenever it suited the purpose of the parties. On the other hand, they have provided the Secretary-General with "eyes and ears".

When Great Powers Ignore the UN

Thus far, we have reviewed peacekeeping operations in which the United Nations was involved in some significant aspect. Two others - Vietnam and Afghanistan - were conflicts in which the UN was unable to become involved. The moderating influence of the UN, fumbling and occasionally unsuccessful though it may have been, was absent. Perhaps the most important lesson learned from each, from a peacekeeping point of view, is that when one of the veto-wielding powers of the Security Council is involved, they have the ability to preclude any effective interference from the United Nations, as suggested in the first of our scenarios of hypothetical nuclear wars. If Vietnam and Afghanistan were not sufficient to demonstrate this circumstance, there was also the Falklands War where the United Kingdom and the United States precluded any effective United Nations action. Indeed, in all three cases, the effective participation of any regional organization without the concurrence of the major power involved was also precluded.

Vietnam[20]

With the French withdrawal and the signing of peace accords in Geneva, two regimes were established: a communist one in the north and a "free" one in the south under Ngo Dinh Diem. When scheduled elections failed to be held in 1956 because of objections raised by South Vietnam, renewed guerilla fighting ensued. The United States provided ever-increasing amounts of aid and assistance to the South Vietnamese. Eventually, full scale U.S. combat forces were deployed, reaching a total of some 550,000 by the late 1960s. Additionally, Thailand, Korea, Australia, and New Zealand also deployed troops. North Vietnam, the Soviet Union, East Germany, Bulgaria, and China provided support, mainly matériel, to the Viet Cong fighting the regime in the south. As the Viet Cong suffered greater and greater attrition, they were replaced by regular North Vietnamese units, particularly after the disastrous Tet Offensive of 1968.

American involvement continued in spite of increasing opposition from the world community, including several of its putative allies, and with substantial opposition domestically. Under the Nixon administration, efforts were begun to "Vietnamize" the conflict, in other words, turn the fighting over to the Vietnamese with only indirect American support. These efforts eventually culminated in a cease-fire being reached under the Paris Accords of 1973. American and Allied troops were withdrawn in 1973.

In 1975, in violation of the Paris Accords, the North Vietnamese staged a full scale invasion of the south. Congress and the Ford administration failed to come to the assistance of the South Vietnamese, as promised in those same accords, and the Republic of South Vietnam ceased to exist.

---

20   The standard account of the Vietnam war is Stanley Karnow, *Vietnam: A History* (New York: Viking Press, 1983). For an analysis of U.S. involvement, see Harry G. Summers, *On Strategy: A Critical Analysis of the Vietnam War* (Novato, CA: Presidio Press, 1982).

Additionally, the domino theory was proven at least partially correct; both Cambodia and Laos fell to the communists.

The lessons for peacekeeping and for the United Nations were evident. Despite opposition from most of the world community, including some of its allies, the United States was able to pursue its policies in Vietnam for two decades with virtual impunity. Attempts to raise the subject in the Security Council or the General Assembly were met with vetoes, threats of vetoes, or simply ignored. However, there were consequences for the United States. Quite apart from the domestic impact on American foreign and military policy, there was a substantial decrease in the influence and credibility of the United States on the world stage. Smaller powers put less trust and faith in the United States and began to seek alliances elsewhere.

Afghanistan[21]

Even more drastic results were to come to the Soviet Union as a result of its incursion into Afghanistan. Afghanistan amply demonstrates the two-tier security system referred to earlier. The superpowers, and, in this case, particularly the Soviet Union, simply ignored or blocked any attempts of the UN or other bodies to interfere in Afghanistan. Just as with the United States involvement in Vietnam, the Soviet involvement in Afghanistan followed a different set of rules than those applied to the non-superpowers.

In April 1978, the government of President Daoud was overthrown. Daoud was assassinated by a KGB-backed coup that placed Noor Mohammed Taraki in power. In the following months, the Taraki government would begin a reeducation and forced modernization program in coordination with Soviet advisers. The bulk of Afghans opposed these moves. By March 1979, resistance to the Communist government had become a full-scale rebellion. The rebel ranks were filled with deserters from the Afghan army. As could be expected in Afghanistan, the rebels were divided into groups along ethnic lines. The situation deteriorated as the rebels gained control of much of the countryside.

In September 1979, Taraki in turn was overthrown and murdered by his premier, Amin, apparently without the approval of the Soviets, even though Amin was a Communist. In December 1979, after a slow build-up of troops

---

21   Although the Afghan crisis is technically not a part of "the founding years" covered in this chapter, it is included here for ease of comparison with Vietnam.

in the Kabul area and along the Afghan-Soviet border, Soviet forces entered Afghanistan in strength. The Soviets subsequently installed Babrak Karmal as president.

The invasion aroused world public opinion. Soviet actions were strongly condemned in various forums. As an outgrowth of this outrage, the United States Senate refused to ratify the SALT II treaty that had been signed earlier in the year. The Carter administration imposed a grain embargo on the U.S.S.R. and withdrew American participation in the 1980 Moscow Olympics. The American actions created substantial controversy domestically and abroad. No real action was taken in or through the United Nations, where the Soviets would have simply exercised their veto. In a reversal of roles from Vietnam, the United States began providing clandestine aid to the Afghan rebels through a surrogate, in this case, Pakistan.

Popular, but disjointed, resistance to the Soviet occupation intensified. The resistance received support not only from the United States and Pakistan, but from other countries such as Saudi Arabia and Iran. A substantial opposition to the war, both within the Soviet bureaucracy and among the Soviet people, began to grow and be expressed more and more openly, creating significant fissures in the Soviet leadership. By mid-1980, Soviet forces had grown to a strength of over 105,000. In contrast to the Americans in Vietnam, the Soviets and the Afghan regimes tried to defeat the insurgents through repressive measures akin to those employed by the French in Algeria. The various ethnic factions among the rebels responded in kind.[22]

As the situation in Afghanistan deteriorated and the Soviet people became more and more disaffected, the KGB overthrew Karmal in May 1986 and installed the head of its Afghan counterpart, the KHAD, initially as head of the Communist Party and later as president of Afghanistan. The new president, Najibullah, attempted a policy of reconciliation, not unlike that attempted by President Minh of Vietnam after American withdrawal. It had limited effect. Pakistan stepped in as a third party negotiator in 1988. The Soviets agreed to the withdrawal of their forces, which was completed in 1989. Simultaneously, the government of the Soviet Union disintegrated.

---

22 Typically, the United States and, to a slightly lesser extent, the Europeans perceived the rebel factions in religious terms. Although there was a religious component, the various factions in Afghanistan were, and are, based on ethnic, tribal, and clan identities of which religious belief is but one part.

Other than resolutions, United Nations involvement in the Afghan War had been minimal. The Soviet veto ensured no involvement by the Security Council. The United States had no desire for UN involvement either, other than to use it as one more venue for its attacks on the "Evil Empire". The involvement in Afghanistan had serious effects on both the domestic and foreign policies of the then Soviet Union, which carried over to those of Russia.

This review of the early formative cases of United Nations peacekeeping reveals how incremental but real the process of institutionalization has been. Each cases presented a unique problem within a context of international distrust. Each peacekeeping mission added a new rule, a new procedure, or a new strategy to the UN's way of coping with international conflict. Through successes, failures, and even neglect, the organization has grown and expanded its military and peacekeeping functions. Peacekeeping has been a parallel track to its arms control efforts. The two - arms control and peacekeeping - have pushed the world inexorably toward a context of political trust.

9 Contemporary United Nations Peacekeeping: Issues

In the fifty years since its founding, the United Nations role has involved more than peacekeeping. Particularly in the late 1980s and early 1990s, it has been able to expand its efforts into prevention of conflict, as exemplified in its operations in Namibia, and in providing assistance for nation building, as in Cambodia and Mozambique. It cannot be coincidental that the most successful operations have been those in which the major powers are only peripherally involved, with the notable exception of Kashmir. On the other hand, the principal failures, Somalia and the former Yugoslavia, for example, are those where there is direct involvement of the major powers. Further, there has been an increasing involvement of regional associations in peacekeeping and peacemaking efforts. On balance, the United Nations had a good deal to celebrate on its fiftieth anniversary.

Institutional Developments in UN Peacekeeping

Numerous institutional trends can be discerned from the United Nations peacekeeping experience, as sampled in the case studies of the preceding chapter. The following recapitulation of the institutionally significant developments in those early cases reveals *the accretion of organizational behaviors, political precedents, and formalization of expectations that has and continues to take place at the United Nations, most of which have contributed to the environment of trust that has been building in the international arena.*

In the Greek case, the effectiveness of publicity as a counter to covert operations (by Russia, in this instance) was demonstrated as was the neutrality of United Nations observers. In Palestine, the UN recommended the conditions for creating Israel as a sovereign nation, a precedent for later involvements in nation building. The General Assembly also proved itself an effective third-party mediator in the various Israeli-Arab armistice negotiations.

237

The issue of UN jurisdiction was raised in the Indonesian case. The Dutch considered Indonesian independence to be a domestic problem, hence outside the jurisdiction of the UN. Nevertheless, the UN offered its good offices in the dispute and again recommended the creation of a sovereign nation (the United States of Indonesia). In Kashmir, the importance of sustained UN pressure for negotiations was demonstrated. A UN-supervised plebiscite - a new duty - was recommended, although not carried out.

Korea revealed the risks and costs of collective security under the guise of a "police" operation. The Uniting for Peace Resolution enlarged the roles of the General Assembly and Secretary-General and redefined the function of peacekeeping. By the time of the Suez Crisis, a major military role was assigned to the Secretary-General. At the same time, financing of UN peacekeeping missions emerged as a serious administrative problem, as did unilateral termination of a peacekeeping mission by one of the parties. The Congo civil war was the largest armed peacekeeping mission to that date and led to an even more serious financial crisis. One consequence was establishment of the Committee of 33 to look into the financial and other requirements of peacekeeping by the UN.

Thus, the articles of the UN Charter were coming to life in often surprising ways and circumstances, and each produced an additional set of goals and procedures for this institution. Even minor institutional changes built up the confidence of nations in the UN, despite the anti-UN rhetoric often heard back home.

In Lebanon, the Arab League undertook the first regional peacekeeping mission, which set precedents for similar regional undertaking elsewhere, e.g., Liberia. The professionalism and even-handedness of the UN Force in Cyprus (UNFICYP) enhanced the reputation of UN peacekeeping. The mission's outstanding intelligence work contributed to a reduction in communal strife.

The India-Pakistan Mission (UNIPOM) demonstrated how a superpower's cooperation may facilitate conflict resolution, particularly if the cooperation of the parties was forthcoming and trustworthy. In UNEF-II, a Soviet proposal for a joint superpower peacekeeping force was rejected, but at this time the Security Council returned to its principal responsibility for establishing a peacekeeping mission when necessary. A member of the Soviet bloc (Poland) was represented on the mission.

The institutional evolution of the UN in its early years was impressive. Regardless of its military weakness, the United Nations has provided a vital third-party role in an impressive number of conflict cases. Whether the

Security Council, the General Assembly, or the Secretary-General, at least one organ of the world body has been available as a channel of communication, a focus of publicity, and a source of mediatory pressure for most major international conflicts. It has even on occasion served this function during confrontations between the superpowers.

The pragmatism of the UN has been demonstrated in its ability to bring military action to a halt and to transfer the conflict to the negotiating table. Although not always successful, the UN has shown the importance of timely intervention between parties locked in military combat. Another positive development is that UN peacekeeping has become a widely shared international activity. When the world's major powers cooperate, peacekeeping functions are usually carried off promptly and smoothly. When the major powers are at opposite sides of an argument, the middle and nonaligned powers are able to implement significant initiatives.

Many nations, not least being the United States and Russia, have accommodated to the requirements of peacekeeping. In fact, it is becoming one of the major functions of their armed forces, as exemplified by the establishment of the office of Deputy Assistant Secretary of Defense for Peacekeeping and Peace Enforcement by the Department of Defense. At the UN itself, changes have been made. For example, the UN Situation Center has been substantially enhanced. In 1993, the center was only partially staffed and had but two telephones. By the end of 1995, it had expanded to a fully staffed center with satellite, computer, voice, and fax communications to the then seventeen field missions as well as direct connections to various news media.

Equally important are moves by selected nations with a peacekeeping tradition to establish some form of UN rapid reaction force that could be deployed immediately to a troubled area. A major problem for the United Nations has been its inability to react quickly in crisis situations. The Friends Group, led by Canada and the Netherlands,[1] created the Vanguard Concept. This would create a mobile military headquarters that would continually conduct contingency planning and be prepared to coordinate the establishment of a force for deployment. This would work in conjunction with the "stand-by" forces requested in the Secretary-General's *Agenda for Peace* and its supplement noted in the preceding chapter. An effective model for such a force exists in the former Allied Command Europe

---

1   Other members include Australia, Denmark, New Zealand, Jamaica, Nigeria, Senegal, and Ukraine.

Mobile Force that existed in NATO. The ACE Mobile Force had a small headquarters planning staff with regular NATO elements "earmarked" for selected contingencies.

As the representatives of national elites have become preoccupied with arguments and decisions regarding when and how to employ peacekeeping missions, they also have developed a certain clarity about the nature of this function and a substantial degree of camaraderie about surmounting the difficulties associated with it. Five decades of United Nations peacekeeping may seem militarily unimpressive to those who equate order with might. However, if we could design an objective measure of political trust, we would undoubtedly find substantial correlation between the United Nations peacekeeping experience and the expansion of trust among the world's leaders. The five decades of peacekeeping have been five decades of confidence building and institutional development.

Contemporary Activities

The institutional development of the United Nations continues. Currently, the UN operates in a more complex and dynamic world than hitherto. An enumeration of some of its more recent operations will partially indicate how the peacekeeping function has broadened and become enmeshed with peacemaking. The end of the Cold War has put peacemaking at the forefront of UN missions and arms control, in many respects, on a "back burner".

Cambodia (UNTAC). The UN mission to Cambodia was officially ended in September 1993. It brought about a cease-fire and conducted (rather than merely observe) free elections and a functioning government. Indeed, the UN mission actually performed many governmental functions while the Cambodian government proper was being organized. It also provided humanitarian and infrastructure support to the government. Several nations, not the least of which was Japan, participated in these UN operations for the first time. In contrast to many other operations, this was not just a peacekeeping mission, but an exercise in humanitarian aid and nation building.

UN Observer Mission in El Salvador (ONUSAL). ONUSAL monitors the agreements between the government of El Salvador and the former insurgents (Farabundo Martí National Liberation Front, or FMLN) that brought an end to that country's civil war. The agreements were essentially self-initiated in September 1989, albeit under substantial external pressure.

The first part of the agreement, prepared with the assistance of the UN, was signed in July 1990, and dealt with human rights. A UN verification mission (ONUSAL) was established as a trust-building mechanism between the parties. This provision was agreed upon prior to the cease fire, so great was the distrust and so important as an antecedent condition was trust building. Negotiations culminated, under UN auspices, with a peace agreement in January 1992 that incorporated all previous agreements. It also called for the substantial enlargement of ONUSAL to take on the various tasks of confidence building, monitoring the cease fire, and establishing a civil police force for the nation. ONUSAL was expanded to include Human Rights, Military (Peacekeeping), Electoral, and Police divisions.

The Electoral Division was disbanded after the successful conduct of elections in April 1994. The Police Division undertook the unique task of establishing an entirely new National Police Force for El Salvador. During the training and establishment of this force, it created and monitored a transitional police force. This experience was later used in a similar operation in Haiti. In addition to monitoring the cease-fire, ONUSAL's military and civilian observers monitor human rights violations. All ONUSAL divisions report directly to the UN Chief of Mission, a practice that was not always used in previous missions. ONUSAL consists of 30 observers and 220 civil police from eight nations. Established in July 1991, its 1994 budget was $24 million.

UN Iraq-Kuwait Observer Mission (UNIKOM). After Coalition forces liberated Kuwait in 1991, the United Nations was asked in April 1991 to provide a mission to monitor the demilitarized zone between Iraq and Kuwait, including the Khawr 'Abd Allah waterway. The observer force was unarmed. Initial units were drawn temporarily from UNFICYP and UNIFIL, thus permitting rapid deployment of already trained and experienced personnel. This applied one of the key lessons learned from previous missions.

By 1992 and 1993, UNIKOM experienced several border incursions by Iraq in an effort to seize abandoned equipment. UNIKOM thereafter was reinforced, armed, and authorized to employ force to prevent small scale incursions. However, once again, the difficulties in raising and deploying peacekeeping forces became evident. Bangladesh provided a mechanized infantry battalion; the force was authorized in April 1993, but deployed in January 1994, almost a year later. Observers were provided by some 33 countries which, for the first time, include observers from all five Permanent Members of the Security Council. Two thirds of the cost of some $69 million annually was provided by the Government of Kuwait. The remainder was to be paid by assessed contributions from UN member states.

The relative success of UNIKOM must be considered in context. Substantial related actions have been taken that preclude Iraq from taking any aggressive act. International resolve, led primarily by the United States, has been demonstrated on more than one occasion through the deployment of forces to neighboring nations any time there appears to be a build-up of Iraqi forces. Iraq is also subject to the continued priority surveillance by national technical means of both the United States and the United Kingdom. Few, if any, other UN operations have had the good fortune of this type of support. It makes UNIKOM unique.

UN Mission for the Referendum in Western Sahara (MINURSO). MINURSO was established to monitor the cease-fire between Morocco and insurgents seeking to establish an independent state. Initially, the mission was to conduct a referendum on the desire of the people to remain a part of Morocco or establish an independent state. Because of confusion and disagreement about who should vote in the referendum, the mission has been restricted to monitoring the cease-fire until the question of voter eligibility is resolved. The annual cost is about $41 million. It has 310 personnel, with support units from Canada and Switzerland and observers from 24 nations, who, as of April 1994, had suffered three fatalities.

Political maneuvering among the parties and lack of interest by most of the world have thus far prevented MINURSO from fulfilling its obligations. However, it has been able to maintain an uneasy truce between Morocco and the insurgents and provide a means of communications between them.

UN Angola Verification Mission (UNAVEM). Angola presents yet another version of Cold War rivalry. Various rebel forces fought the colonial power, Portugal, until domestic pressures in the home country forced the granting of Angolan independence. Shortly after independence a three-way internal civil war ensued. The U.S.S.R. supported one faction, while the United States and its allies supported another. Substantial numbers of Cuban forces were introduced, initially as advisors, and subsequently in actual combat operations in support of the Soviet-backed Marxist government. For reasons having little to do with events in Angola, support by both superpowers was withdrawn by 1988. UNAVEM I was established in January 1989 to monitor the withdrawal of the Cuban forces, which was completed in May 1991.

UNAVEM II was created in June 1991 to verify the cease-fire, monitor elections, and observe the Angolan police. Initially, the force consisted of small numbers of unarmed military observers. The UN also provided technical assistance to the parties to the agreement in preparing for and conducting elections. Meanwhile, the military observer force continued to monitor the progress of the disarmament of the two main militaries at designated assembly areas.

The elections were held in October. The main rebel faction, UNITA[2] and other parties charged widespread election fraud and withdrew their support from both the election results and from the disarmament process. The situation continued to deteriorate as armed conflict escalated. Both sides continued to solicit United Nations' assistance. The conflict had grown, however, to the point where the Secretary-General stated that for all intents and purposes, Angola had reverted to a state of civil war by January 1993. Both the United States and Russia refrained from providing support to their former clients.

Diplomatic efforts under the auspices of the United Nations and the Organization of African Unity, including sanctions imposed on UNITA for not accepting the election results, continued and eventually bore fruit in November 1994. A protocol was signed by the parties at Lusaka that reconfirmed much of the earlier agreements. However, civil war continued, but at a much reduced level.

In February 1995, the Security Council approved the establishment of UNAVEM III, but only on condition that the Secretary-General could certify that substantial progress had been made by the parties to the Lusaka Protocol. On March 25, 1995, the Secretary-General certified that progress had been made (although minor incidents continued), stating inter alia that ". . .it is clear that it is becoming increasingly necessary to assist the parties in overcoming their mutual mistrust. . .".[3] The mistrust to which the Secretary-General referred was based not only on years of civil conflict, but also on ethnic-tribal issues as well.

---

2   UNITA - Uniao National para a Independencia Total de Angola (National Union for the Total Independence of Angola).

3   United Nations. Report of the Secretary-General concerning Angola, March 25, 1995.

UNAVEM III began its deployment in May 1995.[4]   In creating this force, the United Nations capitalized on the experiences it had gained in similar transitions in Namibia, and more especially in Cambodia and Mozambique. The force was substantial enough to protect itself and also to cover the vast expanses of territory involved. Additionally, it contained a large police presence in addition to the military. Perhaps most importantly, procedures have been established to ease coordination and cooperation of the military, civil, and humanitarian activities of the various agencies involved. This type of cooperation and coordination was critical to overcoming the distrust that has been created between the agencies as well as the warring parties.

Disarmament was a critical part of UNAVEM III's mission: land mine clearance and the demobilization of forces, particularly those of UNITA. Land mines had been widely used and few were mapped in accordance with international custom and treaties. Demobilization of personnel involved as it did in Cambodia and Mozambique, a great deal more than simply turning in weapons and uniforms. Many, if not most, of these guerrilla fighters were recruited when they were barely into their teens and have known no other life. They must not only be trained in new job skills, but also socialized into the civilian world. One of the major problems in the transition has been unemployed and disillusioned former soldiers resorting to banditry.

UN Operation in Somalia (UNOSOM) I and II and *UN Unified Task Force (UNITAF)*.   Somalia was one of the UN's more spectacular failures. The mission was terminated in 1995. It had several distinctions and taught the UN many lessons.

After the overthrow of the regime of General Siad Barre, Somalia descended into chaos as clan factions fought each other for control. This only compounded massive starvation brought about by repeated crop failures. The United States moved military forces into the area to protect humanitarian aid workers as well as to provide humanitarian relief. These were relatively new duties for the U.S. war-winning troops.

The U.S. turned to the UN to coordinate and establish a longer term program. In April 1992, UNOSOM was created to monitor the cease-fire among the Somali warlords and protect supply convoys. The U.S., however, continued its operations independently as well as additionally participating in UNOSOM and UNITAF. This violated the age-old principle of unity of

---

4   The advance party of the British logistics element actually arrived on 13 April.

command and led to both the UN and the U.S. becoming involved directly in the Somali civil war.

The U.S. was forced by domestic pressure to withdraw. However, its humanitarian mission had saved millions of people from starvation. UNOSOM and UNITAF attempted, with only limited success, to revert to its original peacekeeping mission, but was increasingly ignored by the local warlords. With the American retreat, other nations also began to withdraw their support from the UN mission. The final Pakistani troops were withdrawn with American cover in 1995.

At its peak, the mission included some 35,000 troops from 30 countries, suffered over 120 fatalities, and learned many lessons, particularly about unity of command and having the consent of the parties to the conflict. Neither condition obtained in Somalia. The UN also recognized the need for advanced planning and coordination, which resulted in the establishment of the UN Peacekeeping Operations Department discussed below.

United Nations Operations in Mozambique (ONUMOZ). If Somalia was a failure, Mozambique was a spectacular success. The mission was established in March 1993 for the purpose of monitoring a cease-fire, demobilizing the opposing forces, actually destroying weapons, and protecting UN personnel in monitoring elections. It was essentially an arms control mission.

At its peak, the mission had 5,453 military and 476 civil police personnel and cost well over $450 million. Units and observers were provided from over 35 countries. Opposing forces were disarmed and elections held. The UN force was withdrawn in late 1994. Experience gained here and in Namibia were subsequently applied to UN operations in Angola. In accomplishing its mission, ONUMOZ suffered approximately eleven fatalities.

The effectiveness of the operation in Mozambique can be attributed to several factors. Ceasefire accords were reached between the two major parties in Portugal (neutral ground) in 1991, with a follow-up agreement in Rome (again neutral ground) in 1992. Elections were subsequently held. However, unlike Angola, ONUMOZ had substantially disarmed and demobilized both factions *prior* to the elections. It also had presided over the creation of a completely "new" military, much reduced in size, that incorporated elements of both factions. Additionally, provisions were made for the transition of demobilized fighters to peacetime employment. Emphasis in the demobilization was placed less on destroying the guns than on *creating trust* between the factions. Admittedly, the end of the Cold War facilitated the process, as did the changes in the government in South Africa. The latter effectively removed external support from both parties.

United Nations Observer Mission Uganda-Rwanda (UNOMUR). The ethnic war and savage slaughter in Rwanda led to Security Council Resolution 846. Under this resolution, a mission of 80 observers was dispatched to the border area between Uganda and Rwanda in June 1993 to insure that military equipment did not reach strife-torn Rwanda across this border. With the subsequent changes that occurred in both Uganda and most especially in Rwanda, the mission was terminated in September 1994. The mission was unable to prevent military equipment from reaching Rwanda, but the observer force did serve as a deterrent that probably reduced the arms reaching the area.

United Nations Assistance Mission for Rwanda (UNAMIR). UNAMIR was formed in October 1993 to monitor an agreement reached between the government of Rwanda and the insurgent Rwanda Patriotic Front (RPF). Shortly after its formation, and before it could really implement its mandate, civil war again broke out. All but 250 of the 2,500 UN troops were forced to withdraw during a period of massacres bordering on genocide.

In June 1994, after the RPF forced out the Hutu dominated government of Rwanda, the Security Council approved a plan to deploy 5,500 peacekeepers to Rwanda at the end of the civil war. UNAMIR monitors the unilateral cease-fire, attempts to protect refugees, and provides security and support for the distribution of humanitarian relief.

The ethnic strife in Rwanda has resulted in enormous numbers of refugees, many of whom are hesitant to return to Rwanda in fear of reprisals. This has generated substantial relief efforts outside the purview of the United Nations. A French force of some 2,500, for example, was deployed into Zaire and Rwanda in June 1994 to establish protected areas for refugees. They were subsequently joined by troops from Senegal and Chad.

In late 1994, the French-led force began to withdraw and turn over the protected areas to the incoming elements of UNAMIR. In July 1994, the United States deployed troops to provide humanitarian relief to the refugee camps in Zaire. After establishing water purification facilities and other technical support, the U.S. effort was reduced to airlift support. Other nations have provided humanitarian relief, but it is not always clear whether they are part of the UN effort or not. These have included medical units from Australia and Israel as well as medical personnel and engineers from the United Kingdom. As the situation has stabilized, unilateral support elements have been withdrawn and their functions turned over to UNAMIR.

The situation in Rwanda remains intractable at this writing. The ethnic violence has exacerbated long held ethnic distrust. This is compounded by the massive refugee problem, particularly in Zaire. Efforts to encourage voluntary return to Rwanda have met with, at best, marginal success. Many of the nations that initially assisted the UN in peacekeeping have grown frustrated, as have many of the NGOs, at the lack of progress in both Rwanda and Burundi. For lack of funds, UNIMIR has had to be reduced from 5,500 to 1,800 troops.

United Nations Observer Mission in Georgia (UNOMIG). In July 1993, break-away ethno-nationalist elements in the Abkhazia area and the government of Georgia concluded a cease-fire. The United Nations has deployed 21 observers from seven countries to monitor the cease-fire and investigate possible violations. An uneasy truce continues as of the end of 1995, but little other progress has been made. Georgia falls within the Russian sphere of influence known as the "near-abroad". As a result, most efforts here have been conducted under the auspices of the Commonwealth of Independent States and Russia.

United Nations Mission in Haiti (UNMIH). Jean-Bertrand Aristide was elected president of Haiti in December 1990, and took office in February 1991. The election had been certified by the UN, the OAS, and the Caribbean Community (CARICOM). In September 1991, Aristide was overthrown by a military coup led by Lieutenant General Raoul Cedras. The coup was condemned by the international community. Various diplomatic and economic actions failed to dislodge the Cedras government. In January 1993, Aristide sent a letter requesting, inter alia, UN assistance in the restoration of his government.

UNMIH was officially established in September 1993 and charged with monitoring the change of government in Haiti. The military government of Haiti initially refused to allow the force to land. In late 1994, a U.S.-led coalition occupied Haiti and installed the previously elected government of President Aristide. In early 1995, the American operation was turned over to the UNMIH, which was made up largely of units that had participated in the multinational force. Meanwhile, President Aristide abolished the army and inaugurated a program for training a professional police force with the assistance of elements of UNMIH.

In early 1996, free elections were held, and for the first time in Haitian history, there was a peaceful transition of government in accordance with the constitution. The UNMIH was to withdraw on February 29, 1996. Several nations, however, led by Canada, have indicated a willingness to maintain training and security forces in Haiti until representative government is institutionalized.

From a peacekeeping standpoint, Haiti must be considered a success. However, only after a U.S.-led multinational force had landed and established order did it become a United Nations mission. One essential difference in this mission was that it included a substantial contingent of both civilian and military police. It was approached more as a police problem than one of a military peacekeeping force in the normal sense. It unquestionably was interference in the internal affairs of a member nation. When, then, is it legitimate for the United Nations to involve itself in the restoration of a government? Was it in violation of the United Nations Charter? Could this event have occurred had it not been in the interest of the United States, Canada, and France.

United Nations Observer Mission in Liberia (UNOMIL). Civil war broke out in Liberia in 1990 with the overthrow of the government of Samuel Doe. As a result of internal fighting among various elements, the situation deteriorated into near chaos. It is estimated that between 100,000 and 150,000 civilians died as a result of the complete breakdown of law and order. Much of the strife among the factions was based on tribal-ethnic groupings. Liberia is also unique in that one of the groupings involves descendants of former slaves from the United States who returned to West Africa to establish the nation in the nineteenth century. The United Nations attempted to cooperate and coordinate actions with the Economic Community of West African States (ECOWAS) and imposed a total arms embargo on Liberia in 1992.

ECOMOG (Military Observer Group of the Economic Community of West African States) is a 3,000-man force composed of regional forces from Nigeria, Ghana, Gambia, Guinea, and Sierra Leone. The force entered Liberia in August 1990 and has, forcibly when necessary, imposed a cease-fire in the multi-party civil war, negotiating a caretaker government until elections could be held. It has arranged several cease-fires and other accords which have almost invariably broken down.

Under the joint auspices of the Organization of African Unity (OAU), ECOWAS, and the UN, a peace accord was successfully brokered among the major factions in July 1993. The agreement laid out a multi-phased program moving from a cease-fire through demobilization to national elections.

UNOMIL was established in September 1993 to investigate cease-fire violations and to monitor other parts of the agreements. UNOMIL will be involved in monitoring elections. The mission includes personnel to train ECOMOG in mine clearance operations. Its 370 observers and trainers closely coordinate their activities with ECOMOG.

In August 1995, yet another cease-fire and accord was reached by the various parties, but only after armed intervention by ECOMOG. This accord restored some semblance of order to the capital, Monrovia, but areas outside the capital were beset by sporadic fighting. ECOMOG also began to have difficulties internally as the result of unsettled conditions in its home countries, e.g., Nigeria and Sierra Leone. However, within Liberia it has earned the respect of the participants to the conflict as well as the international community for its fairness and firmness.[5] This cease-fire also eventually broke down; the civil war continues and seems intractable.

United Nations Protection Force (UNPROFOR). One of the largest and most costly, both in lives and resources, was the UN mission undertaken in former Yugoslavia. UNPROFOR operated in three (Bosnia-Herzegovina, Croatia, and Macedonia) of the five nations that were formed with the break-up of Yugoslavia. It contained military, civilian, and police components and was provided additional military assistance by elements of NATO and the Western European Union (WEU). However, due to UNPROFOR's inability to provide security, not only for the warring parties, but for itself, its operations were terminated at the end of 1995 and the military tasks were taken over by an "implementation force (IFOR)" provided by NATO. UNPROFOR was a classic example of the violation of the military dictum of unity of command and a lack of a clear mission.

By May 1995, the mission had been unable to bring about any lasting agreement or to end hostilities in Croatia or Bosnia-Herzegovina. Only in Macedonia have UNPROFOR efforts been successful, although the situation there was quiescent even before its arrival. While UNPROFOR was unable to bring peace and stability to the region, its presence undoubtedly slowed the fighting and lessened casualties. Its efforts have brought humanitarian relief to refugees and others. As of April 1995, an estimated 340,000 people had lost their lives and over 2 million had been made refugees.

UNPROFOR included over 40,000 personnel at its peak. In April 1995, it had 23,000 personnel and cost almost $2 billion a year. As of May 31,

---

5   Pan Africa News Agency report, "American Helicopters for Peacekeepers", February 12, 1996.

1995, 162 peacekeepers had been killed and over 1,400 wounded. The situation is so complex that several states that offered forces had their offers initially rejected. Nations that have contributed forces have on a number of occasions threatened to withdraw them. The ability of the force to accomplish its task was complicated by the unusual number of players on the scene.

NATO provided assistance in the form of humanitarian relief flights, primarily to Sarajevo. Regularly, however, these flights were suspended due to ground fire. The airlift force also engaged in air-drops of supplies to besieged areas. Although Provide Comfort was a NATO operation in support of the UN, over 20 countries have assisted in the effort. Since October 1992, NATO has provided AWACS coverage and, since April 1993, air combat patrols over the area to enforce the "no-fly" restrictions imposed over Bosnia-Herzegovina. In June 1993, NATO air forces were assigned Operation Deny Flight as an additional mission to provide air strikes in support of UNPROFOR.

The request procedure for such attacks was extremely complex, involving at least two major decision centers: the UN and NATO. In mid-1995, this process was changed. NATO became the sole authorizing agency. As a result, when the Bosnian Serb faction continued to ignore agreements in late July and August, 1995, their cease-fire violations were promptly met with air strikes. This became a major motive for them to come to the peace table that led to the Dayton Accords.

Both NATO and WEU were engaged in Operation Sharp Guard from 1991. This was primarily a naval force engaged in enforcing the embargoes placed on various participants in the war. In June 1993, this force was consolidated as Combined Task Force 440 for operational purposes. In addition, there are elements from the Organization for Security and Cooperation in Europe (OSCE) and the European Union, each conducting various missions in the area.

Typically, major powers involved in various aspects of the Balkan situation found it necessary to have their national forces operating independently in the area. This has taken two approaches. The more innocuous were typified by, but not restricted to, U.S. special operations forces engaged primarily in intelligence gathering from an island off the Croatian coast. The other was an equally clandestine approach involving several smaller powers that for various ethnic and cultural reasons were opposed to aspects of the embargoes. These groups smuggled arms and other supplies to various factions in the conflict.

With the formation of IFOR in January 1996, many of these command and control problems were solved. All forces came under NATO operational control, including those of non-NATO members. The force itself is larger and equipped to use decisive force to enforce the agreement. However, one of the objections to the operation is that instead of setting measurable goals, e.g., separation of forces and demobilizations, a specific time limit (one year) has been imposed. Delays on the part of the parties to the conflict were already in evidence within days after the establishment of IFOR. Generally, IFOR has been succesful. Its mandate was essentially extended in December 1996.

Perhaps the most important long-term outcome of the peacekeeping effort are the war crimes investigations and prosecutions. UN efforts have led to the first international war crimes investigations since World War II. These are not trials of the vanquished by the victors, but trials by an independent authority against particular individuals. The trials will have only a marginal effect in the current crisis. They are, however, precedent-setting and may bring the rule of law and individual responsibility more explicitly into the international realm. The tribunal has been expanded to include investigations of crime against humanity committed in Rwanda.

If Bosnia and Somalia teach any lesson for the institutionalization of peacekeeping, it is that there is a substantial difference between peacekeeping and peacemaking. Peacekeeping implies that the parties to the conflict have accepted the intervention of a third force. Peacemaking, however, occurs when one or more of the parties to the conflict have not agreed to a third-party intervention. The third-party operation then becomes one of peacemaking. This corresponds to the second of our analytical scenarios wherein the UN endeavors to break up a fight between mid-sized powers. However, attempting to separate combatants that are engaged in fighting is extremely dangerous, as any rookie policeman knows. There must be sufficient force and will to separate the parties, despite the substantial risk to the peacemaker.

In the case of the former Yugoslavia, like Somalia, there were a number of "normal" military and diplomatic practices that failed to be followed in UN participation in peacemaking. Unity of command[6], crucial

---

6   Command is used here in its generic sense, rather than the technical sense employed by the military and lawyers. For example, U.S. law forbids the placing of American forces under foreign command. They can, however, be

to the successful accomplishment of military missions and tasks, was absent. Goals and objectives, which must be clear, concise, and measurable, were missing.[7] All participants in the operation must fully understand and agree to its objectives; they were not. As a corollary, missions and tasks must be assigned to elements that do have the skills, training, and equipment to accomplish the goal; skills were lacking.

At the diplomatic level, bluffing is always a dangerous tactic. If ultimatums are to be issued to parties, the "or else" part must be clearly defined. Further, there must be prior agreement among the peacemakers that the "or else" action will be executed promptly should a party not comply with the ultimatum. An unsuccessful ultimatum destroys the credibility of the peacemakers.

Institutional Issues

This review of selected cases of recent United Nations peacekeeping suggests how far along in its institutional development the UN has come since its founding. After its failure at collective security in the Korean War, the General Assembly's Uniting for Peace Resolution salvaged and redefined its peacekeeping mission. It has refined its peacekeeping efforts and, with the end of the Cold War, broadened the participation of nations in this work. Its early involvement in nation building has expanded, with variable success. Peacemaking and election monitoring have augmented and complicated the nation building efforts. Its use of the military resources of its members has grown and involves it increasingly in on-the-ground disarmament and arms control arrangements. It is this latter activity that confirms the intimate connection between contemporary arms control and peacekeeping functions. Despite all this development and accomplishment, however, a number of basic problems remain.

The basic peacekeeping contract is Chapter VII of the United Nations Charter. While the words continue to read as a collective security mandate,

---

placed under foreign "operational control". It is in this latter sense that we use the term, i.e., "who's in charge?"

7   There must be a way of knowing when a specific goal has been achieved. If the goal is to re-open the Sarajevo airport, it has been achieved when all positions from which artillery and air defense fire that can affect airport operations have been occupied. The mission is 50 percent there when half of them have been occupied.

the practicalities of international politics and history have converted them into a set of peacekeeping guidelines. Words and guidelines, however, have raised still unresolved issues of implementation.

Who authorizes? Chapter VII declares that the Security Council shall "determine" when a threat to the peace warrants action by the United Nations. The 1950 Uniting for Peace Resolution allows the General Assembly to assume that responsibility when the Security Council does not. Under Article 99, the secretary-general may not only bring to the attention of either or both bodies any threat to the peace, but may, upon his own initiative, investigate, observe, report, and offer his good offices as initial peacekeeping measures in any crisis.

The Charter also welcomes regional and local peacekeeping interventions. This has been variously interpreted as including actions by regional organizations, such as NATO or the Arab League, as well as the good offices of major powers in whose sphere of influence the conflict may occur, as in the case of the Soviet Union's assistance to India and Pakistan at Tashkent in 1966. It may also include the good offices of a neutral broker with little of no direct interest in the area, such as Norway's role in bringing about agreement between Israel and the Palestine Liberation Organization (PLO) in 1993.[8]

The Organization for Security and Cooperation in Europe Missions[9] have included six active missions as of mid-1994 in Macedonia, Georgia, Estonia, Moldova, Latvia, and Tajikistan. A second regional effort has been the Multinational Force and Observers (MFO), established in 1981 after the signing of a peace treaty between Israel and Egypt. Its task is to monitor force-level compliance and ensure free navigation of the Straits of Tiran.

Perhaps the oldest peacekeeping mission still in existence was formed in 1953 to monitor the cease-fire at the end of the Korean War: the Neutral Nations Supervisory Commission for Korea (NNSC). The European Community (Union) Monitor Mission (ECMM) was established jointly by the then CSCE and European Community (now European Union) in July

---

8   Articles 52-54 of Chapter VIII of the UN Charter encourages peacekeeping by regional associations. Regional arrangements will presumably initiate efforts at conflict resolution before referring them to the UN. Increasingly, regional organizations have been taking up responsiblity for peacekeeping.

9   This used to be the Conference on Security and Cooperation in Europe (CSCE).

1991. It was originally created to monitor the withdrawal of forces of former Yugoslavia from the newly created Republic of Slovenia. When that task was successfully accomplished, the ECMM role was modified to accomplish a similar task in Bosnia and Croatia. The Temporary International Presence in Hebron was a unique operation established in April 1994 following the murder of about 40 Palestinian worshipers in the mosque at the Tomb of Abraham by an Israeli settler. Its mission was to patrol the city of Hebron and to report possible human rights violations. It withdrew in July 1994.

This many potential sources of peacekeeping intervention in international conflicts is in marked contrast to the situation prior to the Congress of Vienna in 1815. Today, it is difficult to conceive of a serious conflict that could escape notice, fail to receive prompt attention, or avoid being subjected to the conciliatory pressures of the international community. In a profoundly important way, so many peacekeepers and peacemakers are reassuring to competing national leaders who must occasionally engage in brinkmanship. The high probability of such intervention was part of the Israeli military calculation when it embarked upon a preemptive strike in 1967. Similarly, it must have been a factor in the Egyptian planning in 1973. Each side could be positive that no war between them would be allowed to last longer than a matter of days.

There is some dispute over which of these many institutional agencies has the prime prerogative and responsibility for peacekeeping. In this debate, the United States has been a loose constructionist in its interpretation of Chapter VII. The American premise is that any agency and anybody who can bring a military engagement to an end should have the right to do so by peaceful means. It was the United States that sponsored the Uniting for Peace Resolution that has become the basis for the enlargement of the General Assembly's involvement in peacekeeping operations. The United States has also supported several plans for broadening and regularizing the military management responsibilities of the Secretary-General.

On the other hand, the former Soviet Union was a strict constructionist regarding Chapter VII. According to the Soviet view, the Charter placed responsibility for collective security with the Security Council, and that is where it should be exercised. Russia continues to espouse this position in general terms, but does make some exceptions. In this connection, the former Soviet Union has from time to time recommended full activation of the Military Staff Committee and the assignment of serious functions to it.

Implicit in the Soviet position, of course, was the special veto prerogative that it could have exercised as a permanent member of the Council. With the end of the Cold War, however, the superpowers and others are cooperating to carry out the United Nations peacekeeping functions.

Those favoring a large peacekeeping role for the General Assembly rest their case upon several propositions. Their first argument usually is that there can be no veto power on the question of a breach of or threat to the peace. A military crisis is a military crisis. Those who refuse to face up to it must be considered a party to it. Modern wars may lead too directly and too readily to the ultimate nuclear catastrophe. There is no room for naysayers. Second, the General Assembly is populated by middle and smaller powers. These are the nations most likely to profit from a resolution of serious conflicts. They are also most likely to participate in peacekeeping missions. Third, the members of the General Assembly tend to have an easier and more varied relationship with the Secretary-General, who has acquired most of the management responsibilities for peacekeeping missions. Fourth, there could be those serious confrontations between the major powers that could be headed off only with the authority of the full membership of the international community. The General Assembly is where that community is best mobilized for such a grave task.

It should not be forgotten that a major source of authority for a peacekeeping mission comes from the parties in conflict themselves. Two features of contemporary peacekeeping are that the consent of the parties is essential and that the peacekeeping mission remains in the field only so long as that consent continues. Yet the experience with UNEF-I in 1967 raised serious doubt about the propriety of unilateral actions by a host government. A demand for withdrawal of a peacekeeping mission should, it is contended, be immediately referred to the organ that authorized the mission in the first place, that is, the Security Council or the General Assembly. We have also witnessed, in Lebanon, Bosnia, and Somalia, the extreme difficulties that face any such force, regardless of size or need, when one or more parties to the conflict do not accept the peacekeeping force's role. The experience of the Multinational Force in Lebanon in 1982 and 1983, along with Somalia more recently, demonstrates the type of disasters that can occur when the peacekeeping force begins to side with one party or the other, or is perceived as doing so.

When may an authorization be made? This question addresses the issues of procedure and immediacy of response. The usual course has been for a party to complain to the Security Council. If the Security Council fails to respond, the matter may be taken to the General Assembly under the Uniting for Peace Resolution. If a regional organization or major power is interested in interceding in the conflict, this must be taken into account. If a crisis is imminent and time is of the essence, the Secretary-General may put it on the agenda in the absence of any other complainant.

The facts of the case, usually difficult to ascertain in the heat of an international confrontation, must be put together authoritatively and objectively as a basis for the judgment to send or not to send a peacekeeping force. These and other procedural requirements take time, staff, and effort, all of which may be in very short supply at the moment of crisis. A new procedure seems to be evolving in the post-Cold War era. This involves a major power or regional association taking immediate action and then turning over responsibility to the United Nations. This, in fact, is what has occurred, for example, in Somalia (United States), Rwanda (France), and Haiti (United States).

The problem of timing is perhaps the most significant. Since surprise attacks are so much a feature of military advantage, it is rare for a party to announce an intended military action: one such rare case was the invasion of Vietnam in 1979 by the People's Republic of China "to teach the former a lesson". However, such surprise attacks are usually only tactical in nature, the result of tensions that have been building for a period of time. Furthermore, international wars are becoming more and more rare. The norm is *intra*nation conflicts that have the potential to implicate other nations. In either case, speed of response and timing of an intervention may make all the difference in the outbreak and course of a military conflict. Elaborate and prolonged institutional procedures of decision making are hardly effective responses.

The need for an immediate response capability raises a number of extremely difficult issues. Should United Nations peacekeeping missions consist of standing military forces instead of the standby forces now employed? Should an executive such as the Secretary-General be allowed, as is the American president, for example, to order peacekeeping forces into action at a moment's notice? Should the United Nations plan ahead for the contingency as tensions heighten? Is the solution that of another actor moving quickly and then turning the action over to the UN, as noted in the previous paragraph? The issues have generated several proposals and much debate.

In 1948, the first Secretary-General, Trygve Lie, proposed the formation of a United Nations Guard. He conceived of the Guard as a standing unit of the secretariat, available for such operational duties as protecting United Nations property and personnel, patrolling cease-fire zones, or supervising elections. He proposed an initial force of only 800 international volunteers, 300 of whom would be permanently located at UN headquarters. He anticipated that the guard might eventually number between 1,000 to 5,000 men. He denied that the guard would be a substitute for the enforcement army that the Military Staff Committee was presumably responsible for creating. The Lie plan found absolutely no support. The major powers had already reached an unspoken consensus against standing forces for the United Nations.

In 1958, Secretary-General Hammarskjold prepared a Summary Study of the UNEF-I experience. It was a thorough-going statement of all of the requirements and issues associated with the development of a peacekeeping force that "could be activated on short notice in future emergencies".[10] The Summary Study and its recommendations were never approved. The then Soviet Union distrusted any such plan; other nations were concerned about the financial burdens; the United States wanted to remain free to send in the Marines unilaterally, and so on. Instead, Hammarskjold began to expand the secretariat's Field Operations Service section, created by Lie in 1949. This was the staff that would increasingly absorb the civilian administrative support of peacekeeping missions. Hammarskjold also gave renewed attention to the preparation of standby agreements with a substantial number of nations. If enough nations were willing to keep peacekeeping units in full preparedness for immediate assignment in a crisis, such standby units could possibly do what was necessary for the problem of immediacy of response.

Subsequently, a UN Department of Peacekeeping Operations (DPKO) was established. It underwent a major reorganization in 1993 in which its military staff was reinforced. It now consists of two offices; Planning and Support, and Operations. It is staffed by over 100 military officers as well as civilians. The Situation Center has been expanded and moved to the main Secretariat building in New York. This permits much closer coordination with the departments of the UN dealing with political and humanitarian affairs. In a departure from past practice, contingency

---

10   UN General Assembly, *Official Records*, 12th sess., Sup. IA (1957). The full Hammarskjold document is *United Nations Emergency Force: Summary Study of the Experience Derived from the Establishment and Operation of the Force*, UN Doc. A/3943, October 9, 1958.

planning is now an accepted function and is staffed by permanent professional personnel who deal with generic planning as well as specific operations. It has also recognized the need to collect information on such matters as terrain, climate, communications, personalities, and military forces.

A special task force on standby forces has concluded its work and the Secretary-General has asked members to advise the DPKO of the status and availability of forces to participate in peacekeeping operations. Almost fifty states had identified such forces by 1994, totalling about 70,000 personnel with their attendant equipment. Each state, however, has agreed with the caveat that commitment of its forces will be on a case-by-case basis, with the right of refusal. This should go far in alleviating difficulties experienced in obtaining technical and specialist units at an early stage.

The basic lessons of doctrine have also been established. These elements, such as impartiality, openly conducted operations, consent, respect for persons and property, freedom of movement, and many others that engender trust, are being incorporated not only into national training programs, but also those of some regional organizations such as NATO.

This is not to imply that all is peace and harmony in the area of authorization; there are significant differences that have yet to be resolved. What is more important is the degree of agreement and movement toward a common approach.

Who may participate? It was the obvious assumption of the authors of the United Nations Charter that the members of the Security Council, particularly the permanent members, would provide the forces necessary to punish an aggressor or maintain the peace. According to Chapter VII, other nations would be invited to help. The Cold War and the Korean War effectively set aside that assumption. Instead, peacekeeping missions authorized by the Security Council or the General Assembly came to be manned by troops volunteered by a slowly expanding company of nations. At first, the Nordic powers - Sweden, Norway, Denmark, and Finland - were the principal providers. Equipment, supplies, and finances came chiefly from the United States and the United Kingdom. Canada, the Netherlands, Austria, Iran, New Zealand, Italy, and others began to develop special peacekeeping units during the 1960s. These nations made standby agreements with the secretary-general and have been called to duty over the years. To this list, particularly in the 1980s and 1990s, have been added a host of nations from all corners of the globe.

In more recent years, there has been concern that participation in peacekeeping missions be widely shared among the five regions of the world. This was explicitly sought in the composition of UNEF-II, which included a member of the then Communist bloc. Calling up peacekeeping units from all parts of the world has the distinct symbolic purpose of giving such forces an aura of universality and worldwide support. Recruitment from such dispersed sources also tends to spread the opportunities for gaining peacekeeping experience and insights. Further, participation tends to reinforce middle and small power commitment to the United Nations generally.

The question of participation by the permanent members of the Security Council continues to be a touchy one. Initially, distrust between the superpowers ran so deep that each side was certain the other would become a spoiler in any peacekeeping mission if given the opportunity to introduce its own troops. With occupied Eastern Europe and Berlin in mind, the West was particularly sensitive to Soviet reluctance to remove its military forces once they have set foot in a nation. However, during the debate over Resolution 340 of October 1973, in which UNEF-II was established, several of the permanent members indicated a desire to participate in future peacekeeping missions.

As the prospects for such participation increase over the years, United Nations peacekeeping missions will assume many of the characteristics of military alliances in which commanders and troops from different cultures and languages must learn how to work together, employ standardized equipment, and coordinate their implementation of specific missions. Such a development, particularly as it tends to involve substantial military cooperation between the superpowers, would be a major step toward the globalization of world military institutions. It is our assumption that this trend is analogous to the centralization of military institutions observed within nations.[11]

For some time to come, however, middle-sized nations are likely to provide most of the peacekeeping forces. The motivations are several and reasonable. Middle-sized nations are likely to prefer having international disputes resolved by mediation rather than by military might. Their contributed troops will have an opportunity to receive training and skills in the use of specialized equipment provided by the superpowers. The costs

11   Ralph M. Goldman, *From Warfare to Party Politics* (Syracuse: Syracuse University Press, 1990).

of their national contingents are reimbursed by the United Nations, resulting in financial savings. Participation in peacekeeping missions lends prestige and influence in both the particular crisis and in world affairs generally. Finally, such participation nurtures the image of nonalignment and a strong commitment to peace, always popular in their own constituencies.

What is to be contributed? This question refers to numbers of troops, kinds and amounts of pertinent equipment, supplies and other logistical support, and financial resources. Manpower contributions have varied widely, ranging from individual officers with special skills to one or more battalions. The special nature of peacekeeping missions increasingly calls for special training. Soldiers ordinarily trained to kill must be taught how to return fire only in self-defense, and even then, selectively. Mediating and pacifying skills are particularly appropriate in many on-site situations. The gathering of evidence in investigatory or observational missions must be learned. Skills in intelligence work, particularly with respect to modern sophisticated early warning systems, is necessary. Most difficult of all is the need to function as a kind of sitting duck for unhappy extremists eager to remove peacekeepers who stand between them and their chosen enemy.

If this assessment is valid, then what is being described is not a military force, but a police force. This is coming to be recognized more and more as increasing numbers of civil police officers are detailed to peacekeeping forces. This is also the problem confronting the U.S. Department of Defense as it prepares its personnel for the 21st century.

The provision of equipment and supplies for peacekeeping missions has become a high-cost item. The United States has absorbed the greatest share of this burden not only because of its desire to have missions succeed, but also as part of its role as the world's principal arms supplier. The United Kingdom has been the second principal supplier. But equipment and supplies require elaborate logistical arrangements. In this area, the secretariat has developed a substantial staff and body of experience with respect to acquisition, storage, delivery, and replacement of the material needed by its peacekeeping missions. Here again is the overlap between arms control and peacekeeping.

Who pays? This is the unpleasant question raised most stubbornly at the conclusion of the UN operation in the Congo. Should the financial resources for peacekeeping be drawn from the regularly assessed funds of the United Nations, or should reliance be placed upon either a special scale of assessment or voluntary contributions? Those who resist the development of a truly international peacekeeping force with substantial autonomy will resist including peacekeeping among the regular costs of the United Nations. Mandatory financial support for missions would remove the leverage of those wishing to discourage such missions. Also, the universal experience with military expenditures is that they tend to become one of the largest items in a governmental budget. This degree of financial support is not yet forthcoming for the United Nations.

There is already serious objection to the United Nations budget, even though the amount seems a pittance given the scope of the United Nations' functions. Most of these objections, however, are based on the practical factors of the proportion in which the costs are allocated and in the perceived managerial ineffectiveness of the secretariat in spending the funds. A major factor that impacts heavily on both regular funding and funding for peacekeeping operations is the domestic politics of the nations involved.

The consensus seems to be leaning in the direction of employing all options: regular assessment, special assessment, and voluntary contributions. The important goal is to get the peacekeeping job done. There are those who look forward to the time when the United Nations, like any public agency, will have regular and independent sources of income, for example, royalties from ocean mining operations. However, that seems far in the future.

Once beyond the questions of financial contributions, there are other fiscal issues to be resolved. Pay scales for military personnel from different nations vary. The question of standardizing these scales for peacekeeping missions continues to be debated. Special training costs for standby units are a matter of concern. A wider sharing of the costs of equipment and supplies is likely to become a troublesome issue as the United States reduces its contribution.

Collections remain a problem. As of May 31, 1995, the United Nations had 64,273 soldiers from over 60 countries serving in various peacekeeping operations. The UN was in arrears to these nations more than $800 million. Additionally, it owes various vendors and suppliers about $375 million, which also remains unpaid. At the same time, the UN is owed over $2.8 billion. The five major debtors to the UN are the United States ($1.2 billion), Russia ($599 million), Ukraine ($217 million), South Africa ($114 million), and France ($81 million).

Who shall have operational control of missions? The Charter presumably assigns this duty to the Military Staff Committee, but history has given it to the Secretary-General. This has been a mixed blessing. The

Secretary-General has been unable, until the late 1980s, to gather a permanent staff of military advisers; most of the arrangements have been, and still remain, ad hoc. Administrative support services have been absorbed in the Field Operations Service within the secretariat. These are headquarters issues. In the field, peacekeeping missions face a more difficult real world. Many field commanders have been permitted substantial autonomy and have exercised it with consummate skill and excellent results. Their story, when fully told and appreciated, may emerge as the principal glory of United Nations peacekeeping. Equally, but unfortunately, better known are several spectacular failures of command.

What goals for peacekeeping? Perhaps the most fundamental question relates to the functions to be served by the peacekeeping activities of the United Nations or, for that matter, regional and other peacekeepers. Several functions come to mind, the most important of which is the promotion of a system of institutionalized trust in world affairs.

One elementary function of peacekeeping of even the mildest sort is its inherent collective disapproval of and resistance to war and other military actions as approaches to international conflict. This disapproval is usually manifest in (a) Security Council or General Assembly decisions to view the particular conflict as a threat to the general peace, (b) similar decisions to investigate such conflicts and offer third-party good offices toward their resolution, (c) United Nations willingness to organize and pay for costly peacekeeping missions, and (d) sustained United Nations attention to the conflict until it does reach some degree of resolution. In the short term, such collective disapproval may seem a weak and ineffectual way of confronting serious conflicts. In the long term, however, consistent, firm, and formal world disapproval of military methods of conflict is likely to contribute significant negative reinforcement of warlike behavior. There are those optimists who believe that such constraints are already beginning to take effect.

A second function of peacekeeping has been to hasten the termination of military hostilities in particular cases. Cease-fires and truces are essential steps in moving adversaries from the battlefield to the conference table. The implementation of cease-fires and truces requires monitoring by a neutral and trusted peacekeeper. Clearly, conflict resolution is easier to accomplish when words and negotiations replace weapons and violence.

A third function is to strengthen, incrementally, the collective security capabilities of the United Nations. As we have seen, it is already the case that successful UN peacekeeping missions have increased the confidence of nations in this United Nations role and have prompted many countries to assume some degree of participation in such missions. Because the United Nations so predictably and promptly expresses a peacekeeping interest in every international, and, increasingly, in intranation conflict, it now appears that some national leaders are willing to risk military engagement on the assumption that UN peacekeeping intervention will keep the engagement brief.

A fourth and perhaps most important function of peacekeeping is the promotion of institutionalized trust in world affairs. As we have seen in an earlier chapter, institutionalized trust requires (a) predictable behavior that (b) produces positive consequences for the transactor in an exchange. Well-established and assertive third-party peacekeeping interventions by the United Nations or regional organizations such as the European Union tend to encourage predictable behavior by the adversaries in a number of ways. When a neutral third party mounts public pressure on both adversaries to negotiate rather than battle, it becomes difficult for the adversaries to refuse; most adversaries are reluctant to be identified as the one who prefers bloodshed. Most adversaries are likely to want a cease-fire in order to preserve their military resources for another day. Finally, an adversary can respond favorably to the peacemaking good offices of a neutral third party without loss of "face" or indication of weakness before the enemy.

As the United Nations and other supranational organizations persist in providing regular and reliable peacekeeping efforts and as the political habits of responding positively to such peacekeeping interventions become established, the predictability of international conflict scenarios, from military engagement to negotiating table, will increase and strengthen the structure of international institutionalized trust. Even such setbacks as Somalia and Bosnia may have peripheral positive effects, although it may not be readily apparent; they are valuable, albeit expensive, learning experiences for all the parties involved.

Institutionalized trust also requires that political transactions produce positive consequences for the embattled adversary parties. Successful peacekeeping can promote the probability of such positive outcomes by making it easier and cheaper for the adversaries to negotiate the substantive issues that led to their war making. The attention of the world is likely to remain fixed on the grievances and issues until they are to some extent resolved. The formal and informal influence of outside parties is likely to encourage moderation and reasonableness in demands. The very process of negotiation improves the prospect that each side will come away from the conflict with "half a loaf", that is, something rather than nothing or everything. The more successive profitable transactions of this type, the more enduring is likely to be the trust that competing elites extend to each other and the greater their confidence in the peacemaking-peacekeeping institutions that facilitated the resolution of their disagreements.

This brief survey of United Nations peacekeeping summarizes not only some of the major examples of that experience and some of the broad issues raised in connection with its future development, it also reveals the large extent to which a great many nations and agencies have become involved in this process. Past, present, and future arrangements for peacekeeping are the continuing concern of the Security Council, the General Assembly, and the Secretary-General, not to mention the Committee of 33, regional organizations, and a large number of non-governmental organizations (NGOs) promotive of a stronger United Nations. Perhaps the most immediate, yet least visible, consequence of all this activity and development is the growth in mutual trust among world leaders that flows from such efforts. In a sense, the nations that peacekeep together are collectively more secure together. The pathway of peacekeeping, as currently practiced, may well be a direct route back to collective security.

10 Types and Functions of Arms Control Treaties

The quantity and quality of public discussion, official negotiations, and international treaties dealing with arms control, global security, and international peacekeeping since the end of World War II have been unprecedented in human history. This degree of international communication has undoubtedly been motivated by the visibility of the world's elites, the technological ease with which communication can be carried on, and The Bomb and the shared fear it has generated. What has all this activity accomplished in building political institutions that can provide security services sufficient for all to feel safe? What have the treaties and agreements provided as building blocks of systems of institutionalized trust among the world's elites?

Political institutions grow as a consequence of rules incorporated into enduring agreements about how political roles and relationships are to be formally organized, what uniform patterns of political conduct are to be expected of participants, and what ratio between conflict and consensus is to be maintained in promoting stability. When the recurrent actions and events of a community attain a high degree of formality, uniformity, and stability, these actions and events are said to be institutionalized. Bureaucratic, judicial, party, commercial, family, religious, and other human institutions evolve in the same way, by uniform, hence predictable, behavioral responses to recurrent social or political situations.

Political institutions promote trustworthy conduct and attitudes of trust when they (a) help make the conduct of members and participants predictable and (b) facilitate transactions among members from which they derive positive consequences, that is, satisfactions and a "sense of profit". In the economic realm, for example, we have used the example of mortgage loans and similar commercial transactions. How, then, have the arms control treaties and agreements that have accumulated since the end of World War II contributed to the development of international institutions promoting trust among leaders? What has been the content of these treaties and agreements? What aspects of relationship and conduct have been formalized, made uniform, and stabilized? Are the outcomes of these arms

265

control treaties and agreements substantial enough to construct systems of international trust and security?

Examination of the arms control treaties and agreements of the past half century reveals a two-tier structure, as alluded to earlier: nuclear and conventional. At the nuclear tier, with its awesome risks of mass annihilation, errors in strategic judgment, theft, and proliferation, motivation to cooperate has been strong and treaties numerous. At the conventional tier, progress has been much slower and are the most recent challenge for policy makers.

Preventive Treaties

One series of treaties, often referred to as nonarmament treaties, have been preventive in character. Their object has been to prevent arms competition where none has yet taken place, but seems imminent. Although never agreed upon, the Baruch Plan (June 1946) was the earliest attempt at prevention. The nonarmament treaties include the Antarctic Treaty (signed December 1, 1959), the Outer Space Treaty (January 27, 1967), the Latin American Nuclear-Free Zone Treaty (February 14, 1967), Seabed Arms Control Treaty (February 11, 1971), and the Environmental Modification Treaty (May 18, 1977). Later treaties have dealt primarily with arms limitations, reductions, and safeguards. Of current interest along these same lines are discussions regarding the establishment of nuclear-free zones in the Indian Ocean region, the Middle East, and Africa. These negotiations continue in hit-or-miss fashion, one of the most recent, in 1994, being an offer by Pakistan to declare South Asia a nuclear-free zone.

The *Baruch Plan*, presented by the United States to the United Nations Atomic Energy Commission, offered to cease the manufacture of atomic bombs, destroy those then in existence, and establish an international agency to which all information pertaining to the production of nuclear energy could be given. All this was to be implemented as soon as a reliable system of inspection and control could be established to apprehend and punish violators. In other words, the United States, fully aware of the unprecedented nature of the weapon it had created, was willing to forgo its nuclear monopoly and move toward international collective controls. Since the United States monopoly was likely to be short term, rational self-interested action, as would be an inclination to confess in the Prisoners' Dilemma model, would unquestionably lead to a costly nuclear arms race. The logical escape from the dilemma seemed to be by way of some system of international cooperation and control, together with procedures of inspection that would help build a system of communication and institutionalized trust.

The Soviet Union rejected the Baruch Plan, viewing it as a potential invasion of Soviet sovereignty, a plot against Soviet economic development, and a threat to Soviet security. What the Soviet representatives did not say was that Stalin was intent upon producing a Russian atomic bomb, an effort well along even as the Baruch Plan was debated in New York. In retrospect, one may speculate what the military state of the world might now be if the Baruch Plan had been adopted and an institution for shared control of atomic energy created in 1946. One may also speculate if and how current world elites could find their way back to the system envisaged by the Baruch Plan as a reasonable approach to collective control over nuclear arms and nuclear energy. Some, albeit limited, moves have been made in this direction in the wake of the end of the Cold War. The open-ended extension of the Non-Proliferation Treaty in May 1995 and the enhancement of the International Atomic Energy Agency can be interpreted to be moves in this direction.

By the early 1950s, some fifteen nations had explored the Antarctic continent. Several had registered claims of sovereignty over some of its areas. Most of the activity in Antarctica was scientific in character, reinforced by the collaborations taking place during the International Geophysical Year of 1957-1958. In May 1958, the United States proposed a conference aimed at keeping Antarctica international and demilitarized. The treaty written by the ensuing conference prohibits military bases, fortifications, weapons, tests, maneuvers, and similar activities on that continent. It also prohibits nuclear explosions or the deposit of nuclear wastes. However, all parties may use Antarctica for peaceful purposes, have free access to all parts of the continent at any time, and may freely inspect any installations on it. Disputes may be referred to the International Court of Justice. Agreement has been so effective in this area that it was not uncommon for teams from the then superpowers to "overwinter" at each others bases, even at the height of the Cold War.

Drawn up with a minimum of fanfare, the *Antarctic Treaty* is loaded with precedents of a confidence-building nature: military and scientific cooperation instead of competition; defined demilitarized territory; free access and open inspection of the facilities of all nations; an institution for dealing with disputes. As the first postwar arms control agreement, the Antarctic Treaty offered a hopeful sign despite the view of some that it dealt with a continent that was remote, barren, and militarily uninteresting. Quite the contrary. Relevant technologies are reducing the distance to Antarctica, discovering its rich resources, and increasing its military potential. The treaty was a positive diplomatic achievement and a model and stimulus for subsequent negotiating efforts.

In October 1957, the Soviet Union launched Sputnik, the first earth-orbiting satellite. The United States' Explorer I satellite followed in January 1958. Shortly after becoming president, John F. Kennedy called for a space program that would land American astronauts on the moon, a goal accomplished by the Apollo program in 1969. The decade of the 1960s witnessed a crescendo of manned satellites orbiting the earth. It also raised qualms about the prospect that nuclear-armed satellites might be sent aloft or stationed on the moon. In September 1960, President Eisenhower, in an address before the General Assembly of the United Nations, recommended that the demilitarized-zone approach of the Antarctic Treaty be applied to outer space and celestial bodies. Prolonged negotiations eventually led to the *Outer Space Treaty* of 1967.

The treaty signatories agreed not to place in orbit around the earth, install on the moon or any other celestial body, or otherwise station in outer space nuclear or any other weapons of mass destruction. The agreement limited the use of the moon and other celestial bodies to peaceful purposes only, calling for international cooperation in space exploration and, in a precedent-setting provision in Article VII, holds launching states "internationally liable for damage" to states or persons caused by objects launched into space. The treaty has not only prevented an arms race in space, but has led to numerous Soviet (and now Russian)-American scientific collaborations in space experiments. With the expansion of technology, joint space ventures among any number of countries has become almost commonplace.

Also signed in 1967 was the *Treaty of Tlatelolco* (Mexico) prohibiting nuclear weapons in Latin America. The Cuban missile crisis of 1962 had pointedly reminded the leaders of Latin America of the risks of involvement in the nuclear arms race and led many of them to propose an agreement to make Latin America a nuclear-free zone along the lines of the nonarmament treaties. The treaty requires the contracting parties to refrain from receiving, producing, testing, or otherwise using nuclear weapons in their respective territories. Nuclear materials and facilities are to be devoted only to peaceful purposes. The contracting parties also agree to follow IAEA safeguard procedures and to cooperate with the verification procedures of OPANAL, the treaty's newly established Agency for the Prohibition of Nuclear Weapons in Latin America. Protocol I to the treaty requires signatory states outside the nuclear-free zone to abide by the treaty's provisions. Protocol II requires signatory nuclear-weapons states to respect the denuclearized status of the zone and to avoid contributing to violations of the pact. Significantly, there are some signatories to this pact, e.g., Brazil, that have not signed the more general Nuclear Non-Proliferation Treaty.

Although enhancing the security of the United States and discouraging the proliferation of nuclear weapons, this treaty presented problems for the United States that led to a later statement of understanding. This statement became part of the U.S. Senate's instrument of ratification in 1971. With Cuba not a party, the United States affirmed that nonparties within the zone would not be protected by the treaty provisions. With Brazil actively interested in nuclear energy at the time, America insisted that the explosion of any nuclear device should be prohibited. As a voluntary constraint upon itself, the United States agreed to detonate its own nuclear devices only under appropriate international arrangements according to the then recently signed (1968) Nuclear Non-Proliferation Treaty.

Oceanographic developments during the 1960s opened the possibility that the ocean floor could be used to launch nuclear and other weapons of mass destruction. Verification of such weapons emplacements was technically difficult. The concept of the seas as the common heritage of mankind was also gaining popularity at this time. Disputes over the extent (12 miles, 200 miles, and so on) of a nation's territorial waters were becoming increasingly intense. There was, nonetheless, international consensus that the question of peaceful uses of the oceans and seas was urgent. The General Assembly appointed a committee to study the issue. The problem was also referred to the Eighteen-Nation Disarmament Committee. Early in 1969, the Soviet Union and the United States both presented draft treaties that, by the end of the year, had become a joint draft treaty. The definition of territorial waters and the procedures for verification were the principal subjects of discussion for the next two years. By February 11, 1971, however, the *Seabed Arms Control Treaty* was written and open for signature.

The treaty prohibits contracting parties from emplacing nuclear and other weapons of mass destruction on the seabed and the ocean floor beyond a twelve-mile coastal zone. Both unilateral and international verification procedures are permitted. A five year review conference was called for and subsequently held in June 1977.

The *Environmental Modification Treaty* of 1978 varies slightly from the preceding treaties, but is closely akin to the Seabed Arms Control Treaty. It deals both with preventing armaments in an area (the environment) as well as a category of potential weapons. Modifying the climate for use as a military weapon had received little practical attention. Potentially, such weapons could be substantially more devastating than nuclear, biological, or chemical weapons. In July 1972, the United States announced that it would not develop, and if developed elsewhere, would not employ techniques that modified the climate for military purposes. In 1973, the United States called for an international treaty that would prevent the development and employment of these techniques. Under the leadership of President Nixon and General Secretary Brezhnev, the two superpowers presented a joint draft treaty to the United Nations Conference on Disarmament in August 1975. On December 10, 1976, the United Nations General Assembly, after debate, voted 96 to 8, with 30 abstentions, to have the Secretary-General open the convention for signature and ratification. This treaty is unique in that it bans a category of weapons before anyone had started to develop them.

In contrast to the above preventive treaties, the spreading militarization of the Indian Ocean region, the Middle East, and Africa reflected continuing contests for national and regional power. Further, it was fairly evident, but never acknowledged, that at least one nation in each of these regions already had a nuclear weapon capability: India in the Indian Ocean area, Israel in the Middle East, and South Africa in Africa. However, South Africa has unilaterally disposed of its weapons, declared itself a non-nuclear state, and acceded to the NPT.

Perhaps even more important than the preventive features of these nonarmament treaties is their promotion of cooperation in several aspects of international security. Exploration and scientific research have been the principal beneficiaries in the Antarctic and Outer Space treaties. The Seabed Treaty undoubtedly facilitated the conferences that developed a law-of-the-seas treaty.

In sum, the nonarmament treaties have specified important areas of collective security interest and set in place significant expectations and arrangements in the structure of institutionalized trust. The fact that these treaties are multilateral and relatively undramatic, in contrast, for example, to the START treaties, is itself a great assurance that they will endure and provide the basis for more comprehensive arrangements.

Duopoly-Maintaining Treaties

In industry or commerce, a duopoly exists when the market is dominated by two sellers, often acting in collusion to set prices, allocate production, and control distribution. This exercise of economic power is not only profitable, but also allows a controllable competition that reduces the probability of devastating surprises, overwhelming marketing victories, or serious challenges by lesser sellers. These same conditions characterized the nuclear duopoly maintained by the United States and the former Soviet Union.

The nuclear duopolists were, of course, interested in military might rather than profit, global political prestige rather than price setting. They were surely competitive, but seeking to be so in a controlled fashion, as exemplified by the SALT treaties. They were deeply concerned about the production and distribution of nuclear weapons, and this is manifest in the test ban and nonproliferation treaties. With the actual reduction, in an unprecedented, almost wholesale manner, under the START treaties and agreements, the United States and Russia continue to manage competition, but in a new and encouraging way. They represent a duopoly of reduction that hopefully will be emulated by others. However, they both continue to maintain control of "market share".

In the absence of a Baruch Plan system of international controls, is the Soviet (Russian)-American nuclear duopoly a form of institutionalized trust that facilitates communication about a particularly dangerous weapons system and achieves arms limitations that would otherwise have been impossible? As prolonged and difficult as the SALT and START talks were, it is argued, they would have been even more so if a larger number of nations had been involved.

While the British have now joined the superpowers in the negotiations for a Comprehensive Test Ban Treaty, this opens the duopolistic process only slightly. The participation of the French and the Chinese, the two other established nuclear weapon powers, in negotiations to maintain control over the nuclear tier of the arms race, has been problematical; each has preferred to go its own way in building a nuclear stockpile, although the French have continued to join the others, except China, in renewing their pledge annually not to test weapons. In March 1996, after completing a series of tests in the Pacific, the French have announced substantial reductions in their nuclear force and have renounced further testing. China remains the odd man out, ironically testing a nuclear device the day after it acceded to an extension of the NPT.

As though keeping the lid on nuclear weaponry among the five nuclear-weapon states were not difficult enough, there are some ten other nations ready and eager to detonate nuclear weapons and join the prestigious and exclusive nuclear club. There are a much greater number that, although they have the capability to develop such weapons, have refrained from doing so. What must be of increasing concern are other weapons of mass destruction and increasingly more formidable weapons systems such as the man-portable laser "blinder" weapon that China put on the market in May 1995.

Nuclear weapons have been present on earth since 1945. Given the Cold War and the intensity of international distrust since World War II, the pace at which the duopolistic superpowers and others have written treaties banning nuclear tests and limiting nuclear stockpiles has been unprecedented. In the deliberate and cautious realm of diplomatic negotiation, the duopolists have been relatively speedy and prolific in the production of nuclear arms control treaties. The negotiations have had not only to deal with complex technical issues, but also to reconcile competing bureaucratic interests that underlay each party's posture. Over the years, superpower negotiators have acquired insight into each other's needs and thinking, experience with negotiating strategies and tactics, and personal friendships built on a shared desire to prevent unwanted catastrophe. At the nuclear tier of the arms race, negotiations and treaties have accomplished much in laying the foundations for systems of institutionalized trust.

When the United States and the Soviet Union exploded their first hydrogen bombs in 1952 and 1953, respectively, the terrifying size of the explosions and the uncontrollable radioactive fallout caused worldwide concern about the dangers of testing. Scientists, military planners, politicians, and the public embarked upon an angry debate, generally with limited knowledge, about the effects of radiation: hereditary defects caused by mutation of reproductive cells; leukemia and bone cancer caused by strontium 90; and the life-shortening consequences of radiation to the body as a whole.[1]

---

1   Details may be found in Herbert F. York, ed., *Arms Control* (San Francisco: W. H. Freeman, 1973), Section 3. Additional information, including the effects

But even as the test ban debate grew in intensity, the technology for monitoring compliance with test bans was being invented and produced by the superpowers. High-resolution photo-reconnaissance equipment was developed by the mid-1950s and carried by high-flying U-2 aircraft. The first U-2 flights over the Soviet Union began in 1956; Sputnik arrived in 1957. By 1960, the United States began orbiting its reconnaissance satellites for detecting nuclear tests and photographing nuclear installations. Remarkably, within the span of a single decade, the superpowers had created programs of dangerous nuclear weapons tests, the technical means for monitoring such tests, and a treaty to ban the most dangerous tests in the atmosphere, in outer space, and underwater. Most importantly, these negotiations, aided by technology, built up sufficient trust so that on-site inspection and verification became possible under the START agreements. In turn, this had a spill-over effect into other categories of weapons.

The *Limited Test Ban Treaty* (LTBT) was signed on August 5, 1963, the outcome of a negotiating process begun in July 1958. Scientific representatives of eight nations met in Geneva in 1958 to discuss how to monitor a ban on nuclear explosions, that is, how to distinguish a nuclear test from an earthquake and how to know a test had occurred a long distance from its site. Meanwhile, the United States, the United Kingdom, and the Soviet Union, each unilaterally, began a temporary nuclear test moratorium that lasted until October 1961 when the Soviets detonated a 57-megaton H-bomb, the largest to that date. LTBT negotiations were continued in 1962 and 1963; the final three-power treaty was concluded within ten days.

The parties to LTBT agreed not to carry out any nuclear weapon test explosion, or any other nuclear explosion, in the atmosphere, underwater, in outer space, or in any other environment if the explosion would cause radioactive debris beyond the borders of the state conducting the explosion. Thus, in the absence of adequate verification controls, peaceful nuclear explosions (PNEs) as well as weapons tests were prohibited. Underground tests continued to be permitted. Over 100 nations have since signed the treaty; France and the People's Republic of China have not.

---

of chemical and biological weapons of mass destruction as well can be found in U.S. Congress, Office of Technology Assessment, *Proliferation of Weapons of Mass Destruction: Assessing the Risks* (Washington: U.S. Government Printing Office, 1993).

During LTBT negotiations, numerous treaty proposals and clarifications of technical issues did much to advance trust-promoting institutional arrangements. For example, in June 1957, the Soviet Union proposed, for the first time, the creation of an international test-ban supervisory commission and a system of inspection installations on the territories of the three nuclear powers in the Pacific Ocean. The Soviets sought an immediate suspension of tests. The United States insisted upon an adequate system of controls.

The requirements of a control system became the focus of contention: (a) the Soviet Union wishing to retain the veto, the United States opposing any limits on the inspection process; (b) the Soviet Union wishing to limit on-site inspections, the United States opposing quotas, geographical limits, or limits on types of events to be inspected; (c) the Soviet Union desiring national ownership of control installations, the United States arguing for internationally owned and operated control posts; and (d) the Soviet Union proposing a tripartite ("troika") administrative council for the international control commission, the United States favoring a single administrator. These differences, appearing at a time of Cold War distrust, were relatively minor and legitimate when measured against the usual demands of national self-interest and security. In fact, the substance of these differences represented a "great leap forward" from the extreme and stubborn disagreement evoked by the Baruch Plan a decade earlier.

When France in 1960 and the People's Republic of China in 1964 detonated their first nuclear devices, it was at least generally acknowledged that nuclear materials were widely available and that nuclear technology was less difficult to master than previously assumed. Further, by 1966, five nations were operating or constructing nuclear reactors for the generation of electric power. Since some types of reactors also produce plutonium, a fissionable material usable in the manufacture of nuclear weapons, it was imperative that anti-proliferation measures be developed promptly.

As early as August 1957, nonproliferation proposals were submitted to the United Nations Disarmament Commission. In 1961, the General Assembly urged the preparation of a nonproliferation agreement. On January 21, 1964, President Johnson offered a nonproliferation plan to the Eighteen-Nation Disarmament Committee. The Soviet Union responded with expressions of doubt about American motivations, noting that the United States was even then discussing a multilateral nuclear force (MLF) with its NATO allies. The MLF project was perceived by the Soviets as a form of proliferation that would eventually give West Germany access to nuclear weapons.

By 1966, the United States gave up plans for MLF, at the same time assuring its NATO allies that a nonproliferation treaty would cover only nuclear weapons and not delivery systems. The United States also assured NATO that the emerging treaty would not prohibit development of U.S.-controlled nuclear weapons on the territory of nonnuclear NATO members nor would it bar a newly federated European community from succeeding to the nuclear status of one of its members. The latter assurance anticipated the time when a united European state would evolve from that continent's steady progress toward political and military integration.

On July 1, 1968, a Nuclear Non-Proliferation Treaty (NPT) was ready for signature. The treaty provided that each nuclear weapon state party to the agreement would refrain from transferring and each nonnuclear-weapon state party to the agreement would decline to receive any nuclear weapons or other nuclear explosive device. The parties agreed to accept international, that is, IAEA, safeguard procedures for preventing the diversion of peaceful nuclear activities to the development of nuclear weapons. The peaceful uses of nuclear energy, including nuclear explosion technology, were to be made available to nonnuclear parties under appropriate international control arrangements. The parties to NPT expressed the determination to work toward comprehensive nuclear arms control and disarmament agreements. The treaty called for an NPT review conference. One was subsequently held in May 1975, with additional reviews at five year intervals.

Several significant concerns emerged during the NPT negotiations that are worth noting. Some were dealt with in whole or in part by the treaty. Regional nonnuclear states, such as those in the European Atomic Energy Community (EURATOM), were eager to maintain their regional safeguard system. This was made possible by allowing them collectively to have direct negotiations with IAEA. Developing countries were apprehensive about the availability of nuclear energy for their rapidly growing energy needs, and the treaty gave assurances in this regard. Nonnuclear states feared military disadvantages if they renounced nuclear weapons, and this brought forth agreement from the nuclear powers that steps toward a cessation of the nuclear arms race would be speeded up. In addition, the United States, the Soviet Union, and the United Kingdom each made formal declarations before the UN Security Council that it would seek immediate Security Council action to provide assistance to any nonnuclear weapon state party to NPT that was the object of nuclear aggression or threats.

Jumping ahead chronologically, a major review of the NPT was held in New York in May 1995. The primary concern at this conference was whether or not to renew the treaty. Resistance to renewal was minimal; the general consensus was that, in overall terms, the NPT had been successful. Particularly effective have been the five-year interval conferences. These review conferences have provided an institutionalized mechanism that encourages dialogue between the nuclear haves and the have-nots that would not have existed without the NPT. While each of the conferences has heard criticisms of the treaty, no state has ever withdrawn, nor has the treaty been amended. Indeed, after each of these conferences, there has been a spurt of increased membership. This is a substantial indication that increasing numbers of states view the NPT as being in their best security interests. As of March 1995, there were 172 signatories to the treaty. There are, however, some significant absences, including three undeclared nuclear states - India, Israel, and Pakistan. Other states that had not signed the NPT as of March 1995 included Andorra, Angola, Brazil, Chile, Comoros, Cuba, Djibouti, Eritrea, Macedonia, Micronesia, Oman, Palau, Serbia, Tajikistan, the UAE, and Vanuatu.

There were several competing issues, some of them politically contentious, at the conference. At both the 1995 conference and each of the four previous review conferences, many, if not most, of the criticisms were brought not by individual states, but by coalitions of states. Each of the groups would meet privately to coordinate their position and then present it to the conference.

Concern was expressed by several of the nonaligned nations that the five declared nuclear states had not made substantial progress at dismantling their nuclear stockpiles as required by Article VI. Included in this issue was the concern of the nonnuclear states that little progress had been made in the establishment of a comprehensive test ban. Another issue was the time period for which the treaty would be in effect. Some states, for example, proposed renewal for twenty-five years, with a conference at the end of that period to consider renewal again. Other states wanted an indefinite renewal. Members of the Arab League, led by Egypt, expressed especial concern over the non-membership of Israel; they felt that not enough effort had been expended by influential states to pressure Israel into joining the NPT. The nonnuclear states continued to express their concern that the nuclear powers continued to be discriminatory in the sharing and fostering of the peaceful uses of nuclear energy. Through adroit behind-the-scenes political maneuvering, combined with assurances from the policy statements of certain states, consensus was reached; the NPT was renewed for an indefinite period.

During the 1960s, the Soviet Union, as the junior duopolist at the time, made major strides toward achieving nuclear stockpile parity with the United States. As noted in Table 3-6, from 1965 to the signing of the SALT I agreements in 1972, Soviet ICBM delivery vehicles grew from 270 to 1,618, surpassing the 1,054 vehicles in the American arsenal. The same rate of growth occurred in submarine-launched ballistic missiles (SLBM): from 120 in 1965 to 740 in 1972, the latter figure representing 84 SLBMs more than the American. The Soviet missiles also carried a much heavier payload, or throw-weight, than the American. The United States, on the other hand, remained ahead in strategic bombers: 457 to 140 in 1972, and in the target accuracy of its missiles.

What was thoroughly clear during the SALT I negotiations from 1969 to 1972 was that the duopolists' production of nuclear weapons and delivery systems had reached a point of diminishing returns. About 400 strategic nuclear weapons, depending on yield and type, are theoretically sufficient to almost completely destroy either the United States or the Soviet Union. With thousands of nuclear warheads in their respective stockpiles, the two superpowers had enough to destroy each other several times over. As overkill capacity grew, the utility of each additional warhead and delivery vehicle diminished. The American development of MIRVs (multiple independently-targetable reentry vehicles) after 1967 only underscored the trend toward diminishing returns in national security. MIRVs enabled an individual missile to carry a number of nuclear warheads, each of which could be directed toward a separate target. A MIRVed "bus" could carry, at that time, from three to ten warheads. The Soviet Union tested its first MIRV in 1973, a year after the SALT I agreements were concluded.

The first series of *Strategic Arms Limitation Talks (SALT I)* opened up all of the issues pertinent to arms limitation efforts in general. How is parity between dissimilar weapons to be measured, for example, superior Soviet throw-weight versus superior American target accuracy? How should agreements deal with technological advances that were achieved even as limitation agreements were being negotiated, for example, the Soviet decision to place an antiballistic missile (ABM) defense system around Moscow versus the American decision to build MIRVs? In the absence of a neutral and powerful international monitoring agency, how would verification of compliance be assured? How could each party's different defense needs be taken into account, for example, the Soviet fear of encirclement by NATO at its west, China at its east, and general uncertainty at its south in the Middle East and the Asian subcontinent versus the United States' commitments to overseas allies in Europe and Asia? How would defensive measures such as antiballistic missile systems and civil defense preparations be balanced against offensive strategic systems such as ICBMs, SLBMs, and strategic bombers?

On May 26, 1972, the first round of SALT negotiations concluded with two documents: an *Anti-Ballistic Missile (ABM) Treaty* and a five-year *Interim Agreement on Strategic Offensive Nuclear Weapons*. The underlying assumptions of the ABM Treaty were that (a) no antiballistic missile system could effectively defend either country against the downpour of nuclear missiles each could deliver and (b) the retaliatory second-strike capability of each was sufficient to destroy the entire population of the other in the event of all-out attack. These were chastening admissions of indefensibility and the capacity to hold each other's populations hostage to a second strike. However, for mutually assured destruction (MAD) to maintain the nuclear stalemate, mutual vulnerability was critical. If one or the other side gained any substantial advantage in defense, the stalemate would be ended. Both sides recognized this, and neither was inclined to commit national suicide.

The provisions of the ABM Treaty allowed each side to have two ABM deployment areas of a restricted size and location. One area could protect the nation's capital, the other an ICBM launch area. The two sites were to be at least 1,300 kilometers apart. Each side could have 100 interceptor missiles and 100 launchers per site. Both agreed to restrict qualitative improvement of ABM technology and to consult with each other if technological breakthroughs occurred. Finally, the treaty provided for a U.S.-U.S.S.R. Standing Consultative Commission to promote the treaty's objectives and implementation. (A protocol to the treaty was signed in 1974 reducing the allowed sites to one: the Moscow system for the Soviets and the Grand Forks, North Dakota, missile defense system for the United States.)

The Interim Agreement placed a temporary limit on the numbers and types of strategic missile delivery systems, in effect freezing them at their level in 1972. This meant a limit of 1,054 ICBMs for the United States and 1,618 for the Soviet Union, 710 SLBMs for the United States and 950 for the Soviets. Each side could improve or replace older missiles, but neither could significantly enlarge the dimensions of the silo launchers. Mobile ICBM systems and strategic bombers were not included in the limitations.

Both parties agreed to pursue further negotiations without delay, that is, embark on *SALT II* discussions.

Two further trust-promoting agreements were achieved in the *Threshold Test Ban Treaty* (TTBT) of 1974 and the *Peaceful Nuclear Explosions (PNE) Treaty* of 1976. Together, these agreements represented further steps toward a sharing of exact knowledge about each other's nuclear weaponry and toward the conclusion of a comprehensive test ban. The parties to the Limited Test Ban Treaty of 1963 had pledged to work toward a comprehensive and final ban on nuclear weapons test explosions, and TTBT was one outcome of that pledge. The treaty prohibits underground nuclear tests having a yield exceeding 150 kilotons (150,000 tons of TNT). Further, for the first time, each party agreed to make available to the other important scientific information regarding test sites and nuclear weapons test programs, for example, location and geological characteristics of the test sites in order to facilitate verification, numbers of tests, and so on. There was to be prompt consultation if explosions accidentally exceeded the 150-kiloton threshold.

In negotiating TTBT, both parties recognized the difficulty then in distinguishing between a nuclear weapons test explosion and a peaceful nuclear explosion or series of explosions such as might be employed in digging a river channel or a reservoir. The Treaty on Underground Nuclear Explosions for Peaceful Purposes, that is, the PNE Treaty of 1976, was the response to these concerns.

The treaty put an aggregate ceiling of 1,500 kilotons on group PNEs, that is, two or more explosions within five seconds. For the first time a provision for on-site inspection by the other party during a test was included, along with mandatory exchanges of technical information. The number of inspecting observers, the geographical extent of their access, and similar details were spelled out. A joint consultative commission would be established to discuss compliance measures and additional on-site inspection arrangements. Both parties declared in 1976 that they would abide by the limits of these two treaties as long as the other did. Meanwhile, the willingness to move toward a comprehensive ban, exchange technical information, and tolerate on-site inspection are to be counted as additional building blocks in the structure of institutionalized trust.

Not yet ratified by the U.S. Senate, the TTBT and PNE treaties may eventually be superseded by a Comprehensive Test Ban Treaty. However, an air-tight comprehensive test ban had still not been achieved by 1996. All of the powers, except China, have stated they would refrain from testing as long as the others did. China's test of a nuclear device in May 1995 does not seem to have affected the position taken by the others. As noted, France conducted a series of tests in the Pacific and subsequently announced that it would no longer conduct testing, at the same time dismantling its test facilities.

SALT II commenced shortly after the SALT I agreements were signed. But SALT II promptly bogged down in old issues and new technologies: the definition of nuclear parity; the inclusion of MIRVs and strategic bombers in the ceilings; the counting of Soviet Backfire bombers and American cruise missiles as strategic delivery vehicles; the inclusion or exclusion of NATO nuclear forces. At a 1974 summit meeting between President Ford and General Secretary Brezhnev in Vladivostok, the principle of equal aggregate ceilings for strategic nuclear delivery vehicles was agreed upon. Each side would be allowed 2,400 vehicles, of which 1,320 could be MIRVed systems. The 2,400-vehicle ceiling included ICBMs, SLBMs, and strategic bombers. The classification of cruise missiles and Backfire bombers remained unresolved. Most important in the long term was their agreement that the key elements of the Interim Agreement, particularly with regard to inspection and verification, would be incorporated into the new treaty.

SALT II, as we have seen, was signed at a time when Hawks in both the United States and the Soviet Union seemed to be on the ascendant. The Soviet buildup in nuclear and conventional arms continued unabated. The United States and its NATO allies undertook to modernize European tactical nuclear forces. The Soviet Union continued to use surrogate military forces, such as the Cubans, to shore up pro-Soviet political parties and movements in Africa and the Middle East. Soviet unwillingness to support the condemnation of Iran for holding American diplomats hostage at the United States embassy in Tehran and the Soviet invasion of Afghanistan all but ended talk of detente and initiated what has been referred to as Cold War II. At no point, however, did the executive leadership of either superpower speak or act as though SALT II would be cast aside. Indeed, the exact opposite was true. Both leaderships continued to make policy statements that they would abide by the limitations as long as the other side did. Even after the United States accused the Soviet Union of breaking the agreement, no substantial changes were made.

The SALT agreements were overtaken by events and were superseded by the START agreements. There were substantial differences between the START and SALT agreements. While the SALT agreements imposed limitations, the START agreements imposed actual reductions and destruction of weapons systems. SALT dealt primarily with delivery systems and throw-weights, while START deals with warheads as well. SALT agreements relied primarily on national technical means for verification, while START established a substantial semi-permanent mutual on-site inspection and verification regimen. However, without the negotiations that went into SALT, the START agreements would probably have not been so comprehensive nor completed as quickly as they were.

Furthermore, at the time of SALT and immediately thereafter, there were other compelling nuclear problems in the wings. Laser technology was progressing rapidly. There were those who believed laser weaponry would make nuclear weapons and strategic delivery systems obsolete within a decade or two. This expectation seemed implicit in the comprehensive test ban negotiations, a kind of recognition that the most and the worst had already been accomplished in nuclear weapons technology and that a new era in the science of weaponry was in the offing. On the other hand, CTB discussions also held, and continue to hold, promise of devising ways of returning to the kind of international cooperation and institutionalized trust envisaged in the Baruch Plan. If a CTB could be completed, even incrementally, it may organize a permanent agency to carry out its provisions. This would be a major step toward effective supranational control of developments at the first (nuclear) tier of the arms race. Such arrangements could well create a multilateral and internationally controlled monopoly of the world's principal instruments of violence.

It must be remembered that the START treaties are bilateral, involving the two principal nuclear powers. Even when reduced to the final levels of START II early in the next century, Russia and the United States will still have substantially larger nuclear arsenals than the other nuclear powers combined. There also is the problem of designing effective nuclear energy safeguards and discouraging the nuclear hide-and-seek being played by the near-nuclear states. Finally, there is the growing prospect of nuclear theft and terrorism, a brand of international lawlessness that could eventually compel the community of nations to hire themselves a global sheriff.

Emergency Communication Treaties

This general category of arms control treaties aims to avoid the most serious pitfall of prisoners' dilemmas, namely, failure or incapacity to communicate with a potential ally. Difficulty in judging the trustworthiness of the other party is increased manifold by lack of communication. The search for common goals and nonviolent strategies is impossible without communication. Emergencies, accidents, errors, and misperceptions cannot be handled adequately without communication. In a nuclear age, when the survival of civilization may depend upon the ability to communicate with a potential ally or an adversary within minutes, emergency communication treaties and agreements have an obvious special importance.

The first of these communications treaties was the *"Hot Line" Agreement* of 1963 between the United States and the Soviet Union. The Soviet Union expressed its concern about surprise attack in 1954. A 1958 Conference of Experts on Surprise Attack focused professional attention on the problem. American and Soviet general and complete disarmament (GCD) proposals in early 1962 mentioned the need for prompt and reliable military communications. This need was dramatized by the Cuban missile crisis of October 1962 during which prompt, direct communication between heads of state was lacking.

By June 1963, the two superpowers completed the first "hot line" agreement establishing a direct telegraphic communication link between Washington and Moscow to be used only in crisis situations involving the security of either nation. The original "hot line" had teletype equipment at both terminals, one full-time duplex wire telegraph circuit using a northern route through Copenhagen, Stockholm, and Helsinki, and one full-time duplex radio telegraph circuit via Tangiers.

Advances in satellite communications technology made it reasonable before long to improve the "hot line". This was done in 1971 with a *"Hot Line" Modernization Agreement*. A system of multiple terminals was installed at each end in Washington and Moscow, and two new circuits were established using the United States Intelsat satellite system and the Soviet Molniya II satellite. The line has been used repeatedly by the heads of the two states.

An agreement to again upgrade and, more importantly, expand the "hot line" was made in 1984. The 1984 agreement adapted newer technology by the addition of high speed facsimile transmission (fax) capability to what heretofore was essentially a teletype. This allowed more rapid and more accurate exchanges, which could now include maps, drawings, and the like. While there is no formal agreement, since the late 1980s the two heads of state have been able to communicate directly with each other over satellite telephone, and have done so repeatedly. President Bush used the telephone, which has a secure link capability, to coordinate efforts dealing with the Gulf War of 1990-1991.

During the SALT I talks, negotiators on both sides began to realize the risks of technical malfunction, human error, misinterpreted incidents, or unauthorized actions that could lead to nuclear disaster. As a consequence, two separate working groups were established, one to arrange for the "hot line" link just described and the other to explore measures to reduce the risk of outbreak of nuclear war. The latter concluded an *Accidents Measures Agreement* in 1971. In this agreement both sides pledged to take measures to improve organizational and technical safeguards against accidental or unauthorized use of nuclear weapons. Arrangements were made for immediate notification should a risk of nuclear war arise from ambiguous incidents, unidentified objects reported by early warning systems, or unexplained detonations of nuclear weapons. Planned missile launches beyond one's own territory and in the direction of the other party would require advance notification.

In 1972, an additional communications-preventive agreement was signed: the *Incidents at Sea Agreement*. There had been several incidents involving the American and Soviet navies, where ships had actually bumped each other and aircraft had "buzzed" the other side's ships and planes. In March 1968, the United States proposed talks on preventing such incidents, any one of which could rapidly escalate into nuclear confrontation. The talks were begun in 1970 and concluded in 1971. The agreement entered into force in 1972. The agreement specified steps to be taken to avoid such close encounters and established a system of communications between the fleets using international signals.

A second consultative agreement was signed shortly after SALT II talks began. The era of Soviet-American detente had just gotten under way. This was the 1973 *Agreement on the Prevention of Nuclear War*. The superpowers agreed to make the removal of the danger of nuclear war a primary objective of their policies and to practice restraint in their relations toward each other and all countries. They also agreed to consult with each other in situations that involved a danger of nuclear confrontation. These consultations would also be communicated to the United Nations and to others such as the NATO or Warsaw Pact allies.

Innocuous though it may seem, the inclusion of a responsibility to notify third parties, particularly the United Nations, was a profoundly significant acknowledgement of the vital role of third parties in international conflict resolution. It was another step in the long-term process of diminishing the prisoners' dilemma predicament in which the nuclear powers often find themselves.

The Direct Communications Link, to give the Hot Line its proper name, is between heads of state only. Under its terms, any communication received *must* be delivered *directly to the head of state*. In September 1987, communications between the two superpowers were further enhanced by the establishment of *Nuclear Risk Reduction Centers*. This agreement is of unlimited duration and continues, with Russia as the agent for the Commonwealth of Independent States (CIS). Each of the parties established centers in their capitals, and, using facsimile transmission and telephone equipment, maintains contact with the other. The centers became operational on April 1, 1988. Their purpose is to supplement the Hot Line by providing for staff level, government-to-government exchanges in addition to heads of state exchanges.

The communications links are the same as, but separate from, the Hot Line. They are not crisis management centers, which are to be dealt with through the Hot Line and diplomatic channels, but rather facilities for the increasing amount of routine information that must be exchanged under various arms control agreements and protocols. These include such actions as ballistic missile launch notifications, prevention of incidents at sea notifications, and the like. The notifications continue to expand by mutual agreement well beyond their initial purpose. Their volume is a major confidence builder.

In 1988, another communications agreement was reached between the United States and the Soviet Union. (As with previous agreements that remain in force, Russia currently acts as the agent for the CIS.) This agreement was an outgrowth of the START negotiations. Both sides had proposed the advance notification of missile launches. Such launches are required to conduct training, testing, and maintenance. The proposals of both sides were relatively similar, hence both sides decided not to wait for the START treaties to be concluded, but to implement immediately this feature of the agreement. Using the Nuclear Risk Reduction Centers, each side now notifies the other of the planned date, launch area, and area of impact for any launch of an ICBM or SLBM.[2] The agreement expands upon the Accident Measures agreement and is included as a part of the START I treaty.

---

2   Under SALT, submarine-launched ballistic missile had not been included in the notification provisions.

Communication and third parties are essential elements of any system for promoting institutionalized trust. These elements have been put in place by the several emergency communication agreements just examined. In many ways, these particular agreements help bring the nuclear tier of the arms race back to earth by acknowledging the human frailties of the leaders and agencies of nuclear-weapon states. Like other humans, these leaders and agencies are subject to misinformation, misperception, error, and accident. Each agreement has been a contribution to the growing international structure of institutionalized trust.

Chemical and Biological Weapons Treaties

The other weapons of mass destruction are chemical and biological devices. Given the volumes that have been written and the enormous amount of effort expended since World War II, it may come as a surprise that both chemical and biological weapons have a much longer history than their nuclear younger brother. Like nuclear weapons, they have the potential to kill or maim on a massive scale. Unlike nuclear weapons, chemical and biological weapons are much more difficult to detect. They are also much more difficult to store and employ. However, as was graphically illustrated in the Gulf War of 1990-1991, particularly in the Scud attacks on Israel, just the threat of their possible use is enough to cause substantial panic.

The use of biological weapons throughout history has been sporadic. In part, this was because medical science did not understand the cause of many diseases until the last 300 or so years. One of the better known historical instances of biological warfare was the British use of smallpox-infected blankets against the American Indian allies of the French in the French and Indian Wars. However, the real potential for the use of biological weapons had to await the modern understanding of pathogens, which has occurred only in this century. The devastation that can be done with even small amounts of material is illustrated by laboratory experiments with anthrax, a bacteria. If effectively disseminated and inhaled, a mere 10 grams of this bacteria could produce as many casualties as a ton, i.e., one million grams, of nerve agent. Imagine what might have happened on the Tokyo subway had anthrax been employed rather than the chemical agent sarin.

The reasons for not employing biological agents also provides a form of elementary protection against them. Collection or creation of the toxins is easy and the industrial microbiological personnel required to accomplish it are readily available. Facilities for their manufacture have no special identifying characteristics, as do nuclear weapons. The equipment for their manufacture is dual use and readily available at most medical supply facilities. If they are so readily available and easy to use, why have they not been? In the first place, as living organisms, these toxins are highly perishable. Unlike a nuclear weapon, they cannot simply be placed in a warhead and stored in a bunker. If conditions are not properly maintained, the toxin dies, whether natural or synthetic. To paraphrase Shakespeare, there's the rub. It is extremely difficult to maintain the necessary conditions from creation through storage and transportation to employment.

In the second place, discrete employment is difficult. The toxin employed must generally be delivered in an aerosol form to affect a wide area. Delivery systems to accomplish this were developed in the 1960s. However, effective employment, more than any other weapon system, is dependent on weather conditions. Not only will wind direction and speed affect it, witness the Dugway, Utah, sheep fiasco,[3] but adverse weather will affect it quickly, causing the toxin to perish.

Although these and many other factors mitigate against the use of toxins, there are nations, and, more ominously, terrorist and criminal groups that persist in attempting to find the right mix. What must be of major concern is the rapid advances in genetics; it may become possible through genetic splicing to overcome the disadvantages of storage, transportation, and distribution. Nations that are generally accepted as having an interest in offensive biological warfare programs are Iran, Iraq, Israel, Libya, Syria, China, North Korea, and Taiwan.[4] Both the United States and the Soviet Union also had programs at one time. The United States and Russia have both renounced these programs.

The detection of biological weapons programs and the toxins themselves is extremely difficult. The facilities used to develop vaccines for many diseases also have to produce the toxin for research purposes. Even

---

3   During tests conducted at the Dugway Proving Ground, winds shifted and blew the agent off the installation, killing large numbers of sheep that were grazing in the area.

4   One of the major difficulties in dealing with chemical and biological weapons is in the intelligence gathering aspect. All such programs are kept highly secret. This secrecy is aided by the fact that it is extremely difficult to separate the appearance of these programs from legitimate activities. Indeed, they can be carried on simultaneously in the same facility.

more enigmatic is the fact that these weapons can be employed, and yet have no one know they have been! An outbreak of a virulent epidemic can be from natural causes as easily as from employment of a biological weapon. There is almost no way to tell which was the source. This seems to be a factor with regard to the Gulf War Syndrome reported by American and other veterans.

The *Geneva Protocol of 1925* included a prohibition against the use of biological weapons. The *Biological Weapons Convention* of 1972 is the latest effort to stop the development, production, and storage of biological weapons. The 1972 Convention is more strict and takes into account the massive strides that have been made in the biomedical field. Both the United States and the Soviet Union offered plans for the general disarmament and elimination of both biological and chemical weapons at the Eighteen-Nation Disarmament Committee (ENDC). There was some degree of resistance because of the linkage between the two. In 1969, the United Kingdom offered a draft convention to the ENDC that dealt solely with biological weapons. When President Nixon assumed office, he ordered a review of U.S. policy in the area of biological weapons. On November 25, 1969, he unilaterally announced that the United States would renounce use of biological warfare and would continue research only on defensive measures. Several nations, e.g., Canada, Sweden, and the United Kingdom, followed suit.

It was recognized that unilateral actions, though welcome, were insufficient. The UN General Assembly, after discussion, referred the matter to the Conference of the Committee on Disarmament, formerly the ENDC and now the Committee on Disarmament (CD), in Geneva in 1970. Initially, there was little progress. In March 1971, however, the Soviet Union and its allies agreed to separate the issues of chemical and biological weapons. Movement thereafter was swift. The United States and the Soviet Union, as co-chairmen, introduced identical texts. The convention was opened for signature in April 1972. Under the terms of the treaty, the signatories undertake not to develop, produce, stockpile, or acquire biological agents or toxins "of types and in quantities that have no justification for prophylactic, protective, or other peaceful purposes". Equally, they agree not to develop or adapt other systems for the delivery of such weapons. All existing stocks and delivery systems are to be destroyed. All parties agree to share, to the maximum extent possible, data on peaceful uses and defensive measures.

At subsequent periodic review conferences, particularly that of 1987, signatories established a regimen for the exchange of data to enhance cooperation and build confidence. All states have the right and obligation of reporting possible violations to the Security Council. When Russia admitted that the Soviet Union had a program in violation of the convention, the U.S., U.K., and Russia prepared and signed a joint declaration that provided for inspection of each other's facilities. No other inspection mechanism is in place. However, the signatories, in 1992, established an international Ad Hoc Group of Governmental Experts on Verification (VEREX) to examine possible means of inspection and verification.

Chemical weapons provide a somewhat thornier problem. Like biological weapons, expertise for their development is widespread. Facilities for their manufacture are generally dual use in nature. Their development, manufacture, and storage are difficult to detect. The storage bunker, at least externally, for chemical shells does not differ from that used for the storage of conventional munitions. Unlike biological weapons, however, chemical weapons are relatively easily stored and transported, particularly with the advent of binary munitions.[5] Also unlike biological weapons, chemical weapons have a substantial record of use in the twentieth century. "Poison gas", as it was then termed, caused over 100,000 deaths and over one million casualties in World War I. Since World War II, toxic chemical weapons have been known to be employed in Yemen, Iraq, Iran, Afghanistan, Cambodia, and probably elsewhere. They have now also entered the arsenals of terrorists.

Chemical weapons have been referred to as the "poor man's atomic bomb", and rightly so. They are relatively inexpensive to manufacture and can be delivered in any number of ways. However, like biological weapons, they appear to be easy to use, but depend in large measure on proper weather conditions. A heavy rainstorm will dissipate their effects. If the wind changes as the weapons are deployed, the user may end up "gassing" an empty field instead of the target area. When employed tactically, as has happened on more than one occasion, the user may end up attacking his own troops instead of the enemy. The effectiveness of even the threat of chemical weapons employment was demonstrated repeatedly in the Gulf

---

5   In binary munitions the active components are separated so that each portion is essentially inert. When the warhead is fired, the two compounds mix to become the active chemical agent.

War of 1990-1991. For example, although they were never used, to the best of our knowledge, the threat of their use often necessitated troops donning protective gear, which substantially impeded operations.

Once agreement to separate chemical and biological weapons issues was reached, work began on developing a chemical weapons ban treaty. The issues involved were more complex than those involved in the biological warfare problem. In the biological warfare realm, unlike chemical weapons, although substantial research had been done, no one had really developed a practical program. It is always easier to give up something you have never had (biological weapons) than to give up something you do have (chemical weapons).

Another difficult aspect was in defining what constituted a chemical weapon. There was little question that such things as sarin, mustard gas, etc., were types of weapons to be included. The problem arose at the other end of the scale with such things as riot control agents, napalm, magnesium bombs and shells, and the like. Another major issue was inspection and verification.

After lengthy negotiations, a *Chemical Weapons Convention* (CWC) was opened for signature in 1993. By late 1994, 157 nations had signed it. By November 1996, the necessary 65 ratifications to implement the treaty had been made. The 65 do not include the United State, which may, therefore, find itself at a disadvantage unless ratification is made by April 1997. Like the START agreements, this convention commits the signatories not to limitations, but to actual disarmament, including the destruction of existing stocks of chemical munitions. Further, it bans the development, production, use, and possession of such weapons. Most importantly, the CWC has the most extensive, intrusive on-site verification regimen of any convention signed. The bureaucracy to administer the CWC, the Organization for the Prohibition of Chemical Weapons (OPCW), is still in process of formation.

Conventional Arms Treaties

At the second (nonnuclear) tier of the world's arms races are the conventional arms transfers and buildups. Most of the treaty activity in this second tier continues to be in the discussion stage and remains concentrated in Europe. However, with the end of the Cold War, progress is being made. The lessons of START are being applied to conventional arms. This process is made easier because of the diminution of the nuclear threat. Nevertheless, much surplus conventional weaponry continues to find its way, legitimately and otherwise, into markets around the world. Often lost in the atom bomb discussions is the fact that the fire bomb air raids on Tokyo killed about 100,000 people and similar attacks on Dresden killed over 200,000.

Two conventional weapons areas are receiving the greatest attention. On July 17, 1992, the *Conventional Armed Forces in Europe Treaty* (CFE) came into force. Details of this treaty have been noted previously. By late 1993, all of the states were to have reduced their forces from the Atlantic to the Urals (ATTU) area by 25 percent. This goal was achieved, except for Armenia and Azerbaijan. Verification inspections as of the end of 1994 noted no flagrant treaty violations.

The one difficulty has been due to the changed role of Russia; the signatory to the treaty in 1990 was the Soviet Union. Russia has raised the issue of altering the limits placed on equipment deployed along its southern flank. Russia's argument is that when the limits were created, much of this area was internal to the Soviet Union. Now it is Russia's southern border; the amounts to which it is restricted are too small for its legitimate security needs. The other signatories are opposed to Russia's request, not least because of Russian operations in Chechnya, a part of the territory under discussion. In June 1996, a temporary *modus vivendi* was achieved that essentially froze Russian equipment in place until a more permanent solution can be reached.

The second area receiving some attention is the United Nations Register of Conventional Arms. This register came into force in 1993. Selected items of equipment imported or exported during the preceding year are to be reported to the United Nations. The register deals only with imports and exports, and not directly with domestic production or stocks. The normal growing pains of a new process are being experienced; reports are late, incomplete, inaccurate, and so forth. It is, however, a welcome effort toward transparency and exact knowledge on a worldwide scale.

As described in an earlier chapter, the motivations for buying and supplying conventional arms are still very strong. The newly emerging nations continue to experience internal political instability and security threats from hostile neighbors. Developing nations purchase arms not only in reaction to purchases by neighbors, but also as ways of promoting their regional and global political prestige. Sellers continue to do so not only for profit, domestic employment, and balance-of-trade considerations, but also as a technique for building or maintaining alliances. As a consequence, the conventional arms race has become another meeting ground for the twin problems of conventional arms control and United Nations peacekeeping. Civil wars and regional wars are fed by conventional arms transfers on the one hand; the resulting conflicts activate the UN peacekeeping process on the other hand. This interaction is likely to go on until all nations acquire stable domestic institutions and clarify sovereign relations between themselves and their neighbors, developments that are likely to require a long time.

The interaction has, if anything, become even more complex and aggravated in the post-Cold War era with not only the advent of formerly repressed ethno-nationalist groups, but also the growth of organized crime in many new parts of the world. Some of these criminal organizations have reached such proportions that they actually endanger governments. They are international in scope, not in the sense of the Mafia of the 1930s and its import-export of narcotics, but in the same sense as multinational corporations. Crime cartels actually have profits that are larger than the GDP of some of the smaller developed countries. Some of these operations control "armies" of up to 25,000. While they have yet to equip themselves with warplanes or tanks, a few do have light artillery, and in some countries they represent a substantial paramilitary force. A great deal of attention is given to arms moving between states, but not nearly enough to flows to non-state actors such as ethno-nationalist groups and organized crime.

The Conference on Mutual and Balanced Force Reductions in Central Europe (MBFR) was both a nuclear and a conventional arms limitation negotiation. It was essentially a non-starter from the outset, but it did provide a forum for the exploration of issues. A direct outgrowth of these talks was the CFE described above. The MBFR was plagued by events both internal to the talks and to external politics. A major internal difficulty was the attempt to determine equivalent force structures. How many anti-tank missiles does it take to equal one tank? There were also very substantial differences of opinion as to the actual strength of Warsaw Pact forces, NATO estimates being higher than those claimed by the Warsaw Pact. When the United States deployed medium range missiles to Germany and England in 1983, the Soviets protested and walked out of the medium range nuclear force talks (MNF), START, and MBFR talks. MBFR was not directly resumed. Instead, later negotiations resulted in the CFE.

In May 1977, President Carter announced a policy intended to restrain United States arms exports, particularly to nations in the more volatile regions of the world. Whereas previously United States military aid to another government was automatically considered a positive contribution to American security, the new policy would view arms transfers as an "exceptional" foreign policy instrument. The burden of proof that the proposed transfer will contribute to United States national security rested with those who favored such a proposal. Guidelines were established for limiting the level of sophisticated weaponry that could be exported. The policy further stated that the United States would refrain from being the first supplier to introduce advanced weapons into a region.

By 1978, fully two-thirds of the world's conventional weapons transfers involved the United States (32 percent) and the Soviet Union (34 percent) as suppliers. The new arms transfer policy thus acknowledged that, as one of the principal suppliers, the United States had a special responsibility for initiating the search for limitations on the trade in conventional weaponry. Therefore, in 1977, the United States called on supplier and recipient nations to join together in such an effort.

Domestic politics and external realities, such as the Iranian Revolution and the Soviet invasion of Afghanistan, ended these attempts. During this period, from prior to 1975 until 1983, the Soviet Union had deployed very substantial numbers (in the tens of thousands) of military advisers and technicians throughout the Third World. Additionally, beginning in 1976, the U.S. intelligence agencies had determined that the U.S.S.R. was striving to achieve strategic nuclear superiority. It also appeared that by 1979, as a part of their build-up, the Soviets had begun to invest seriously in developing a first strike capability. When combined with the increase of conventional forces in the Warsaw Pact from 140 divisions to 170, it became apparent that the realities were working against the Carter policy. In 1979, the policy essentially reverted to the policies on arms exports that had prevailed in previous administrations. The Reagan, Bush, and Clinton administrations brought the export volume back to where it was in 1978.

The first formal document explicitly supporting the concept of limitations on conventional arms transfers was the Final Document of the UN General Assembly's 1978 Special Session on Disarmament (SSOD). The 149 members of the United Nations at that time agreed in Paragraphs 22-24, 54, and 81-85 that the question of conventional arms transfers required prompt consultation and agreement among suppliers and recipients regarding methods for limiting all types of international trade in such weapons. Significantly, SSOD urged that such talks be "based on the principle of undiminished security of the parties" and "also taking into account the inalienable right to self-determination and independence of peoples under colonial or foreign domination". These were references to the very conditions that seem most to propel the conventional arms race, namely, the desire for regional security on the part of new and developing nations recently risen from the ashes of old empires. Political interest in achieving domestic order within many of these new and developing nations was substantial and presented the most serious hurdle to limitation of the conventional arms trade.

MBFR, the Soviet-American CAT working group, and the Final Document of SSOD suggest that, during the 1970s, the conventional arms race had at last come into the focus of attention of the world's major suppliers and buyers. However, in the 1980s, it was evident that such thoughts were more apparent than real. The two superpower alliances engaged in a massive arms race in the 1980s. Both also engaged at this time in an equivalent race to arm their clients and potential clients in the Third World, the most active theaters of competition being in the Middle East and sub-Saharan Africa. This arms race ended only when the economics of the situation, combined with domestic political unrest caused in part by the devotion of so much of the economy to the military, led to the unraveling of the Warsaw Pact and the Soviet Union.

Weapons of mass destruction, particularly nuclear devices, have continued to receive the attention of the world. In the conventional arena, some attention has gone to the "big ticket" items, e.g., high performance aircraft, missiles, main battle tanks, but little or no attention has been paid to those weapons systems that have been responsible for most deaths since World War II. Small arms, land mines, light machine guns, mortars, light artillery and the like, actually arm many of the developing countries, ethno-national groups, terrorists, and, increasingly, organized crime. While the systems for delivery of nuclear and other strategic weapons are being stored away, massive amounts of tactical weapons systems are being made available, often at below cost. The situation is further compounded as arms industries, particularly of the United States and Russia, scramble to find new customers.

Rather than refocusing its effort, the Coordinating Committee on Export Controls (COCOM) was disbanded in 1994. COCOM was organized by fifteen western nations to compile a strategic embargo list, primarily high technology, not to be sold to the eastern bloc. With the end of the Cold War, its original purpose ended, but its experience had the potential of slowing the qualitative arms race in many parts of the world. There are discussions about reconstituting it to meet post-Cold War realities.

There are other encouraging signs. The CFE agreements do bring some degree of order and conventional arms reductions to Europe. The Conference on Disarmament also provides a forum for addressing some of the concerns. The United Nations Register of Conventional Arms, although far from perfect, is at least a beginning. The START agreements, the NPT, and the Chemical Weapons Ban Treaty indicate that nations have increasingly accepted mutual or third party on-site inspection and verification, a major confidence-building measure. Perhaps the most encouraging has been the growing role peacekeeping has taken in both the United Nations and in regional alliances.

It has also become evident that if some international agency had the capacity to help maintain internal order, justice, and safety within developing nations, who are now the most active conventional arms buyers, many of the most compelling motivations for the international conventional arms trade would be reduced or removed. If, for example, United Nations or regional peacekeeping forces were sufficient to keep unfriendly neighbors from invading each other or discourage foreign powers from promoting domestic civil wars, national regimes would have far less need to arm themselves to the point of economic ruin and gross militarization of their maturing societies.[6] From this perspective, the need for a global sheriff may once again be recognized as critical for safety and much-reduced national military budgets.

---

6   In 1993, for example, of the top twenty nations ranked by military expenditure as a portion of GNP, only Russia (arguably), and perhaps Israel, could be considered developed countries.

11 Arms Control Forums: Backing into a Collective Security System?

War and preparations for war are costly, risky, and primitive techniques of self-protection. When antagonistic but astute leaders understand this, they often become predisposed to negotiate with each other. Negotiation is cheaper, less risky, and more civilized. The problem then becomes one of choosing a forum for negotiating, given particular contexts of power and events.

Historically, each negotiating context presents a different set of practical problems. In one context, for example, victorious leaders may dictate to the vanquished what new external arrangements are going to prevail for their country. Usually this means that the loser will be incorporated into the victor's political system, as were the Central Powers under the League of Nations. Or, the victors may impose a new internal system on the losers, as did the Allies in Germany and Japan after World War II. In another context, stalemated adversaries may create new institutional arrangements that preserve the political *status quo*, to allow time for the improvement of opportunities for nonviolent conflict, for example, the Egyptian-Israeli peace treaty produced at Camp David.

Another example may be in progress at this time. United Nations and regional peacekeeping arrangements may be providing opportunities for building more effective institutions of nonviolent international interventions. Simultaneously, arms control negotiations may be helping rearrange the world's military institutions. Peacekeeping and arms control, taken together, could presumably lead to global institutions that transform war-making into the order-maintaining duties of defenders of constitutional governments, order, and justice.

Globalization of military institutions requires that distinctions be drawn between war-making and order-maintaining. Order-maintaining changes the perception of "them-*versus*-us" simply to "us". As a result, resolving conflicts becomes more important than victory. Globalization would necessarily be organizational, with management responsibilities shared by all nations. The essential antecedent condition for this is a confidence-building, trust-promoting political process. Such a process has antecedents in the history of nations such as Great Britain, the United States, and Mexico, as described earlier, and has been evolving internationally over the past half century. Through successful negotiation, the major powers and their allies have been, as the evidence of this book suggests, expanding the area of political trust and may well be backing the world into a viable, effective, and stable collective security system. Wars and revolutions will hopefully become obsolete because of their lack of cost effectiveness.[1] Terrorism and crime will be the principal concerns of the international collective security system.

At the present time, however, rationality is still in short supply and political distrust continues in many parts of the world. There are obvious examples of uncertainty. Russia may revert to its historic authoritarian and aggressive ways. Or, both the United States and Russia remain unsure about future developments in Communist China. Arabs and Israelis remain stalemated after decades of negotiation. There are the Saddam Husseins and the Quaddafis. In short, the prisoners' dilemma is operative in many contexts. The transition from armed distrust to institutionalized trust and from pervasive conflict to sturdy cooperation will continue to be a long, tedious, incremental, backsliding human process. Successfully negotiated phases of the transition may be recorded in treaties and constitutions, but the records cannot make the transition happen.

The Significance of Changing Forums

The above said, we proceed with our review of the arms control and disarmament process. Specifically, we examine where they are negotiated, who are the officials involved, and what is achieved by negotiating.

There is the matter of terminology, that is, the current usage of such terms as "arms control", "arms limitation", and "disarmament". Some definitions are long-standing and are reiterated in the U.S. ACDA publication, *World Military Expenditures and Arms Transfers, 1993-1994*.

> Arms control includes all those actions, unilateral as well as multilateral, by which we *regulate* the levels and kinds of armaments in order to reduce

---

1   John Mueller, *Retreat from Doomsday: The Obsolescence of Major War* (New York: Basic Books, 1988).

the likelihood of armed conflicts, their severity and violence if they should occur, and the economic burden of military programs. Disarmament, a somewhat older term, describes a particular kind of arms control - efforts specifically to *reduce* military forces and perhaps ultimately to eliminate them.[2]

While "arms control" is a more popular generic term, most agreements and negotiations may be more strictly referred to as "arms limitation". The parties to an arms limitation agreement place mutually acceptable constraints upon particular types of military forces and weapons systems. Such agreements also strive to stabilize an established military balance of power, slow an arms race without loss of military advantage or security, reduce international tension, and introduce predictability into the military balance. Arms limitation agreements seem to place limits on weapons systems that may become obsolete within the foreseeable future. The content of such agreements may be less important than the confidence-building political process, if any, that they engender.

"Disarmament" is not only an older term, but also a term that evokes more emotion and ideological implications. Extreme proponents of disarmament tend to be extreme anti-militarists, pacifists, and advocates of brotherly love as the solvent of human conflict. As anti-militarists, disarmers see military leaders as bloodthirsty managers of human carnage, ever delighted by new weapons and by opportunities for battle (a view that most generals and admirals, with first-hand experience with the carnage of war, would hardly share). As pacifists, disarmers rarely offer a program for deterring unwarranted attacks and maintaining order and physical safety. In fact, some disarmers propose one or another form of unilateral disarmament in the belief that other nations, including determined adversaries, may be trusted to follow the noble example. Such proposals assume, erroneously, that trust is something that is given rather than a set of attitudes that parties earn transactionally.

Disarmament is nevertheless regularly placed on the agenda of world politics: in Chapter VII of the United Nations Charter; in proposals for world disarmament conferences (interestingly, rarely for a world security conference); in the convening of General Assembly special sessions on disarmament; in the titles of programs and agencies, such as the U.S. Arms

---

2   U.S. Arms Control and Disarmament Agency, *Arms Control Report* (July 1976), 3.

Control and Disarmament Agency; and in the rhetoric of world leaders as they try to identify themselves with their people's universal yearning for an end to war and violence. Once on the agenda, disarmament usually refers to the liquidation of all national military forces except those needed to maintain domestic order. This goal is presumably to be achieved by phased, simultaneous, and balanced reductions in the military forces and weapons stockpiles of all nations.

Such a policy and process is, of course, contrary to all human experience and an unfortunate example of placing the cart before the horse. Political elites disarm only when they (a) have been conquered, (b) have become a coalition member or satellite of some larger military power, or (c) have agreed to subordinate themselves and their military forces to a centralized military institution controlled by a system of collective decision making in which they have a share, for example, civilian parliamentary control over military policies and budgets. No leadership will disarm itself until the requirements of physical safety and military security are established and assured. The necessary antecedent condition of world disarmament is a system of world security that includes arrangements that build on institutionalized trust.

With these terminological considerations in mind, we may now examine the negotiating forums on questions of arms control, arms limitation, and disarmament. This may consist of many elements that reflect a power struggle, reveal trends in the evolution of a political institution, or measure the level of political trust among the parties. Specifically, it is useful to examine the following factors: the occasion for a negotiation; the parties to the negotiation; the topics of concern; the procedures of decision and settlement; the duration of the negotiation (and whether long duration is due to complexity of issues or dilatory tactics), and the outcomes in terms of trade-offs, formal treaties or agreements, the creation of institutional or bureaucratic structures, and, contextually, the improvement of political relations and trust.

The first such arms control and disarmament forum was conducted before the end of World War II at the San Francisco Conference that wrote the Charter of the United Nations. The charter was signed June 25, 1945, and came into effect on October 24, 1945. Between these dates, events took place that altered many of the basic assumptions of the Charter and radically changed the nature of world politics. On July 16, the United States secretly exploded the first nuclear bomb on the desert of New Mexico. In August, the United States Army Air Force dropped atom bombs on

Hiroshima and Nagasaki. The Charter's arrangements for dealing with issues of arms control and disarmament were thus outmoded even before they came into effect.

Under the Charter's original design, the Security Council, and particularly the five Permanent Members, was to have primary responsibility for maintaining international peace and providing for collective security. This was to be accomplished with "the least diversion for armaments of the world's human and economic resources (Article 1)". To assist the Security Council in performing these responsibilities, Article 47 established the Military Staff Committee (MSC) consisting of the chiefs of staff, or equivalent, of the five Permanent Members of the Council: the United States, the Soviet Union, the United Kingdom, France, and China.

The Military Staff Committee, as described in a previous chapter, was charged with advising and assisting the Council "on all questions relating to the Security Council's military requirements for maintenance of international peace and security, the employment and command of forces placed at its disposal, the regulation of armaments, and possible disarmament". If the discharge of its responsibilities required, MSC could invite other states to serve with the Committee. Following the traditional function of chiefs of staff, MSC was to be responsible for "the strategic direction of any armed forces placed at the disposal of the Security Council". According to Chapter VII of the Charter, member states were expected to hold military units immediately available for collective international enforcement actions when authorized by the Security Council.

At the close of World War II, collective security, in practical terms, meant collective enforcement actions by the five Permanent Members against any international "outlaw" engaging in acts of aggression or other breaches of the peace. Members were concerned with inter-state wars, the prevention of World War III, and aggression by one state against another, rather than the ethno-nationalist conflicts and insurgencies that would come to dominate human history after the 1960s. In the late 1940s, however, the invention of the atom bomb made traditional notions of military action obsolete. The Cold War made the expectation of collective military action unrealistic.

These consequences were quickly manifest in the demise of the MSC as a forum for arms control negotiations and collective security preparedness. To address the totally unprecedented issues raised by nuclear weapons, in January 1946, the General Assembly created the United Nations Atomic Energy Commission, composed of representatives of all states on the Security Council and Canada. UNAEC was to be the nuclear forum. It lasted only until January 1952, when the General Assembly replaced it with the Disarmament Commission.

American proposals before the UNAEC, generally known as the Baruch Plan (after Bernard Baruch, a famous financier and adviser to United States presidents), offered to turn over to the United Nations full information about nuclear technology and full control over sources of raw materials (uranium, thorium, and so on) and means of production, provided that the veto power of permanent members be abrogated in enforcement decisions pertaining to the development and control of atomic energy and further provided that an International Atomic Development Authority be created with powers to control and inspect all atomic activities throughout the world.

The Soviet Union, taking the position that the United Nations was merely an organ of American power, rejected the Baruch proposal, particularly with respect to the veto and inspection of all atomic activities. The former was viewed as diminishing Soviet influence in the United Nations and the latter as an invasion of Soviet sovereignty. In September 1949, the Soviet Union tested its first atomic weapon and thereby ended the American monopoly.

American, Soviet, Canadian, and other nuclear arms proposals remained stalemated in AEC deliberations and the General Assembly until January 1950 when the Soviet Union withdrew from the discussions in an effort to apply pressure to have Nationalist China replaced at the United Nations by a representative of the People's Republic of China. This forum for possible nuclear arms control was abandoned in 1952.

The UN Military Staff Committee was faring poorly, too. At its first meeting on February 4, 1946, MSC embarked upon a study of the organizational implications of Article 43. Under this article member states were to make armed forces available to the Security Council "on its call and in accordance with a special agreement or agreements" with regard to numbers and types of forces, their degree of readiness and general location, and so forth. While the Permanent Members agreed that they were likely to be the principal suppliers of national contingents for peacekeeping, they were in almost complete disagreement about the structure and composition of such forces. MSC's report of April 30, 1947, to the Security Council reflected the impasse. While the report's forty-one articles contained many broad areas of consensus, each of the five powers made extensive comments on points of disagreement. By August 1948, MSC abandoned its efforts and held its last substantive meeting. MSC met thereafter perfunctorily every fortnight for a few minutes "as a symbol of disappointed hopes which are not dead, but have been put aside for a better day".[3]

Unable to determine what its collective security forces should be, MSC was even less able to deal with arms control and disarmament questions. On December 14, 1946, the General Assembly addressed itself to the latter concerns in a unanimously adopted resolution that noted the relationship between world security and disarmament, called for reduction and regulation of armaments and armed forces under an international system of control and inspection, and recommended the withdrawal of armed forces from former enemy territories, the latter referring to the massive Allied occupation forces in Europe and elsewhere. Two months later, the Security Council established the Commission for Conventional Armaments (CCA) to examine these issues.

CCA consisted of representatives of all members of the Security Council. The reports of the Commission between 1948 and 1950 ran up against counter-proposals from the Soviet Union and the Ukrainian SSR. The commission recommended, among other things, that full publication of level of armed forces and conventional armament be reported by all members. The Soviets argued that such a requirement was "militaristic" in its assumption that security should precede disarmament. The General Assembly adopted the commission's proposals. However, in April 1950, the Soviet Union challenged the membership status of the representative of Nationalist China and boycotted the work of the commission. Thus, another forum was hurt by the Cold War, and, very shortly, destroyed by the Korean War.

Hoping to keep alive the security, peacekeeping, and arms control discussions begun in the Atomic Energy Commission and the Commission on Conventional Armaments, the General Assembly, in 1952, created a Disarmament Commission to consist of representatives from all Security Council states plus Canada. The new commission was directed to examine (a) questions of disclosure and verification of force levels of all states, (b) limitation and reduction of the size of these forces, (c) nuclear as well as conventional armament limitations, and, what turned out to be most significant, (d) procedures by which states could more readily negotiate arms limitation treaties. By 1954, the Disarmament Commission had

---

3   Trygve Lie, *In the Cause for Peace* (New York: Macmillan, 1954), 98.

received a substantial number of arms limitation and disarmament proposals from its principal members and decided to create a Subcommittee on Disarmament to facilitate negotiations. The subcommittee included Canada, France, the Soviet Union, the United Kingdom, and the United States. This membership included the powers with nuclear programs and avoided the distracting issue of the two Chinas.

The proposals in the Subcommittee on Disarmament during the 1950s were many and the debates often acrimonious. The competing views were well-prepared and vigorously presented. By 1956, it was evident to the members of the subcommittee that their efforts were not likely to bring forth any comprehensive program of arms limitation or disarmament. Instead, it appeared more reasonable to work toward limited rather than comprehensive disarmament objectives. The subsequent proposals and deliberations of the subcommittee have been credited with paving the way for the establishment of the International Atomic Energy Agency in 1957, the Antarctic Treaty of 1959, the Limited Test Ban Treaty of 1963, the Outer Space Treaty of 1967, and the Non-Proliferation Treaty of 1968. All of these treaties related to problems of nuclear weaponry and nuclear energy, and the Subcommittee on Disarmament, made up initially of four nuclear powers, was indeed the most competent forum for exploring these problems.[4]

In 1956, the Western members of the subcommittee began to suggest that forums and agencies outside the United Nations be created to negotiate and implement arms limitation agreements. The veto, the composition of the Security Council, and the politics of the General Assembly were obstacles to the serious negotiating tasks at hand. Further, with the United States and the Soviet Union now embarked on a nuclear arms race, the power structure of the world had become bipolar, thoroughly dominated by the two superpowers and their respective alliance systems. When the Disarmament Commission of twelve members was expanded in 1959, at the Soviet Union's behest, to include all members of the United Nations, it was recognized that the commission could no longer be, if ever it was, an effective forum. The commission met from time to time during the 1960s and early 1970s to receive reports and hear proposals for a World Disarmament Conference, but it remained otherwise inactive. At the General Assembly's Special Session on Disarmament in 1978, the Final

---

4   China did not join the "acknowledged" nuclear powers until 1964 and did not gain a seat at the United Nations until 1971.

Document called for reactivation of the full Disarmament Commission, and this occurred in 1979.

With the Disarmament Commission going out of business in 1959, a new forum came into being: the Ten-Nation Disarmament Committee (TNDC). The Committee reflected the new global balance of power: Canada, France, Italy, the United Kingdom, and the United States for the West; Bulgaria, Czechoslovakia, Poland, Romania, and the Soviet Union for the Communist bloc. TNDC immediately fell into charges and counter-charges, the West claiming that the Eastern powers were unwilling to undertake the necessary planning for a real reduction of armaments under effective international controls, the East declaring that the West was avoiding the General Assembly's declared objective of general and complete disarmament.

As the 1960s began, the arms competition was further complicated by the American commitment to the development of MIRVs (multiple independently-targetable reentry vehicles), which made it possible for each side to have many more warheads than the other side had missiles.[5] A further source of tension was the shooting down of an American U-2 reconnaissance plane by the Soviet Union just prior to a scheduled Eisenhower-Khrushchev summit meeting. The dispute led to the demise of TNDC and creation of a successor Eighteen-Nation Disarmament Committee (ENDC) in 1962. ENDC was enlarged in 1969 to twenty-six members and renamed the Conference of the Committee on Disarmament (CCD), now more commonly known as the Geneva Conference on Disarmament (CD). One of the more important items on the CD agenda in 1994-1995 was the continuing effort to negotiate a comprehensive test ban treaty.

ENDC and CCD were both arrangements for moving arms control and disarmament questions out of the formal structure and constraints of the United Nations. Although formally detached from the United Nations, both forums have been staffed by the secretariat and financed by the General Assembly, to which they have submitted annual reports. The Geneva Conference continues in the same manner. Both ENDC and CCD, through expansions of membership, as well as the CD, have sought to represent not only the superpower alliances, but also the growing number and influence of nonaligned nations. In 1969, the CCD balance was seven members from

---

5   The destabilization resulting from MIRV became a major dilemma during the SALT II negotiations in later years.

the West, seven from the Soviet bloc, and twelve nonaligned. In 1975, five other nonaligned states were added to make a total membership of thirty-one. The United States and the Soviet Union have served as co-chairmen of both ENDC and CCD, and continue those responsibilities with the CD. In 1980, the Geneva Conference (CD) was expanded to include forty members, including China, and became the Conference on Disarmament.

When Secretary-General U Thant recommended the transformation of ENDC into CCD in 1969, he also proposed that the General Assembly declare 1970-1980 a Disarmament Decade, which it did. Unburdened by glittering publicity and dramatic confrontations and all too often discounted as an ineffectual academic seminar and debating club, ENDC had nonetheless served as an indispensable site for communication and negotiation about difficult questions of arms control and disarmament, and would continue to do so as the Geneva Conference. ENDC's composition was also politically realistic, for the nonaligned nations had come to realize the vital importance and risks that the superpower and other arms races held for their own security and development.

The nonaligned states have not only served as a third force in global military and political affairs, but have also become a relentless pressure group for the design and achievement of multilateral arms limitation agreements. This nonaligned role emerged in ENDC and was expanded in CCD during the Disarmament Decade. It was in fact one of the reasons for expanding the CD in 1980, along with the inclusion of China. The role of the nonaligned states has continued within the CD, as well as in other forums, such as the recent extension of the Non-Proliferation Treaty (NPT).

As the seedbed of arms control and disarmament initiatives, proposals, and agreements, the record of ENDC, CCD, and CD, often unnoticed, has been impressive. ENDC picked up and carried forward the work of the Disarmament Commission. ENDC also did the drafting and other preparatory work of major treaties and agreements, many of which were concluded in other forums. ENDC became a clearinghouse and codification committee for nearly every significant security, arms control, and disarmament proposal put forth before and during its tenure. Even draft proposals that were shelved were highly important as a record of official governmental thinking about many issues and as a source of ideas that subsequently bore fruit.

The major documents initially before the Eighteen-Nation Disarmament Committee in 1962 were the "Draft Treaty on General and Complete

Disarmament under Strict International Control", submitted by the Soviet Union on March 15, and the "Outline of Basic Provisions of a Treaty on General and Complete Disarmament in a Peaceful World", submitted by the United States on April 18. Early versions of these proposals were offered by the Soviet Union in April and June 1957 and by the four Western powers on the Subcommittee on Disarmament in August of that year. More detailed plans were submitted to the Ten-Nation Disarmament Committee by both sides in March 1960. The 1962 documents became the basis for discussions over the next three years. By 1964, the GCD proposals revealed the best official Soviet and American thinking about how the superpowers might lead the world into an era of disarmament and international peacekeeping at the end of a three-stage process. Although all but forgotten, the two competing approaches reflect principles of action that are of more than passing interest, *particularly in their recognition that any reduction in armaments must be accompanied by a related increase in United Nations peacekeeping forces.* Furthermore, features of the two proposals may be discerned in several of the arms control treaties actually consummated during the late 1960s and thereafter.[6]

The topics and concepts introduced, analyzed, and refined in ENDC and CCD have been wide-ranging. Discussions of nuclear weapons test bans prepared the ground for the Limited Test Ban Treaty (1963), the Threshold Test Ban Treaty (1974), the Peaceful Nuclear Explosions Treaty (1976), and current negotiations toward a comprehensive test ban within the CD. The concept of nuclear-weapons-free zones spawned the Outer Space, the Latin American Nuclear-Free Zone, and the Seabed treaties (1967, 1967, and 1971, respectively), and has kept alive proposals for other regional nuclear-free zones such as south Asia, sub-Saharan Africa, and the Middle East.

Attention to the economic and social consequences of the arms race and disarmament has succeeded in linking the plight and prospects of

---

6 The full texts continue to provide important insights into Soviet and American policies and proposals. Texts may be found in Department of Political and Security Council Affairs, United Nations, *The United Nations and Disarmament, 1945-1970* (United Nations, 1970), Appendixes II and III. Full texts and a summary description of negotiations of arms control and disarmament treaties to which the United States is a party can be found in U.S. Arms Control and Disarmament Agency, *Arms Control and Disarmament Agreements* (Washington: Government Printing Office, 1990).

developing nations to the wastefulness of excessive military expenditures and unwanted wars. Proposals for the reduction and elimination of nuclear weapons stockpiles have led to the Non-Proliferation Treaty (1968), the Strategic Arms Limitation Talks (SALT) and Strategic Arms Reduction Talks (START) between the two superpowers, and the broadening of the responsibilities of the International Atomic Energy Agency. Another major concern has been the achievement of a comprehensive ban on chemical and biological weapons, which eventually produced a Biological Weapons Convention (1975) to which the United States, reluctant for years to do so, has subscribed. A comprehensive weapons ban also grew out of the ENDC-CCD-Geneva Conference: the Chemical Weapons Convention of 1993. Its overall intent is to ban totally such weapons, including the destruction of current stocks. Most importantly, it establishes a substantial mechanism for inspection and verification. Subsequent negotiations and treaties, such as the START (1991 to present), Nuclear Material Convention (1980), Intermediate-Range Nuclear Forces Treaty (1987), extension of the NPT (1995), and others find their roots in this organization. In sum, ENDC, CCD, and CD have been notable and effective arms control and disarmament planning and negotiating forums, so much so that the 1978 Special Session of the General Assembly (SSOD) took steps to incorporate more fully CCD into the operations of the United Nations.

The Final Document of SSOD noted that "for maximum effectiveness, two kinds of bodies are required in the field of disarmament, deliberative and negotiating", the former to include all members and the latter a much smaller number (Paragraph 113). Declaring that the General Assembly "has been and should remain the main deliberative organ" in the disarmament field, SSOD's Final Document restricted the future work of the Assembly's First Committee to security and disarmament questions and reactivated the Disarmament Commission composed of all members to conduct deliberations regarding a comprehensive program for disarmament. As a consequence, France and China were brought into the negotiating process and transformed CCD into a Committee on Disarmament open to all nuclear-weapon states plus thirty-two to thirty-five other states to comprise the negotiating body for this field.

By declaring itself the main deliberative organ in the disarmament field, the General Assembly assumed a major role in a function initially assigned to the Security Council. This action is comparable to the Assembly's assumption of a key role in peacekeeping through its Uniting for Peace Resolution in 1950. As students of two-house legislatures will appreciate, this type of arrogation of function is a predictable feature of normal political competition within bicameral legislatures. As evidence of this tendency, the General Assembly concluded the first Special Session on Disarmament by scheduling a second Special Session for 1982. From the point of view of progress in the field of arms control and disarmament, the growing involvement of the General Assembly may be a salutary effort to overcome the constrained ability of the Security Council to provide an effective forum.

Not all security, arms control, and disarmament forums are universal (General Assembly) or bilateral (SALT/START). Regional forums and negotiations have also been undertaken. The European region is the principal case in point. In 1973, the Conference on Security and Cooperation in Europe (CSCE), made up of thirty-three nations of Europe plus the United States and Canada (as members of the NATO alliance), began meetings that led to the signing of a Final Act in 1975. Aimed at reducing barriers between Western and Eastern Europe, the Final Act set forth three sets (or "baskets") of principles for governmental action by the thirty-five states. The principles dealt with "confidence-building measures" bearing upon the improvement of human rights, protection of the environment, movement of people, scientific and technological exchanges, settlement of disputes, and military security. The latter, of particular interest here, included agreements to give prior notification of major military maneuvers, exchange observers to these maneuvers, and encourage negotiations for effective arms control. CSCE established a Commission on Security and Cooperation in Europe to receive and consolidate semiannual reports on the implementation of the Final Act.

In 1993, the CSCE established a Permanent Committee to accomplish day-to-day operations, focusing on its peacekeeping and preventive diplomacy functions. In late 1994, the organization was made even more formal and became the OSCE (Organization being substituted for Conference). The OSCE maintains various peacekeeping and assistance missions throughout Europe. It has a permanently established Sanctions Coordinator attached to the European Union. Thus, the subjects - human rights, security, environmental protection, and so on - are now matters of public information, institutionalized attention, and, inevitably, propaganda and debate, although this has been muted with the end of the Cold War. As of 1996, OSCE has fifty-five member states.

In 1973, another regional forum got under way: the Conference on Mutual and Balanced Force Reduction (MBFR). MBFR was composed of seven voting members representing NATO (the United States, the United Kingdom, Canada, Belgium, West Germany, Luxembourg, and the Netherlands), four from the Warsaw Pact (Russia, East Germany, Poland, and Czechoslovakia), and eight nonvoting participants (five from NATO and three others from the Warsaw Pact). The objective of MBFR was to reduce the size and weaponry of the armed forces in Central Europe and to make their locations less apparently confrontational. Each side consistently challenged the numbers and interpretations of the other and little progress was made in this forum. However, it did lay the groundwork for other venues that would substantially contribute to a plethora of arms control agreements in the 1980s and 1990s, not the least of which were SALT and START, and most especially, the Conventional Armed Forces in Europe (CFE) Treaty. In addition to its European concerns, perhaps the most significant feature of MBFR was the fact that it was the first serious attempt to deal with the control of conventional arms. MBFR laid the foundations for the eventual signing of the Conventional Armed Forces in Europe Treaty in July 1992.

From the point of view of popular interest, the Strategic Arms Limitation Talks (SALT) were undoubtedly the most dramatic of the arms control forums. The advent of the Strategic Arms Reduction Talks (START) talks and agreements superseded them. In the SALT discussions, the two nuclear giants were face to face on a problem that was perceived as vividly threatening the survival of human civilization.[7]

The United States SALT delegations, whose negotiating positions were theoretically coordinated through the National Security Council, included

---

7   For a scenario contemplated by a group of NATO officers, see, John Hackett et al., *The Third World War, August 1985* (New York: Macmillan, 1978). From a military point of view, the account is strikingly realistic. It describes, in retrospect, the one-month war in which the Soviet Union makes a lighting strike into Central Europe at a time when the Allies are ill-prepared. There is a limited nuclear exchange which triggers the internal collapse of the Soviet Empire. In this "report", presumably written after the war, the authors observe: "The purpose of the war had after all been largely political, to exploit the conventional weakness of the West in order to humiliate the U.S. and to re-establish absolutism in Eastern Europe as the only safeguard against dissidence and fragmentation". A series of scenarios applicable to the post-Cold War era can be found in Trevor N. Dupuy, *Future Wars: The World's Most Dangerous Flashpoints* (New York: Warner Books, 1992).

representatives of the secretary of state, the secretary of defense, the chairman of the Joint Chiefs of Staff, the director of the Arms Control and Disarmament Agency, and the director of the Central Intelligence Agency. The chief of the U.S. delegation was the head of the U.S. Arms Control and Disarmament Agency. On the Soviet side, there were two overlapping decision making structures: the Communist party and the Soviet government. The Politburo of the party, backed up by the staff of the Central Committee, was the principal decision maker for SALT. In the governmental bureaucracy, SALT policy research preparations were the concern of the Supreme Military Council, the Ministry of Defense, the Ministry of Foreign Affairs, and the Academy of Sciences Institute of World Economy and International Relations, and the Institute on the U.S.A.

With such important agencies and officials on each side, there was little doubt that the two governments placed supreme importance upon the SALT process, commensurate with their responsibility to themselves and to the rest of humanity. SALT I extended from 1969 until 1972; SALT II, which resulted in an unratified treaty, extended from 1972 until 1979. SALT I resulted in the Anti-Ballistic Missile Treaty and the Interim Agreement on Strategic Offensive Weapons.

In 1962, the Soviet Union deployed a limited antiballistic missile (ABM) system around Leningrad. In 1964, the Russians displayed an ABM missile during a parade in Moscow, thereby anticipating the deployment of an ABM system, called the Galosh, around Moscow. The purpose of these ABMs was to intercept and destroy incoming nuclear missiles. The technology for ABM systems was available in the early 1960s, but it soon became clear to most planners that no antiballistic system could be created that would provide a completely effective shield against attack. Nevertheless, Congress insisted upon appropriating funds for an ABM system.

After many attempts by Presidents Kennedy and Johnson to draw the Soviets into a negotiation about ABM, Johnson, in responding to congressional pressure in 1967, agreed to begin deployment of an ABM system unless the Soviet Union promptly and seriously entered into an arms limitation discussion. Premier Kosygin agreed to do so in 1967, but the Russians were unwilling to commence until after the pending Non-Proliferation Treaty (NPT) had been completed. At the signing ceremony for the NPT in July 1968, President Johnson announced that agreement had been reached to begin talks. Before a date could be arranged, the Soviets invaded Czechoslovakia, and the United States suspended further discussion. However, with the election of President Nixon, the suspension was lifted and meeting dates established. The first SALT sessions were held in Vienna from April 16 to August 15, 1970, and in Helsinki from November 2 to December 18, 1970. Their purpose was the "limitation and reduction of both offensive and defensive strategic nuclear-weapon delivery systems and systems of defense against ballistic missiles".

The first SALT talks produced two agreements in 1972: the Anti-Ballistic Missile (ABM) Treaty, still in effect, which limited each side to two ABM sites, subsequently reduced to one;[8] and a five-year Interim Agreement on strategic offensive nuclear weapons, which froze the number of ICBM and submarine launchers on both sides at the levels deployed or under construction in 1972. Strategic heavy bombers were not restricted. The Interim Agreement allowed the Soviet Union more launchers than the United States, 2,350 to 1,710, but also prohibited further deployment of Soviet launchers, which they were doing at the rate of several hundred per year. The object of the subsequent SALT II negotiations was to convert the Interim Agreement into a permanent arms arrangement.[9]

In August 1972, the United States Senate approved the ABM Treaty. During the second half of September, both houses of Congress approved the Interim Offensive Arms Agreement. This paved the way for the SALT II negotiations. SALT II began on November 21, 1972, in Geneva. The agenda included the extension of numerical restrictions on the delivery systems of strategic weapons, the development of qualitative restrictions on the rapidly advancing missile technology, and the inclusion of bombers and

---

8   The American ABM site at Grand Forks, South Dakota, was placed in an inactive status in 1976 and has remained so ever since.

9   Details of the SALT I negotiations are available in several publications. For example, see John H. Barton and Lawrence D. Weiler, *International Arms Control: Issues and Agreements* (Stanford, CA: Stanford University Press, 1976), ch. 9, and Mason Willrich and John B. Rhinelander, eds., *SALT, The Moscow Agreement and Beyond* (New York: Free Press, 1974). Also see U.S. Arms Control and Disarmament Agency, *Arms Control and Disarmament Agreements* (Washington: Government Printing Office, 1990) and U.S. Congress, Office of Technology Assessment, *Proliferation of Weapons of Mass Destruction: Assessing the Risks* (Washington: U.S. Government Printing Office, 1993).

other new systems in the accounting of a strategic balance between the superpowers.

The issues before the SALT II negotiating forum were intrinsically difficult. The negotiating situation was further complicated, however, by the fact that the United States had replaced almost all the personnel of its SALT I delegation, and the Soviet Union had significantly changed the composition of its SALT decision structure by admitting the Soviet defense minister to full membership in the Politburo. In addition, Watergate was, by 1974, distracting the Nixon-Kissinger leadership on these matters.

During 1973, a Nixon-Brezhnev statement expressed the hope that a new SALT agreement would be reached by 1974. When it appeared that this would be impossible, two side agreements were concluded instead: a protocol to the ABM Treaty limiting each side to one ABM system instead of the two in the original treaty, and a new Threshold Test Ban Treaty restricting underground nuclear tests to explosions with a yield no greater than 150 kilotons. Both agreements were signed on July 3, 1974.

Domestic political, bureaucratic, and technological developments continued to impede the SALT II negotiations. Another major difficulty was the definition of "parity" between the two strategic weapon and delivery arsenals. As a consequence, the regular delegation negotiations were intermittently supplemented by summit meetings between President Nixon and General Secretary Brezhnev, and, later, President Ford and Brezhnev. In November 1974, the latter two met in Vladivostok and agreed in principle to equal aggregate ceilings for strategic nuclear delivery vehicles, including bombers. However, when the negotiators resumed their discussions in Geneva in 1975, new disagreements appeared regarding the classification and treatment of certain new delivery technology, namely, the American cruise missile and the Soviet Backfire bomber.

Shortly after the inauguration of President Carter in 1977, the new administration proposed lower ceilings than those agreed upon at Vladivostok, thereby reopening several issues and prolonging the negotiation process. When the Interim Agreement expired in 1977, both parties continued to conduct themselves as though it were still in effect. Not until June 1979 was a SALT II agreement signed by President Carter and now President Brezhnev as heads of state, subject to ratification by Congress and the Supreme Soviet.

The SALT II agreement consisted of three parts: (1) a treaty setting quantitative limits on numbers of delivery systems and qualitative constraints on new types of weapons, to last until the end of 1985; (2) a short-term protocol effective until December 1981, dealing with mobile ICBM launching systems and cruise missiles; and (3) a joint statement of principles and guidelines for subsequent SALT III negotiations.

The timing of the SALT II treaty-signing was less than fortuitous. It took place amid growing strains in Soviet-American detente and at the beginning of the quadrennial American presidential election contest. Before 1979 concluded, the American hostage crisis in Iran and the invasion of Afghanistan by Russia propelled Soviet-American relations into a major clash, with SALT II ratification a major victim. Nevertheless, there seemed little doubt among foreign policy officials on both sides that the SALT negotiating process would eventually be resumed. There were those, particularly at the United Nations, who looked forward not only to SALT III, but also to an eventual SALT IV that would bring into the negotiating process the other principal nuclear powers. Their optimism, with one exception, proved misplaced. SALT III never happened. The exception was that both governments, starting with the Carter administration in 1980, continued to announce that even though SALT II had not been ratified, they would continue to abide by it as long as the other side did. With some minor disagreements, they continued to do so until the provisions were superseded by the START agreements in 1991.

A new period in U.S.-Soviet relations was ushered in during 1981. The three-pronged policy of the Reagan administration has been detailed in previous chapters: engage in a massive arms build-up, including support for anti-Soviet movements such as those in Afghanistan; call repeated attention to human rights violations by the Soviet Union both domestically and in its foreign actions; but, all the while, maintain communication with the Soviet leadership in all the forums discussed above, particularly in the area of arms control. The Bush administration, in turn, capitalized on the foundations laid by the Reagan administration that finally brought an end to the Cold War and led to some of the most comprehensive arms limitations agreements ever signed.

In May 1982, President Reagan reaffirmed that the United States would continue to abide by the SALT II treaty as long as the Soviets did. President Reagan pointed out, in 1984 and 1985, that the U.S.S.R. was violating the accords in several ways. He announced that the United States would refrain from undercutting the SALT and other agreements to the extent that the Soviets did and further made it a condition that the Soviets actively pursue nuclear and space talks in Geneva. On May 26, 1986, Reagan announced that the Soviets had not complied with their commitments to SALT and other agreements, so ". . . in the future, the United States must base decisions regarding its strategic force structure on the nature and magnitude of the threat posed by Soviet strategic forces and not on standards contained in the SALT structure. . . ".[10] In fact, there was no appreciable change in U.S. strategic forces. The changes that occurred were primarily technological, including the Strategic Defense Initiative (SDI), development of the B-1 bomber, and implementation of stealth technology.

START negotiations began in Geneva in 1982 and were a vital part of the Reagan policy. However, they were not limited to the venue in Switzerland, but included a series of summit conferences, ancillary agreements, and some of the venues described earlier. START very much broadened the scope of items to be considered, including warheads and delivery systems. Perhaps the two most important features of the START agreements were their shift from dealing with limitations to their emphasis on reductions and their setting up a mechanism for on-site inspections and verifications.

In December 1987, the leader of the U.S.S.R., Mikhail Gorbachev, and President Reagan signed the Intermediate-Range Nuclear Forces (INF) Treaty in Washington. This treaty effectively eliminated medium and short range nuclear missiles in Europe. Under provisions of the treaty, ground-launched ballistic missiles and ground-launched cruise missiles (GLCM) with ranges of between 500 and 5,500 kilometers, if located in Europe, were to be destroyed, including their support equipment. The treaty entered into force in June 1988; by 1992, the program for destroying equipment was begun.

Although the INF treaty was bilateral in nature, much of the initial negotiations and detailed work involved NATO and the Warsaw Pact. The U.S.S.R. had started to upgrade its intermediate range missiles (IRBM) by replacing them with the SS-20. In 1979, NATO decided on a dual track approach to the situation by encouraging direct arms control negotiations between the United States and the Soviet Union and by approving the deployment to Europe of American GLCM and Pershing II IRBM. Agreement for the talks was reached in 1981. The talks proceeded fitfully until the United States began to deploy the missiles in 1983. The talks were resumed in 1985, parallel to, but not a part of, the START process. The

---

10   U.S. Arms Control and Disarmament Agency, *Arms Control and Disarmament Agreements* (Washington: Government Printing Office, 1990), 263.

treaty included a verification regimen that included, among other things, on-site inspection. In 1987, Germany announced unilaterally that if the U.S. and the Soviet Union reached agreement, they would also destroy the Pershing missiles under their command.

The Ballistic Missile Launch Notification Agreement was signed on May 31, 1988, in Moscow. It was a further effort on the part of the two major nuclear powers to prevent a nuclear exchange because of misinterpretation, miscalculation, or accident. It was a direct outgrowth of the START talks. In simple terms, the agreement provides for advance notice of the launch of strategic ballistic missiles for testing and training purposes.

In December 1991, the Soviet Union ceased to exist. Its break-up left four new nations - Russia, Belarus, Ukraine, and Kazakhstan - to inherit the Soviet nuclear weaponry. In the Tashkent Declaration of 1992, the four agreed in principle that all except Russia would become non-nuclear nations and that Russia would act as their agent in this process. For ease of description, therefore, agreements and conditions concerning the START treaties and other agreements that followed will assume that Russia acts for them all.

START I was signed in Moscow by President Yeltsin and President Bush on July 31, 1991. The treaty reduces offensive strategic weapons by roughly thirty percent. The treaty requires the destruction of warheads and delivery systems, the destruction to be monitored and verified on-site. Implementation is scheduled to take seven years in three phases. The treaty has a special significance in that it represents the first agreement that requires actual reduction of nuclear weaponry as opposed to limitations and redeployments. START I is also indicative of the change in the climate of mutual trust. Significantly, both sides began to destroy weapons and deploy the required inspection teams before the treaty was ratified, which occurred officially in 1995.

START II was signed by President Bush and President Yeltsin in January 1993. It may well be the broadest arms reduction pact in history. It requires the two former superpowers to reduce their strategic nuclear arsenals to about one-third of their Cold War size within ten years. Further, it totally eliminates land-based multiple re-entry warheads. It will be implemented, upon ratification, after START I is well under way.

From a collective security point of view, the SALT-START process is of crucial importance. These were, by and large, bilateral negotiations between the two superpowers and occurred outside the purview of the

United Nations or any other organization. They were narrowly focused on a specific class of weapons: nuclear and their delivery means. The agreements had no provisions for other powers to be directly involved. However, if the Big Two substantially reduce the numbers of nuclear weapons, it may begin a process which can be joined by other nuclear states. The United Kingdom and France have unilaterally begun reductions in their strategic nuclear forces in the spirit of START. Beyond the practical benefits, all this reinforces the development of trust

Of paramount importance was the return of arms control action to the UN General Assembly where the long-awaited, much-debated Comprehensive Test Ban Treaty was consummated. On September 10, 1996, over the strenuous objection of India, the General Assembly voted 158 to 3 (India, Libya, and Bhutan) to end nuclear weapons testing. There were five abstentions (Cuba, Lebanon, Mauritius, Syria, and Tanzania). Nineteen other nations were absent or barred from voting because of failure to pay assessments. The pact is on the table for countries to sign. If signed and ratified by the 44 nations possessing nuclear reactors, including the five nuclear weapons powers, an organization for monitoring and enforcing the treaty will be established. A review conference is planned in three years.

Arms Control Bureaucracies

There is one type of arms control forum that has been given relatively little attention, but which may carry the seeds of enduring institutional development in this field, namely, the various ongoing, sometimes tiny, bureaucracies created in connection with post-World War II arms control agreements. These bureaucracies consist of the permanent staffs of several supranational agencies such as: the International Atomic Energy Agency (IAEA) created in July 1957; the Agency for the Prohibition of Nuclear Weapons in Latin America (OPANAL) established under the Treaty of Tlatelolco, Mexico, in 1967; the Standing Consultative Commission (SCC) established by the United States and the Soviet Union in 1972 to monitor the SALT I agreements; and the United Nations Centre for Disarmament organized in 1977.

There are other bureaucratic forums, e.g., the Conferences on Security and Cooperation in Europe (CSCE, now OSCE) to administer periodic reviews of the Helsinki agreements of 1974. Also, in March 1977, the United States and the Soviet Union established eight task forces or "working groups", each to deal with one of the following problem areas: a comprehensive test ban; control of radiological weapons; arms limitation in the Indian Ocean zone; control of conventional arms transfers; civil defense; antisatellite capabilities; and arrangements for prior notification of missile test flights.

Many bureaucracies, including the supranational ones just cited, have qualities that may make them excellent long run forums for arms control negotiations. A substantial and well-organized bureaucracy often represents diverse concepts, theories, and interests relevant to the public policy issue with which it is concerned. Personnel usually have long tenure, with the advantages and disadvantages of daily ongoing interaction with each other. This results not only in familiarity with each other's modes of thought and actions, but also tends to inhibit dramatic surprises in the behavior of the parties represented. In time, the staff of such bureaucracies develop a shared interest in their common goals and take on the perspectives and style of third parties mediating competing interests. Bureaucracies also become a repository of essential information and experience relevant to the agreements and policies they administer. They serve as a clearinghouse for proposals and plans that otherwise would be lost or ignored. Bureaucracies also tend to break up larger policy issues into smaller, more manageable ones, a process that is often critical for conflict resolution.

To return to the International Atomic Energy Agency as one of the major supranational bureaucratic forums related to arms control, the IAEA had its origin in President Eisenhower's 1953 Atoms-for-Peace proposal. With the endorsement of the General Assembly in 1954, the American proposal creating IAEA became a statute that was signed by seventy governments. IAEA came into operation in 1957. Unlike many specialized United Nations agencies, it does not report through the Economic and Social Council, but directly to the General Assembly. Its General Conference is the annual meeting of all signatory members, as of 1994 numbering 114. The conference elects half of the members of a thirty-four-member board of governors, approves the selection of the director general, and sets the IAEA budget.

IAEA has become a staff of several hundred, with responsibilities for nuclear research and development, health and safety standards, civil liability, technical assistance and, since the adoption of the Nuclear Non-Proliferation Treaty in 1968, the administration of a safeguard program to ensure that peaceful nuclear energy activities are not diverted to military uses. As a consequence of India's surprise nuclear explosion in 1974, IAEA has accelerated its efforts to tighten nuclear safeguard controls. It is in this function that IAEA's staff has expanded most rapidly in order to perform activities increasingly significant for nuclear arms control. In the aftermath of the Gulf War, the inspection role of the IAEA has taken on even greater importance. Further rapid growth of the agency's arms control responsibilities over the next decades may be expected.

Regional agencies such as OPANAL and CSCE conferences may also be expected to evolve in keeping with their broadening experience and assignments. OPANAL consists of a General Conference made up of all contracting nations, a five-member council selected by the General Conference, and a secretariat whose staff is concerned with administering meetings, verifying compliance, negotiating IAEA safeguard agreements, conducting special inspections upon request and acquiescence by contracting parties, maintaining relations with other international organizations, and carrying out other arms control and mediating duties.

The Final Act of the Conference on Security and Cooperation in Europe adopted in 1975 by the thirty-five participating nations sought to establish a "CSCE process" that would maintain a continuing oversight of the implementation of its provisions on military security in Europe, cooperation in the fields of economics, science, and technology, and cooperation in the fields of human rights and related humanitarian matters. The vehicle for this process was to be follow-up conferences, the first of which was held in Belgrade from October 4, 1977, to March 9, 1978. A second review conference began in Madrid on November 11, 1980, and a third in 1986 in Vienna. Subsequently, as previously noted, a permanent Organization on Security and Cooperation in Europe (OSCE) has been established.

The Standing Consultative Commission established by a memorandum of understanding between the United States and the Soviet Union in 1972 was charged with implementing the provisions of various strategic arms agreements, including the ABM Treaty, the 1972 Interim Agreement, and the 1971 Agreement on Measures to Reduce the Risk of Outbreak of Nuclear War. The SCC meets in private, deals with questions of compliance, endeavors to remove uncertainties and misunderstandings about the agreements, and entertains proposals for improving implementation of the agreements. Each side has a "component", or delegation, supported by a small staff that engages in almost continuous review, discussion, and negotiation. It may be assumed that this particular forum also serves as a convenient place for sharing intelligence about each other's nuclear and strategic technology and policies. The SCC is perhaps the most likely agency for preventing either side from carrying off any technological surprises in the strategic weapons field. Relatively unnoticed, the SCC may be one of the more successful means for promoting institutionalized trust between the two major nuclear powers.

Yet another growing bureaucracy is the United Nations Centre for Disarmament. The Centre, previously the Disarmament Affairs Division of the Secretariat, was upgraded in 1977 and assigned an assistant secretary-general as director. The Centre's responsibilities were expanded by the 1978 Special Session On Disarmament (SSOD). These new responsibilities include an augmented program of study, research, information, and contact with nongovernmental organizations (NGOs). Prior to SSOD, the Centre's staff numbered about thirty-five to forty, and its biennial budget was $2,145,700. Both the budget and number of personnel have continued to grow and expand. SSOD also created a board of eminent persons to advise the secretary-general on various studies and policies in the field of arms control and disarmament, this board to be administered by the staff of the Centre. There is little doubt that the Centre for Disarmament will have a solid career as a forum in the arms control negotiating process.

Another new organization (actually an expansion of the already existing UN Secretariat) that has come into being is the United Nations Register of Conventional Arms. The purpose of the register and its bureaucracy is to try to keep track of the import and export of major items of conventional equipment.

We shall forgo mentioning, for example, the bureaucracies of the Geneva Conference on Disarmament or those created as a result of various treaties and conventions such as START. Each has become a mini-forum for the arms control field.

The large number of arms control and disarmament forums noted in this survey reinforces the impression that problems of international security, the arms race, arms control, and disarmament are high on the agenda of the world's leaders and receive a substantial investment of leadership time and thought. With struggle for international power and influence always in the background, much more than talk and propaganda have come out of these forums. The large accumulation of treaties and agreements in the historically brief period of fifty years has been impressive and, in many respects, well-institutionalized.

Most especially, the tempo of peacekeeping, already detailed, when combined with the rapid increase in arms control and arms reduction efforts of the first half of the 1990s, seems to allow for a substantial degree of optimism regarding global security, despite inevitable setbacks and failures along the way. Most encouraging has been the manner in which several rather serious, politically motivated barriers have been overcome in order to extend the Nuclear Non-Proliferation Treaty indefinitely in 1995.

Encouraging, too, has been the quality of many nations' involvement in the arms control process. Unilateral gestures such as the Baruch Plan and the several testing moratoriums have been supplemented by bilateral and multilateral negotiations. Middle and small powers have insisted upon enlarging their participation and have been relatively effective in bringing pressure for action on the superpowers. The General Assembly, by conducting special sessions on disarmament and augmenting its organizational capacity for dealing with disarmament matters, has been a major factor in universalizing attention to and planning for security and arms control debates.

The importance of universalizing arms control forums cannot be overstated, despite the success of the bilateral negotiations such as of START. All nations have a vital interest. The nonaligned nations of the world have a tremendous interest in reducing their own and major power military expenditures better to afford economic development budgets. Universal forums are more likely to maintain arms control negotiations as a public process subject to popular pressures. Above all, the large array of negotiating forums reviewed here reveals how numerous are the marketplaces for security, arms control, disarmament, and peacekeeping transactions where almost none existed before.

The Functions of the Negotiating Process

There is a substantial body of behavioral science theory regarding negotiation and transaction in politics and other fields of human interaction. William Zartman declares simply: "Ours is an age of negotiation". Anselm Strauss observes: "A social order - even the most repressive - without some forms of negotiation would be inconceivable. Even dictators find it impossible and inexpedient simply and always to order, command, demand, threaten, manipulate, or use force; about some issues and activities they must persuade and negotiate". According to Peter Blau, social exchange relations evolve slowly, usually starting with minor transactions in which little trust is required, but neither is there much risk. By discharging obligations for goods and behaviors received, individuals demonstrate their trustworthiness, leading to a gradual expansion of exchanges accompanied by growth of mutual trust.[11]

Negotiations are an essential communications process that precedes any transaction. It specifies the goods, behaviors, or other currencies available for exchange between the transactors. It compels each transactor to clarify his or her value priorities sufficiently to be able to decide, according to his or her own subjective criteria, whether the thing to be received is worth more than that which is to be given in exchange. This can be money for goods or services (the typical economic transaction), deference for advice (as suggested by Homans and Blau in connection with socio-psychological exchanges), a vote for a political favor (common in legislative logrolling), or cruise missiles for Backfire bombers (as in SALT II negotiations). Negotiations also help reveal those values that transactors may share more or less equally (as in the Ballistic Missile Launch Notification Agreement of 1988). Knowing these shared values often facilitates the discovery of common ground for exchanges and cooperation. Thus, for example, the shared values that seem to motivate powerful adversaries to negotiate arms control agreements include (a) common fear of mutual destruction, (b) unpredictable and uncontrollable consequences of military engagement, (c) satisfaction with the status quo, and (d) the economies of preventable armed conflict.

---

11   I. William Zartman, *The 50% Solution* (Garden City, N.Y.: Anchor Books, 1976), 2; Anselm Strauss, *Negotiations: Varieties, Contexts, Processes, and Social Order* (San Francisco: Jossey-Bass, 1978), ix; Peter M. Blau, *The Dynamics of Bureaucracy* (Chicago: University of Chicago Press, 1955); Ralph M. Goldman, "A Transactional Theory of Political Integration and Arms Control", *American Political Science Review*, 62 (September 1969), 719-733; and *Contemporary Perspectives on Politics* (New Brunswick, NJ: Transaction Books, 1976), Ch. 4. See also, George Homans, *Social Behavior: Its Elementary Forms* (New York: Harcourt, Brace and World, 1961); Alfred Kuhn, *The Study of Society* (Homewood, IL: Dorsey Press, 1963); I. William Zartman, ed., *The Negotiation Process; Theories and Applications* (Beverly Hills: Sage Publications, 1978); Thomas A. Reilly and Michael W. Sigall, *Political Bargaining* (San Francisco: W. H. Freeman, 1976); Robert O. Matthews, Arthur G. Rubinoff, and Janice Gross Stein, edits., *International Conflict and Conflict Management* (Scarborough, Ontario: Prentice-Hall of Canada, 1984). Michael D. Intriligator and Urs Luterbacher, *Cooperative Models in International Relations Research* (Hingham, MA: Kluwer Academic Publishers, 1994).

Political transactions differ from economic ones in that the currencies exchanged are somewhat less clearly specified. The units of currency exchanged in political transactions are not as precisely measurable as in most economic exchanges. Nonetheless, the other attributes of transaction are present in all types of exchange. One of these is time, which can be an important aspect of transaction. The simplest transactions are those in which two parties transfer goods between themselves simultaneously. However, when the transfers take place at different times, anticipation and trust become significant psychological elements in the situation.

These theoretical observations about negotiating and transacting permit us to better appreciate the special significance of arms control negotiations and treaties as processes and events promotive of international institutionalized trust. A few brief illustrations drawn from arms control negotiations may further illuminate this view.

Negotiations help reveal adversary values and priorities. In the case of the CSCE Helsinki agreements and follow-up conferences, it was evident that the former Soviet Union was most interested in the security arrangements, particularly those that tended to confirm its dominance of Eastern Europe, whereas the United States preferred to focus on issues of human rights.

Negotiations may be revealing of adversary military and diplomatic strategies. For example, as a vast land mass with one-fourth of the world's population, the People's Republic of China was more interested in modern conventional weaponry than in nuclear weapons, feeling safe by adopting policies that helped maintain the nuclear stalemate between the former Soviet Union and the United States. However, as technology changed, particularly in delivery systems, this policy also changed, as exemplified by China's testing of a nuclear device in May 1995. A change in attitude was also revealed by China's more aggressive posture regarding the Spratly Islands in 1994 and the beginning of the development of a blue water navy in 1995.

During negotiations, opposing expectations may become explicit, whether accepted by the other party or not. Thus, during the SALT II negotiations, the United States made clear its expectation that the Soviet Union would refrain from stepping up the rate of production of its Backfire bombers. At first, the Soviets demurred, then, eventually, they acknowledged and made concessions regarding their production plans.

On-going negotiations may be a vital preventive of surprise maneuvers and unexpected crises. This is certainly one of the functions of the START negotiating process, the CSCE process, the Conventional Forces in Europe (CFE) process, the "hot lines", and similar continuing discussions.

Two other trust-promoting functions of negotiation are less evident, but equally significant. The various negotiating forums have, over the years, served to give structure to the world's "marketplaces" for deals regarding security services. Thus, there has evolved a set of nuclear marketplaces in which the superpowers have arranged a duopolistic dominance over strategic weapons systems. Near-nuclear powers have continued to try to break into this marketplace. But the smaller nonnuclear nations have begun to challenge the very existence of nuclear weaponry as pillars of global security. There have also been conventional weapons marketplaces. Some of the marketplaces are global and others are regional. As we have seen, these marketplaces, or forums, are increasingly visible and organized. Over future decades, these locations are where issues of international security are most likely to be negotiated.

A second, less evident function of negotiation is its role in the pursuit of "exact knowledge" of military capabilities. Hitherto, this pursuit has been almost entirely the function of military intelligence. More recently, the negotiating process has presented its own occasions for learning about the military capabilities of others. Just as Harry Truman told Joseph Stalin of the detonation of the first atom bomb during their conversations at Yalta, we must assume that such developments as cruise missiles, antisatellite satellites, Backfire bombers, anti-optic lasers, and similar technological advances have been shared between negotiating parties at some time before the news reached the popular press.

As for arms control negotiations proper, these would be literally impossible if each side did not have precise and verified data about the other's military hardware and deployments. To these sources have been added a number of non-governmental organizations, some of which rival intelligence agencies, that publish large amounts of data on the world's armed forces, including technology, for example, the International Institute of Strategic Studies, Jane's Information Group, World Priorities, Stockholm International Peace Research Institute, and others.

Turning to treaties and international agreements, we find similar confidence-building implications. Treaties and agreements, after all, are literally the creations of the contracting parties. Each party not only assumes that the other is less than trustworthy, but also is vitally concerned with agreeing only to those arrangements that are unilaterally verifiable and enforceable. There is no developed world judicial process as yet that can determine, on the basis of presented evidence, whether one or another party has breached a contract. Nor is there a world enforcement agency at hand to punish the guilty party. Nevertheless, treaties and international agreements do comprise much of the body of international law. As do laws of any kind, treaties and international agreements serve as public instruments for clarifying and stabilizing expectations about each other's behavior. Such clarification and stabilization are essential institutionalizing activities for the development of social and political order at all levels of human self-governance.

Treaties and agreements enable the contracting parties to publicly specify areas of common interest as well as shared goals. Even though such declarations are often dismissed as "mere verbiage", they are an indispensable antecedent for cooperation and organized activity. The "verbiage" becomes more compelling if it spells out specific observable guidelines for behavior. Such behavioral requirements and expectations may subsequently be the basis for signaling danger if one of the parties is preparing to breach the contract. For example, in the case of the Helsinki security arrangements, the conduct of NATO or Warsaw Pact military maneuvers *without due notice* to the other party would have to be interpreted as a clue that something unsavory is going on. Israel's preemptive strike against its Arab neighbors in 1967, as another example, was justified as a defensive action in response to threatening maneuvers by Egypt, Syria, and others. United Nations threats to employ NATO air strikes against the Bosnian Serbs provided yet another example of punitive action taken in response to breaches of expected behavior.

Treaties and agreements may also provide grounds for response to potential breaches or betrayals by one of the contracting parties. This is usually provided for in abrogation, inspection, and verification clauses. A nation that seeks to abrogate rather than renegotiate a treaty is undoubtedly preparing to make trouble. If inspection or verification arrangements are obstructed, a similar conclusion may be drawn. The inclusion of such provisions in treaties and agreements provides a device whereby each party may have some warning of danger and some opportunity for preparation and response. A classic example of this type of behavior, and the conclusions drawn as a consequence, is North Korea's unwillingness to allow IAEA personnel inspect its nuclear weapons program in 1994. Because Iraq persisted in throwing up obstacles to UN inspectors that sanctions against it were maintained as the firm policy of the United States.

Finally, treaties and agreements may provide organizational mechanisms, such as the aforementioned bureaucratic forums, for continuing, perhaps permanent, negotiation about issues too difficult to resolve immediately or in the near future. Such are the arrangements that lead to the social order alluded to by Anselm Strauss. In this sense, theoreticians speculate that conflict is an important prerequisite of political integration so long as conflict is accompanied by negotiations and some successful political transactions. If this is a valid proposition, then arms control negotiations, treaties, and agreements have been essential for the development of institutionalized trust and shared control over the security services of the world.

Domesticating Security: Should the Ranchers Hire a Sheriff?

When all the bits and pieces of international arms control and peacekeeping activity since the end of World War II are tied together, do they add up to a structure sufficient to house the attitudes, conduct, and guarantees of international institutionalized trust? Our answer is optimistically in the affirmative. Highly dangerous and lethal weaponry, profound ideological differences, bitter political diatribe, and cumbersome bureaucracies notwithstanding, the major powers and numbers of middle-sized and small states have involved themselves in elaborate and sustained negotiations, bilateral and multilateral agreements and treaties, universal declarations of arms control and peacekeeping policies, and new supranational bureaucratic operations that have welded together whole networks of cooperation and institutionalized trust. By these means, expectations about the conduct of international actors have been clarified, constrained, and made more predictable. The consequences of "good" conduct have become more decisively positive for most parties: reduced cost of military preparations; less risk of accidental war; growing awareness of cheaper nonmilitary modes of conflict resolution, and greater opportunity for identifying and pursuing common goals worldwide.

Several conclusions may be drawn from this survey. First, the arms race is not likely to be ended without the development of systems of institutionalized trust among the world's competing elites. Second, among the most critical systems of institutionalized trust are those provided by arms control agreements and various types of peacekeeping.

Third, the implementation of arms control agreements, because of its potential for promoting and institutionalizing relationships of trust, are often more important than the military weaponry and force-level features of these agreements. The quantitative provisions about military hardware give only an illusion of objectivity about military balance. By implication, the negotiation and implementation procedures acknowledge that balance is inevitably a subjective and debatable judgment. By institutionalizing negotiation and implementation processes, the parties to arms control agreements are better able to update, match, and discuss their different subjectivities, senses of security or insecurity, and solutions, thereby discovering common security goals and testing each other's trustworthiness on an ongoing basis.

Fourth, world security services are likely to evolve on a two-tier basis for some time into the future. At the nuclear tier, the greatest risks of mass disaster are likely to come from horizontal proliferation, nuclear theft, and terrorist possession. International policing agencies will probably develop rapidly, perhaps jarred into place by some unfortunate, and possibly preventable, nuclear disaster.

At the conventional tier, world security services are likely to evolve from the present peacekeeping function. To the extent that United Nations and regional peacekeeping missions eventually provide security forces capable of displacing the unilateral, armed, self-defense forces of individual nations, to that degree will the arms race(s) at the conventional tier diminish and collective security increased. However, the process of building collective security organizations, that is, supranationalizing national armed forces, is likely to be a long and challenging one.

In matters of world security services, the notion of a supranational sheriff may be something more than an amusing figure of speech. The history and functions of sheriffs provide a relevant, human, institutional experience for the needs of a contemporary world in which international crime, terrorism, and aggression abound and grow increasingly dangerous.

The office of sheriff had its origins in pre-Conquest England and persists to this day as a county law enforcement office in the United Kingdom and the United States. During the first century after the Conquest, the English sheriff convened and led the military forces of the shire (county), executed all writs, and judged criminal and civil cases. Over time, the sheriff's judicial functions were taken over by the king's itinerant judges. His remaining duties involved investigation of allegations of crime, preliminary examination of the accused, trial of lesser crimes, and detention of the accused in major crimes. In modern England, the sheriff also brings together panels of jurors, provides for the safe custody of prisoners, and conducts the returns in parliamentary elections.

In the United States, the sheriff is usually an elected public officer of his county. He has major police, court, and prisoner detention duties related to the enforcement of the criminal law. In literature and in film, American sheriffs, particularly those in the West, including their federal equivalent, the U.S. Marshals' Service, have been glamorized and glorified as civic protectors against gangs of rustlers, gamblers, murderers, and other evildoers. In order to preserve public order, the sheriff has had the power to call out the *posse comitatus*, that is, to deputize persons to serve temporarily as an armed force in the county. Such sheriff's posses could be compared to UN peacekeeping missions gathered ad hoc by the Secretary-General in crisis circumstances. UN peacekeeping missions do not quite ride to capture an outlaw; the criminality of nations or national leaders do not have an established place in international law and practice. However, the time may not be too distant when such missions may include the capture of nuclear thieves or gangs of terrorists. The conflict in Bosnia has already seen some movement in this direction in the apprehension and trial, by an international court, of war criminals.

It is also worth noting that the election of county sheriffs as well as the financial and military support of international peacekeeping missions succeed when endorsed and funded by leaders with a common security interest, for example, by wealthy ranchers in the American West and by powerful states or multinational corporations in contemporary international peacekeeping. In a practical sense, the sheriff and the peacekeeping mission may be viewed as "hired guns" charged with maintaining order within informal systems of law and justice. Peace, after all, is, among other things, "good for business".

The institutionalizing trends alluded to in this survey will probably be among the most critical factors in future arrangements for promoting and maintaining an environment of trust in a world seeking to end arms races and conduct its disagreements without war. Some of these trends have been going on for some time, others have just begun, and still others have yet to appear. Optimists and Doves will pay attention to the undramatic and the gradually aggregating institutional developments. Pessimists and Hawks will focus on the dramatic confrontations and past dangers that are an inescapable part of the international conflict process. Both perspectives will be laden with subjectivity, distinct attitudes of trust and distrust, and widely differing senses-of-security. The architects of a world without arms races and wars will necessarily continue to cope with both, undoubtedly for a long time.

If the development of world and regional peacekeeping and security services follows along the same historical lines as that of county sheriffs, the way may already be paved for the gradual integration of national armed forces into a network of supranational security organizations. In this way, the military organizations of competing national elites, under the guidance of some representative civilian institution such as the Security Council or the General Assembly or both, may be able to merge step-by-step into a collectively controlled world security force. The time may come when transnational political parties, functioning through a representative institution such as the General Assembly, will provide an institutional alternative to warfare under a system of shared civilian control over the emerging world collective security force. The institutional model is already established in the European Parliament, the Western European Union, the Organizational for Cooperation and Security in Europe, NATO, and related organizations. What lies ahead are further details of global arms control and peacekeeping arrangements yet to unfold.

Appendix: A Chronology of Significant Security, Arms Control, and Peacekeeping Events

1945
* Germany surrenders to Allies, May 8.
* Establishment of United Nations.
* Atomic bombs dropped on Hiroshima, August 6, and Nagasaki, August 9.
* Japan surrenders, September 2.

1946
* First session of the United Nations General Assembly.
* Atomic Energy Commission (UNAEC) created by United Nations General Assembly. Baruch Plan presented to AEC.
* Atomic bomb tested at Bikini by United States.

1947
* Commission for Conventional Armaments (CCA) created by United Nations General Assembly.
* Cold War begins. U.S. initiates "containment" policy.

1948
* Israel declares independence. Arab League commences war with Israel. United Nations Truce Supervision Organization in Palestine (UNTSO) established.
* Kashmir crisis leads to United Nations Commission for India and Pakistan (UNCIP) and United Nations Military Observer Group in India and Pakistan (UNMOGIP).
* Malaya civil strife leads to United Nations Commission for Indonesia (UNCI).
* Organization of American States (OAS) established as collective security system.

1949
* North Atlantic Treaty Organization (NATO) established.
* Soviet Union detonates atomic bomb.
* UN mediates cease-fire between India and Pakistan ending two years of fighting over Kashmir.
* UN mediates cease-fire between Israel and Arab states.
* Coordinating Committee for Multilateral Export Controls (COCOM) established.

1950
* North Korea invades South Korea. Korean War. United Nations General Assembly adopts Uniting for Peace Resolution

1951
* Australia, New Zealand, and United States sign ANZUS Treaty.

1952
* United Nations Disarmament Commission replaces Atomic Energy Commission and Commission for Conventional Armaments.
* United Kingdom detonates atomic bomb.
* United States detonates first hydrogen bomb.

1953
* Soviet Union reports possession of hydrogen bomb.
* Eisenhower presents Atoms-for-Peace proposal at United Nations.

1954
* Southeast Asia Treaty Organization (SEATO) established.
* United States-Japanese mutual defense treaty signed.
* Mutual defense treaty between Nationalist China (Taiwan) and United States.
* Western European Union (WEU) established for mutual defense.

1955
* Baghdad Pact (Iraq, Turkey, United Kingdom, Pakistan, and Iran) formed, later (1959) to become Central Treaty Organization (CENTO).
* Soviet Union and its satellites create Warsaw Pact Organization.

1956
* Hungarian Revolution suppressed by Warsaw Pact.
* Suez crisis. Nasser nationalizes Suez Canal. Britain and France occupy Suez, with collusion of Israel. United Nations Emergency Force (UNEF-I) created for Middle East.

1957
* United Kingdom detonates hydrogen bomb.
* European Community created by Rome Treaty.
* International Atomic Energy Agency (IAEA) established as suggested in Atoms-for-Peace proposal.

1958
* Conference of Experts to Study the Possibility of Detecting Violations of Possible Agreements on a Suspension of Nuclear Tests (with representatives from the United States, the United Kingdom, France, Canada, the Soviet Union. Poland. Czechoslovakia, and Romania).
* Comprehensive test ban talks (CTBT) begun by the United States, the Soviet Union, and the United Kingdom.
* Lebanese crisis leads to creation of United Nations Observation Group in Lebanon (UNOGIL).

1959
* Ten-Nation Disarmament Committee (TNDC) created. In 1961 TNDC succeeded by Eighteen-Nation Disarmament Committee (ENDC). in 1969 ENDC becomes Conference on the Committee on Disarmament (CCD) with 26, later 31, members. In 1979 it becomes the Conference on Disarmament (CD), known as the Geneva Conference.
* Khrushchev proposes complete world disarmament at United Nations.
* Antarctic Arms Control Treaty signed.

1960
* Congo crisis. United Nations Operation in the Congo (UNOC) begun.
* France joins "nuclear club".
* Downing of American U-2 over Soviet Union.

1961
* Non-Aligned Movement organization established.

1962
* First meeting of Eighteen-Nation Disarmament Committee (ENDC).
* Cuban missile crisis. United States "quarantines" Cuba.
* United States and Soviet Union present General and Complete Disarmament (GCD) proposals to ENDC.

1963
* Organization of African Unity (OAU) established.
* Limited Test Ban Treaty signed ending nuclear tests in atmosphere, in outer space, and underwater.
* "Hot Line" Agreement signed.

1964
* Communist China detonates atomic bomb.
* United Nations Force in Cyprus (UNFICYP) established.

1965
* Special Committee on Peacekeeping Operations (Committee of 33) set up by United Nations General Assembly.
* United Nations India-Pakistan Observation Mission (UNIPOM); new Kashmir crisis.
* Organization of American States (OAS) sends regional peacekeeping mission to Dominican Republic.

1966
* France withdraws from NATO military forces.

1967
* The new European Union established, as the European Community (EC), from the European Coal and Steel Community, European Economic Community (Common Market), and European Atomic Energy Community.
* Association of South East Asian Nations (ASEAN) established.
* Outer Space Treaty signed.
* Latin American Nuclear-Free Zone established by Treaty of Tlatelolco.

1968
* Nuclear Non-Proliferation Treaty (NPT) signed.

1969
* Eighteen-Nation Disarmament Committee membership expanded to twenty-six and renamed Conference of the Committee on Disarmament (CCD).
* SALT I talks begin.
* United Nations General Assembly declares Disarmament Decade.

1970
* General Assembly passes the first internationally accepted principles on seabed beyond territorial waters.

1971
* Seabed Arms Control Treaty is signed.
* "Hot Line" Modernization Agreement is signed.
* Soviet-American Agreement on Prevention of Accidental Nuclear War is signed.
* Communist China replaces Nationalist China at United Nations.

1972
* Biological Weapons Convention prohibiting the development, production, and stockpiling of biological and toxin weapons, and the destruction of current stocks.
* Salt I Interim Agreement and Anti-Ballistic Missile (ABM) Treaty signed.
* Conference on Security and Cooperation in Europe (CSCE) begins in Helsinki.
* Incidents at Sea Agreement signed by United States and Soviet Union.

1973
* Conference on Mutual and Balanced Force Reductions in Europe (MBFR) begins.
* Conference on Security and Cooperation in Europe established.
* October War in Middle East. United Nations Emergency Force (UNEF II) reestablished.
* Congress passes War Powers Act.
* Soviet-American Agreement on Prevention of Nuclear War.
* United Nations Law of the Sea Conference begins.

1974
* India detonates a nuclear device.
* Soviet-American ABM Protocol signed.
* Threshold Test Ban Treaty (TTBT) signed.
* Vladivostok Agreement between Ford and Brezhnev.
* United Nations Disengagement Observer Force (UNDOF) established along Golan Heights.
* Nuclear Suppliers Group (London Suppliers Group) established to coordinate guidelines for limiting exports of technical information and

nuclear materials and equipment to proliferation countries and areas of instability.

1975
* Nuclear Non-Proliferation Treaty (NPT) Review Conference held.
* Helsinki Summit Accords produced by CSCE.
* Biological weapons ban takes effect.

1976
* Peaceful Nuclear Explosions (PNE) Treaty signed.

1977
* Environmental Modification Convention signed.
* Formal trilateral negotiations begin on comprehensive nuclear test ban.
* OAU Border Mediation Committee unsuccessfully attempts to mediate conflict in Ogaden.
* U.S.-IAEA Safeguards Agreement signed.

1978
* United Nations Interim Force in Lebanon (UNIFIL) established.
* Camp David Summit Agreement between Israel and Egypt.

1979
* SALT II signed.
* U.S. and U.S.S.R. jointly submit a draft Radiological Weapons Treaty to Committee on Disarmament in Geneva.
* Soviet forces invade Afghanistan.
* Security Council votes to eliminate UNEF I and rely on observers from UNTSO.
* Arab League mediates temporary cease-fire in Yemen.
* NATO proposes medium range nuclear force (MNF) negotiations, but also agrees to upgrade obsolete U.S. tactical missiles.

1980
* French test neutron bomb in South Pacific.
* Soviets test killer satellite.
* United Nations General Assembly condemns, 104-18, Soviet intervention in Afghanistan.
* Second Review Conference on Nuclear Non-Proliferation Treaty attended by 75 of treaty's 114 signatories.
* Ratification of SALT II Treaty stalled in United States Senate.
* Convention on the physical protection of nuclear material signed.

1981
* Congress passes Reagan's proposed defense build-up.
* OAU sends peacekeeping force to Chad.
* MNF talks begin in Geneva.

1982
* Falkland Islands War.
* Brezhnev announces unilateral freeze on deployment of SS-20 missiles in Europe.
* Initial START talks begin; U.S. states it will abide by SALT as long as Soviets do.
* French and Italians send peacekeeping forces to Lebanon.
* French announce nuclear force modernization.

1983
* Reagan calls for funding of Strategic Defense Initiative (SDI).

1984
* U.S. claims Soviets violating SALT II and biological warfare conventions.
* Conventional Forces in Europe talks begin (replacing MBFR).
* Hot Line expansion agreement signed.
* Australia Group of 26 nations established to consult and coordinate export controls on chemical and biological weapons.
* Group of Six (Argentina, Greece, India, Mexico, Sweden, Tanzania) formed to work for nuclear disarmament.

1985
* START talks resume.
* Gorbachev announces unilateral freeze on deployment of IRBM.

1986
* Explosion of nuclear power plant an Chernobyl.
* Stockholm confidence and security building measures document signed.

1987
* Intermediate-range Nuclear Force (INF) Treaty signed.
* Nuclear Risk Reduction Centers Agreement between U.S. and Soviet Union signed.
* U.S. Navy begins escort of Kuwaiti flag tankers in Persian Gulf.
* Third Reagan-Gorbachev summit in Washington, agree to dismantle medium range missiles in Europe.
* Missile Technology Control Regime established.

1988
* Ballistic Missile Launch Notification Agreement signed.
* UN mediates withdrawal of Soviet forces from Afghanistan.
* Gorbachev announces unilateral conventional force reduction.

1989
* Fall of East German government and Berlin Wall dismantled.
* UN mediates withdrawal of Cuban troops from Angola and South African troops from Namibia.
* UN sends peacekeeping mission and advisers to conduct elections in Namibia.
* UN sends mission to Nicaragua to monitor elections.

* Arab League assists in mediation that leads to end of Yemeni War and unification of Yemen.

1990

* Conventional Forces in Europe (CFE) Treaty signed.
* Iraq invades Kuwait; U.S. led coalition formed leading to the "Persian Gulf War" which demonstrates high tech weapons such as stealth bombers, smart bombs, GPS, etc.
* UN supervises elections in Haiti.
* Conference on Security and Cooperation in Europe (CSCE) established on permanent basis.

1991

* U.S.S.R. (CIS) and United States sign START I (Strategic Arms Reduction Treaty) to reduce nuclear weapons by 30 percent.
* Negotiations for START II begin with the goal of reducing nuclear weapons by 60 percent.
* United Nations Iraq-Kuwait Observation Mission (UNIKOM) established.
* United Nations Mission in El Salvador established.
* United Nations Mission for the Referendum in Western Sahara (MINURSO) established.
* Secretary-General negotiates interim cease-fire in Angola.
* General Assembly establishes a register of international, government to government arms sales.
* United States Congress passes Soviet Nuclear Threat Reduction Act (Nunn-Lugar) authorizing $400 million to assist new republics of former Soviet Union to dispose of nuclear weapons.

1992

* Bush and Yeltsin sign joint statement proclaiming end to the "Cold War".
* Bush announces end to US production of weapons grade plutonium and uranium and a moratorium on nuclear weapons tests.
* U.S. commits troops to humanitarian relief in Somalia.
* U.S. and Russia announce nuclear arms reduction to 1960s level of 3,500 and 3,000 warheads respectively.
* United Nations negotiates end to civil war in El Salvador.
* United Nations sends over 20,000 personnel to re-establish government and peace in Cambodia.
* United Nations Protection Force (UNPROFOR) established in former Yugoslavia.
* United Nations Verification Mission in Mozambique (ONUMOZ) established.
* Conventional Forces in Europe (CFE) Treaty comes into effect.
* Open Skies Treaty signed.

1993

* United Nations Register of Conventional Arms comes into effect.
* Over 120 nations initially sign the chemical weapons convention banning production, stockpiling and use; first such ban of entire category in history. All stockpiles to be destroyed.
* United Nations Operation in Somalia (UNOSOM) established.
* United Nations Observer Mission Uganda-Rwanda (UNOMUR) established.
* UN mission in Somalia changed to add attempts to suppress local political gangs; results in US casualties.
* United Nations Observer Mission in Georgia (UNOMIG) established.
* United Nations Observer Mission in Liberia (UNOMIL) is established.
* United Nations Assistance Mission in Rwanda (UNAMIR) established.

1994

* Conference on Security and Cooperation in Europe institutionalize and rename themselves Organization for Security and Cooperation in Europe.
* Clinton and Yeltsin announce that strategic missiles will no longer be targeted. British subsequently announce that their strategic missiles will be targeted on the open sea.
* The United States, Russia, Ukraine, Kazakhstan, and Belarus formally implement START I to reduce nuclear weapons by 30 percent.
* UN Conference on Disarmament reestablishes *ad hoc* Nuclear Test Ban Committee.
* Coordinating Committee for Multilateral Export Controls (COCOM) is ended on March 31.

1995

* Nuclear Nonproliferation Treaty (NPT) extended indefinitely.
* Ukraine, last of the START participants to do so, accedes to the Nuclear Non-Proliferation treaty, permitting full implementation of START I to begin.
* United Nations Verification Mission in Mozambique (ONUMOZ) completes it task.
* Final elements of United Nations Operation in Somalia (UNOSOM) are withdrawn.

1996

* UN adopts Comprehensive Test Ban Treaty

Bibliography

Allison, Graham T., *Essence of Decision* (Boston: Little, Brown, 1971).

Arbatov, Alexei G., and Gennady K. Lednev, eds., *Implications of Strategic Defense Deployments for U.S.-Russian Relations* (Washington, DC: Henry L. Stimson Center, June 1992).

Arend, Anthony Carl, and Robert J. Beck, *International Law and the Use of Force.* New York: Routledge, 1993.

Arkin, William, *Research Guide to Current Military and Strategic Affairs* (Washington, DC: Institute for Policy Studies, 1981).

Arms Control Association, *U.S. Arms Tranfers to the Middle East Since the Invasion of Kuwait* (Washington, DC: Arms Control Association, 1993).

Aronson, Shlomo, *The Politics and Strategy of Nuclear Weapons in the Middle East: Opacity, Theory and Reality* (New York: State University of New York Press, 1992).

Art, Robert, J., and Kenneth N. Waltz, eds., *The Use of Force: International Politics and Foreign Policy* (2d ed., Lanham, MD: University Press of America, 1980).

Aspen Strategy Group, *New Threats: Responding to the Proliferation of Nuclear, Chemical and Delivery Capabilities in the Third World* (Lanham, MD: University Press of America, 1990).

Ball, Nicole, and Milton Leitenberg, *Disarmament, Development and Their Interrelationship* (Los Angeles: Center for the Study of Armament & Disarmament, California State University, 1980).

Bamford, James, *The Puzzle Palace* (New York: Penguin Books, 1983).

Barber, Bernard, *The Logic and Limits of Trust* (New Brunswick: Rutgers University Press, 1983).

Barnaby, Frank, *The Invisible Bomb: The Nuclear Arms Race in the Middle East* (London: I.B. Taurus, 1989).

Barnet, Richard J., and Richard A. Falk, eds., *Security in Disarmament* (Princeton, NJ: Princeton University Press, 1965).

Barton, John H., and Lawrence D. Weiler, *International Arms Control: Issues and Agreements* (Stanford: Stanford University Press, 1976).

Beeler, John, *Warfare in Feudal Europe, 730-1200* (Ithaca: Cornell University Press, 1971).

Beres, Louis Rene, *Terrorism and Global Security: The Nuclear Threat* (Boulder: Westview Press, 1979).

Bhupendra, "Ukraine's ICBM Arsenal", *Janes Intelligence Review*, vol.6 (March 1994) no. 3.

Blackwill, Robert D., and Albert Carnesale, *New Nuclear Nations* (New York: Council on Foreign Relations, 1993).

Blair, Bruce G., *The Logic of Accidental Nuclear Warfare* (Washington, DC: Brookings Institution, 1993).

Blau, Peter M., *The Dynamics of Bureaucracy* (Chicago: University of Chicago Press, 1955).

Blechman, Barry M., and Stephen S. Kaplan, *Force Without War: U.S. Armed Forces as a Political Instrument* (Washington, DC: Brookings Institution, 1978).

Bloomfield, Lincoln P., *The Power to Keep Peace* (Berkeley: World Without War Council Publications, 1971).

Bowett, D. W., *United Nations Forces: A Legal Study of United Nations Practice* (New York: Praeger, 1964).

Brogan, Patrick, *The Fighting Never Stopped* (New York: Vintage Books, 1990).

Brown, Harold, *Annual Report to the President and the Congress* (Washington, DC: Department of Defense, 1979).

Butterworth, Robert Lyle, *Managing Interstate Conflict, 1945-74: Data with Synopses* (Pittsburgh: Center for International Studies, University of Pittsburgh, 1976).

------, *Moderation from Management: International Organizations for Peace* (Pittsburgh: Center for International Studies, University of Pittsburgh, 1978).

Buzan, Barry, *People, States and Fear* (2d ed., Boulder: Lynne Rienner Publishers, 1991).

Cahn, Anne, et al., *Controlling Future Arms Trade* (New York: McGraw-Hill, 1977).

Christopher, Warren, "Budget Priorities in Shaping a New Foreign Policy", *The DISAM Journal*, 15 (Spring 1993), 3.

Central Intelligence Agency, *The World Factbook 1994* (Washington, DC: Central Intelligence Agency, 1994).

Chopra, Jarat, and Thomas G. Weiss, "Sovereignty Is No Longer Sacrosanct: Codifying Humanitarian Intervention", *Ethics & International Affairs*, 6 (1992) 95-117.

Cimbala, Stephen J., *Military Persuasion: Deterrence and Provocation in Crisis and War* (University Park, PA: Pennsylvania State University Press, 1994).

Clarke, Duncan L., *Politics of Arms Control; The Role and Effectiveness of the U.S. Arms Control and Disarmament Agency* (New York: Free Press, 1980).

Claude, Inis L., Jr., *Swords Into Plowshares* (3d ed.; New York: Random House, 1964).

Clinton, William J., *A National Security Strategy of Engagement and Enlargement* (Washington, DC: The White House, July 1994).

Cohen, John, *Chance, Skills, and Luck: The Psychology of Guessing and Gambling* (Baltimore: Penguin, 1960).

Commission on Global Governance, *Our Global Neighborhood* (New York: Oxford University Press, 1995).

Conner, Walker, *Ethnonationalism: The Quest for Understanding* (Princeton: Princeton University Press, 1994).

Coser, Lewis A., *Continuities in the Study of Social Conflict* (New York: Free Press, 1967).

Damrosch, Lori Fisler, ed., *Enforcing Restraint: Collective Intervention in Internal Conflicts* (New York: Council on Foreign Relations, 1993).

------ and David J. Scheffer, eds., *Law and Force in the New International Order.* (Boulder: Westview, 1991).

Danaher, Kevin, *In Whose Interest? A Guide to U.S.-South African Relations* (Washington: Institute for Policy Studies, 1984)

Daniel, Donald C.F., and Brad C. Hayes, ed., *Beyond Traditional Peacekeeping* (New York: St. Martin's Press, 1995).

Davis, Lynn, "Export Controls and Non-Proliferation Regimes in the Post-Cold War World", *The DISAM Journal*, 16 (Spring 1994) 3.

Davis, Zachary S., *Nonproliferation Regimes: Policies to Control the Spread of Nuclear, Chemical, and Biological Weapons and Missiles* (Washington, DC: Congressional Research Service, 1993).

Dawkins, Richard, *The Selfish One* (New York: Oxford University Press, 1976).

Day, Alan J., ed. *Border and Territorial Disputes* (2nd ed.; Harlow, UK: Longman Group, 1987).

Dean, Jonathan, *Ending Europe's Wars: The Continuing Search for Peace and Stability* (New York: Twentieth Century Fund Press, 1994).

Defense Assistance Agency, *Security Assistance Manual*, Change 6, October 1, 1988.

Defense Institute of Security Assistance Management, *The Management of Security Assistance* (12th ed.; Wright-Patterson AFB, OH, 1994).

Deutsch, Karl W., *Politics and Government* (Boston: Houghton Mifflin, 1980).

Deutsch, Morton, *The Resolution of Conflict: Constructive and Destructive Processes* (New Haven: Yale University Press, 1973).

Deutsch, Morton, "Trust and Suspicion", *Journal of Conflict Resolution*, 2 (1958).

Diehl, Paul F., *International Peacekeeping* (Baltimore: Johns Hopkins University Press, 1993).

Divale, William Tulio, *Warfare in Primitive Societies: A Bibliography* (Santa Barbara, CA: ABC-Clio, 1973).

Donelan, M.D., and M.J. Grieve, *International Disputes; Case Histories, 1945-1970* (New York: St. Martin's Press, 1973).

Dougherty, James E., ed., *The Prospects for Arms Control* (New York: MacFadden Books, 1965).

Dougherty, James E., and Robert L. Pfaltzgraff, *American Foreign Policy, FDR to Reagan* (New York: Harper & Row, 1986).

Douglass, Joseph D., Jr., and Amoretta M. Hoeber, *Soviet Strategy for Nuclear War* (Stanford: Hoover Institution, 1979).

------, *Soviet Military Strategy in Europe* (New York: Pergamon Press, 1980).

Downs, George W., *Collective Security Beyond the Cold War* (Ann Arbor: University of Michigan Press, 1994).

Dupuy, R. Ernest, and Trevor N. Dupuy, *The Harper Encyclopedia of Military History: From 3500 B.C. to the Present* (4th ed.; New York: HarperCollins, 1993).

Dupuy, Trevor N., and Cay M. Hammerman, *A Documentary History of Arms Control and Disarmament* (Ann Arbor: R.R. Bowker, 1973).

------, et al., *The Almanac of World Military Power* (4th ed.; San Rafael, CA: Presidio Press, 1980).

------, *Future Wars: The World's Most Dangerous Flashpoints* (New York: Warner Books, 1992).

Edmonds, Martin, ed., *Central Organizations of Defense* (Boulder: Westview Press, 1985).

Eldridge, Albert E., *Images of Conflict* (New York: St. Martin's Press, 1979).

Evron, Yair, *Israel's Nuclear Dilemma* (London: Routledge, 1994).

Fabian, Larry L., *Soldiers Without Enemies; Preparing the United Nations for Peacekeeping* (Washington, DC: Brookings Institution, 1971).

Fain, Tyrus G., ed., *The Intelligence Community: History, Organization, and Issues* (New York: R.R.Bowker, 1977).

Farrar, Lancelot L., Jr., *War: A Historical, Political, and Social Study* (Santa Barbara, CA: ABC-Clio Press, 1978).

Ferencz, Benjamin B., *Defining International Aggression: The Search for World Peace* (2 vols., Dobbs Ferry, N.Y.: Oceana, 1976).

Ferris, Elizabeth G., ed., *The Challenge to Intervene: A New Role for the United Nations?* (Uppsala: Life & Peace Institute, 1992).

Fetherston, A.B., *Towards a Theory of United Nations Peacekeeping* (London: Macmillan, 1994).

Fischer, David, *Stopping the Spread of Nuclear Weapons: The Past and the Prospects* (New York: Routledge, 1992).

Flournoy, Michele A., *Nuclear Weapons After the Cold War: Guidelines for U.S. Policy* (New York: HarperCollins, 1993).

Freedman, Lawrence, *Arms Control: Management or Reform?* (New York: Routledge & Kegan Paul, 1986).

Freedman, Lawrence, ed., *Military Intervention in European Conflicts* (Oxford: Blackwell Publishers, 1994).

Fromkin, David, *A Peace to End All Peace: Creating the Modern Middle East 1914-1922* (New York: Henry Holt and Company, 1989).

Fry, M.P., N.P. Keating, and J. Rotblat, eds., *Nuclear Non-Proliferation and the Non-Proliferation Treaty* (New York: Springer-Verlag, 1990).

Gacek, Christopher M., *The Logic of Force: Limited Wars in American Foreign Policy* (New York: Columbia University Press, 1994).

Galtung, Johan, *Human Rights in Another Key* (Oxford: Polity Press, 1994).

Garthoff, Raymond L., *The Great Transition: American-Soviet Relations and the End of the Cold War* (Washington, DC: Brookings Institution, 1994).

Gelb, Leslie H., and Richard K. Betts, *The Irony of Vietnam: The System Worked* (Washington, DC: Brookings Institution, 1979).

Godson, Roy, ed., *Intelligence Requirements for the 1990s* (Lexington, MA: Lexington Books, 1989).

Goldblat, Jozef, *Arms Control: A Guide to Negotiations and Agreements* (Thousand Oaks, CA: Sage Publishers, 1994).

Goldman, Ralph M., *Contemporary Perspectives on Politics* (New Brunswick, NJ: Transaction Books, 1976).

------, *From Warfare to Party Politics* (Syracuse: Syracuse University Press, 1990).

------, "A Transactional Theory of Political Integration and Arms Control", *American Political Science Review*, 63 (September 1969).

Goodman, Hirsch, and W. Seth Carus, *The Future Battlefield and the Arab-Israeli Conflict* (New Brunswick, NJ: Transaction, 1990).

Gordon, Michael R., and General Bernard E. Trainor, *The Generals' War: The Inside Story of the Conflict in the Gulf* (New York: Little, Brown and Company, 1995).

Graham, Norman A., ed., *Seeking Security and Development: The Impact of Military Spending and Arms Transfers* (London: Lynne Rienner, 1994).

Grant, Michael, *The Army of the Caesars* (New York: Charles Scribner's Sons, 1974).

Haas, Ernst B., *Beyond the Nation-State: Functionalism and International Organization* (Stanford: Stanford University Press, 1965).

Hackett, John, et al., *The Third World War, August 1985* (New York: Macmillan, 1978).

Halberstam, David, *The Fifties* (New York: Ballantine Books, 1993).

Hammond, Paul Y., David J. Louscher, Michael D. Salomone, and Norman A. Graham, *The Reluctant Supplier: U.S. Decisionmaking in Arms Sales* (Cambridge, MA: Oelgeslager, Gunn & Hain Publishers, 1983).

Harkavy, Robert E., *The Arms Trade and International Systems* (Cambridge, MA: Ballinger, 1978).

------, and Stephanie G. Neuman, eds., *Arms Transfers in the Modern World* (New York: Praeger, 1979).

------, and Stephanie G. Neuman, eds., "The Arms Trade: Problems and Prospects in the Post-Cold War World", *Annals of the American Academy of Political and Social Science* (Thousand Oaks, CA: Sage Publications, September 1994).

Hart, Liddell B.H., *Strategy* (New York: Praeger Publishers, 1967).

Held, Colbert C., *Middle East Patterns: Places, People, and Politics* (Boulder: Westview Press, 1989).

Hersch, Seymour M., *The Sampson Option* (New York: Random House, 1991).

Hickman, Martin B., *The Military and American Society* (Beverly Hills, CA: Glencoe Press, 1971).

Higgins, Rosalyn, *United Nations Peacekeeping; 1946-1967: Documents and Commentary* (4 vols., New York: Oxford University Press, 1969-1980).

Hilsman, Roger, *The Politics of Policy Making in Defense and Foreign Affairs* (New York: Harper & Row, 1971).

Hoffmann, Stanley, "A New World and its Troubles", *Foreign Affairs,* 69 (Fall 1990).

Homans, George, *Social Behavior: Its Elementary Forms* (New York: Harcourt, Brace & World, 1961).

Hooson, David, *Geography and National Identity* (Oxford: Blackwell Publishers, 1994).

Huntington, Samuel P., *The Soldier and the State* (New York: Vintage Books, 1964).

International Institute for Strategic Studies, *The Military Balance 1994-1995* (London: Brassey's, 1995).

------, *The Military Balance 1995-1996* (London: Brassey's, 1995).

International Peacekeeping. Edited by Michael Pugh. Ilford, Essex, Great Britain: Frank Cass Publishers. Published quarterly.

Intrilagator, Michael D., and Urs Luterbacher, *Cooperative Models in International Relations Research* (Hingham, MA: Kluwer Academic Publishers, 1994).

Ippolito, Dennis S., *Blunting the Sword: Budget Policy and the Future of Defense* (Washington, DC: National Defense University, 1994).

Jacobson, Harold K., *Networks of Interdependence: International Organizations and the Global Political System* (New York: Knopf, 1979).

James, Alan, *Politics of Peacekeeping* (New York: Praeger, 1968).

Janis, Irving L., *Victims of Groupthink: A Psychological Study of Foreign-Policy Decisions and Fiascoes* (Boston: Houghton Mifflin, 1972).

Janowitz, Morris, *The Professional Soldier: A Social and Political Portrait* (New York: The Free Press, 1960).

------, *Military Institutions and Coercion in the Developing Nations* (Chicago: University of Chicago Press, 1977).

Jervis, Robert, *Perception and Misperception in International Politics* (Princeton: Princeton University Press, 1976).

------, *The Logic of Images in International Relations* (New York: Columbia University Press, 1989).

Jones, Rodney W., and Stephen A. Hidreth, *Modern Weapons and Third World Powers* (Boulder: Westview Press, 1984).

Kahan, Jerome H., *Security in the Nuclear Age: Developing U. S. Strategic Arms Policy* (Washington, DC: Brookings Institution, 1975).

Kahn, Herman, *On Thermonuclear War* (Princeton, NJ: Princeton University Press, 1961).

Kahn, Riaz, *Untying the Afghan Knot; Negotiating Soviet Withdrawal* (Durham, NC: Duke University Press, **1991**.).

Kanter, Arnold, and Linton F. Brooks, ed., *U.S. Intervention Policy for the Post-Cold War World* (New York: W. W. Norton & Company, 1994).

Kapur, Ashok, *International Nuclear Proliferation; Multilateral Diplomacy and Regional Aspects* (New York: Praeger, 1979).

Karnow, Stanley, *Vietnam: A History* (New York: Viking Press, 1983).

Keegan, John, *World Armies* (New York: Facts on File, 1979).

------, *A History of Warfare* (New York: Vintage Books, 1993).

Keller, William W., *Arm in Arm: The Political Economy of the Global Arms Trade* (New York: Basic Books, 1995).

Keohane, Robert O., *After Hegemony: Cooperation and Discord in the World Political Economy* (Princeton: Princeton University Press, 1984).

Kincade, William H., and Jeffrey D. Porro, eds., *Negotiating Security* (Washington, DC: Carnegie Endowment for International Peace, 1979).

Kohn, George C., *Dictionary of Wars* (New York: Doubleday, 1986).

Kolkowicz, Roman, et al., *The Soviet Union and Arms Control: A Superpower Dilemma* (Baltimore: Johns Hopkins University Press, 1970).

Kolodziej, Edward, and Patrick Morgan, eds., *Security and Arms Control* (2 vols.; New York: Greenwood Press, 1989).

Krause, Keith, *Arms and the State: Patterns of Military Production and Trade* (New York: Cambridge University Press, 1992).

Krepon, Michael, Amy Smithson, and James Schear, *The U.S. ACDA: Restructuring for the Post Cold War Era* (Washington, DC: Henry Stimson Center, 1993).

Larson, Jeffrey A., and Gregory J. Rattray, *Arms Control Toward the 21st Century* (Boulder, CO: Lynne Rienner, 1995).

Laue, James H., "Contributions of the Emerging Field of Conflict Resolution", in W. Scott Thompson and Kenneth M. Jensen, *Approaches to Peace: An Intellectual Map* (Washington, DC: United States Institute of Peace, 1991).

Laurenti, Jeffrey, *National Taxpayers, International Organizations: Sharing the Burden of Financing the United Nations* (New York: United Nations Association of the United States,1995).

Lawrence, Robert M., *Arms Control and Disarmament; Practice and Promise* (Minneapolis: Burgess, 1973).

Lee, William T., *Understanding the Soviet Military Threat: How CIA Estimates Went Astray* (New Brunswick, NJ: Transaction Books, 1977).

Lefever, Ernest W., *Nuclear Arms in the Third World: U.S. Policy Dilemma* (Washington, D.C.: Brookings Institution, 1979).

Levi, Werner, *The Coming End of War* (Beverly Hills, CA: Sage, 1981).

Lewis, William H., *Military Implications of United Nations Peacekeeping Operations, McNair Paper Seventeen* (Washington, DC: National Defense University, 1993).

Lie, Trygve, *In the Cause for Peace* (New York: Macmillan, 1954).

Liska, George, *Nations in Alliance* (Baltimore: Johns Hopkins Press, 1962).

Liu, F.T., *United Nations Peacekeeping and the Non-Use of Force* (Boulder: Lynne Rienner Publishers, 1992).

Lyons, Gene M., and Michael Mastanduno, eds., *Beyond Westphalia? State Sovereignty and International Intervention* (Baltimore: Johns Hopkins Press, 1995).

Marwah, Onkar, and Ann Schulz, eds., *Nuclear Proliferation and the Near-Nuclear Countries* (Cambridge, MA: Ballinger, 1975).

Matthews, Robert O., Arthur G. Rubinoff, and Janice Gross Stein, eds., *International Conflict and Conflict Management* (Scarborough, Ontario: Prentice-Hall of Canada, 1984).

Mazarr, Michael J., *The Military Technical Revolution: A Structural Framework* (Washington, DC: Center for Strategic and International Studies, 1993).

McGowan, Patrick, and Charles W. Kegley, Jr., eds., *Threats, Weapons, and Foreign Policy* (Beverly Hills, CA: Sage, 1980).

Mearsheimer, John J., "Back to the Future: Instability in Europe After the Cold War", *International Security*, 15 (Summer 1990).

Meese, Edwin, III, *With Reagan: The Inside Story* (Washington, DC: Regnery, Gateway, 1992).

Meisler, Stanley, *United Nations: The First Fifty Years* (New York: The Atlantic Monthly Press, 1995).

Menges, Constantine, *Inside the National Security Council; The True Story of the Making and Unmaking of Reagan's Foreign Policy* (New York: Simon & Schuster, 1988).

------, *The Twilight Struggle: The United States v the Soviet Union Today* (Washington, DC: American Enterprise Institute, 1990).

Midlarsky, Manus I., *On War; Political Violence in the International System* (New York: Free Press, 1975).

Miller, Steven E., and Stephen Van Evera, *The Star Wars Controversy: An International Security Reader* (Princeton: Princeton University Press, 1986).

Morgenthau, Hans J., *Politics Among Nations* (5th ed.; New York: Knopf, 1973).

Morris, Charles, *Iron Destinies, Lost Opportunities: The Arms Race Between the USA and the USSR, 1945-1987* (New York: Harper & Row, 1988).

Moynihan, Daniel Patrick, *Pandaemonium: Ethnicity in International Politics* (New York: Oxford University Press, 1993).

Mueller, Harold, David Fischer, and Wolfgang Koetter, *Nuclear Non-Proliferation and Global Order* (Oxford: Oxford University Press for SIPRI, 1994).

Mueller, John, *Retreat from Doomsday: The Obsolescence of Major War* (New York: Basic Books, 1988).

Neuman, Stephanie G., and Robert E. Harkavy, eds., *Arms Transfers in the Modern World* (New York: Praeger, 1979).

Odom, William E., *America's Military Revolution: Strategy and Structure After the Cold War* (Washington, DC: American University Press, 1993).

Organization for Economic Cooperation and Development, *Globalization of Industrial Activities* (Paris: OECD, 1992).

Pearson, Frederic S., *The Global Spread of Arms: Political Economy of International Security* (Boulder: Westview Press, 1994).

Perlmutter, Amos, and Valerie Plave Bennett, eds., *The Political Influence of the Military* (New Haven: Yale University Press, 1980).

Perry, William J., *Annual Report to the President and the Congress* (Washington, DC: Department of Defense, February 1995).

Platt, Alan, and Lawrence D. Weiler, *Congress and Arms Control* (Boulder: Westview Press, 1978).

Purver, Ronald G., *Arms Control: The Regional Approach* (Kingston: Queen's University, 1981).

Ra'anan, Uri, Robert L. Pfaltzgraff, Jr., and Geoffrey Kemp, eds., *Arms Transfers to the Third World: The Military Buildup in Less Industrial Countries* (Boulder: Westview Press, 1978).

Rabinovich, Moysey, *Soviet Conventional Arms Transfers to the Third World: Main Missile and Artillery Directorate, 1966-1990* (Alexandria, VA: Global Consultants, 1993).

Raman, K. Venkata, *Dispute Settlement Through the United Nations* (Dobbs Ferry, N.Y.: Oceana, 1977).

Randle, Robert F., *Origins of Peace* (New York: Free Press, 1973).

Ranger, Robin, *The Arms Control Experience Re-Examined: Arms Control in Theory and Practice, 1958-1981* (Kingston: Queen's University, 1981).

Renn, Ludwig, *Warfare* (Freeport, NY: Books for Libraries Press, reprinted 1971).

Richelson, Jeffrey T., *Foreign Intelligence Organizations* (Cambridge, MA: Ballinger Publishing, 1988).

------, *The U.S. Intelligence Community* (New York: Harper Business Publishing, 1989).

Roberts, Brad, ed., *Ratifying the Chemical Weapons Convention* (Washington, DC: Center for Strategic and International Studies, 1994).

Robles, Alfonso, *The Denuclearization of Latin America* (Washington, DC: Carnegie Endowment, 1967).

Romanucci-Ross, Lola, ed. *Ethnic Identity: Creation, Conflict, and Accommodation* (3rd ed.; Walnut Creek, CA: Altamira Press, 1995).

Rosecrance, Richard, *Action and Reaction in World Politics: International Systems in Perspective* (Boston: Little, Brown, 1963).

Rosi, Eugene J., ed., *American Defense and Detente* (New York: Dodd, Mead & Co., 1973).

Rourke, Francis E., *Bureaucracy and Foreign Policy* (Baltimore: Johns Hopkins Press, 1972).

Ruggie, John Gerard, *Multilateralism Matters: The Theory and Praxis of an Institutional Form* (New York: Columbia University Press, 1993).

Sanders, Ralph, *The Politics of Defense Analysis* (New York: Dunellen, 1973).

Sanderson, Stephen K., *Civilizations and World Systems: Studying World-Historical Change* (Walnut Creek, CA: Altamira Press, 1995)..

Scheer, Robert, *With Enough Shovels: Reagan, Bush & Nuclear War* (New York: Random House, 1982).

Schelling, Thomas C., *Arms and Influence* (New Haven: Yale University Press, 1966).

Shaker, Mohamed Ibrahim, *The Nuclear Non-Proliferation Treaty: Origin and Implementation, 1959-1979* (Dobbs Ferry, N.Y.: Oceana, 1980).

Sherry, George L., *The United Nations Reborn: Conflict Control in the Post-Cold War Critical Issues*, (New York: Council on Foreign Relations, 1990).

Singer, J. David, *Deterrence, Arms Control, and Disarmament; Towards a Synthesis of National Security Policy* (Columbus: Ohio State University Press, 1962).

------, and Melvin Small, *The Wages of War, 1816-1965: A Statistical Handbook* (New York: Wiley, 1972).

Sivard, Ruth Leger, *World Military and Social Expenditures* (Washington, DC: World Priorities, annually).

Smith, Anthony, *The Ethnic Origins of Nations* (Oxford: Blackwell Publishers, 1988).

Snyder, Jed C., and Samuel F. Wells, Jr., *Limiting Nuclear Proliferation* (Cambridge, MA: Ballinger Publishing Co., 1985).

Spaulding, Oliver L., Jr., H. Nickerson, and J.W. Wright, *Warfare* (New York: Harcourt, Brace, 1925).

Spector, Leonard S., *Nuclear Ambitions* (Boulder: Westview Press, 1990).

Spiers, Edward M., *Chemical and Biological Weapons: A Study of Proliferation* (London: Macmillan, 1994).

Staley II, Robert Stephens, *The Wave of the Future: The United Nations and Naval Peacekeeping* (International Peace Academy Occasional Paper Series, 1992).

Stockholm International Peace Research Institute (SIPRI), *World Armaments and Disarmament; SIPRI Yearbook* (Stockholm: SIPRI, annual).

Stoessinger, John G., *Why Nations Go to War* (2d ed.; New York: St. Martin's Press, 1978).

Strauss, Anselm, *Negotiations* (San Francisco: Jossey-Bass, 1978).

Summers, Harry G., *On Strategy: A Critical Analysis of the Vietnam War* (Novato, CA: Presidio Press, 1982).

Sun Tzu, *The Art of War*, trans. by Samuel B. Griffith (Oxford: Oxford University Press, 1963).

Tammen, Ronald L., *MIRV and the Arms Race: An Interpretation of Defense Strategy* (New York: Praeger, 1973).

Tefft, Stanton K., *Secrecy: A Cross-Cultural Perspective* (New York: Human Sciences Press, 1980).

Truman, David B., *The Governmental Process* (New York: Knopf, 1951).

UNESCO, *World Directory of Peace Research and Training Institutions* (Oxford: Blackwell Publishers).

United Nations, *Economic and Social Consequences of the Arms Race and of Military Expenditures* (New York: UNIPUB, 1978).

------, *Study on Ways and Means of Promoting Transparency in International Transfers of Conventional Arms* (New York: UNIPUB, 1992).

------, *The Limits of Sovereignty* (United Nations Department of Public Information, 1992).

------, *An Agenda for Peace: Preventive Diplomacy, Peacemaking and Peace Keeping* (Report of the Secretary General [A/47/277-S/24111], 17 June 1992).

------, *Supplement to An Agenda for Peace* (Report of the Secretary General [A/50/60-S//1], 3 January 1995).

------, *Report of the Secretary General on Standby Arrangements for Peacekeeping* (S//943)., 10 November 1995.

------, *General and Complete Disarmament* (Report of the Secretary General to the General Assembly [A/50/115], March 23, 1995).

------, *Report of the Special Committee on the Charter of the United Nations and the Strengthening of the Role of the Organization* [A/50/361], August 22, 1995.

U.S. Arms Control and Disarmament Agency, *Arms Control and Disarmament Agreements* (Washington, DC: U.S. Government Printing Office, 1990).

------, *World Military Expenditures and Arms Transfers, 1991-1992* (Washington, DC: U.S. Government Printing Office, 1994).

U.S. Congress, Office of Technology Assessment, *The Effects of Nuclear War* (Washington, DC: U.S. Government Printing Office, June 1979).

------, *Proliferation and the Former Soviet Union* (Washington, DC: U.S. Government Printing Office, 1994).

------, *Proliferation of Weapons of Mass Destruction: Assessing the Risks* (Washington, DC: U.S. Government Printing Office, 1993).

U.S. Department of Defense, *Military Forces in Transition* (Washington, DC: Department of Defense, 1991).

U.S. Department of State, *Security and Arms Control: The Search for a More Stable Peace* (Washington, DC: Bureau of Public Affairs, 1984).

Vagts, Alfred, *A History of Militarism* (New York: Meridian Books, 1959).

Van Cleave, William R., and W. Scott Thompson, *Strategic Options for the Early 80s: What Can Be Done?* (New Brunswick, NJ: Transaction Books, 1979).

van Creveld, Martin, *Technology and War: From 2000 B.C. to the Present* (New York: The Free Press, 1989).

van Ham, Peter, *Managing Non-Proliferation Regimes in the 1990s: Power, Politics, and Policies* (New York: Council on Foreign Relations Press, 1994).

Wainhouse, David W., et al., *International Peace Observation; A History and Forecast* (Baltimore: Johns Hopkins Press, 1966).

Waltz, Kenneth, *Theory of International Politics* (New York: Random House, 1979).

------, *The Spread of Nuclear Weapons: More May Be Better* (Adelphi Paper No. 171, London: International Institute for Strategic Studies, 1981).

Warner, Edward, *Next Moves: An Arms Control Agenda for the 1990s* (New York: Council on Foreign Relations, 1989).

Wehr, Paul, *Conflict Regulation* (Boulder: Westview Press, 1979).

Weigley, Russell F., *The American Way of War: A History of United States Military Strategy and Planning* (Bloomington: Indiana University Press, 1977).

Weiner, Tim, *Blank Check: The Pentagon's Black Budget* (New York: Warner Books, 1990).

Wells, Donald A. *The War Myth* (New York: Pegasus, 1967).

Worden, Simon P., *SDI and the Alternatives* (Washington, DC: National Defense University Press, 1991).

Wright, Quincy, *A Study of War* (2 vols.; Chicago: University of Chicago Press, 1942).

Yoder, Amos, *The Evolution of the U.N. System* (Bristol, PA: Crane Russak, 1989).

York, Herbert F., *Race to Oblivion; A Participant's View of the Arms Race* (New York: Simon and Schuster, 1970).

------, *The Advisors: Oppenheimer, Teller and the Superbomb* (San Francisco: W.H. Freeman, 1976).

Young, Brigadier Peter, *A Dictionary of Battles, 1816-1976* (New York: Mayflower Books, 1977).

Zartman, I. William, ed., *The Negotiation Process* (Beverly Hills, CA: Sage, 1978).

Index